REVIVING THE ETERNAL CITY

ROME AND THE PAPAL COURT, 1420–1447

Elizabeth McCahill

HARVARD UNIVERSITY PRESS
Cambridge, Massachusetts
London, England
2013

Library of Congress Cataloging-in-Publication Data

McCahill, Elizabeth M., 1974–
Reviving the Eternal City : Rome and the Papal Court, 1420–1447 /
Elizabeth McCahill.
p. cm.
Includes bibliographical references and index.
ISBN 978-0-674-72453-2
ISBN 0-674-72453-4
1. Papacy—History—1378–1447. 2. Eugene IV, Pope, 1383–1447.
3. Rome (Italy)—History—1420–1798. I. Title.
BX1270.M33   2013
262'.1309024—dc23   2013007877

To my parents, Michael and Barbara Ann McCahill,
with love and thanks

CONTENTS

LIST OF ILLUSTRATIONS

Following Chapter 6:

REVIVING THE ETERNAL CITY

Introduction: Rome ca. 1420

R OME was and is a city of myth, a city whose aura and associations have, time and again, proven larger than her physical reality. From Romulus to Lucretia, from Caesar to Nero, from Constantine to Augustine, from Michelangelo to Bernini, from Garibaldi to Burckhardt, from Mussolini to Fellini and from Russell Crowe to Dan Brown, men (and sometimes women) have fought, painted, sculpted, filmed, described, and ruled the city as something more than a city, as an idea or symbol of grandeur, barbarity, citizenship, Christianity, *imperium*, and beauty. The city has grown slowly over time, each era and ideal superimposed on the last. Rome is a palimpsest, its epochs bleeding through onto other epochs.[1] Thus, one of the most difficult aspects of studying early fifteenth-century Rome is stripping away the later accretions, recognizing the city for what it was in the Quattrocento rather than what it had been in antiquity or what it has become in the last six centuries.[2] Most obviously, it is necessary to return Saint Peter's to its late medieval form, remove the Via dei Fori Imperiali, tear down the monument to Victor Emmanuele (this with some glee), and take away anything that is Baroque. Try for a minute to imagine Rome without the Baroque. . . .

If this task of physical dismemberment is difficult, stripping the city of its ideological accretions presents even more of a challenge. A vulgarized version of a Burckhardtian Renaissance, a version in which most of Burckhardt's nuance and ambivalence have been lost, still shapes the general conception of fifteenth- and early sixteenth-century Rome.[3] Michelangelo and Raphael, the triumphant exponents of mankind's potential, serve as the standard-bearers of this Renaissance, and Michelangelo's *Creation of Man,* not his tortured poetry or his *Dying Slaves,* is its paradigmatic image. Popular views of the Renaissance also shape attitudes toward antiquity, which in many quarters is idealized and glorified with a naiveté that would make even the most avid of humanists blanch. Thus, to study Rome in the early Quattrocento, one must first strip the city down and see what was there—physically, institutionally, and politically. Only then is it possible to start—cautiously and with sensitivity to encroaching anachronisms—to reconstruct the intellectual ethos and cultural milieu of Rome almost a century before Michelangelo's arrival.

This introduction will offer a brief sketch of Rome as it looked in 1420, when Pope Martin V finally brought the papacy back to its historic home. It will then take a step back, addressing the larger problems the institution of the papacy had inherited from the Avignon Exile and the Western Schism. Finally, the introduction will discuss the reasons why Rome and the papacy between 1420 and 1447 have not received much attention, at least in English scholarship, and it will identify some of the main characters of this book, the classical scholars who worked in the papal Curia during the first half of the fifteenth century.

Rome, ca. 1420

In September 1420, Pope Martin V (d. 1431) made his solemn entrance to the seat of Saint Peter. The pope had been elected almost three years before, on November 11, 1417, at the Council of Constance and had spent the intervening period moving ever closer to the Eternal City.[4] In 1417, condottieri dominated the Papal States, and Martin had to negotiate, plot, and raise money for an army before it was safe—and even possible—for him to return to Rome.[5] The city that Martin finally entered in 1420 was not, however, a fitting stage for a triumphant celebration of papal power—or, indeed, any type of power. Rome had suffered during the almost one hundred year absence of the papacy.[6] The natural disasters of the mid-Trecento, especially the earthquake of 1349, had wreaked havoc on the city's fragile urban fabric; the Colosseum lost its southern wall in this quake.[7] The absence of a firm political authority had proven at least equally deleterious; during the popes' absence, a succession of papal legates, local barons, foreign condottieri, and short-term republican regimes ruled Rome, and during the brief periods when popes were in residence, their position was far from secure.[8] Rome's 1363 municipal statutes excluded the great baronial families (including the Colonna, the Orsini, the Savelli, and the Conti) from government, and these clans had left the city for their castles in the *campagna*. Nevertheless, they still exerted powerful influence through networks of clients; their partisans frequently resorted to brawls to uphold their patrons' overlapping rights to various parts of the city, and this urban violence was exacerbated by thieves, bandits, and the incursions of foreign mercenaries.[9] The Anonimo Romano wrote about Rome in the 1350s, but his description could just as easily describe the situation of the early 1400s.

> The city of Rome was living through great troubles. It had no appointed rectors. Combat raged every day. People were robbed everywhere. Virgins were defiled. There was no protection. Little old maids were assaulted and led off to dishonor. Wives were seized from their husbands in their own beds. Farm workers going out to labor were robbed. Where? Within the gates of Rome. Pilgrims, who had come to the holy churches for the good of their souls, were not defended but were robbed, their throats slit. Priests began committing crimes. Every lust, every evil, no justice, no restraint. No longer was there a remedy. The individual was perishing. The man who could wield the sword best was the one who had most claim to the right. There was no safety unless each man defended himself with the help of his relatives and friends. Every day saw musters of armed men.[10]

Accounts of Rome around the time of Martin's arrival echo this gloomy picture of danger and deprivation.[11] In the early 1400s, condottieri added to the general instability of the fourteenth century, with the 1413 sack of the city by Ladislaus of Naples proving particularly devastating.[12] In 1417, when Braccio da Montone took control of Rome, the city's barons, municipal authorities, and the populace welcomed the warlord and his troops; they were all too hungry and too weary of war to think of resistance.[13] Visiting Rome in 1411, Manuel Chrysoloras wrote to the Byzantine emperor Manuel II Palaeologus that "almost nothing in Rome has come down to us intact: you will not find anything that is undamaged, either crumbling beneath the natural forces of time or due to the violence of human hands. Like our own city, Rome uses itself as a mine and quarry, and it both nourishes and consumes itself. It is exhausted, so to say, in every way."[14] Although Chrysoloras was focusing on Rome's ancient structures, his image of exhaustion applied also to the economy and to the city's population. In the early Quattrocento, Rome's population was no greater than 30,000 and may, in fact, have been much less.[15]

According to the diary of Stefano Infessura (1435–1500), in spite of (or perhaps because of) the sorry state of their city, the Romans welcomed their new pontiff with open arms:

> In the year 1420, on Saturday, the twenty-eighth of September, Pope Martin came to Rome and entered through the Porta del Popolo. He spent the night at Santa Maria del Popolo, and Sunday morning, he went to the palace of Saint Peter's and through the rione Colonna and then finally to San Marco. He went along the Via Papalis, wearing a pallium around his neck, and in every rione eight gentlemen acted as players for the pope and made sport with greatest honor.[16] The Conservators and the caporioni with many citizens of Rome walked around the hills with lighted torches in their hand for several evenings always calling "long live Pope Martin, long live Pope Martin."[17]

In short, according to Infessura, both the city government and ordinary Romans did their best to ensure the pope a warm reception. The three Conservators and the thirteen caporioni were the city's principal municipal officials; their presence demonstrated the communal government's acceptance and appreciation of its new overlord.[18] The "gentlemen" strove to render the occasion festive, as did the torches, which represented a substantial outlay of the citizen's limited resources; in 1414, Rome lacked the money to pay for a single lamp for the feast of Saints Peter and Paul.[19] Thus, the profusion of light, as much as the loud cheering, attested to the populace's enthusiasm for the new pontiff, but this enthusiasm could hardly match the reception Martin had enjoyed in the far larger and more prosperous cities of Milan and Florence.[20]

What did Martin see as he traveled from the Piazza del Popolo to the Vatican and then from the Vatican to the Colonna enclave near the Forum? Information about Rome at this time remains sparse, but one of the oddities of the city was that, rather than having one clear center, it had (as it still does) a myriad of dispersed but important sites.[21] Thus, an account of Martin's progress, like a journey through the Quattrocento urban landscape, moves between well-known, ideologically fraught landmarks and large zones of desolation. In the mid-thirteenth century, the Augustinians had established a convent at Santa Maria del Popolo, Martin's starting point. Although the Piazza del Popolo served as the occasional scene of civic events, church, convent, and piazza were all part of the *disabitato,* the large uninhabited area within the Aurelian Walls.[22] The *disabitato* consisted mostly of vineyards, gardens, and occasional dwellings or religious institutions; it included much of Rome south and east of the Forum, as well as the northern end of the Via Lata (the modern Corso).[23] Leaving Santa Maria del Popolo for the Vatican, Martin most likely proceeded down the Via Lata to the Via dei Coronari and then to Ponte Sant' Angelo, the only bridge connecting the Vatican to the rest of the city. (Since his main processional route, as described by Infessura, began at the Vatican, we will transport him there, saving an account of the regions of Ponte, Colonna, and the Borgo for his return journey across the river.)

Arriving at the Vatican palace, Martin did not find the splendid structure to which Boniface VIII (1294–1303) had put the finishing touches. Most of the palace was built in the thirteenth century by some of the most proudly monarchical of the medieval popes, Innocent III (1198–1216) and Nicholas III (1277–1280).[24] By the 1420s, however, the palace was no longer habitable, and Martin V chose to spend the early part of his time in Rome in a residence near Santa Maria Maggiore.[25] Saint Peter's was in a similar state of disrepair. The original basilica of Constantine had been expanded and embellished for more than ten centuries, but essential restoration work had been neglected during the Trecento and early Quattrocento.[26] A commission established by Gregory X between 1271 and 1276 determined that the walls of the church were about to collapse and needed to be rebuilt.[27] The roof leaked, and the main nave lacked a proper ceiling. Its visible beams gave a look of impermanence to the great basilica, as did the uneven floor, which was constantly disturbed by the insertion of new funeral monuments.

In spite of Saint Peter's dilapidation, Martin would have seen plentiful reminders of the exalted position he was expected to fill. During the eighth century, the church's portico was decorated with scenes from the first six ecumenical councils. Five centuries later, frescoes were added depicting events from the lives of Peter and Paul, as well as the construction and consecration of Saint Peter's by Constantine and Pope Sylvester. Inside the basilica, Nicholas III commissioned portraits of all the popes. Although Saint Peter's iconography also included scenes from the Bible, these scenes were faded, and the predominant visual message affirmed the power and pretensions of the later medieval pontiffs. The seat of the Apostle would have reminded Martin of his special role as Peter's successor, even as it highlighted the penury that prevented him from matching the largesse of his predecessors.

Leaving Saint Peter's, Martin encountered what was, for much of the High Middle Ages, a prosperous tourist region.[28] In the very atrium of Saint Peter's, known as the *Paradiso,* pilgrims entering or leaving the basilica could buy sacred images, rosaries, and replicas of the Veronica; the canons of Saint Peter's, who had the rights to this area, were happy to lease commercial permits for profit. There were also shops on the stairs of the church and at the base of the campanile.[29] In the piazza in front of Saint Peter's, hawkers sold bread and salted fish, as well as books and other artisanal goods. The area around the basilica, the Borgo Leonino, had not been a part of the ancient city, but ever since the great basilica was built, and especially after Leo IV (847–855) surrounded the area with protective walls, the region had grown and prospered. In the twelfth and thirteenth centuries, it was densely populated with monasteries, taverns, inns, and hostels, and innkeepers were so eager for customers that they reportedly stole guests by physical force to ensure a healthy profit.[30] The Borgo was divided by three main roads that led from Saint Peter's to the Ponte Sant' Angelo, and thus the rest of the city. Along these roads, vendors had once provided straw for bedding, icons, fruits, vegetables, rosaries, shoes, and wine, but the absence of the popes and the dangers of the *caput mundi* had dramatically reduced pilgrimage traffic by the early Quattrocento. Although there are no estimates for the number of pilgrims who came for the Jubilees of 1390, 1400, and 1423, the crowds paled in comparison with those that attended the great Jubilees of 1300 and 1350.[31] After the 1413 attack of Ladislaus, the streets were in such bad condition that pilgrims could only reach Saint Peter's with difficulty, and Santo Spirito, the great charitable complex near the Tiber, was forced to suspend all its work as it was almost completely destroyed.[32]

To leave the Vatican region and enter the older part of the city, Martin had to cross the Ponte Sant' Angelo and thus to pass the Castel Sant' Angelo, formerly Hadrian's Mausoleum. In 1379, furious at the election of the antipope Clement VII (1378–1394), the Romans had done their best to destroy the stronghold and had stripped it of its marble. Boniface IX (1389–1404), one of the only popes to have made a significant political and architectural impact on Rome during the Avignon Exile and the Schism, restored the Castel and made it his principal stronghold, but the depredations of 1379 had permanently turned the white marble tomb into a hulking black mass.[33] If the Castel had lost its ancient elegance, it retained its strategic significance; it was the last papal stronghold to fall to Ladislaus in 1413, and once it did, the entire city was in his hands. Throughout the Middle Ages and Renaissance, whoever controlled the Castel Sant' Angelo controlled Saint Peter's and the Borgo. The proximity of the Orsini stronghold at Monte Giordano (the Orsini were long-time rivals of the Colonna) would have reminded Martin of his precarious hold on the Castel and on his bishopric more generally.[34]

Having crossed the Tiber, Martin started down the Via Papalis, one of the three streets leading from the Borgo to key areas of the city.[35] The Via Papalis more or less followed the path of the modern day Corso Vittorio Emmanuele, passing the southern tip of the Piazza Navona, the Largo Argentina, and the northern end of the Campidoglio; it then headed east to the Colosseum and the Lateran. The Via Papalis thus served as Rome's main processional route and the route for pilgrims going between the Lateran and Saint Peter's; its western end, the part traversed by Martin on September 29, led through the densest quarter of the Quattrocento city, the area within the bend of the Tiber. Because the ancient aqueducts had fallen into disrepair, Rome's inhabitants huddled near the river, where they were close to water. Unfortunately, the Tiber flooded several times a century, often with devastating consequences. In a flood of 1277, the high altar of the Pantheon was four feet under water, and a flood of similar severity inundated Rome two years after Martin's return to the city.[36] Still, proximity to potable water was so alluring that Romans refused to move to higher ground, and, as a result, the inhabited part of the Quattrocento city was small and densely packed, a "labyrinth of irregular, narrow and twisted streets, badly built houses, and baronial towers."[37]

Five years after his entrance to Rome, Martin commented on the deterioration of municipal oversight and the sorry state of the city's streets:

> The office of magistrates [*Maestri di strada*] was instituted and ordained long ago for the administration of the property rights and repairs of roads, ways, courtyards, and other places, public and private, and also of stone and wooden buildings, walls, building materials, stalls, roofs, floors, balconies, storehouses, bridges, gates, paths, water courses, canals, and passages, and finally of urban and rural farms, meadows, gardens, and vineyards, both encumbered and unencumbered. As is plainly evident, due to the failure of this magistracy, the city and aforementioned districts, which we embrace with paternal affection, have suffered great destruction and a very terrible ruin in all and each of these structures. Furthermore (as we have heard) some of the citizens and inhabitants of the sweet city and the aforementioned districts, such as butchers, fishmongers, shoemakers, tanners, and craftsmen of diverse types, inhabiting the places and workshops of the city and exercising their arts there, have thrown and hidden viscera, intestines, heads, feet, bones, blood, and also spoiled skins, flesh, fish, and other fetid and corrupt things into the streets, ways, courtyards, and public and private places.[38]

Martin goes on to note that these practices endanger health and air quality; long before the fumes of leaded gasoline spread over the Eternal City, this pragmatic pope was concerned about pollution. His complaints about viscera, intestines, and the dangers they posed were not specific to one region. Although some Roman craftsmen congregated in a single rione (such as the armourers of Parione, the woolmakers of Pigna, and the merchants of luxury goods in Ponte), many trades spread throughout the city.[39] Butchers and leather dealers worked in the populous Campus Martius and the Campo dei Fiori, and there were slaughterhouses in the rioni of Ripa and Sant' Angelo; in fact, some were even housed in the theater of Marcellus. Thus, the remains of butchered cattle threatened the health of many parts of Rome, and the fact that cattle were the main source of prosperity for the new municipal aristocracy that arose in the late Trecento did nothing to improve communal oversight of the problem. Fish posed another danger. Most towns established one fish market and did not allow fish to be sold in other places because of the health risks involved, but in Rome they could be sold anywhere and at any time. Convenience rather than hygiene had determined the location of businesses in Rome, with potentially serious health implications.[40]

For the most part, Romans lived where they worked; houses typically had a workshop on the ground floor and then one or two stories of living quarters; most houses also had a small garden.[41] Because of repeated floods, warfare, and general old age, many structures in the most populous rioni, such as Ponte and Parione, were partially or completely ruined. In spite of this, they were sold or rented for long periods with plans for repair; the general tendency was to reuse existing structures rather than embark on new building.[42] Many medieval houses lay on ancient foundations or were tucked into surviving ancient structures like the theaters of Marcellus and Pompey. The great baronial families dominated these structures because ruins provided good fortification, and they added towers to strengthen their strongholds further. There is evidence that there were as many as three hundred and eighteen of these towers in the twelfth or thirteenth century, and although many of them were torn down in 1257, they remained a striking—or menacing—part of the urban landscape.[43] On the Via Papalis, Martin would have seen one of the Cenci towers, which stood until 1536 and may have imprisoned Gregory VII in 1075. The towers did have a certain aesthetic appeal; while looking down on Rome from the Alban Hills in 1444, Biondo Flavio described the city as a forest of towers or castles.[44] Nevertheless, from Martin's perspective, each tower marked a potential bastion of resistance to papal authority.

If the barons represented one threat to Martin's rule over Rome, the republican aspirations of the Roman commune represented another. Toward the end of his tour, Martin passed the Campidoglio which, more than any other place in the city, stood for the commune and its historical stance against papal interference. The Campidoglio was the site of the Senator's palace, and the platform from which Cola di Rienzo had chosen to proclaim Rome's newfound (if very temporary) republican liberty in 1347.[45] Large public meetings took place on an unpaved patch of ground in front of the palace, and smaller groups met in Santa Maria in Aracoeli, the church of the commune.[46] The Campidoglio was more than simply a political center, however. The stairs leading up to the church, which had been constructed in 1348 in thanks for the end of the plague, were the principal public works project of the fourteenth century and represented the strength of local, as opposed to papal, piety. On Saturdays, merchants gathered to sell their goods at the foot of the Campidoglio, and the Senator and Conservators used this occasion to punish offenders against the commune, ensuring maximum publicity for municipal justice. The Saturday market was also the principal city market throughout the Middle Ages.[47] Merchants sold their wares from stones that they bought or rented, from small stalls or from porticoes; religious institutions, barons, and *bovattieri* (those who gained their wealth through the cattle trade) owned the rights to these commercial spaces. Thus, the Campidoglio represented the economic as well as the political forces that the new pope would have to challenge or placate.

Martin's visit to the rione Colonna and to San Marco would have been more reassuring. Soon after the Colonna pope's election, his brother began repairs to the church of Santi Apostoli, and the family left its old residence on the Quirinal to establish itself nearer to the church.[48] Although Martin himself did not take up residence in the new family base until 1424, this area represented the center of Colonna power. San Marco was one of the better preserved churches in the early Quattrocento; in fact, one of Martin's Quattrocento successors, Paul II, chose to make it, and the adjoining palace he built while still a cardinal, into his main residence.[49] Martin's apartments at Santi Apostoli were a harbinger of Paul's decision to live near Rome's ancient center, but while Paul II built a luxurious palace, the structure at Santi Apostoli was a fortress, reflecting Martin's awareness of his own vulnerability.[50] Infessura suggests that Martin's trip ended at San Marco, but if the pope had continued to the city's other major basilicas he would have seen plentiful reminders of this vulnerability. Santa Maria Maggiore and the Lateran were both surrounded by small islands of habitation, but for the most part, the *disabitato* included all of Rome east of the Forum. The Lateran had suffered significantly from fires as well as the 1349 earthquake, and it had been abandoned as a papal residence during the Avignon era. Thus, the bishop of Rome could not inhabit and, indeed, hardly dared to visit his Episcopal seat.

The State of the Church and of Papal Historiography

In short, Martin did not find himself the master of a flourishing religious capital; instead, after three years of fighting and diplomacy, he had won precarious hold of a small medieval town, a town unused to papal authority and accustomed to political turmoil. But the state of Rome was only one of the problems facing the Colonna pope; upon his election, international respect for the papacy was at an all-time low. From 1309 to 1377, the popes had resided in Avignon, and this had led, fairly or unfairly, to the claim that the descendants of Saint Peter were puppets of the French kings.[51] The opulence of the Avignon papacy likewise encouraged anticurial feeling, and skepticism toward the Holy See was only increased when, in 1378, the cardinals decided they were not happy with the pope they had elected and gathered to choose another. Thus began the Western Schism, the period when Europe had to face the farce of two men, each claiming to be the one legitimate descendant of Saint Peter.[52] To make matters worse, the first serious attempt to end the Schism only exacerbated the divisions of the Church. In 1409, a council met at Pisa, deposed the Roman and Avignonese pontiffs, and elected a new pope, Alexander V.[53] The rival claimants to the throne refused to resign, however, and there were thus three popes, rather than two. Although the competing pontiffs routinely promised to step down if their opponents would do the same, none of these promises were realized, and a new council assembled at Constance in 1414.[54]

To establish their authority to end the Schism, the members of the Council of Constance issued two important and controversial decrees. In *Haec sancta* (March 1415), the council declared that general councils are the highest power in the Church, that they receive their authority directly from Christ, and that all Christians, including the pope, must obey their decrees on matters of faith, the extirpation of schism, and the reform of the Church. In *Frequens* (October 1417), the council declared that general councils should meet frequently and that they cannot be transferred or dissolved except by their own members. At the time, these decrees seemed to be the necessary canonical prerequisite to election of a legitimate pontiff, but they were to plague Martin, his successor Eugenius IV (1431–1447), and later popes well into the sixteenth century.

Although the various nations at Constance were able to agree on *Haec sancta* and *Frequens,* in other matters they were hampered by conflicting political aspirations and allegiances.[55] The English and Germans argued that the Council needed to institute reforms before electing a pope; the French, Italians, and Spanish insisted that the choice of a new pontiff was the first, and most pressing, order of business.[56] In the end a compromise was reached, and some reforms were instituted at the time of Oddo Colonna's election as Martin V.[57] It was no accident that the electors at Constance chose a member of one of Rome's leading noble families; they hoped that Martin's ties to the Eternal City would help him return the papacy to Rome.[58] Many of the problems that the Council of Constance had been summoned to resolve still remained when the meeting was closed in 1418, however, and the future of both reform and negotiation with the Hussites depended on Martin V's priorities and his willingness to adhere to the council schedule outlined in *Frequens.*

In spite of the fact that a council was responsible for his election, Martin was no great friend to conciliarism, and even after he settled in Rome he faced an intimidating array of practical problems, as well as the vaguer issue of reform. In addition to losing spiritual prestige, the papacy had also lost effective control of the Papal States during the period in Avignon and the Schism. Because certain papal revenues had been repealed as part of the reforms at Constance, Martin needed this territory as a source of income, and he devoted much of his pontificate to regaining it.[59] His efforts to do so were not simply diplomatic; in spite of the depleted resources of the papacy, on average Martin spent close to 100,000 ducats a year on his mercenary army.[60] Surrounded as he was by enemies and intrigues, the Colonna pope relied on members of his family to help him reconstruct and administer his unruly realm, and he rewarded his relatives and dependents generously. While Martin was not the holiest man to adorn the seat of Saint Peter, thanks to both his family connections and his personality, he was well suited to rule an Italian state in the cutthroat environment of Quattrocento Italy. His pontificate represented an important reassertion of the papacy's temporal power, but he bequeathed to his successor a swarm of avaricious Colonna relations and a council that was scheduled to be held at Basel and was thus dangerously independent of papal control. In the early years of his pontificate, the Venetian Gabriele Condulmer, who chose the name Eugenius IV, proved himself ill-equipped to face these challenges. Chased from Rome, he spent much of his reign in Florence and all of it warring with the Council of Basel. In 1439, the Council elected its own pope, Felix V, who did not step down until 1449, two years after Eugenius's death.

Plan of Reviving the Eternal City

Based on the military and religious issues described in this introduction, it is easy to see why historians have not included Martin and Eugenius in accounts of Rome's Renaissance. Their papacies were defined by political unrest rather than by cultural rebirth. Furthermore, their successor, Nicholas V (1447–1455), was credited by his own contemporaries, most notably his biographer Giannozzo Manetti, with beginning a distinctively Roman revival of ancient culture, and modern scholars have followed Manetti's lead.[61] Only under Nicholas was the papacy firmly established in Rome, the threat of conciliarism finally removed, and a true devotee of antiquity seated on the throne of Saint Peter. Only under Nicholas did the Curia recognize the full propagandistic potential of Rome's classical legacy and begin a systematic effort to restore and beautify the *caput mundi*. Martin and Eugenius appear briefly in hopeful introductions to works on Nicholas and the later Roman Renaissance; the very darkness of the early Quattrocento and of their pontificates has been used to highlight later achievements.[62]

Scholars interested in Renaissance Rome are not the only ones who have shied away from the period between 1420 and 1447. If Martin and Eugenius do not fit neatly into accounts of Rome's cultural revival, their reigns also represent an abrupt shift from some of the most interesting currents of the Trecento city. Political historians of this period have examined the heady aspirations of Cola di Rienzo, the Romans' repeated efforts to craft a working republican government, and the rise of a new noble class with close political ties to the commune.[63] From their perspective, Martin and Eugenius appear as representatives—or at least harbingers—of papal tyranny, determined to end a long-standing, if spasmodic, effort to free Rome from papal rule. Although the return of the papacy in 1420 was not yet permanent, it marked the end of the Avignon and Schism eras, eras that hurt Rome financially but gave the city unprecedented political freedom.

The Schism also provoked and promoted complex and exciting political theories about the nature of power in the Church. For many legal and intellectual historians, as well as scholars of theology, the real sphere of activity in the early Quattrocento was not the Curia but the councils that challenged its authority. Studies of the pontificate of Eugenius focus on the meetings at Basel and Ferrara-Florence rather than on the pope and his Curia.[64]

The lack of attention to Rome in the early Quattrocento is, however, more than an accident of historiography. The years from 1420 to 1447 were a liminal period in the city's history, a time when both Rome and the Curia were caught between conflicting realities—between the Middle Ages and the Renaissance, between conciliarism and papalism, between an image of Rome as a restored republic and a dream of Rome as a papal capital. Rather than trying to argue that the reigns of Martin and Eugenius were part of the Middle Ages or the Renaissance, this book embraces their liminality. It argues that Rome between 1420 and 1447 was a hotbed of initiatives that borrowed from the city's medieval legacy and also presaged its Renaissance future. In spite of the challenges facing the Curia and the city, both secular and spiritual leaders had some important assets: the traditional reverence due the papacy, a Curia that had grown into a sophisticated bureaucracy during its time in Avignon, an elaborate and evocative ceremonial system, and an urban landscape which, if physically denuded, was rich in myths and associations.

The city also had a very special set of publicists. In the sixteenth century, humanism was to become the intellectual orthodoxy of Europe, but in the early Quattrocento it was still an avant-garde intellectual movement.[65] Humanists were united by their commitment to certain disciplines—grammar, rhetoric, history, poetry, and moral philosophy—that were not at the center of scholastic curricula.[66] But they were also united by their passionate love of classical antiquity. For these men, Rome really was the *caput mundi,* the eviscerated, but still living, embodiment of a grandeur that they longed to revive. The contrast between the architectural and political glory described in ancient texts and the derelict reality of Rome and the papacy stoked the imagination of these scholars.[67] They came to Rome in search of jobs, most especially the coveted post of papal secretary. But they did much more than write official papal letters.

The works of scholars such as Leonardo Bruni (1370–1444), Poggio Bracciolini (1380–1459), and Leon Battista Alberti (1404–1472) have been extensively analyzed as representative of the Florentine intellectual milieu, but their ties to Rome and the papal Curia have received much less attention.[68] Yet both Bruni and Poggio enjoyed the prestigious post of papal secretary (Bruni from 1405–1414, Poggio from 1414–1415 and 1423–1453). Alberti was active as a papal abbreviator from about 1430–1437 and more loosely connected with the Curia throughout the 1440s. In spite of the close ties of these much studied scholars to the papal court, Celenza's rich study of Lapo da Castiglionchio the Younger's *De curiae commodis* (1438) offers the only extended discussion of curial humanism prior to the pontificate of Nicholas V.[69] In part this reflects an Anglo-American bias toward Florentine studies, a bias that has survived the many criticisms of Hans Baron's conception of "civic humanism," but it also reflects the emphases of the humanists' own writings.[70] Whereas texts such as Bruni's *History of Florence* and Alberti's *Books on the Family* express their authors' deep commitment to the city on the Arno, few humanist works address Quattrocento Rome and the papal court so explicitly. Curial humanists often seem surprisingly ostrich-like in their lack of engagement with the specific crises shaking the papacy, especially given the fact that the political events of the early fifteenth century Curia shaped their peripatetic careers. If these scholars showed minimal interest in politics, however, they were still civically minded, commenting extensively, even obsessively, on other aspects of the urban environments around them.[71] Their writings offer journalistic insights into the state of marriage, the mores of clerics, the wiles of prostitutes, the pretensions of princes, the idiocy of their curial colleagues, the facial hair of Greek visitors, the festivities surrounding the consecration of the Florentine cathedral, and a host of other contemporary events and practices. Thus, they trace a rich, evocative image of the Curia and its various homes at a time when other sources are scarce and fragmentary. By combining the testimony of the humanists' complex rhetorical texts with some of the surviving archival materials, it is possible to reach a deeper understanding of both the papal court and the city of Rome in the period from 1420 to 1447.

Throughout the Middle Ages and the early modern period, political and religious leaders as well as artists and intellectuals looked to the past when they wanted to solidify their own positions. For members of the early Quattrocento papal Curia, newly returned to Rome, the legacy of antiquity was inescapable and endlessly evocative, but there was not, as of yet, any consensus on how to use it. Every chapter of this book explores appropriations of antiquity to some extent, but the theme is particularly pronounced in the first and last chapters. Upon entering Rome in 1420, Martin V faced a restive and somewhat skeptical populace that wanted to develop a new balance between their traditional overlord and municipal government. Chapter 1 traces some of Martin's interventions in his bishopric and his attitudes toward local authority. It also explores the *Descriptio urbis Romae* of the communal bureaucrat Niccolò Signorili, a description that looks back to the chronicle tradition of the High Middle Ages even as it incorporates certain elements of humanist scholarship. By analyzing two of Martin's major initiatives—the revival of the *Maestri di strada* and the completion of a splendid double-sided triptych for Santa Maria Maggiore—chapter 1 argues that Martin's vision of Rome complemented and confirmed that of Signorili.

Like other courts and bureaucracies of the period, the Curia was expanding, and humanists had to compete with swarms of other job seekers eager for the financial benefits, stability, and prestige of curial posts. Thus, even as they sought to establish an intellectual program, classical scholars also had to market that program to prospective patrons and employers, and the beginning of chapter 2 explores their efforts to do so in their dedications of translations of Greek works. As they crafted these dedications, scholars resorted to familiar platitudes about the glories of the *studia humanitatis*. Such an optimistic attitude did not, however, pervade the majority of humanist writings. Curial applicants and those scholars who won a place within the institution were critical of courts generally and of their own court in particular. The second part of chapter 2 examines anticourtly sentiment in a number of humanist writings. The chapter as a whole thus traces two of the most familiar themes explored by curial scholars between 1420 and 1447.

Although there were certain elements of continuity in curial culture during the reigns of Martin V and Eugenius IV, there were also striking differences. Thanks especially to two recent collections of essays, much more is known about Martin's pontificate than that of his successor.[72] The beginning of chapter 3 summarizes the many political challenges that Eugenius IV faced. It then examines how Poggio Bracciolini and Leon Battista Alberti responded to the tumult of Eugenius's reign. As the Curia was rocked by contemporary events, these humanist bureaucrats sought to craft a distinctive intellectual identity. Not content to describe the world they saw, they also sought to shape it, to excoriate evil practices, and to offer alternatives. They wanted to make society more like the ancient world they admired, but where ancient precedents were unavailable, they simply sought to make their world better.

One of the ways in which Alberti and Poggio hoped to improve contemporary society was through reform of the Church. Their ideas differed sharply from those of the conciliarists at Basel, whose plans for church reform have been more widely recognized and studied. They did, however, share certain elements with the reforming initiatives of Eugenius IV and one of his cardinals, Domenico Capranica. While the humanists' visions of an improved Church were considerably more secular than those of the pope and cardinal, they suggest that classical scholars were not just critical outsiders and that they may have played a role in shaping the ethos and ideals of Eugenius's Curia. Chapter 5 continues this line of analysis, collating humanist descriptions of papal ceremony with a contemporary pontifical. It considers how Eugenius's Curia used magnificent display to bolster its shaky authority in Rome and other cities, and it examines how humanist descriptions of papal ceremonies helped to promote a monarchical vision of Church authority.

Returning to the question of what Rome meant in the early Quattrocento, chapter 6 parses the ways in which Biondo Flavio (1392–1463), Eugenius, and Filarete (ca. 1400–1465) collaborated—and competed—as they sought new rationales for urban renewal. Both Biondo and Filarete combined study and imitation of ancient models with enthusiastic praise of the pontiff, and in doing so, they looked forward to the propagandistic uses of humanism by pontiffs of the later Quattrocento. It is, however, too simplistic to suggest that the ethos of Martin's reign was still medieval, whereas that of Eugenius was characteristic of the Renaissance. Instead, chapters 1 and 6, and this work more generally, demonstrate the endless fluidity and malleability of Rome's legacy. The Renaissance that developed in the later fifteenth century was not a natural response to renewed interest in the past but, instead, a product of conscious, calculated choices about how Rome's past could enrich her present and future. This book examines Poggio, Alberti, Biondo, and their fellow curialists not as "midwives to modernity" but as individuals determined to use the classical legacy both to manage and to shape the chaotic, rapidly changing world in which they found themselves.[73]

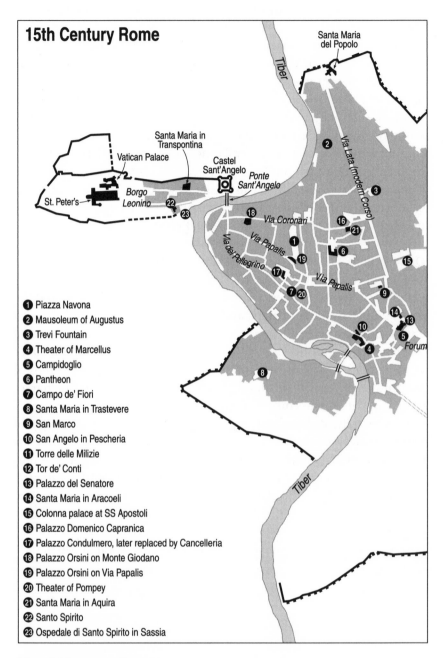

15th Century Rome

Santa Maria
del Popolo

Tiber

Via Lata (modern Corso)

Santa Maria in
Transpontina

Vatican Palace

Castel
Sant'Angelo

Ponte
Sant'Angelo

St. Peter's

Borgo
Leonino

Via Coronari

Via Papalis

Via del Pellegrino

Via Papalis

Forum

Tiber

❶ Piazza Navona
❷ Mausoleum of Augustus
❸ Trevi Fountain
❹ Theater of Marcellus
❺ Campidoglio
❻ Pantheon
❼ Campo de' Fiori
❽ Santa Maria in Trastevere
❾ San Marco
❿ San Angelo in Pescheria
⓫ Torre delle Milizie
⓬ Tor de' Conti
⓭ Palazzo del Senatore
⓮ Santa Maria in Aracoeli
⓯ Colonna palace at SS Apostoli
⓰ Palazzo Domenico Capranica
⓱ Palazzo Condulmero, later replaced by Cancelleria
⓲ Palazzo Orsini on Monte Giodano
⓳ Palazzo Orsini on Via Papalis
⓴ Theater of Pompey
㉑ Santa Maria in Aquira
㉒ Santo Spirito
㉓ Ospedale di Santo Spirito in Sassia

Map: 15th century Rome

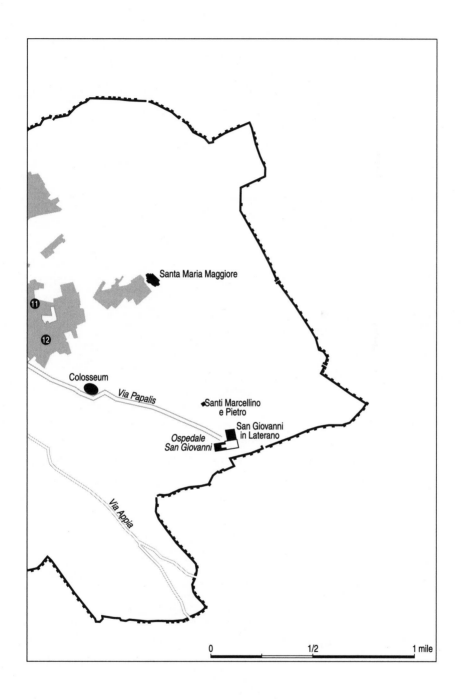

Santa Maria Maggiore

⓫

⓬

Colosseum

Via Papalis

Santi Marcellino
e Pietro

*Ospedale
San Giovanni*

San Giovanni
in Laterano

Via Appia

0   1/2   1 mile

1

Rome's Third Founder? Martin V, Niccolò Signorili, and Roman Revival, 1420–1431

A s THE introduction to this book argues, it is possible, in part, to recreate or at least imagine what Martin V saw the day he entered Rome as pontiff. It is, however, much more difficult to know how he interpreted what he saw, what the city meant to him. Manetti memorably recorded Nicholas V's vision of what Rome could and should be, and Pius II left his own *Commentaries*, giving his opinion not just on the city but on Italy more generally. Unfortunately, Martin and his successor left no such personal responses to the urban center they fought so hard to rule. Thus, their attitudes to Rome have to be pieced together from their actions and from contemporary interpretations of the city. While these literary sources do not provide direct insight into the urban goals of Martin or Eugenius, they demonstrate an array of interpretative frameworks through which the city could be viewed and some of her Quattrocento meanings. They thus offer guidance as to the parameters within which the popes' ideas developed.

Some Readings of Rome, 1330–1430

One of the most influential fourteenth-century responses to Rome was Petrarch's letter to Giovanni Colonna. When Petrarch visited Rome in 1337, he found a city impoverished by the absence of the Curia, and writing to Colonna, he further exaggerates Rome's emptiness and desolation, transforming her into a blank slate on which his imagination can have full play. By claiming to see a legion of famous Romans including Evander, the she-wolf, Ancus Martius, Lucretia, Lars Porsena,

Horatius, Coriolanus, Curtius, Jugurtha, Caesar, Augustus, Nero, Peter, Paul, and Constantine, Petrarch offers a virtuosic summary of his knowledge of Roman history.[1] His letter is an exercise in rhetorical imitation, a rewriting and reinterpretation of Evander's prophecy to Aeneas, but unlike Vergil, Petrarch does not offer a triumphal promise of political grandeur. Instead, he bewails the fact that "nowhere is Rome less known than in Rome"; rather than summarizing a common cultural heritage, his historical catalogue displays knowledge that is only accessible to a few experts. Although Petrarch acknowledges the possibility that "Rome would rise again instantly if she began to know herself," the rest of his letter questions the feasibility of a revival of ancient civilization. In fact, Petrarch suggests that Rome may be nothing but a projection of his own, classically trained imagination, an emblem of his own reading.

During the last few years of Martin's reign, Niccolò Signorili, the secretary to Rome's magistrate, dedicated his *Descriptio urbis Romae eiusque excellentiae* to the pope.[2] Whereas Petrarch focuses on the extent to which Rome has fallen, Signorili takes a more optimistic tone. He does bewail the fact that writings about Rome's laws, honors, and general history have been lost, and he explains that the Conservators of the *Camera urbis* urged him to remedy this situation. As in so many dedications, he waxes on about his own lack of knowledge, eloquence, and ability but concludes that, even if he can only offer a sketch of Rome's grandeur, it will be better than nothing.

> Starting from this, Holy Father, one thing is constant and most true with credible evidence and without doubt; indeed it is very evident to all nations and it does not require proof that Rome alone shines clearly throughout the world in spiritual and temporal affairs with a special law and dignity, since the seats of both the highest Apostle and the supreme emperor are located here. And from this it follows, not surprisingly, that this city deserved to be decorated with such lofty structures, to be distinguished with such great titles and to be raised to such superiority, with divine clemency permitting. Thus Rome is called the head of the world, the head of faith, the mother of laws, the common fatherland and mistress of all people and their teacher, both from the disposition of her laws and from the universal usage of her speech. Your holiness is able to grant the truth of this testimony. For you, who are considered lord throughout the world so that you are honored as Rome's protector by the munificence of great kings and princes, you should

hold fast to this city, take care to conserve her honors and dignities, and not permit her, who ought by every right to be honored by all, to be held in small esteem by her subjects.[3]

Here, in short, is the other side of a coin that Rome offered to her Quattrocento interpreters. At the same time that she was nothing, a ruined shell, she was also a landscape whose meaning was so multivalent, so predetermined, that no number of superlatives could capture it. The temporal and spiritual capital of the world, Rome was as great, as awe-inspiring as she was elusive. Signorili goes on to argue that Martin was raised by God in order to restore the city, which he describes as the pope's "oppressed true wife."[4] In other words, Signorili does not deny that Rome is in a sorry state, but he believes—or at least claims to believe—that Martin can easily effect a cure and restore her to the honors she deserves. After all, together pope and city are the head of faith and the head of the world.

Signorili's dedication demonstrates that even the most extravagant exponents of Rome's grandeur realized the city had fallen on hard times. The question was how to interpret this depression. Was it a sign of how completely and irrevocably Rome had fallen from her past glory? Was it a downturn of the wheel of fortune that controlled all human endeavors? Or was it a temporary blip, a minor interruption in the grand, eternal story of the *caput mundi?* At least in the passage above, Petrarch subscribes to the first of these readings, and the nostalgia he expresses has been described as one of the great achievements of the humanists, connoting as it does an awareness of anachronism and of the differences between antiquity and the present day.[5] This appreciation of anachronism was not, however, the exclusive property of humanists.[6] A Spanish traveler to Rome, Pero Tafur, who was certainly no humanist, describes a reaction similar to Petrarch's:

> I stayed at Rome during the whole of Lent, visiting the sanctuaries and ancient buildings, which appeared to me to be very wonderfully made, but not only am I unable to describe them, but I doubt whether I could appreciate them as they deserved. Therefore I may be pardoned, such is the grandeur and magnificence of Rome, if I fall short in my account, for I am not equal to so great an undertaking in view of the extent to which these ancient buildings have been destroyed and changed, and are decayed. Nevertheless, to all who behold them it is clear that they were once very magnificent, in spite of the tumults which they witnessed

after the beginning of the downfall of Rome, in the discords between the princes who were her citizens, the destruction wrought by powerful kings who fought against her, and the hand of time which consumes everything. Moreover, Pope St. Gregory, seeing how the faithful flocked to Rome for the salvation of their souls, but that they were so astounded at the magnificence of the ancient buildings that they spent much time in admiring them, and neglected the sacred object of their visit, the Pope, I say, sent orders to destroy all or the majority of the antiquities which had survived from ancient times.[7]

Tafur works to give historical reasons for Rome's dilapidation, more concrete explanations than those offered by Petrarch. The basic thesis of his statement is nevertheless the same; Rome is in ruins, but Tafur claims that appreciation of Rome's duality is not confined to experts but is, in fact, "clear to all" who behold [the ruins.]" Thus, while it is difficult to know whether to credit Tafur's inclusivity or Petrach's elitism, it seems that some late medieval visitors saw Rome with a double vision—ruin and past majesty were distinct but simultaneously apparent.[8] Such an attitude hardly seems remarkable to modern Westerners. Visitors to Rome today, like visitors in the eighteenth and nineteenth centuries, are struck by Rome's ruins and the haunting sense of lost grandeur they convey.[9] But in the early Quattrocento there was far less agreement about the relationship between Rome's past and her present. Rather than being subject to neat (or arbitrary) modern periodization, Rome's pagan, republican, imperial, and Christian pasts intermingled in complementary ways. Rome stood for empire and the loss of empire, grandeur and the loss of grandeur, a Christianity that completed Rome's classical legacy, and a Christianity that systematically sought to destroy that legacy; yet for even its most gloomy visitors it also held out the possibility of renewal.[10] If humanist rhetoric encouraged dialectical reasoning, so too did the city that symbolized both the greatness and the loss of antiquity.

Martin V and Rome

As the preceding section suggests, Martin was presented with a grab bag of possible interpretations of Rome. Which ones did he find most compelling? This question is particularly fraught because it relates to a broader historiographical debate about the balance of communal and papal authority and about when Rome became a Renaissance city, ruled by a papal *signore*. According to one compelling interpretation, in 1398 Boniface IX effectively ended the communal government that had emerged in the twelfth century and was briefly restored during the papacy's absence in Avignon, first under Cola di Rienzo and then under the *Bandaresi*.[11] Thereafter, even when the popes were away from Rome, struggles between their representatives and municipal authorities were only about minor details; the principal battle for a strong popular government had been lost.[12] An alternative reading defines the reign of Nicholas V as an essential turning point; before him, the papacy was still struggling to gain a footing, but he succeeded in making Rome into his own seigniorial state and introducing the era of the "papal prince." Recently, other historians have painted a more complex picture, in which the balance between papal and municipal authority was, if not constantly shifting, at least constantly tested throughout the Quattrocento.[13] The frequent plots against fifteenth-century popes serve as just one manifestation of how the communal ideal endured. In the aftermath of one such plot, Martin's successor, Eugenius IV, had to flee from Rome disguised as a monk and a republic was again declared, albeit briefly. Eugenius's plight suggests that much of Martin's success in regaining control of Rome was personal rather than institutional.

During Martin's life, humanists praised his restoration of the Papal States and, more particularly, of Rome; his return to and revival of the city made him a third Romulus, a third founder of the city.[14] After Martin's death, curial scholars tended to view his reign nostalgically, transferring the myths of the golden ages of Augustus and Cola di Rienzo onto his pontificate.[15] In the twentieth century, the studies of Peter Partner were less complimentary, portraying Martin as more concerned for the aggrandizement of himself and his family than the amelioration of conditions in Rome and the Papal States. Two recent Italian collections of essays on the Colonna pope have revived some of the humanists' enthusiasm for Martin's innovations, albeit in more muted and cautious terms.[16] If Martin's intentions and priorities are open to debate, however, certain facts are not in dispute. As a member of the august Colonna family, Martin V had deep and complex ties to Rome and the *campagna*.[17] Like the thirteenth-century popes who came from Rome and Lazio, he was a feudal baron who saw the territorial strength of the Colonna as a long-term goal, one that would outlast his pontificate.[18] In other words, Martin's perspective on how to rule Rome was both local and traditional. Whatever his more general and theoretical ideas about Rome may have been, he instituted reforms that promoted papal monarchy but that also favored a new urban elite. Because of their debts to the pontiff, the members of this elite did not necessarily see the promotion of a strong communal administration as the best means of furthering their own interests.

In 1425 the pope renewed the statutes of 1363, an apparent sign of respect for Rome's municipal autonomy. Nevertheless, in a variety of ways Martin co-opted or undermined communal authority. While he did not make sweeping changes on par with those of Boniface IX, Martin seems to have chosen most city officials himself rather than allowing them to be elected.[19] Although the Senator (selected by Martin) was theoretically Rome's governor, in fact the papal Vice-Chamberlain served as the true administrator of the city, taking an active role in the Capitoline court, overseeing the *gabelle,* and controlling the flow of money from the *Camera urbis,* much of which went to the Apostolic Camera.[20] Not content with the oversight of the Vice-Chamberlain, Martin promoted Colonna clients in the Curia, in his own *familia,* and in the municipal government. These men brought to Rome the peace and order for which Martin was so frequently praised, but they also helped his brother Giordano and his nephews to create a Colonna state in Lazio. Thus, even as Martin quashed the political aspirations of other baronial families who threatened papal authority, he greatly expanded the power of the Colonna.

Martin's political and economic policies proved beneficial not just to Colonna clients. He also provided critical assistance to a broader social group—Rome's emerging urban nobility—and while some of these nobles were loyal to the Colonna, the group as a whole spread well beyond the tentacles of one family's patronage.[21] Thanks to the expulsion of the barons from Rome in the mid-Trecento and their subsequent impoverishment, cattle farmers, merchants, and notaries had invested in land, first in the Roman *campagna* and then in the city itself.[22] By the 1420s, these new nobles typically owned a house in Rome, urban properties (commercial and/or residential) that they could rent, and farms and vineyards in the *campagna,* but land ownership was only one of the ways in which Rome's new nobles sought to increase their social and economic prestige.[23] They embarked on legal and medical careers in hopes of curial positions, bought titles of nobility, moved to prestigious neighborhoods, built or expanded their family chapels, and married into baronial families.[24]

Martin played an important role in supporting this new group and ensuring that its members would become key players in later fifteenth- and sixteenth-century Rome. He appointed nobles to both curial and communal offices, and he treated these officials with deference and respect; in other words, he gave the new *nobiles* the sort of social legitimation they sought, and the benefits he offered were not simply social.[25] The presence of the papacy brought money into the city, and for this reason Martin was welcomed by merchants and investors in real estate.[26] By the mid-Quattrocento, thanks in part to the Colonna pope, the new nobility had merged into a homogenous social class with a shared value system and shared strategies for social promotion. Long after the Colonna had lost the power they enjoyed under Martin, Rome's nobility continued to play an important role in the city's political, cultural, and economic life.

Niccolò Signorili, the author of the *Descriptio urbis Romae*, was both a member of Rome's new nobility and a Colonna client.[27] In addition to serving as the secretary to Rome's Senator, he was also one of the *caporioni* of the Monti region when he wrote the *Descriptio*. During his active career, he held a variety of other posts in the municipal government and the guild of the *bovattieri;* thus he followed the sort of career path typical of Rome's new nobility. Because of Signorili's affiliation with the social group Martin favored and his clientage ties to the Colonna pope, the *Descriptio* has been described as a sort of manifesto for Martin's Rome.[28] In spite of this often-made claim, scholars have tended to mention but not discuss the significance of the *Descriptio,* or they have focused on one particular part of the text; for this reason, the next section will discuss the entirety of Signorili's eclectic work. The remainder of the chapter will then relate the *Descriptio* to two of Martin's most distinctively Roman initiatives, his revival of the office of the *Maestri di strada* and his commission (or at least interest in) the Santa Maria Maggiore triptych painted by Masaccio and Masolino. By examining Signorili's text and Martin's projects, the nature of the pope's collaboration with Rome's new nobility becomes clearer as does the cultural ethos of Martin's reign. The evidence suggests that the pope saw the city not primarily as a museum to ancient glory or a transhistorical symbol of power but as a region in need of and open to renewal.

Signorili's *Descriptio*

After the dedication that begins Signorili's *Descriptio,* the first substantial section of the text offers a summary of Roman history. Signorili does not open this section with the apostles or the emperors, the men who, in his eyes, gave Rome her twofold authority. Instead, he details the earliest history of the city with some care. According to Estodius, Rome was founded by Noah who moved there after his sons built the Tower of Babel.[29] His son Janus and nephew Japhet constructed a mausoleum on a mountain beyond the Tiber, giving the Janiculum its name. The city continued to prosper under Noah's descendants, and Saturn, after he was defeated by Jupiter, came to Rome and built an arch on the Capitoline. Jupiter followed his father and destroyed him, and he, in turn, was followed by his own son Hercules. Only at this point did Evander and Latinus arrive in the area, shortly thereafter followed by Aeneas.

Although this account may sound strange to devotees of Livy, it was very much in keeping with the Italian tradition of communal chronicles; in fact, the story of Rome's founding by Noah was popular from at least the twelfth century.[30] It is not clear who first made the claim (nothing is known about the supposed Estodius, who is frequently cited as the source for this bit of Rome's history), but it was found, among other places, in the *Mirabilia urbis Romae;* in fact, Signorili's account almost exactly follows that of the *Mirabilia.*[31] More generally, Signorili's concern with Rome's prehistory accords with the conventions of chroniclists of the Italian communes. These chroniclists sought to increase their cities' prestige by crafting elaborate founding myths, and while the majority of such myths drew on Roman history, they also combined an eclectic range of pagan and biblical figures.[32] For example, some Venetian chroniclists claimed the Trojans as their founding father; others chose a foundation date of March 25, 421, the time at which the invading forces of Attila the Hun established themselves on the main island of Venice. Venice had Christian as well as pagan origins; Venetians boasted that the city was founded on the feast of the Annunciation and

Saint Mark established the first bishopric in the area.[33] In his famed *Chronica nuova,* the Florentine chroniclist Giovanni Villani began his account with the Tower of Babel.[34] Thus, Signorili makes up for Rome's relative dearth of chronicles by regurgitating a chronicle-like founding myth.[35] While other cities tried desperately to match Rome's authority, Signorili had at his fingertips the material that non-Roman authors strove to approximate or appropriate.

Once Signorili reaches the story of Aeneas, his narrative speeds up. Four hundred and twenty years after the fall of Troy, Romulus and Remus were born, and at this point Signorili starts citing sources regularly, especially Orosius, Livy, and Florus.[36] He moves quickly through Romulus's reign and even more quickly through the reigns of Rome's other six kings; rather than giving a complete historical account, Signorili offers a summary that he assumes will refresh the memory of his readers. Once the kings are expelled and the republic founded, Signorili's chronological account ends. He does not guide his readers through the triumphs and tragedies of the republic but instead devotes several pages to discussing the ages of Rome—how long it was ruled by the kings, the republic, and the emperors—and to describing its conquests.[37] Thus while the beginning of the *Descriptio* reads like a chronicle, Signorili stops writing a chronological account of Rome's development as soon as the historical record becomes more certain. His relative lack of interest in Livy and in the details of Roman history serves as just one of the many indications that the *Descriptio* is not a humanist work.[38]

As Signorili moves away from summary, he turns to panegyric, quoting and paraphrasing a range of sources on the reasons for Rome's greatness.[39] According to Quintilian, Vegetius, and Valerius, Rome's army and its discipline served as the foundations of Roman power. Conversely, Orosius, Valerius, and Apuleius praised the Romans' lack of concern for personal wealth, and Signorili supports this explanation by citing the general paeans to poverty of Aristides, Socrates, and Homer. He is not, however, content to focus on ancient sources. The author Signorili cites most often in his celebration of the Roman empire is Augustine, and he explains Augustine's argument that the Romans' defense of liberty and desire for glory were the two things that made their city great.[40] While Signorili's paraphrases of Augustine are accurate, he utterly ignores Augustine's main point—that Rome represents the limits of what human virtue alone can accomplish and that from the Romans' devotion to their earthly city, Christians can imagine the far greater devotion they should show to the City of God.[41] Signorili's reading of Augustine demonstrates the filter through which he interprets his sources; all things must redound to the credit and glory of Rome, and anything that questions or minimizes the grandeur of the city should be ignored.

Thus, already at this early stage, Signorili works to smooth any apparent conflict between Christian and pagan Rome. Augustine's critique of Roman concern with fame becomes, in his handling, yet another celebration of the glory of the classical past. And if Augustine's authority is not sufficiently weighty, Signorili has at his fingertips indisputable evidence of the complementarity of Christian and pagan Rome.

> Our lord Jesus Christ led this city founded, developed and defended by his will to the pinnacle of affairs. And the greatest of its glories is that when he came, he wished to be a Roman citizen according to the register of the census. O happy race of Romans, to be placed before all other nations by law! O happy Rome, whom the creator of the world, the Highest God raised up to such a great and lofty height. He determined that his son should be born under your empire and gave Rome a census. He wished his son to be crucified under the same empire for the salvation of the human race. And inasmuch as he deemed you, O Rome, worthy of his death, you are stained with the blood of the holy Apostles and infinite martyrs.[42]

Christ's birth thus serves as the definitive proof of Rome's preeminence. The fact that His crucifixion and the blood of the apostles and martyrs also add to the glory of Rome reveals the extent to which Signorili, in spite of his misreading of Augustine, adheres to an Augustinian view of Providence: all of human history must be a part of God's ultimate design.[43] Since Christ's crucifixion saved humankind and martyrdoms increased the faith, these actions redound to Rome's credit rather than condemning her as brutal and pagan. By conflating Augustine's divine and earthly cities, Signorili makes Rome (rather than heaven) the true pinnacle of God's design, and thus Rome's religious history, far from being an alternative to or criticism of her imperial pagan past, validates, affirms, and consecrates that past. Rome is simultaneously both city and empire, both pagan and Christian. In fact, simultaneity can be seen as the hallmark of the city. Rome as empire saw the birth and death of

Christ, while Rome as city saw the torture and killing of the apostles and martyrs, but for Signorili this distinction is not significant. His *Descriptio* lacks the intimate involvement with civic life that was characteristic of communal chronicles because, for him, Rome is much more than a city; she is the stage on which all the world's great events have occurred.[44] Just as this stage minimizes the problem of geography, so too does it mute distinctions of time. Signorili sees no reason to despair about the future of Rome because in his eyes all of Rome's pasts are her present.[45] Rome's history ensures her continuing success, at least as long as Martin and other popes follow both imperial and apostolic typologies. Here, Signorili's work offers a harbinger of the ceremonies of the High Renaissance, which interwove Rome's imperial and Christian pasts in order to celebrate the city's fifteenth- and sixteenth-century pontiffs. This propaganda, which hardly bothered with niceties such as anachronism, may in fact have owed more to Signorili's cheerful mishmash of authorities and enthusiasm than to the historical sophistication of humanist scholars.

Apparently, however, even Signorili could not continue indefinitely with superlatives, because at this point he changes topics abruptly, turning to the physical reality of the city. This remains his concern for much of the rest of the work. After praising Rome's location, he enumerates the regions of the city and the ancient gates. He gives a brief survey of the city by region, noting the main attractions of all thirteen medieval rioni. He then names the city's bridges, mountains, fields, fora, basilicas, baths, roads, palaces, and arches.[46] In enumerating the arches, he includes the inscriptions on them, and this, along with his use of an ancient regionary catalogue, is the principal reason that Signorili's work has been included in accounts of early antiquarianism.[47] But Signorili's devotion to the city's antiquities comes through most clearly not in these dry lists but in the impassioned passages from Cassiodorus, which he quotes at length. For example, rather than trying to speak of the city's statues, he leaves it to the great rhetorician to do it for him. The first excerpt is from a formula addressed to the prefect of the city on the appointment of an architect.

> Let him [the architect] read the books of the ancients; but he will find more in this City than in books. Statues of men, showing the muscles swelling with effort, the nerves in tension.[48] The whole man looking as if he had grown rather than been cast in metal. Statues of horses, full of fire, with the curved nostril, with rounded tightly-knit limbs, with ears

laid back—you would think the creature longed for the race, though you know that the metal moves not.[49]

Cassiodorus goes on to say that while the ancients speak of the wonders of the world, the statues of Rome surpass them all. And in Signorili's next excerpt from the *Variae,* Cassiodorus discusses repairs to the Cloaca and asks "what city can dare to rival your towers, when even your foundations have no parallel?"[50] In spite of his obvious enthusiasm for Rome, Signorili cannot match the aesthetic appreciation of this sixth-century prefect, and so he does not try, quoting him at length where he earlier paraphrased the words of Augustine, Livy, etc. Signorili's predilection for Cassiodorus may be due to historiographical as well as aesthetic factors. Just as the bureaucrat of Theodoric worked to present a case for the continuity between Rome's imperial and Gothic traditions, so too did Signorili strive to integrate the broader arc that stretched from Noah to Martin V. And if, as one modern scholar has suggested, "only a real disaster can stir up interest in Cassiodorus" (and more specifically the *Variae),* the end of the Schism certainly provided dislocation and instability that made Cassiodorus's illusion of continuity appealing.[51]

In privileging the testimony of Cassiodorus, Signorili also adds a new technique to his repertoire. Having praised Rome in his own words, summarized her early history, discussed her various ages, paraphrased (and misinterpreted) the accolades of ancient and patristic authors, and enumerated her ancient structures, Signorili now begins to include long excerpts from documents and literary works. This practice was typical of medieval chronicles and served as a means of preserving official records of historical importance. For Signorili, these excerpts may offer a welcome break from composition, but they also demonstrate the centrality of late antiquity to his vision of Rome. After a brief account of Constantine's vision of the cross, his defeat of Maxentius, his cure from leprosy, his conversion and erection of churches, and his move to Constantinople, Signorili includes the entire text of the Donation of Constantine, the Donation of Pippin and Charlemagne, and confirmations of the Donation by Louis the Pious, Otto I and Henry I, and Henry II.[52] In short, whereas Signorili was content to rely on his own research to describe the early passage of *imperium* from the kings to the republic to the emperors, he meticulously documents the (supposed) granting of imperial authority to the popes; this passage from the *Descriptio* reads like a collection of primary sources designed to bolster the Donation myth. At one level, Signorili's decision to accept the Donation at face value is surprising given the fact that it was already subject to widely different interpretations—many of them antipapal—in the late Middle Ages and especially the fourteenth century, but even after Valla's well-known attack on the Donation, Renaissance pontiffs continued to cite Sylvester's gift of temporal authority as a source of their prestige.[53] For earlier and later propagandists, as for Signorili, the Donation was too potent a historical myth to be ignored simply because of a few grumpy monks and heretics.

Having firmly established papal *imperium,* Signorili returns to praise of the city:

> This is most happy Rome, which omnipotent God wished to be head of the whole world and of orthodox faith. This is most holy Rome which he chose as the prop of faith and consecrated with the blood of his blessed apostles, martyrs, and saints. This is the glorious city which deserved to be graced with so many and such holy gifts, ennobled with the splendor of so many wonderful deeds, and decorated with the brilliance of so many ornaments, that the spirit is stupefied in contemplation.[54]

This passage not only reiterates some of Signorili's earlier praises, it also presages the remaining major points of the *Descriptio.* After a long excerpt from Petrarch's letter to Colonna, Signorili emphasizes that Rome is the one and only true seat of apostolic authority. He uses Peter's famous interrogation "Domine, quo vadis?" to remind pontiffs that even fear of death should not prompt them to leave the seat chosen for them by God. He then goes on to remind all secular rulers and religious leaders that they owe their position to the popes and cannot be legitimately chosen or confirmed by any other authority.[55] After listing these rulers, and thus proving that the entire world is subject to the jurisdiction of Rome in both temporal and spiritual matters, Signorili lists Rome's churches.[56] In the midst of this list, he discusses the cardinalate and explains the protocol for papal elections, the protocol ensuring that the elected pope is Peter's legitimate successor. Finally, he devotes the last thirty folios of his work to a detailed description of the relics of Rome's churches; these relics represent a rich, unique part of the city's legacy and offer yet another proof of God's favor.[57]

In short, Signorili's *Descriptio* includes a fascinating mixture of genres and ideas. It combines an origin myth, a historical summary, a collection of sources on Rome's grandeur, a compendium of ancient inscriptions, a meticulous listing of ecclesiastical property, an impressive series of panegyrics, and an extended defense of papal authority. In bringing together these different genres and types of information, Signorili represents the Quattrocento city as hovering on the cusp between the Middle Ages and the Renaissance; his Rome evokes both the city of credulous twelfth-century pilgrims and the capital of papal princes such as Julius II. But what motivated Signorili to create this strange compendium? While the tradition of medieval chronicles helps to explain certain aspects of the work—especially its account of Rome's prehistory—the *Descriptio* is not a chronicle. Like civic descriptions of the thirteenth and fourteenth centuries, it emphasizes the advantages Rome enjoyed. But Signorili was writing primarily for a prince rather than for an audience of fellow-citizens, and he relies on richly rhetorical quotes rather than statistics to support his assertions.[58] As in many of the guides to Rome, the *Descriptio* focuses on the city's holy places, yet its meticulous detailing of relics and relative dearth of stories make it unlikely to appeal to the casual visitor. Signorili also evinces some of the interest in ruins that was initiated by Petrarch, but no one would mistake him for a humanist.

In short, by combining elements from different genres, Signorili creates a piece that cannot be classified. Certainly, the *Descriptio* is an exercise in propaganda, designed to flatter Martin and to extol the glories of Rome, but even the amorphous goal of propaganda does not account for its eclectic combination of elements. Nor does it account for Signorili's most persistent theme—the continuity of Rome's power. Most medieval chroniclers assumed that the conditions of the world were stable, that men of the past and the present lived by the same societal rules. Signorili does not just assume this—he insists on it with almost ferocious intensity. At one level, Signorili's insistence on continuity betrays anxiety and suggests that he realized the passage of *imperium* from Noah to Martin V was not quite as seamless as he claims.[59] Certainly, there were historical reasons for such anxiety; Martin had only brought the papacy back to Rome in 1420, and both another schism and another papal defection from Rome must have seemed like potent dangers in the 1420s. If the papacy left Rome, so too would much of the prosperity that Signorili and other *nobiles* enjoyed.

Signorili's insistence on continuity suggests more than fear, however;

it suggests that he and his fellow nobles were not entirely content with papal domination of Rome. In the first sentence of the main text of the *Descriptio,* Signorili explains that after the *translationem imperii* from the republic to the emperors, Rome was again made into a prefecture.[60] Everything within a radius of one hundred miles was under the jurisdiction of the city, which remained a republic. The prefect had power over roads, public waters, ports, taxes, and many other things, and Rome retained the fiscal privileges that it had possessed before the translation; in other words, it had immunity from certain taxes. Romans or their governors, such as senators and prefects, could make laws and could recall an emperor, restoring command to themselves when a legitimate cause arose.[61] In short, in spite of his celebration of the papacy, Signorili makes a firm claim that Rome, by historical right, was and remains a functioning republic.[62]

One modern scholar argues that this assertion of the city's rights coincides neatly with Signorili's emphasis on the pope's temporal power.[63] But it does so only on one condition; the pope must leave the city free to exercise her traditional liberties. He must exercise his temporal dominion not in Rome herself, but in the rest of Europe. From the beginning of Signorili's *Descriptio,* it seems that Martin has temporal authority everywhere *except* in Rome. The condition of his inhabiting the seat of the apostles is his recognition of the republican rights of Rome's citizens, rights that dramatically predate Peter's visit to the Eternal City. Yet Signorili is hardly a Cola di Rienzo or a Porcari.[64] His claim of republican rights forms only a small part of a large work, mostly devoted to praise of Rome's greatness. It seems that he hopes to present Rome's power and might in such glowing terms that Martin, far from being offended by this mild declaration of municipal independence, will appreciate his own place as Rome's spiritual leader and the inheritor of *imperium* outside the confines of the city. It also seems that Signorili is trying to manage the tension experienced by so many members of the new aristocracy, the tension between longing for old republican liberties and appreciation of the benefits that loyalty to the papacy brought.[65]

One of the ways in which this tension could be resolved or mitigated was through civic pride, a pride that, in the absence of real municipal autonomy, found its surest foundation in Rome's cultural and historical preeminence.[66] Signorili's *Descriptio* serves as a manifesto of this pride, and Martin's cultural projects, especially his revival of the *Maestri di strada*, his efforts to rebuild the city, his decision to live near the Campidoglio, seat of Rome's municipal authority, and the creation of the Santa Maria Maggiore altarpiece, demonstrate how the pope could and did promote the Romans' self-esteem.[67] While it is possible to see Martin as a Machiavellian monarch, cunningly manipulating Rome's aristocracy in order to achieve his own personal and familial ends, these projects suggest instead that the pope saw members of Rome's new nobility as his allies. For Martin, who grew up within a network of barons and vassals, the promotion of papal power, the aggrandizement of family members and clients, and the amelioration of conditions in Rome were interdependent and mutually supportive enterprises that, like the city's classical and Christian identities, could not be separated. If the opposition between papal and municipal authority seems clear to many modern historians, such opposition was not so stark in early Quattrocento Rome.

Rome's Streets and Urban Revival

While Signorili expatiated on Rome's beauty and argued that the city is ideally situated to fulfill all human wants, Martin was less impressed with its appearance.[68] In particular, as quoted in the introduction of this book, in the 1425 papal bull *Etsi in cunctarum*, the pope expresses his shock and dismay at the state of Rome's streets. Having complained of the decay of public and private buildings and the ubiquitous presence of animal refuse, Martin goes on to explain how he will address this threat to civic health and aesthetics:

> We do not wish to neglect and conceal the aforementioned defects and aberrations of this sort any longer, and we are mindful that there was neglect in this city for a long period of time and that it grew widespread. We wish to counteract altogether the aforementioned inconveniences; thus with apostolic authority we renew, raise, recreate, and restore the office of the magistrate [of the streets] according to the ancient institution of said office.[69]

The office to which Martin refers, the *Maestri di strada* (or the closely related office of the *Magistri edificiorum et stratarum*) was a long-standing part of Rome's communal government.[70] The *Maestri* of the thirteenth and fourteenth centuries were judges who dealt with disputes between property owners, and the protocol for their election by municipal authorities was carefully laid out in the statutes of 1363.[71] A document of 1410 (probably a copy of an earlier statute on the duties of the *Maestri*) begins by emphasizing that protection of ancient structures should be their special care. Once the premium is over, however, the statute quickly turns to the practicalities of managing Rome's streets, practicalities suggesting that the *Maestri* spent the majority of their time regulating new construction.[72] These officials could demand the removal of buildings that blocked Rome's streets and penalize those responsible; they could also fine anyone who dumped refuse in public areas. At least in theory, the office of the *Maestri* was not solely punitive; they were expected to oversee the repair of streets, buildings, fountains, bridges, and aqueducts. Repeatedly, the 1410 statute emphasizes the power of the *Maestri* to act according to their own discretion, but it also specifies that if the officers do not do their duties, they themselves will be fined.

At the beginning of his pontificate, Martin treated the *Maestri* as communal officers, responsible to the Conservators and the Senate. In a mandate of 1423, "leaning diligently to those things which look to the peace of disputing citizens and the reformation of the said city," he named two men to the position of *Maestri edificiorum et viarum*.[73] At the same time, however, he asked the Conservators to confirm the officials' oath and to replace them with other *Maestri* when they thought fit. Thus, he appeared at least to include communal authorities in his decision-making process. Two years later, the papal bull *Etsi in cunctarum* suggested a different approach; Martin wrote not to the Conservators but directly to the *Maestri,* and in lamenting Rome's urban problems, he presents himself as the city's sole guardian:

> Although we are delighted by the grace and flourishing of all the provinces of the world, according to the office entrusted to us from above, nevertheless not undeservedly we think it fitting and appropriate that we must have a greater care of our city of Rome, which was dampened by the spilling of the blood of the Prince of the Apostles, Peter, and of Paul, who was called to a similar lot, who are the central point of orthodox faith as well as of innumerable victorious martyrs, so that this city, which once flourished under divine and human laws, and it and its district now in our time, by the favor of divine clemency, should rise with good and should win approval with good success in the future.[74]

Like Signorili, Martin underscores the interrelationship of Rome's many stages. But unlike Signorili, he does not mention the commune's ancient liberties; the reference to "human laws" serves as the only possible allusion to Rome's classical government. While this is hardly surprising in a papal bull, the emphasis on the special relationship between pope and city is striking. Most papal bulls begin by stressing the connections between individuals, the benevolence of the pope, and the obedience owed by a bishop, ruler, or other addressee. Here, Rome takes the place of the individual, and the pope alone has duties and responsibilities. Without taking up Signorili's language of an oppressed spouse, the bull suggests that the pope and city are bound by a relationship of conjugal intimacy and exclusivity. In this bull, Martin appears as the divinely appointed guardian of Rome, and he addresses the *Maestri* as papal servants, not as independent officials.[75]

Thus, at one level, Martin's bull of 1425 seems to fly directly in the face of Signorili's aspirations for Rome. By circumventing the Conservators' authority and the electoral process, the pope undermines the city's *imperium*, but even as he does this, he also gives considerable powers to the *Maestri*. They may inspect buildings and roads, and, if anything impedes these spaces, they are responsible for having it removed or destroyed without any judicial proceeding. They can repair and build from scratch what they see fit, and they are also free to use whatever penalties, fines, and condemnations they approve. Although Martin claims simply to reinvest the *Maestri* with the rights and duties laid out in the 1410 statute, he also throws the considerable weight of papal authority and curial finance behind these officials.[76] In other words, he takes on the active leadership role for which Signorili calls, demonstrating a keen awareness of the gritty physical realities of Rome. Whereas the 1410 statute addresses the problem of filth calmly and without emotion, Martin infuses outrage into his discussion of Rome's streets.

It is not clear that this impassioned rhetoric, or, indeed, the revival of the *Maestri*, did much to ameliorate the condition of Roman thoroughfares, but the pope's agenda was certainly practical. He used *Etsi in cunctarum* to condemn the more politically radical elements of Rome's population, and he also passed legislation to ensure that the state of Rome's infrastructure would not prevent pilgrims from visiting (and spending money in) the Eternal City.[77] Furthermore, Martin, like his successors and predecessors, tended to grant the post of *Maestri* to members of Rome's new nobility. Thus, even as the pope's takeover of the *Maestri* undermined the political aspirations of Signorili and his fellow nobles, it furthered their economic and social interests.[78]

Martin's building projects, like his revival of the *Maestri,* reveal both his determination to increase his own power (and that of his family) and his desire to restore his bishopric. He constructed a Colonna residence adjoining Santi Apostoli and lived there, rather than at either of the traditional papal residences, for the majority of his pontificate.[79] Yet in spite of his decision to live in the center of Rome, Martin sponsored work on Saint Peter's, especially its portico, which was to be painted with scenes from the life of Peter and Paul.[80] The pope showed particular interest in the Lateran, where he had a Cosmatesque floor and ancient columns installed and where he commissioned Gentile da Fabriano to create an elaborate fresco program of scenes from the life of John the Baptist and Old Testament prophets.[81] Before his election, Martin had been archpriest of the Lateran, and this personal tie, as well as his family's connection to the basilica, helps to explain his special care for the Lateran and his unusual request to be buried before the high altar of Rome's Episcopal seat.[82]

Martin did not limit his concern to the city's two main basilicas, however. The pope undertook repairs in other prominent churches, including Santa Maria Sopra Minerva and Santa Maria del Popolo, and even as he concentrated his efforts on those churches that received the greatest number of pilgrims, he also demonstrated a more general concern for the religious fabric of the city.[83] In 1425, Martin entrusted two *Riformatori* to inspect all the sacred places of Rome, and he urged his cardinals to undertake repairs in the religious institutions under their care.[84] Moreover, Martin did not ignore the secular parts of the city; he sponsored work at the Castel Sant'Angelo, the Hospital at Santo Stefano dei Ungheresi, the Campidoglio, along the Via Papalis, on the walls and ports of the city, and on its bridges (especially the Ponte Milvio and the Ponte Santa Maria.)[85] As a result of these papal projects, the value of Roman real estate began to rise and the population began to increase.[86]

Based on these urban improvements, the humanist's decision to dub Martin a third Romulus does not seem wholly absurd. Nevertheless, twentieth-century historians and art historians have been more cautious in their assessment of the pope's achievements; they have focused on the ways in which Martin presaged the urban developments of later pontiffs rather than on the extent of his own urban restorations. One scholar describes him as "the initiator of many policies which were developed more fully by his successors."[87] Another argues that while the pope probably did not have an overall plan for urban development, he did begin to transform the pecuniary value and ideological significance of some of Rome's key areas.[88] Sadly, all such arguments must remain somewhat speculative. None of Martin's major projects have survived. The fresco program of Gentile da Fabriano was destroyed in the seventeenth century; the Colonna family fortress was sacked after Martin's death and then subsumed in the later development of the Palazzo Colonna.[89] Thus, assessments of Martin's role as a restorer of Rome will continue to rely on reports of the pope's contemporaries and near contemporaries and on the few remaining testimonies to his activity.

The paucity of evidence renders the surviving artifacts from Martin's reign particularly important, and one of the most splendid of these is the Santa Maggiore altarpiece, which was commissioned by Martin, members of his family, or one of his cardinals.[90] The double-sided triptych, completed sometime in the 1420s, was divided into three separate panels in the eighteenth century.[91] Largely because of Vasari's claim that Masaccio painted the triptych, much of the scholarly literature on the piece has explored problems of attribution; most scholars now agree with Clark that Masaccio painted *Saints Jerome and John the Baptist* and had a minimal role in the rest of the triptych.[92] The iconographical complexity of the piece has also attracted considerable attention, however. The triptych includes a rich mixture of familial promotion, self-aggrandizement, Marian devotion, and civic celebration. This complexity elucidates the reasons why it is so difficult to pigeonhole Martin's pontificate and suggests that his conception of Rome and of his own role in it was as richly multivalent as Signorili's *Descriptio.*

The Santa Maria Maggiore Triptych

As the principal center of Marian devotion in Rome, Santa Maria Maggiore had long included an array of visual representations of the life of the Virgin. The Colonna altarpiece was no exception. One of the two center panels commemorates the legend of the basilica's foundation: Mary caused a snow shower on August 4, and the snow showed Pope

Liberius (352–366) exactly where the church should be built.[93] In Masolino's rendition of the event (Figure 1), Martin V is pictured as Pope Liberius, and he appears at the forefront of a scene that includes both Gothic and Renaissance elements.[94] The buildings at the far left and right of the painting are clearly inspired by classical structures and demonstrate an awareness, if not full mastery, of the three-point perspective that Masaccio was perfecting in Florence. The onlookers, especially those toward the back of the painting, have the *contraposto* poses and Quattrocento garb characteristic of Renaissance group scenes. But the background of the painting is gold, and, looking only at the foreground, one sees the outlines of a traditional Maestà, with Christ and Mary enthroned above and lines of reverent worshippers below.[95]

In addition to telling a familiar Roman story, the *Miracle of the Snow* emphasizes the building and rebuilding of the city. The figure of Liberius/Martin wears a triple tiara (perhaps based on the one Martin commissioned from Lorenzo Ghiberti) and an attendant holds his cloak. Yet in spite of his grand garb, the pope is hoeing or digging along the outlines of the basilica. Such active intervention on the part of Liberius does not accord with the basilica's legend and emphasizes Martin's personal participation in the rebuilding of the city.[96] The painting's background also underscores the scene's Romanness: Masolino carefully depicted the tomb of Gaius Cestius, Testaccio, a section of the Aurelian walls with Porta San Paolo and the Sabine Hills. The painting thus captures the view from the belltower of Santa Maria Maggiore toward the southeast. Here as in his works from the 1430s, Masolino displays his precocious interest in realistic portrayals of Rome's urban landscape, and he simultaneously connects Martin to Rome's ancient, as well as its late antique, past.[97] Many scholars now believe that the triptych was designed for the main altar and that the *Miracle of the Snow* faced the front of the church.[98] Thus, the imagery of this painting would have been visible only to the select group of those in the choir, a group that sometimes included the pope himself. Martin could have pondered his role as a "third Romulus" as he sat through the lengthy papal ceremonies described in chapter 5, and the panels to each side of the *Miracle* would also have prompted the pope to think of himself and his family.[99] The panel that stood to the left of the *Miracle* depicts Saints Jerome and John the Baptist (Figure 2) while the panel that stood to the right portrays Saints John the Evangelist and Martin of Tours (Figure 3). Martin chose his papal name because he was elected on the saint's day of Martin of Tours, and to emphasize the connection between the pope and his namesake, the French bishop also has the face of Martin V.[100] The saint's cope and John the Baptist's red cross are both decorated with columns *(colonne)*, a clear reference to the pope's family. John the Baptist was the titular saint of the Colonna chapel at Santa Maria Maggiore, and the family had been closely connected to the basilica since the thirteenth century.[101] Thus, the back of the triptych serves as a multilayered homage to the connections between the Colonna and the Church, connections not just to the beleaguered Church of the Quattrocento but to the heroic Church of John the Baptist, the writers of the Gospels, the Latin Fathers, and early proselytizing bishops.

Even as the triptych celebrates Martin and his family, it also celebrates Santa Maria Maggiore. The reverse of the *Miracle of the Snow* shows an *Assumption* (Figure 4), which would have been facing the congregation), and the feast of the Assumption was one of the most important days for the basilica. On that day, a grand procession brought the *Acheropita* (an icon of Christ) from the Lateran to Mary's church, and after the son "greeted" his mother (the *Regina caeli*) the icons were placed on two separate altars.[102] The saints on several of the side panels are also closely related to the basilica. Some of the minor relics of John the Baptist and Saint Jerome were housed in Santa Maria Maggiore, and the relics of Saint Matthias (who originally stood to the right of the *Assumption*, Figure 5), were among the basilica's most important possessions.[103]

There has been considerable debate about the figure depicted along with Saint Matthias—originally he was identified as Pope Liberius, and some scholars still accept that attribution. In the 1960s, however, Vayer made a convincing case that the figure represented Gregory the Great, which is now generally accepted.[104] Gregory may, like Martin of Tours, bear the visage of the Colonna pontiff, and his achievements combined the personal and ecclesiastical associations of the triptych. Gregory made Santa Maria Maggiore a stational church, and in 590 his procession with the *Regina caeli* was credited with ending a terrible plague. The famous pope thus played an essential role in establishing the church as one of Rome's principal basilicas, and he simultaneously worked to rebuild the city, surmount schism, and assert papal authority. Thus, even as Gregory's figure recalls the history of Santa Maria Maggiore, it simultaneously celebrates Martin as a pontiff who hoped to equal Gregory's achievements. While Renaissance painters increasingly depicted themselves and their patrons as famous figures (Raphael's multiple portraits of Julius II in the *Stanze* being one of the most obvious examples), this practice was relatively new; according to Meiss, the portrait of Martin V as Saint Martin (and perhaps Pope Gregory) is the first example of an artist depicting any contemporary figure as a saint.[105]

All of these associations have been made by other scholars. What has not, however, been emphasized is that there are at least two ways in which the triptych accords with the spirit of Signorili's *Descriptio*. First, it almost obsessively emphasizes simultaneity. The ages of John the Baptist, the Apostles, the Church Fathers, the sixth century, and the Quattrocento are all intermingled. Thus, a complex process of sedimentation creates the authority of the Church, the Colonna, Santa Maria Maggiore, and Rome herself. By literally making Martin V into Pope Liberius, Martin of Tours, and Gregory the Great while indirectly linking him to Matthias and Jerome and Peter and Paul (who stood to the left of the *Assumption*, Figure 6), Masolino does for the pope what Signorili did for the city. Martin is not one pope but several, not one leader of the Church but all of those leaders combined.

Moreover, the triptych does not simply honor Martin. He was, at least before his election, a member of one of the richest and most influential confraternities in the city, the *Societas raccomandatorum Santissimi Salvatoris ad Sancta Sanctorum*.[106] This confraternity was the steward of the *Acheropita*, housed in the pope's private chapel at the Lateran. Its members came from among the city's elite, bringing them together for prayer, processions such as that on the day of the Assumption, and charitable work.[107] In the early 1400s, this charitable work was especially important, as the *Raccomandati* were responsible for the city's only functioning hospitals: Ospedale di Sant'Angelo near the Lateran, a hospital for women by San Giacomo al Colosseo (now destroyed), and a third hospital at the church of Santi Pietro e Marcellino.[108] (These hospitals thus circled the area that is now Ospedale S. Giovanni.) Martin saw the *Raccomandati* as his allies in the region between the Colosseum and the Lateran and gave them the right to police this area. While the pope relied on the confraternity, he also helped it, most notably by allowing the baronial *ostiarii,* the custodians of the *Acheropita,* gradually to be replaced by members of the *Raccomandati.* This new privilege increased the confraternity's membership and the charitable donations to it, thus enabling the hospitals to grow. It was one more way in which the pope supported the pretensions of the new *nobiles* against the city's feudal barons. Signorili, to take one example, was a secretary of the *Raccomandati* and was responsible for the 1419 inventory which, in addition to listing the confraternity's assets, also recorded its statutes, the possessions of the society and its members, and a book of anniversaries.

O'Fughludha has noted that the Masolino triptych includes the colors of the *Raccomandati.*[109] By indirectly celebrating his confraternity and directly celebrating its most important feast day, Martin's triptych honors this elite group and emphasizes a shared allegiance to its priorities. Furthermore, the triptych presents both the pope and Santa Maria Maggiore as deeply embedded in Rome—her geography, her history, her feast days, her relics. In fact, the triptych itself—with its heavy use of gold and its rich coloring—seems like a reliquary, connecting the multiple significances of Santa Maria Maggiore (a product of the miracle of the snow, home to the relics of John the Baptist, Jerome, and Saint Matthias, and center of Marian devotion in Rome). At the same time, the triptych's richness makes it a marvel, to be admired and exclaimed over just like the city's ancient ruins. Thus, even as the triptych adopts a familiar late medieval artistic form (the altarpiece), it also bears some relation to earlier types of holy or magical objects. As both relic and marvel, the triptych fits neatly into the eclectic material sphere that plays such an integral role in Signorili's ideological portrait of Rome. The form as well as the content of the work emphasizes simultaneity, the simultaneity so valued by Signorili.

Martin V and Rome—Some Concluding Thoughts

In supporting the *Maestri di strada* and in commissioning (or at least providing a major subject of) the Colonna triptych, Martin does not appear as a tyrant, intent on destroying republican liberties. But neither does he look like a papal prince in the manner of Sixtus IV or Julius II. As Verdi argues, Martin's directives to the *Maestri* seem to have been motivated more by frustration with the city's filth than with any grand political scheme.[110] Likewise, the Santa Maria Maggiore triptych is hardly the cornerstone of a sophisticated personal or familial propaganda program.[111] Instead, it is a beautiful object to be admired and examined, an object that links Martin and the Colonna with Rome and the papacy in a personal, stylized fashion. Would Martin's aspirations have been grander if his resources had allowed it? Perhaps, but that is like asking what his pontificate would have been like were it not for the Schism. Unlike some of the historians who have studied him, Martin shaped his aspirations for Rome according to the conditions he faced. He would have been puzzled to be described as a tyrant and would not have known what it meant to be a Renaissance prince. The humanists' comparisons between antiquity and their own day have made it easy to read titanic ancient struggles into Quattrocento Italian politics, and Burckhardt's claim that the Renaissance ushered in modernity has encouraged historians to analyze it according to the standards of later nation-states.[112] But Martin was not the successor to Augustus nor was he the predecessor of Louis XIV.[113] He was a family man, a Roman, a baron, a pope, an aesthete, a benefactor, and a member of a confraternity. If Signorili's *Descriptio* serves as a good representation of Rome under Martin V, it is because the pope saw both himself and the city as filling multiple roles, roles that might seem contradictory or even mutually exclusive to later ages but that, in the early Quattrocento, managed to contain and control the mayhem of Rome and post-Schism Christendom. While he initiated some of the programs and policies associated with the Renaissance papacy, Martin's nepotism, his self-aggrandizement, his patronage of art, and his imprint on Rome's urban structure had at least as much in common with the initiatives of his medieval predecessors as they did with the sophisticated ideological programs of the pontiffs of the High Renaissance.

Figure 1: Masolino, *Miracle of the Snow,* Museo Nazionale di Capodimonte, Naples

Photo Credit: Scala/ Ministero per i Beni e le Attività culturali

Figure 2: Masaccio, *Saints Jerome and John the Baptist,* National Gallery of Art, London

Figure 3: Masolino, *Saints John the Evangelist and Martin of Tours*, Philadelphia Museum of Art, Philadelphia, PA

Photo Credit: The Philadelphia Museum of Art/ Art Resource, NY

Figure 4: Masolino, *Assumption*, Museo Nazionale di Capodimonte, Naples
Photo Credit: Scala/ Art Resource, NY

Figure 5: Masolino, *Saints Gregory the Great and Matthias*, National Gallery of
Art, London

Figure 6: Masolino, *Saints Peter and Paul,* Philadelphia Museum of Art, Philadelphia, PA

Photo Credit: The Philadelphia Museum of Art/ Art Resource, NY

2

In the Theater of Lies: Curial Humanists on the Benefits and Evils of Courtly Life

I<small>F</small> N<small>ICCOLÒ</small> Signorili served as a spokesman for Martin V's vision of Rome, what was the role of the humanist scholars whom Martin employed? Did their comparisons of the pope to Romulus have any impact on the Curia or did Martin and his cardinals resist the allure of the new scholarship? The answer is "yes" and "yes." During the reigns of Martin and his successor, Eugenius IV, the Curia began gradually to accept and adopt the humanist idiom. For example, the 1422 bull that granted Roman citizenship to the Vicenzan scholar Antonio Loschi stated that the presence of Loschi and others like him was desirable because it would help to recall the morality and culture of the ancients.[1] In keeping with the spirit of this bull, Martin collected an impressive group of intellectuals in the Curia, and Eugenius, by bringing the Curia to Florence, increased the institution's contact with the new learning.[2]

Neither Martin nor Eugenius, however, was a humanist by training, and there is no evidence that the two pontiffs took a personal interest in the imitation or translation of classical texts.[3] A few cardinals—most notably Francesco Zabarella, Giordano Orsini, Giuliano Cesarini, and Prospero Colonna—were known and admired as supporters of the new learning. Yet Zabarella, to take one example, was a canon lawyer by training, and his own writing shows relatively few traces of classical learning. In his funeral oration for Zabarella, Poggio praises him as a great orator in the style of the ancients, but this probably involved almost as much rhetorical invention as Poggio's nearly contemporary description of Jerome of Prague.[4] While the support of men like Zabarella was crucial in the early days of curial humanism, their knowledge of antiquity was limited and traditional.[5] In short, classical scholars were not preaching to a group of fellow devotees. Instead, their audience consisted of busy men, most of them trained in the scholastic learning against which humanists defined their own intellectual programs. It is an exaggeration to say that curial humanism only enjoyed "its first major advance" under Nicholas V, but the arrival of a humanist pope did change the landscape dramatically.[6]

This chapter examines the ways in which humanists infiltrated the Curia in the period between 1420 and 1447. While the pontificates of Martin and Eugenius were dramatically different, certain themes, such as the moral value of the study of antiquity and scholars' struggles between the intellectual rewards of *otium* and the practical rewards of *negotium*, reappear in humanist writings throughout this period. Many more works survive from the reign of Eugenius than the reign of Martin, and, while acknowledging this imbalance, the chapter uses the available material to argue for significant continuities in the central preoccupations of curial scholars during the first half of the Quattrocento. Humanists drew on the ideas of Petrarch, Salutati, and Chrysoloras even as they responded to the practical realities of life in and around the papal court.[7]

The chapter first explores the ways in which individual humanists used dedications of translations of Greek works to appeal to curial patrons who could help them procure permanent positions. Applications to the rich and powerful contain their share of sycophancy, but they also offer a party platform, explaining the benefits to be gained from the *studia humanitatis* and arguing for their authors' value as cultural mediators. If dedications present a rosy picture of the complementarity of classical study and curial life, in their independent literary works, both aspiring claimants and well-established bureaucrats expressed deep skepticism about the institution for which they worked. Thus, the final section of the chapter examines some of these critiques and argues that anticourtly polemic, like praise of the *studia humanitatis*, was a common preoccupation of classical scholars throughout the period from 1420 to 1447. The recurrence of similar themes in a variety of different types of text suggests that, in spite of their fierce competitions with each other and minimal support from other curialists, humanists at the papal court began to define a common intellectual program in the first half of the Quattrocento. This program included both elements of propaganda, designed to appeal to potential patrons, and a more select language of cultural criticism, which was confined to the humanist elite.

Humanists and the Development of the Roman Curia

One of the major developments of the Avignon papacy was a dramatic expansion of the curial bureaucracy.[8] Among their many duties, curial bureaucrats produced the voluminous papal correspondence, and thus the Curia, like so many Italian chanceries, needed skilled Latinists and provided a natural home for classical scholars, who were the professional heirs of medieval notaries. During the Schism, the rival popes hired notable humanists (including Leonardo Bruni, Antonio Loschi, and Poggio Bracciolini) as secretaries.[9] After the Council of Constance, however, there were three complete Curias, one for each of the rival pontiffs, and some curialists, including Poggio, lost their positions as a result.[10] By 1423, Poggio had returned to the papal court, but a letter to Bruni suggests that he was still concerned about his status, and that of his fellow secretaries, three years later.

> There is an argument, indeed a dispute, really almost a fight between the secretaries and the lawyers. We each claim the more honorable position relative to the pope in coronations, masses, and processions. The dispute arose because during a recent papal procession, we asked the bishop of Alet where we should go and he said "after the lawyers, nearer to our lord." When we did this, the lawyers took it badly, saying that we ought to go before them. Finally this reached the pope's ears because of the clamor of those who always argue and fight, and he entrusted the case to the cardinals of Sant' Eustachio and San Marco, who were to hear our cases and respond. (The pope is on our side, but you know his humanity; he does not know how to resist the importunity of the lawyers.) The lawyers say that during the coronations of the highest popes, the secretaries always went first and they themselves were in the more honorable place closer to the pope. The bishop of Aretino denies this, and he is the only one here who was present at the coronations of popes. Therefore you, who cherish the dignity of our office, assist us against these foreign declaimers and write what you saw

done and how it seems to you. Then write to the pope, so that he may cherish the dignity of his familiars. For there is no doubt that those men who manage the secrets of the pope have a more dignified office than those who, as publicans, bark for gain at the will of one pimp. . . . If it happens that the secretaries were once nearer to the pope and now are neglected, this will be an eternal ignominy to our office.[11]

At one level, this seems no more than a petty squabble between bureaucrats, an early example of office politics. And yet, as Poggio realized, a great deal was at stake in this battle for precedence. Processions represented the hierarchy of early modern society, establishing the relative authority of various groups.[12] In the mid-fourteen-twenties, the future shape of the Curia remained uncertain. Would Martin return it to its more modest, pre-Avignon size or would he yield to the pleas of the many office seekers? The secretaryship was a relatively new office; perhaps it would not survive the attacks of rapacious lawyers.[13] More generally, the status of humanism at the papal court remained uncertain; given the pope's lack of interest in classical studies, it was possible that humanists generally would be marginalized in, or even excluded from, the new, post-Schism Curia.

In spite of Poggio's fears, the prestige of the secretaryship, and of curial offices generally, increased rather than diminished in the Quattrocento. The financial problems of the Schism had contributed to the rapid growth of the Curia beyond its Avignon size; to raise money, rival pontiffs levied fines on their staff and, in return, gave them certain immunities, benefices, and the rights to charge fees.[14] By the early 1400s, the Curia was the largest, most sophisticated, and best organized bureaucracy in Europe. Its bureaucrats did not simply sit and benefit from lucrative offices; there was a great demand for the complex documents issued by the Curia.[15] Thus, while the Council of Constance called for a dramatic reduction in curial staff, there was a superabundance of qualified—or at least experienced—curialists who insisted that the post-Schism popes maintain the established order. Under Martin V, the Curia included almost five hundred officials; the papal *familia* and the *familiae* of the various cardinals offered additional sources of employment.[16] Even during the tempestuous reign of Eugenius IV, the Curia also provided a considerable degree of job stability.[17] Not surprisingly, a wide array of office seekers targeted these positions; in theory, even poor claimants with the right patrons could (and occasionally did) ascend to prominent and lucrative posts, and each success story increased the number of young men who came to Rome in search of preferment.

While this general expansion of the Curia worked to the advantage of men like Poggio, only some curial positions, most especially those in the papal chancery *(Cancelleria Apostolica),* were appropriate for classical scholars.[18] The chancery produced official papal bulls and the newer, less formal papal briefs.[19] Scriptors copied documents issued by the chancery, and this relatively modest position often served as a stepping stone to more prominent offices. Abbreviators, who were somewhat higher in the curial hierarchy, helped to prepare abridged versions of papal bulls. The most desirable and remunerative post for humanists, however, was that of papal secretary. The creation of the secretariat was one of the many developments of the Avignon period, and the importance of the position grew during the Schism, when the rival pontiffs found chancery protocol too time-consuming and too public.[20] Although the secretaries produced papal correspondence, they were not officially part of the chancery but swore their oath of office in and received their stipend from the *Camera Apostolica,* which managed papal finances; this liminal status between two branches of the Curia gave them unusual freedom.[21] Working in close concert with the pope himself to draft bulls and briefs, they enjoyed exceptional unofficial influence, and the post could also be highly remunerative, as secretaries received a generous fee for each letter they produced.[22] Secretaries were well versed in the political agendas of the popes for whom they worked, and those who enjoyed particular papal favor were frequently sent on diplomatic missions. In short, by the mid-Quatrocento, the Curia was one of the most glamorous and lucrative places of employment for humanists. Competition raged for the relatively few posts appropriate for classical scholars, and the fact that humanists did not even dominate the secretariat in the fifteenth century exacerbated this competition.[23]

Modern scholars have considered when, how, and why the curial bureaucracy began to welcome and reward classical scholarship, but they have tended to focus on general trends within the Curia rather than the ways in which individual humanists attained their positions.[24] To win a permanent, well-paid post, all aspiring curialists required the support of a dense network of brokers and patrons. The dedications of eager job seekers show how scholars thought they could best market their skills to busy clerics, and the similarity of the arguments in humanist dedications underscores the extent to which humanists had a cohesive, coherent (if rather superficial) program to offer to their ecclesiastical bosses. The Curia could only be converted man by man, and so humanists, whose intellectual interests were still novel and controversial, sought to infuse the ethos of antiquity into their quotidian dealings with members of the papal court.[25]

Humanist Dedications and Curial Patronage

In the early Quattrocento, when most humanists were still struggling to master Greek, translations even of relatively brief works represented major investments of time and intellectual energy. Some scholars who had secure intellectual and professional situations (for example, Francesco Barbaro and Guarino Veronese) dedicated translations to their humanist friends, but most scholars chose to send their translations to men who might be able to offer them jobs or to further their careers in some important material way. At least in theory, dedications obligated their recipients to make some sort of return gift. In the early years of the Quattrocento, Alfonso of Aragon (1396–1458) gave especially generous rewards in exchange for translations, and while this sort of largesse was not typical of the curial environment, scholars hoped that an appropriate gift could help them to win or retain a comfortable position.[26] At the same time, dedications conferred an aura of disinterestedness and altruism on both giver and receiver, promoting interpersonal relations even as they facilitated the exchange of goods and services.[27] Dedications offered a space where authors or translators could personalize their work and advertise their intimacy with their dedicatees to a broader audience.[28] Given that the tripartite relationship between a humanist translator, a busy cardinal or pope, and a first- or second-century Greek text was far from obvious, dedications required some clever sleight of hand. Dedicators tended to focus on two subjects: first, the benefits to be gleaned from a particular gift and, second, the virtues and importance of their dedicatee. They also, albeit more cautiously and at less length, discussed their hopes as to how the dedicatee would respond to their gift.

In discussing why they chose a particular text, dedicators emphasized the moral benefits of their presents. This was a particularly appropriate argument in dedications to Plutarch's *Lives,* and because of their length, didactic messages, and the popularity of Plutarch, translations of the *Lives* were common presents in the early Quattrocento Curia, especially in the 1430s and 1440s.[29] Dedicators argued that the study of heroes of the past could, indeed must, inspire readers to emulation. In his dedication of the *Life of Fabius Maximus* to Cardinal Lejeune (written between 1439 and 1451), the aspiring curialist Antonio Pacini asked a series of rhetorical questions:[30]

> For who is there who would not burn with love of justice if he read Aristides the Athenian? Who is there who would not extinguish the lust of his spirit and cultivate chastity if he heard that Alexander most carefully left the daughters of Darius untouched, although they were graced with amazing and unparalleled beauty? Who in reading of Fabricius would not marvel at and revere his fortitude? Because of the greatness of his will, cruel Pyrrhus could not corrupt him with gold or with terror of the fierce beast. Truly I do not know what is more capable of inducing our spirits to cherish virtue than knowledge of history. Who could fail to devote himself heart and soul to literature if he read of Plato journeying to Egypt for the sake of learning or if he heard of Apollonius visiting Arabia, Syria, the Persians and the Medes in pursuit of knowledge?[31]

In spite of his tone of assurance, Pacini is explaining to his readers how they should approach Plutarch's text; rather than looking for information or specific political lessons, they should seek moral edification. They should soak up the spirit and virtues of the great men whose deeds they study. They should read for models, for heroes, for exemplars. In emphasizing the exemplary value of history, humanists adopted the arguments of ancient Greek and Roman historians and orators, arguments that Petrarch revived in his *De viris illustribus.*[32] Plutarch's own emphasis on exemplarity fit neatly with the humanists' ideas, and their dedications cheerfully regurgitate old arguments about how the lives of ancient heroes provide an education in virtue.[33]

Although translators devoted large sections of their dedications to discussion of the general value of their work, this by itself was insufficient; because dedications were intended to be personal gifts, the proffered works had to be peculiarly suitable for the person to whom they were addressed. This could cause some difficulties; no dedicator wanted to insult his dedicatee by implying that he was in need of advice or improvement. Often, dedications emphasized that while certain lessons could be learned from a translation, the dedicatee himself had no need of them. In his dedication of Pseudo-Plato's *Axiochus* to Cardinal Orsini (probably written in 1436 or 1437), Cencio Romano notes that his dedicatee is more concerned about the health of the church than he is about his own life. Thus, Socrates's explanation as to why death should not be feared will confirm Orsini's own beliefs, and reading the work will give him pleasure.[34] Other dedications also present the dedicatee as being in complete accord with, and frequently as embodying, the wise moral lessons of the dedicated work.[35] The dedicatee can himself serve as an exemplar to a broader audience.

The authors of some dedications do cautiously suggest that their presents will be useful to their recipients. In his dedication of the *Life of Chrysostom* to Eugenius IV, Ambrogio Traversari explains that he translated the *Life* in order that others might be moved to imitate the great Church Father. He claims that he himself found solace and strength from reading about Chrysostom and says that the *Life* could go to no one more fitting than Eugenius, "you who were bound by some peculiar obligation of love to this holy man and who, even in the papal office, have persevered in striving to imitate the holiness of his life."[36] Here, Traversari effects a delicate balance; he claims that the *Life* will help Eugenius to imitate Chrysostom but insists that this was already the pontiff's wish. Traversari by this period enjoyed a reputation for sanctity that certainly put him in a different position than most humanists, but even he used caution in suggesting that Eugenius could receive instruction.[37]

Other dedicators claimed that their translations would be useful not for their dedicatees' moral well-being but, instead, in their public activities. In the dedication to Cardinal Francesco Condulmer of a translation of an oration by Demosthenes (ca. 1445), Rinuccio da Castiglione claims that "I translated it in your name because I thought it worthy of inquiry and most useful to the governance of the republic, and for a long time you have been and are still constantly occupied in the governance of the ecclesiastical *res publica*. If your lordship should read this somewhat diligently, because of Demosthenes' excellent erudition in speaking and his singular intelligence, you will find by what endeavors and techniques the republic perishes and by what means it is preserved and increased."[38] Thus, like Traversari, Rinuccio claims that Condulmer can learn from the work he is dedicating, but this learning is impersonal and practical rather than moral. In an even more practical offering, Traversari says that he is dedicating Martin Calecas's *Against the Errors of the Greeks* to Martin V because it will help the pope lead the Greeks back into the Catholic fold.[39]

In his dedication of Plutarch's *Life of Solon* to Eugenius IV (written in 1434 or 1435), the eager job seeker Lapo da Castiglionchio the Younger does not explain how the *Life* will instruct the pontiff but instead suggests a more subtle benefit:

> On account of this [all of Eugenius's great deeds], I wanted (not because of some private favor from you, but affected by your beneficence to all) to give thanks to you insofar as I can, and, in the life of some most excellent philosopher, to extol your divine and admirable virtues. Even though I can find no one in all of ancient history whose virtues can be compared with yours, nevertheless the deeds of Solon the Athenian seemed to me to come closest to all your merits. He alone of the seven was wise and alone of the seven he was the initiator of laws. You are superior to him not only in virtue but in fortune. For he despised the treasures of Croesus, the richest king of the Lydians, because he often acted with pride and insolence, whereas you poured forth your own treasure. He could not contain one city with his laws, whereas all people submit to yours. He received his fatherland free and master of a great part of Greece but left it oppressed and enslaved by a tyrant. You have returned liberty and imperium to the Roman Church, which was despoiled and pressed by a yoke. Wherefore, most blessed father, as I promised long ago, I give Solon to your holiness not so that you may imitate him (for that is not a task for you) but so that you may enjoy how much you have surpassed him. The principles of his life, if they seem pleasing to you as you read them, ought to remind you to encourage and help (as you used to do) those men who, raised by the hope of your humanity, strain to attain to the learning and wisdom of Solon in their studies, insofar as they are able.[40]

Before this passage, Lapo has already indulged in copious praise of Eugenius and his achievements, revealing his skill at demonstrative oratory. Here, he shows how the life of an ancient hero can be used to highlight and advertise Eugenius's supposed achievements. The comparison to Solon adds a certain *gravitas* to the pope; it presents him in the light of a great lawgiver. More generally, it shows that antiquity can serve as a type of handmaiden to contemporary, practical needs and careers.[41] In a rudimentary form, Lapo crafts the type of propaganda that was to become so popular in the High Renaissance, the propaganda that equated Julius II with Julius Caesar or Leo X with Augustus. Indirectly but forcefully Lapo presents knowledge of the past as useful to Eugenius, while at the same time suggesting the value of his humanist skills. Lapo is the essential intermediary between the rich political myths of antiquity and a patron in need of an image makeover. Perhaps, like other learned publicists before and after him, he enjoyed the hyperbole that mocked, even as it honored, his embattled dedicatee; by the time Lapo finishes with poor Solon, he has notably diminished the honor of being compared to the great lawgiver.

In trying to convince popes and cardinals of the importance of imitating the past, scholars also emphasized their own role as cultural mediators.[42] Cencio decried word-for-word translation, specifically citing the authority of the august Chrysoloras.[43] Between 1440 and 1443, Rinuccio criticized an earlier translation of Lucian's *Charon* and claimed that, thanks to his efforts, the text can now be "read with pleasure and understood without difficulty."[44] But scholars did not confine themselves to discussing the mechanical aspects of translating. They also talked about what both translation and dedication meant. In 1436, Lapo claimed that even if the translator does not deserve as much praise as the original author, he nevertheless works with a similar spirit and will.[45] Pacini too sought to validate his work of dedication by comparing himself to other authors:

> We read, most excellent Lord, that when the early philosophers, both Greek and Latin, by vigilantly watching the actions of their fellow men recorded something that was worthy of praise, they generally dedicated it either to their dearest friends or to kings. Thus they honored their dedicatees with immortal praise and glory, and they made their books renowned through the authority of these dedicatees. We perceive that not only Plato and Aristotle but Homer and Vergil and in truth even Jerome and Augustine, who wrote on holy subjects, did this. . . . Thus, they illuminated excellent deeds as an example to men, and they made the virtue of their dedicatees famous and venerable.[46]

Here, Pacini carries favorite tropes of dedications to their logical conclusion. If reading Demosthenes will help Francesco Condulmer quiet the

Papal States, if contemplating the trials of Athanasius will help Eugenius cope with the problems of his papacy, then ancient authors should also serve as models, companions, and colleagues of their translators. Just as Renaissance painters dressed their classical heroes and early saints in marvelous Renaissance garb, so too Pacini transports ancient and patristic authors to a thoroughly Quattrocento literary environment. Literary dedication discouraged the understanding of historical differences for which humanists are famed. Instead, scholars exploited anachronisms in order to clothe their job applications in the august aura of antiquity.

Dedications reveal the difficulty of finding a job as a humanist within the Curia of the early Quattrocento. They express, albeit in cautious terms, a sense of dependence and a plea for consideration. They flatter the dedicatee and strive to make him receptive to the proffered gift by their praise of his merits. But they also summarize what classical scholars thought they could offer potential patrons. Dedications describe the past as a rich storehouse of exemplary figures. They praise the greatness of the intellectual legacy of both Greece and Rome. They argue that church notables of the past can be a source of inspiration and comfort. They claim that classical works offer more practical and specific forms of knowledge, and they display their authors' skill at copious praise. In short, humanists portray the Greek literature that they make accessible as an emotional crutch, a moral inspiration, a source of pragmatic advice, and a potent rhetorical model. Dedications insist that classical works can have a transformative effect, and their translators thus claim that they, experts in these texts, have a moral, as well as intellectual, preeminence.

Finding a Place in the Curia

It is difficult to gauge the success of humanist dedications. Often, it seems that classical scholars and their curial employers inhabited two separate worlds. While the former translated ancient texts, the latter faced the specter of Schism, calls for reform, and the ideological attacks of conciliarism. More practically, they had to win back and protect the Papal States, to maintain relations with their Italian neighbors, and to combat the princes who strove to assume ever greater control over their national churches. Pastor, indignant that the popes nursed representatives of "the false Renaissance" at their bosom, claims that they were simply too busy to notice the exploits of their humanist employees.[47] Without accepting his value judgment, Pastor's argument that the clerical elite was preoccupied seems difficult to refute. Dedications remind readers that every humanist client was in competition with others for a limited amount of financial, political, and social support, and they illustrate the fact that investing substantially and critically in cultural production was not yet an obvious choice for the curial princes of the early Quattrocento.

While aspiring scholars were willing to grovel in their dedications, they resented the difficulties of their position and bewailed the lack of attention paid to humanist studies. In their eyes, the challenge of engaging popes and cardinals in antiquity was not just a product of political events; it was also a sign of how inferior their own day was to the classical world. In this instance, as in their praise of the moral benefits of the *studia humanitatis*, they adopted a familiar theme of Petrarchan humanism, but their laments are infused with the desperation of hungry job applicants as well as the ire of moral philosophers.[48] Such desperation is particularly apparent in the letters of Lapo da Castiglionchio the Younger.[49] Although Lapo came from an old and prominent Florentine family, by the mid-1430s the family's social and economic status had plummeted, and thus from 1435 until his premature death in 1438, Lapo struggled to win a comfortable post, preferably in the Curia. He worked briefly for three cardinals, but death, political instability, and perhaps Lapo's own failure to please cut short these positions. In a 1436 missive to Leonardo Bruni (to whom he looked as a broker in his job search), Lapo begins by apologizing for not having written previously and assures Bruni that he did not fail to do so from forgetfulness, negligence, or ingratitude.[50]

> In truth, I was upset by an unexpected and unthought of occurrence and event so that I even began to hate our studies, studies which I have always cherished and to which I have devoted a great part of my life. I determined that from these studies I would seek all my protection, distinction, honor, dignity, and peace. Indeed, in the beginning, I was prompted by no desire for fame and glory but rather by inclination and pleasure and some hope of improving my life; with all other things despised and cast off, I devoted myself to the study of these noble and

humane arts. Nevertheless, having advanced a little in these subjects, I read and heard very often how much they were honored by the ancients, and how many and how great rewards, splendors and dignities scholars were accustomed to obtain from the most famous princes of antiquity. At this point, with my earlier opinion changed and a little shaken, I began to turn my spirit to such rewards, not because I thought I would be casting off honesty for them, but I sought to join the two. Thus, with ancient examples before me and wholly ignorant of today's times, men, customs, and doctrine, I thought that when I should come forth not imbued and ornamented but lightly tinged by these studies, an easy path would lie open to all the most ample honors and types of dignity and I would not need to seek or long for these honors but they would be conferred even on one who was reluctant and refused them . . . Things happened far differently than I had expected. For we have chanced on these times in which no honor is offered to noble and good arts and no place seems to be left for virtue and probity.[51]

Although Lapo's sense of ill-usage is apparent at other places in his letter collection, here he chooses to portray it in quintessentially humanistic terms. He suggests that, like Petrarch, he is caught between two worlds—an ancient world in which learning was respected and valued and a modern one in which talents like his are ignored.[52] By describing his plight in this way, Lapo insists on his familiarity with both the glories of ancient Rome and the vagaries of modern courts. To prove his humanist credentials more firmly, he goes on to claim that he can consider his experiences from a Stoic perspective, and other letters are even more explicit about how Lapo's own predicament has exacerbated his sense of the power of fortune, the stupidity of men, and the lack of respect for true learning.[53]

Yet Lapo's letters hardly offer a direct outpouring of his personal moral vision. They are carefully crafted works of persuasion, designed to win and maintain the loyalty and support of his addressees. Lapo struggled to transform reality through his letters; he used rhetoric to craft the social relations he wanted to have.[54] In writing to Bruni, Lapo universalizes the problem of his joblessness, presenting it not just as an individual misfortune but as a systemic social issue. His inability to find a suitable position reveals the disjunction between an idealized view of study (with which humanists so enthusiastically belabored to all who would listen) and the dismal reality of trying to make classical skills appealing to employers.[55] Unless this disjunction is remedied, the whole humanist project seems to be threatened. Perhaps Lapo is implicitly comparing his own experience to Bruni's virtuosic winning of a secretarial post through the composition of one elegant letter.[56] Although Lapo faced a tougher job market than that of the previous generation, the dichotomy he sets up is a cultural not a generational one.[57]

Much of Lapo's bitterness can be attributed to his jobless state, but even those humanists who were well established criticized contemporary society, contemporary courts, and the milieu of the Curia. Their knowledge of this milieu enabled them to turn Lapo's generalized laments into pointed social satire. Both because of his long tenure as a papal secretary and because of his incisive and vivid observations of Quattrocento society, Poggio Bracciolini served as one of the leaders of this project. At Constance, he attacked the mores of contemporary clerics, enumerating the many ways in which they failed to live up to the standards of the early church, and he continued to excoriate clerical hypocrisy throughout his career. Poggio devoted particular care to eviscerating the writings, the sexual lives, and the reputations of fellow scholars and members of the Curia he did not like. Yet even as Poggio attacked his contemporaries, he also presented many, if not most of his projects as collaborative enterprises, designed to stimulate the talents of others. One of his most popular works was the *Facetiae* (1438–1452), a collection of 273 Latin jokes and humorous stories. At the end of the work, Poggio offers an evocative origin myth for the collection.[58]

> In the day of Martin V, we used to choose a certain place in the more private part of the court—the Bugiale or Theater of Lies. There the news was reported, and we used to converse about all sorts of things, both for relaxation, which was usually our purpose, and sometimes in a serious way. There we spared no one when we set out to debunk all things of which we did not approve, and our criticism very often started with the pope himself. Therefore many would come, fearing that we would start with them. The chief roles were played by Razello of Bologna, that brilliant conversationalist, some of whose anecdotes I have included here, Antonio Loschi, a very witty man, who appears here often as well, and Cencio the Roman, a man whose vocation lay in joking. I have also added a good many stories of my own, which I thought not without flavor.[59]

In short, Poggio declares that his strange, often pornographic work represents the milieu of curial humanism in a unique fashion. Although he does not define the "we," Antonio Loschi, Cencio Romano, and Razello of Bologna, were all papal secretaries and enthusiastic classical scholars; Poggio, it seems, is presenting the Quattrocento equivalent of the Nixon tapes, a detailed record of the inner machinations of a courtly society.[60]

There is obvious danger in taking Poggio's claim at face value. Perusal of the collection shows that, far from being a map of the papal Curia or a guide to the intellectual ideals of humanist scholars, the *Facetiae* resembles a dense code that cannot be cracked with any one interpretive tool. Most of Poggio's jokes have no framing material, and it is thus difficult to determine how they relate to their specific courtly environment or the avant-garde program of the humanist scholars who inhabited it. The protagonists of the jokes exacerbate this uncertainty; stupid cuckolds, doltish peasants, mendacious wives, lustful widows, and lascivious clerics gambol cheerfully through Poggio's collection, offering evidence of his engagement with a medieval tradition of storytelling.[61] Yet in spite of Poggio's indebtedness to vernacular humor, by choosing to write in Latin he limited his potential audience to a tiny subset of those who enjoyed late medieval bawdy tales. Like most other early Quattrocento humanists, Poggio directed his independent literary works, including the *Facetiae*, to fellow classical enthusiasts, men on whom he depended and who, in turn, depended on him for friendship, editorial assistance, manuscript loans, and intellectual sparring.[62] Although humanists seldom referenced each other directly, their works include a dense web of allusions to contemporary, as well as ancient, texts. Thus, charting the ties between their writings serves as a way of delineating the values and assumptions they shared.[63]

The section that follows focuses on a subset of Poggio's jokes—those that discuss or illuminate courtly life—and compares them to Poggio's moral dialogues and the writings of his colleagues. Such a comparison demonstrates that while classical scholars at the Curia shared many of the interests and concerns of Petrarchan humanism, their perspective was shaped in important ways by the institution for which they worked.[64] Together, these texts, like the letters of Lapo, paint a vivid picture of the difficulties of life in early modern courts generally and in the Curia more specifically.

Humanists as Court Philosophers

The Misery of Courtiers

Alongside a nameless collection of friars, prostitutes, and townspeople, famous figures of Trecento and Quattrocento Italy make cameo appearances in the *Facetiae*. The well-known condottiere Facino Cane insists that his soldiers could not have been responsible for the theft of a cloak because they would never have left the victim with his tunic. Another warlord, Ridolfo Varano, when asked why he frequently deserts his allies to serve his enemies, replies that he cannot lie on the same side for any period of time. Bernardo Manetti, a Venetian ambassador, rebukes the friar who dares to wish him "peace" during the war between Milan and Florence, as the duke of Milan has declared that anyone who speaks of peace will be judged guilty of a capital offense.[65] Thus, amidst the general human drama of the *Facetiae*, the political unrest of an age dominated by condottieri is revealed. While mercenary captains and diplomats cheerfully mock the violence to which they contribute, courtly jokesters appear less lighthearted in their quips about political realities. In one *facetia*, Giovanni Maria Visconti's cook asks his master to make him an ass, and when the duke questions this unusual request, the cook replies: "I see all those whom you have raised to the heights, to whom you have given honors and magistracies. Inflated and insolent with pride and arrogance, they have become asses. Therefore I want you to make me an ass too."[66] In spite of its playful tone, this joke speaks to the cook's frustration; the opportunities of the Renaissance court, far from ennobling those who seek them, serve only to corrupt. This joke, and the many others like it that pepper the *Facetiae*, reflect Poggio's lifelong ambivalence about public life. From his early days as a struggling scholar in England to his late work on the misery of the human condition, Poggio repeatedly urged himself as well as his readers to abandon earthly rewards in favor of study, tranquility, and virtue.[67]

Poggio was not alone in this struggle between the demands of *negotium* and the rewards of *otium*.[68] He and his fellow scholars sought both to preach and to practice the Stoic detachment and self-reliance praised by Cicero, Seneca the Younger, and other Roman authors, but their writings suggest that they could not escape from doubts about how to survive at court and anxiety about contemporary political developments.[69]

The most forceful humanist indictment of courtly employment was offered by none other than the future pope Pius II (born Aeneas Silvius Piccolomini) in his *De curialium miseriis* (1444).[70] Piccolomini spent the 1430s and early 1440s at the Council of Basel, and thus experienced a somewhat different courtly milieu than his Italian colleagues, but he aptly sums up many themes that curial humanists also emphasized. Poor choices in preferment are only one of a host of evils Piccolomini identifies; his acerbic little treatise portrays the Renaissance court as a prison, inhabited by suffering fools. True honor and fame cannot be found at court because no virtue survives there. Power and wealth are similarly illusory; even if one happens to win them, they will soon be taken away. A man motivated by a virtuous desire to advise a prince will most likely be killed, as historical precedent makes clear. At court, there is no solitude, no room for conscience, and no possibility of making true friends. While Piccolomini presents these indictments with great force, he becomes particularly eloquent when he describes the supposed sensory pleasures of courtly life.

> "And what a dinner! You are given wine that fresh wool would refuse to swallow."[71] When you drink the vinegary, watery, heavy, bitter stuff, which has spoiled, possesses a bad color and taste, and is either too cold or lukewarm, you will become mad. And I will not even mention those princes who esteem beer so much, which, although it is bitter everywhere, is most bitter and hard on the stomach at court. Do not think that you are given silver or glass goblets, for they fear that the first will be stolen, and the second broken. You will drink from a wooden cup, black, ancient, and disgusting. There is scum stuck to the bottom, and often the masters have urinated in it. This cup is not given just to you so that you can mix the wine with water or drink it pure, according to your pleasure. Instead, you will drink from a common cup, and your mouth will touch where a lousy beard or drooling lip or very foul teeth were. Meanwhile, ancient wine will be served to the king in your presence, the fragrance of which is so great that the whole hall is filled with its perfume. He drinks muscatel or malvatic wine. He will order that it be brought to him from France, from Crete, from the vineyards of Genoa, from Hungary and from Greece itself, and he will never share

the smallest glass with you, even if you suffer from cardiac pains. Thus although a good wine is before you, it will not taste good, since your nostrils drink in the fragrance of a better one. Sometimes, you will want to drink, but you will not dare, unless your betters begin. The servants will not place wine before you until after the middle of the meal, and if you ask for it earlier, you will be judged rude, petulant, and a drunkard. Furthermore, in addition to this disgrace, you will not receive what you seek, and you will not drink to your own health but the health of your betters. Once the wine is on the table, it will pass through many hands before it comes to you. And do not hope that the goblet will be cleaned when the butlers mix it, even if the dregs stick to the bottom or someone has belched into it. For as in churches the recep-tacle of holy water is emptied and cleaned once a year, so too the same schedule is observed at court even with the royal wine goblets, from which the family drink.[72]

Piccolomini devotes the same care to his description of the moldy, ined-ible food at court, the interruptions that prevent a good night's sleep, and the discomforts of camp life. The courtier does not see and hear anything splendid or beautiful, only those things that are tedious and tragic. Far from cheering him, the arts of Venus only exacerbate his woe. Efforts to advise the prince and to be a good man are equally fruit-less, and the learned are despised. All in all, *De curialium miseriis* suc-cessfully robs Renaissance courts of much of their romantic aura, suggesting that the celebration of classical learning found in humanist dedications masks a grubby and agonistic reality.

In his invective, Piccolomini hardly introduces a new polemic. Criticisms of court life abounded during the Middle Ages, especially during and after the twelfth century.[73] Having itemized the failings of King William II of England (1087–1100), William of Malmesbury bewails the morals of his courtiers: "Spineless, unmanned, they were reluctant to remain as Nature had intended they should be; they were a menace to the virtue of others and promiscuous with their own. Troupes of effeminates and gangs of wastrels went round with the court."[74] Other denizens of late medieval courts went even further. Peter of Blois claimed that if courtiers were enduring their sufferings on behalf of Christ, they would be true martyrs and sure of eternal salvation; instead all their misery will do nothing but send them to hell.[75] (Like Piccolomini, Peter indulges in detailed descriptions of the gustatory aspects of this misery; he even claims that courtiers frequently die from bad food.) Walter Map equates courts with hell and asks "what torment has hell which is not present here in an aggravated form?"[76] In fact, Piccolomini's criticisms accord so well with those of his predecessors that one modern scholar simply integrates *De curialium miseriis* into his discussion of twelfth- and thirteenth-century anticourtly polemics.[77] While Piccolomini enlivens his treatise with distinctively humanistic *copia*, he repeats longstanding and familiar complaints.

What was the social reality behind this polemical tradition? Men who proved unsuccessful in the courtly lottery frequently penned anticourtly tracts, and this explains some of their negative bias. On top of this, the condemnation of courts became a standard literary trope; the absence of competing opinions and the repetition of familiar complaints suggest the extent to which the "misery of courtiers" was as much a linguistic convention as an institutional reality. Thus, part of the challenge in examining humanist criticisms of the Curia consists in comparing these criticisms with other late medieval diatribes against courtly life. Changes to familiar tropes, or shifts in emphasis, can reveal the peculiarities of the curial perspective even when they are embedded in traditional complaints.

The Misery of Princes

Maffeo Vegio joined the Curia in 1436 as an abbreviator and later became a datary and a canon of Saint Peter's.[78] By 1445, when Vegio penned *Palinurus* (also called *De felicitate et miseria*), he had plenty to say about the miseries of princes. This Lucianic dialogue takes place in the underworld and consists of a discussion between the famous boatman Charon and Aeneas's unlucky pilot, Palinurus.[79] At the beginning of the dialogue, the title character insists that sailors have the worst of all lives, but Charon forcefully disagrees. He devotes particular energy to proving why the life of the sailor is superior to that of the prince. At court, one sees the "elevation of flatterers, the acceptance of adventurers, the boldness of soldiers, the greediness of usurers, and the wickedness of supplicants."[80] But the real misery of princes' lives comes not from their corrupt courtiers but from their psychological predicament. To finance their wars, they must extort money from their citizens. As hatred of them grows, they resort to prescriptions and assassinations, which exacerbate public dissatisfaction.

Then you may see them grow pale, they are grieved, destroyed, they fear all things, they are tortured by the consciousness of their crimes, which is the first of all punishments; they fear the plots of enemies, the conspiracies of citizens, the attacks of their servants, and the vengeance of those they have oppressed. Then, they judge that nothing is secure unless they are protected by force and iron. Meanwhile, they do not believe themselves safe with anyone, not with servants, not with relatives, not with siblings, whose authority they fear more than that of any others. They hide themselves from sight and the presence of all, they surround themselves with trenches and walls, they close themselves in citadels as if damned to a perpetual prison.[81]

Vegio's litany does not stop here, but this passage encapsulates the major attributes of his prince. Hated by all, trusting no one, the prince lives as a slave to fear and suspicion, denied even the most basic of human pleasures. This figure of the tyrant has good ancient precedent; Vegio may well owe a greater debt to Bruni's translation of Xenophon's *Hiero* than he does to his stylistic model, Lucian. But, with its emphasis on flux and instability, Vegio's long account of the misery of princes also bears a striking resemblance to Burckhardt's analysis of Italian politics and to one of its most important sources, Machiavelli's *Prince*.[82] Early Quattrocento scholars did not have to rely on ancient models in their discussions of the instability of princely rule; they had plenty of modern evidence on which to draw, and those who worked in the papal Curia, most especially the papal secretaries, were uniquely positioned to analyze the workings of contemporary politics.[83]

Poggio's *Facetiae* assumes this breadth of vision, this ability to reach into the inner political sanctums of the early Quattrocento. In one of Poggio's jokes, Giovanni Maria Visconti receives an unfavorable message about the progress of the war against the Florentines. At a feast later that day, he criticizes some of the dishes and scolds his ever-witty cook for being ignorant of his art. The cook replies: "Why is it my fault, if the Florentines have taken away your hunger and your appetite? My dishes are well-flavored and made with the greatest skill, but the Florentines are heating you up and stealing your desire for food."[84] The duke, whom Poggio describes as *humanissimus*, laughs at his servant's joke, yet this clever remark complements some of the central themes of Poggio's *De infelicitate principum* (1440).[85] In this dialogue, the speakers debate the advantages and disadvantages of princely rule. Although

Carlo Marsuppini praises the princely state and Cosimo de' Medici argues that good princes, at least, can be happy, Niccolò Niccoli systematically and emphatically counters their arguments with a bleak picture of regal misery. Obsessed with ambition, desire, pride, violence, guilt, ingratitude, and fear, princes are, of all men, the furthest from the Stoic goal of freedom, a goal that even beasts recognize as essential to their well-being.[86]

The character Niccolò dominates *De infelicitate principum* and gives only ancient examples. He admits that he does not know princes personally and that his understanding of the princely state comes from his reading. He also acknowledges his Stoic point of view; in his opinion, princely rule simply exacerbates the natural evils of the human condition.[87] In *De varietate fortunae* (1432–1448), however, Poggio again insists on the misery and instability of princely rule, and here, rather than relying on ancient authorities to illustrate his points, he introduces a dazzlingly unfortunate array of fourteenth- and fifteenth-century figures. According to Poggio and Antonio Loschi, the interlocutors of books I and II of the work, the deeds of these rulers equal those of the ancients in magnificence and glory; what modern princes lack are wise men who can record and thus immortalize their actions.[88] While this sounds like a radical and unusual affirmation of the Quattrocento's ability to compete with the hallowed world of antiquity, Poggio soon reveals that it is actually a competition of evil and ineptitude.[89] The humanists agree that the career of Giacomo II, count of the Marche, supports the proverb that "Fortune never favors a stupid man for long," that Antonio Scaligeri prepared his own destruction by his crimes and laziness, that Corrado Trinci di Foligno's beheading was a fitting revenge for his murder of his brothers, and that Guidantonio di Montefeltro should have paid the penalty for his atrocious crimes (which include murder, rape, and burning a young boy alive) sooner.[90] Although books II and III of *De varietate* contain a few examples of men who fall through no fault of their own, the speakers emphasize the results of wickedness more than the power of fortune.[91]

The Misery of Curialists?

While Vegio's *Palinurus* and Poggio's *De varietate fortunae* poignantly demonstrate humanist skepticism about life at court, they do not offer a wealth of detail about the Curia itself or vivid images like those in Piccolomini's *De curialium miseriis*. Some of this detail is supplied by Lapo da Castiglionchio the Younger. Shortly before his death, Lapo wrote *De curiae commodis* (1438); although the work—as its title promises—discusses the benefits of the Curia, Lapo manages to incorporate plentiful criticisms in his well-barbed dialogue. Many of the themes he addresses—including luxury, relations between courtiers, and the prince's attitude toward learned men—are staples of courtly polemic. Yet in each case, Lapo includes details specific to the Curia, flaunting his familiarity with its milieu. The conversation is set in Ferrara, where Lapo is visiting his friend Angelo da Recanate. After they bewail the death of Lapo's patron, Cardinal Orsini, Angelo urges Lapo to leave the Curia, which is "absolutely wretched and morally bankrupt."[92] Lapo insists that the Curia offers many unique benefits and sets out to convince Angelo that he is right. Describing the magnificence of curial liturgy, he argues that God prefers to be worshipped by many people and that, among a large group of priests, some at least must be good. Recounting the wide array of treaties, controversies, and diplomatic deliberations discussed at the Curia (and the rich garments of the princes and ambassadors who pursue these weighty matters), he argues that the Curia provides a prime locale for perfecting prudence, "the guide and teacher of living well."[93] Scholars flock to the Curia in order to display their talents, and the chance to associate with them is no small benefit. (Here Lapo includes a list of prominent humanists, complete with effusive catalogues of their virtues.) Lapo ends his dialogue by defending the wealth of curial prelates, and Angelo admits that he is convinced.

Yet the questions and criticisms that Angelo raises throughout the dialogue remain, and Lapo himself often condemns the Curia in the course of defending it. Many of the benefits he lists, including his claim that among many priests there must be some good ones, are highly ambiguous. And at times he resorts to more direct condemnation. In response to Lapo's claims about the Curia's suitability as a school for virtue, Angelo notes that many people assume that a good curialist is a wicked man. Lapo expresses his fervent wish that the pope should work to curb this tendency and describes the experience of a curialist of the period.

Really what wretchedness is there that is so great that it could be likened or compared to that of the curialists? Despite the existence at the curia of quite a number of honorable, outstanding men, still, just as many are hated and despised by all because of the vice and filthiness of a few; they are subjected to a fire of envy that has long oppressed them. The audacious and the rash call down insults on the head of the pope. Every day they hurl one disaster or another on him and the rest. We see that the goods and fortunes of the church have been exposed to the most corrupt of thieves for the purpose of pillage and devastation, and we see that the entire patrimony has been ruined and stripped of its worth by force of their weapons. And unless we hasten to meet them and their audacity, it seems that soon, any day now, the ultimate annihilation of the curia is at hand.[94]

As discussed in this chapter, the wickedness of courtiers is a familiar trope, and in his personal letters, Lapo bewails the lack of appreciation of the *studia humanitatis* that pervades the Curia. Here, however, Lapo's dire warnings seem to relate to more specific historical events. The "audacious and rash" are identifiable as members of the Council of Basel, and "the most corrupt of thieves" are, presumably, the condottieri who fought for control of the papal territories. Given Eugenius IV's position in the 1430s, Lapo's doubt and dread appear appropriate. Forced to flee from Rome and threatened by the election of yet another antipope, both the Curia and Eugenius were in very real danger.

Historical exigencies did provide literary opportunities. The problems facing the Curia made it appropriate for Lapo simultaneously to praise the institution and to insist on the need for change and reform.[95] The dialogic form of the work and the shifting arguments of the speaker Lapo enable the author Lapo to create an elegant example of argument *in utramque partem*. He defends the Curia with a concatenation of stylish humanist topics, showing that he can apply the "hot issues" being debated by more prominent scholars to the milieu of the papal court.[96] Thus, both the form and content of the dialogue flaunt Lapo's humanist credentials.

At the same time, Lapo self-consciously displays his knowledge of the Curia; his descriptions of corrupt curial practices are some of the most vivid moments of the dialogue. He introduces clients learning the minutiae of potential patrons' daily routines, clerics squandering their fortunes on fabulous banquets that are served by beautiful boys, foreign cooks burying themselves in grease in the hopes that they will be rewarded with valuable benefices, and prostitutes setting their lapdogs to lick the private parts of unaroused clients. Thus while Lapo's arguments about the corruption of courts and courtiers are familiar, he strives to situate them in a distinctively curial setting. As he describes curial life, however, he himself appears as a spectator rather than a participant. Whereas Piccolomini opens the doors on the inner sanctums of the Renaissance court, Lapo only provides the insights of a hanger-on.[97]

Like Piccolomini, Poggio wrote with the irreverence of an insider, and in the *Facetiae* he offers unflattering pictures of prominent curialists. A Spanish cardinal (presumably Alfonso Carillo de Albornoz) promises the pope's soldiers that those who die on the field of battle will feast that night with God and the angels; when asked by them why he does not join the fighting, he responds that he is not yet hungry. Cardinal Tommasso Brancaccio farts to show his disdain for the admonitions of a man who is urging him to give up his dissolute lifestyle. Cardinal Landolfo Maramaldo sends his agent to straighten out the finances of a hospital he owns; the agent tells the patients that they can only be cured by an unguent made from human fat, and the hospital is quickly emptied.[98] Poggio's main target, however, is Cardinal Angelotto Foschi (or Fosco). One man rejoices at Foschi's election because he claims to be even crazier than the cardinal and thus very hopeful of receiving a red hat; another says that the devil himself would refuse to eat such a man. Thus, the Foschi jokes emphasize Eugenius IV's culpable credulity (a central theme of Poggio's *De varietate fortunae*), and the jokes about cardinals generally portray the members of the college as selfish, dissolute, greedy, crazy, wicked, and all too willing to sacrifice others for their own benefit.[99] Although these jokes reiterate the lament, which occurs repeatedly in the *Facetiae,* that only the wicked and stupid are favored by princes, they read more like a scathing editorial column than like the generalized reflections of Niccolò in *De principum infelicitate.* Poggio here demonstrates how jokes can unite humanist moralizing, humanist political commentary, and humanist invective.[100]

What motivated Poggio to mock the institution for which he worked in this way? After all, in spite of men like Cardinal Foschi, Poggio served as a papal bureaucrat for almost half a century. And while his fellow curial scholars did not all enjoy such long, prestigious, and lucrative careers, they too (with the exception of poor Lapo) retained their curial posts in spite of their negative assessments of courtly life.[101] How did they reconcile their disgust with the Curia with the long hours they spent writing bulls and briefs? Many of them were driven by necessity; most classical scholars did not have the financial resources to devote themselves to lives of quiet study, and habit worked its weird magic as Piccolomini explains.[102]

> It is not because court pleases me that I remain here, but so that I may not be accused of fickleness, as one who is not able to follow the type of life on which he embarked. I think the same reasoning keeps you here. What happens to married people has happened to us. There are very many people who while their spouse is living damn marriage and in their longing for freedom, desire their spouse's death . . . but after they have gotten their freedom, they soon take another spouse, and they can scarcely await the funeral of the dead one. Thus it is a disease of men that they do not know how (and are not able) to change the life which they live and have lived for a long time, even if they know that it is bad.[103]

Piccolomini here offers a powerful statement of the force of inertia, and Poggio's letters echo a similar lament; he knows that he should leave public life, but he simply lacks the strength to live without dependable means.[104]

The humanists' relation with the courts they inhabited, most particularly the Curia, involved more than inertia and financial dependence, however. In voicing their doubts about and disdain for these institutions, scholars were reviving not only the themes but also the tensions of Roman Stoicism. As Petrarch lamented in his letters to Cicero, the great Roman rhetorician hardly practiced the philosophical detachment he preached.[105] Thus, in spite of the fact that many Stoic works in Latin were reducible to platitudes, humanists' professional experiences pushed them to wrestle with the personal and practical implications of Roman moral philosophy. They also entered into a dialogue with Petrarch and Salutati, their more immediate predecessors.[106] If their conclusions about the relative merits of *otium* and *negotium* were not always consistent, this ambiguity accorded with the ambiguity of their favorite Roman author and his Trecento followers.

Furthermore, while the writings of curial scholars express doubts about the merits of courtly life, their bureaucratic careers offer a different sort of testimony to their commitments. In spite of the criticisms leveled at Hans Baron's theory of civic humanism, those scholars who sought employment from republics are still popularly seen as the surest embodiments of humanist public commitment. Yet, as important studies of humanism outside of Florence have stressed, classical scholars could and did also play influential public roles in principalities and despotisms. For all the laments of the characters Palinurus, Niccolò, Loschi, and Angelo da Recanate, the authors Vegio, Poggio, and Lapo affirmed their engagement with the civic world through their curial careers. If these men "knew what the ancients knew . . . tried to write as the ancients wrote, . . . and began to think, and soon to feel, as the ancients thought and felt" this was due not just to their careful perusal of classical writings.[107] It was due also to the fact that the chaos of the early Quattrocento brought to life Cicero's anguished musings about the fate of the republic and his constant vacillation between engagement and withdrawal. In writing of the evils of court life, Poggio and his colleagues were thus combining personal experience and literary tradition. The tension between *otium* and *negotium*—between the idealized view of humanist study presented in dedications and the grim realities of courtly life described in other works—was not just something about which scholars wrote; it was a tension that they experienced daily through the vicissitudes of the early Quattrocento Curia.

3

A Reign Subject to Fortune: Guides
to Survival at the Court of Eugenius IV

Asa CHAPTER 2 reveals, more humanist writings survive from the reign of Eugenius IV than from that of Martin V. While some texts explore themes that had been popular among classical scholars since the fourteenth century and among courtiers throughout the Middle Ages, other works comment on the distinctive milieu of the early Quattrocento Curia. In the third book of *De varietate fortunae*, Poggio offers an explicit, thorough, and damning analysis of the Condulmer pontiff's reign.

> Rarely did the pontificate of another pope bring such great ruin to the provinces of the Roman church and such great calamity to men. Regions crushed and afflicted with wars, cities devastated, towns ruined, fields pillaged, roads infested with highwaymen, many things seized with iron and fire, more than fifty places either demolished or cruelly torn asunder by soldiers: all these escaped no type of barbarity. Many men were sold from ruined towns into slavery; some wasted away from hunger in jail. Desperation compelled Rome, afflicted with ongoing war, abandoned by Fortune and devoid of any hope of aid, to undertake new things and rebel from the pope. . . . It is certain that in no earlier pontificate did those subject to the Roman church suffer such evil fortune.[1]

This picture of mayhem echoes descriptions of Rome before the return of Martin V, and Poggio explicitly contrasts the peace and prosperity of Martin's reign with the misery of Eugenius's. Once Poggio begins discussing specific events, he acknowledges that many of the pope's mistakes were due to his advisors, but he does not excuse Eugenius for falling prey to unscrupulous courtiers. At the end of book III, he claims that no one should be surprised at the calamities that bedeviled Eugenius's reign because "he always involved himself in continual wars, as if impatient of peace and calm."[2] Thus, here as elsewhere in *De varietate fortunae*, Poggio argues that Fortune is always powerful but that individuals exacerbate her power because of their lack of wisdom and virtue; through his involvement in war, Eugenius allowed Fortune to cause more chaos and disruption than she could have under a stronger, less impulsive pontiff, a pontiff like Martin V.

As Poggio's overview of Eugenius's reign suggests, from a curial and Roman perspective, the councils were not the defining events of Eugenius's reign. The pope's local and Italian political problems shaped the agonistic, unstable environment in which his humanist employees worked and his Roman subjects lived; they also played an important role in shaping Eugenius's understanding of his position as pontiff, his ideas about Church reform, his penchant for extravagant ceremony, and his attitude toward the city of Rome. This chapter begins with a brief introduction to the major events of Eugenius's reign, emphasizing the Italian ramifications of his conflict with Basel. It then explores how Poggio and Leon Battista Alberti sought to navigate a Curia in crisis. Some of their literary strategies were common to humanists of the early Quattrocento, especially curial scholars, but at other points they responded directly to the challenges of Eugenius's pontificate, using their rhetorical prowess as a strategic tool as well as a vehicle for social commentary.

An Overview of the Pontificate of Eugenius IV

From the moment he emerged from the conclave at Santa Maria Sopra Minerva on March 3, 1431, as the newly elected pontiff, Eugenius IV's position in Rome was insecure.[3] One of his first acts as pope was to revoke the privileges of the Colonna and confiscate many of the properties Martin V had bestowed on them; to add insult to injury, he presented some of these properties to their arch-nemeses, the Orsini.[4] The Colonna responded by rousing the Roman people against the pope, and they revolted in the spring and summer of 1431.[5] Although papal troops put down the uprising and the Colonna were temporarily reconciled to Eugenius, the pope was not beloved by his Roman subjects. His reliance on Florence and Venice soon won him a more dangerous enemy, Filippo Maria Visconti, duke of Milan, who in 1433 loosed his unemployed condottieri on the Papal States. In desperation, Eugenius decided to buy the services of one of these condottieri, Francesco Sforza, and to pay Sforza's troops, he was forced to yield yet more territory and to impose new taxes on the Romans. On May 24, 1434, at the urging of the Colonna, Milanese ambassadors, and the condottieri Niccolò Fortebraccio and Niccolò Piccinino, the populace of Rome again revolted and then made a treaty with the Visconti. Faced with this open insurrection, Eugenius fled down the Tiber disguised as a monk as angry Romans chased him.[6] For most of the next nine years, the pope made Florence his home, and he was thus implicated in the diplomacy of the republic, especially its strong opposition to Milan. Meanwhile, the Romans declared that their city was an independent commune.

The Colonna and Eugenius's other enemies in Italy opposed the pope for territorial reasons rather than from any great devotion to conciliarism, but their positions were strengthened by Eugenius's troubles with the Council of Basel.[7] Following the schedule established in *Frequens* (the decree that ordered councils to meet in 1423, 1430, and every ten years thereafter), Martin V had appointed Cardinal Giuliano Cesarini as the council's president shortly before his death in 1431.[8] The exact powers of Cesarini and the other clerics at Basel were not clear, however, and this was largely due to *Haec santa*, the most controversial of the Constance decrees.[9] In this decree, the council's participants declared that general councils are the highest power in the Church. Part of the decree reads as follows:

> In the first place, we declare that this synod, legitimately brought together in the Holy Spirit, being a general council, and representing the church militant, has power directly from Christ. Anyone, of whatever state or dignity, even if there is a pope, is constrained to obey this council in those things which pertain to faith and the extirpation of the said schism and the general reform of the church of God in head and in members.[10]

In 1415 when it was promulgated *Haec sancta* was the necessary precondition for deposition of the three Schism popes and the election of one new pontiff, but it posed a strident challenge to papal authority. Was a council's preeminence in matters of faith and reform peculiar to the

Schism? Or were all councils superior to all popes in matters pertaining to faith and reform of the Church? As the Council at Basel grew in size, its members increasingly took the second of these positions, and the reforms they advocated placed additional limitations on papal authority.[11] These reforms (which had been proposed at Constance and were revisited at Basel) included reduction in the revenues of the Curia, diminished papal control over the provision of benefices, and a set procedure for the removal of a pope who caused *scandalum*. Even as it challenged papal supremacy in the short term and threatened to diminish Eugenius's scant resources, the meeting at Basel also sought to increase the power of secular rulers and cardinals, thereby establishing in perpetuity an oligarchical as opposed to a monarchical Church hierarchy. European rulers, who were eager to control their own churches, supported at least this part of the council's agenda and used Eugenius's problems with Basel to increase their control over the secular and regular clergy in their lands.[12]

In December 1431, Eugenius followed Martin's example in dealing with the 1423 Council of Pavia and used poor attendance as an excuse for ordering the dissolution of the gathering at Basel.[13] While Martin's suspension of the meeting at Pavia had not met with opposition, the members of the Council of Basel were determined to continue their conference, and their determination inspired others to journey to Switzerland.[14] In February 1432, the council reaffirmed *Haec sancta* and *Frequens,* and in September of the same year, the council's prosecutors demanded that Eugenius be declared in contempt because of his effort to dissolve the council without its own consent.[15] Weak both in Italy and abroad, Eugenius yielded to the reconciliation efforts of the Emperor Sigismundo. On May 21, 1433, he crowned the emperor in Rome, and he formally recognized the council in December of the same year. The pope did not give up his hope of transferring the council to Italy, but, in 1435, he made a new and extremely powerful enemy when he opposed Alfonso of Aragon's claim to the throne of Naples. Alfonso soon joined forces with the duke of Milan, and the two rulers proceeded to attack the Papal States.[16]

In spite of his troubles in Italy, in 1436 Eugenius resumed an offensive position toward the Council of Basel; he sent a *libellus apologeticus* to the secular rulers of Europe, laying out his grievances against the council. He claimed that the council's insistence that he had to obey it

"is nothing other than totally to destroy the power of the highest pontiff and the vicar of Christ on earth and to place the supreme power,
given by Christ, into the hands of the multitude, which is not so much
erroneous as completely alien according to all the doctrine of the holy
fathers and also truly pernicious to the whole condition of Catholic
princes, since in the same way their people, if they congregate together,
can pretend their power is greater than that of the princes and they can
overturn the position of bishops and the Christian polity, which is least
of all to be admitted or tolerated."[17] In short, Eugenius connected his
predicament with that of the princes, suggesting that they could suffer
the same indignities foisted on him. Eugenius also objected to specific
rulings of the council on annates and the power of the College of Cardinals,
but much of the *libellus* simply enumerates the council's wickedness in
setting itself up as an independent body, daring to judge Eugenius, and
failing to recognize his unique, God-given authority.[18] In the spring of
1437, Eugenius called for the transfer of the council to Ferrara, and
although only a minority of those at Basel—almost all of whom were
Italians—approved the transfer, Eugenius opened a new council at Ferrara
in April 1438.[19] The avowed purpose of the council was reconciliation
with the Greek Orthodox Church, but it also strengthened Eugenius's
position in relation to the assembly at Basel. Faced by a rival council,
the representatives at Basel deposed Eugenius and elected a new pope,
Felix V, on November 5, 1439. The secular rulers of Europe were uncom-
fortable with the idea that an assembly could choose to depose a ruler,
and their support for the gathering at Basel began to dwindle.[20]

Although the Council of Ferrara-Florence improved Eugenius's
political standing, it was not a happy occasion for the Greeks. They were
motivated more by their desperate need for military assistance against
the Turks than by interest in the theological positions of the Latins, and
for most of their time in Italy, they claimed to be weary, dispirited, frus-
trated by Eugenius's delays in paying them, and eager to return home.[21]
The majority of the sessions at both Ferrara and Florence (where the
council moved in early 1439 because of the plague) were taken up with
contentious debates about whether the Holy Spirit proceeded from the
Father or from the Father and the Son *(Filioque)*, and the other subjects
at issue (papal primacy, Purgatory, the moment at which the Sacrament
of the Eucharist is effected, and the use of leavened or unleavened
bread) proved equally divisive. On July 5, 1439, the Greek delegation

agreed to union in the hopes that their cooperation would be rewarded; most of the Greek delegates then disavowed the union on their return to Constantinople.[22] While the union proved illusory, however, the council gave Eugenius many chances to act as the sole legitimate pontiff; thanks to the council, he could claim that both Greeks and Latins agreed on papal primacy.[23] In September 1439, after the departure of the Greeks, the council (which now consisted only of Italians) endorsed the papal bull *Moyses vir,* in which Eugenius condemned the members of the Council of Basel as heretical and schismatic for their insistence on the continuing validity of *Haec sancta* and *Frequens.*[24] Two months later, Eugenius was able to announce another decree of union, this with the Armenians.[25]

The Council of Florence was not the only reason that Eugenius's prospects were improving in the late 1430s. By the time the council got underway, Rome was again securely under Church authority. Although a popular government had briefly been established after the pope's departure in May 1434, by October of the same year Giovanni Vitelleschi, patriarch of Alexandria and papal commissioner in Rome and the western papal provinces, had captured Rome and terrorized the city into submission. He then proceeded against a series of local magnates.[26] During Vitelleschi's absence from Rome between 1435 and 1436, some baronial families led another rebellion in the city, but the patriarch quickly responded by sacking the strongholds of the Colonna and the Savelli. On his return, the Romans welcomed Vitelleschi with a triumphal parade, calling him the "Father of the City of Rome."[27]

Vitelleschi ruled the city with an iron fist, but the exhausted Romans were grateful for the return of order.[28] The Roman notary Paolo di Liello Petrone claimed that "never, up to the present day, has anyone done so much for the welfare of our City of Rome; if only he had not been so cruel, although he was almost brought to this because of the corruptions that prevailed in Rome and its neighborhood to such a degree that murders and robberies were committed by the citizens and peasants by night and by day."[29] Although the Romans had reveled in their short-lived commune, by 1436 they realized that the authority of the Church was preferable to a state of absolute lawlessness. In 1440, Vitelleschi died in the Castel Sant' Angelo under suspicious circumstances, probably with the pope's consent if not at his instigation. For all of Vitelleschi's faults, however, it was he who made Rome again subservient to papal authority.[30]

Eugenius's authority was increasing not just in Rome but throughout Italy. Vitelleschi had made important conquests, and Cardinal Ludovico Scarampo (also known as Ludovico Trevisan), who took over Vitelleschi's military duties, proved a capable commander.[31] Although Eugenius had granted the Marche of Ancona to Francesco Sforza, he was increasingly dissatisfied with the man he had made a standard-bearer of the Church. The pope and his old enemy Filippo Maria Visconti united to attack Sforza's lands in Umbria and the Marche, and at this point, Visconti switched his allegiance from his father-in-law Felix V to Eugenius.

In 1442, Alfonso of Aragon finally took the Kingdom of Naples, and although Eugenius had supported the rival claimant, Rene of Anjou, in 1443 he accepted Alfonso as the true ruler of the kingdom. As Eugenius's temporary alliance with Visconti fell apart, Alfonso moved north to join with the papal forces (led by Scarampo) against Sforza; having been an enthusiastic supporter of Felix, Alfonso henceforth espoused the papal cause. Thus, through shifting military alliances and complex diplomatic negotiations, Eugenius's control over the Papal States gradually increased. By the last years of his reign, the Papal States, though far from secure, were again almost as large as they had been under Martin V, and Eugenius's strengthened position in Italy emboldened him to refuse any proposals of rapprochement with the Council of Basel.

The year 1443 proved to be an important turning point for Eugenius. After nine years of exile, he was finally able to return to Rome on September 28.[32] During the four years until his death, Eugenius remained in Rome, continuing the Council of Florence, which had been officially translated to the Lateran on February 24, 1443. Eugenius celebrated unions with the Syrians (September 1444) and the Cypriots (August 1445).[33] He worked to promote a crusade against the Turks, which ended disastrously at the Battle of Varna on November 10, 1444. Most importantly, Eugenius's campaign against the gathering at Basel continued to prosper, at least in western Europe. When Felix V was first elected, both King Charles VII of France and Emperor Frederick III tried to maintain a neutral position and argued for a third council that would arbitrate between the two popes. By 1446, the emperor announced his allegiance to Eugenius. In spite of enduring rancor over the Pragmatic Sanction of 1438 (which allowed the French clergy to enact the reforms proposed by Basel without papal approval), the pope's relationship with Charles VII also improved.[34]

Meanwhile, Scarampo ruled Rome with as firm a hand as Vitelleschi, but he, unlike his predecessor, was adept not only at military campaigns but also at governing. Rather than trying to maximize the authority of the Curia at the expense of Roman municipal authority, Scarampo worked with communal officers to craft a concordat between the pope and the commune, which was effective as of August 30, 1446.[35] This concordat did not recognize all the liberties of the 1363 statutes, but it nevertheless gave the municipal government greater control over the city's senator. It regularized the rules for notaries and thus the process for legal appeals.[36] It established taxes for the importation and exportation of various goods and made rules about who could and who could not serve as a civic official. The concordat signaled a departure from the high-handed ways of Martin and of Eugenius himself in his early years as pontiff, but there is no way to know how faithfully Eugenius would have adhered to it.[37] Six months after it was signed, the pope died. According to Vespasiano, Eugenius said on his deathbed "O Gabriello, how much better it would have been for the health of thy soul if thou hadn'st never been pope or Cardinal, but had'st died a friar! Wretched are we all, that we only know ourselves when we are come to our end."[38]

Charting the Labyrinth

Although the prospects of the papacy were improving by the end of Eugenius's reign, his pontificate can hardly be described as a political success. The various wars in which he was embroiled forced the Curia to move from Rome to Florence and then back to Rome, creating an atmosphere of instability and danger that classical scholars lamented.[39] Yet they were hardly passive chroniclers of the events that rocked the papacy. As discussed in chapter 2, curial humanists condemned the courtly life they experienced, warning their readers against excessive dependence on external goods and emphasizing the benefits of the self-reliance that devotees of the *studia humanitatis* enjoyed. These lessons in moral philosophy were, presumably, intended for all those interested enough in classical studies to peruse the humanists' letters and dialogues. At the same time, scholars like Poggio and Lapo could not resist more pointed attacks on individuals, attacks that would have been especially amusing to those who shared their experiences and knew the cardinals and courtesans whom they mocked.

Poggio, in particular, also offered more concrete guidance as to how scholars should put their philosophical knowledge into practice and use it to manage the daily challenges of life at court. In *De varietate fortunae*, even as Poggio emphasizes Fortune's power, he also argues that a wise and virtuous man can insulate himself from her. At the end of Book I, the character Poggio expresses his preference for Stoic, as opposed to Aristotelian, definitions of Fortune, and he defends his position because of the practical value of Stoic (and more particularly Ciceronian) philosophy.

> Thus I have always preferred the *De officiis* of Cicero to the *Ethics* of Aristotle because of its useful instruction on how to live our lives. One author offers definitions of the virtues inquiring what they are and how they may be categorized. The other brings forward these virtues in the line of battle and in the field, he stations them in exercise, he makes clear the right way of living, as if the virtues themselves were speaking and instructing, he gives precepts explaining what each virtue allows, what it prohibits, to what extent something is permitted, to what extent it is suitable; in short he explains the duty of a good man.[40]

Thus, Poggio claims to prefer Cicero to Aristotle not because the opinions of the former are truer but because they are more instructive. This belief in the pedagogical value of historical events helps to explain Poggio's strong predilection for descriptive writing. Like translators of Plutarch, he argued that men learn best by example, and his account of Eugenius IV's reign was meant, at least in part, to teach men of the dangers of trusting to Fortune.

Poggio's distinctive pedagogical style is also apparent in the *Facetiae*, which can be read as a series of interactions "in the line of battle and in the field." Even as individual jokes address favorite humanist topics, they also model social interchanges, presenting moral problems as flexible and open to debate.[41] In the introduction to the *Facetiae*, Poggio takes care to emphasize that his stylistic choices are conscious and, in fact, central to his enterprise.[42] He associates his work with the ancient tradition of humorous writings, but he also defends his casual style by classifying it as a form of primary rhetoric: "there are some things that cannot be written ornately because they must be copied from actual conversations."[43] Here, Poggio indirectly cites the humanists' ultimate authority, Cicero, who, at the beginning of *De oratore*, insists that oratory is based on common, everyday language.[44] By simultaneously referencing Cicero and claiming to memorialize conversation, Poggio suggests that his collection offers an account of how scholars used their much-lauded rhetorical prowess to negotiate the competitive environment of the papal court.[45] Style was as important as content in Poggio's joke collection; even a man who could spout Stoic platitudes might find himself an object of ridicule in the competitive environment of the Bugiale if he failed to express his ideas with sufficient elegance. Thus, like Cicero, Poggio offers a guidebook to aspiring orators, but throughout the guidebook, he reminds his readers that rhetorical success, not to mention rhetorical greatness, is elusive and indefinable. By comparing the *Facetiae* to *De oratore*, to *Momus* (a roughly contemporary dialogue), and to a later courtly guidebook, *Il libro del Cortegiano* (1528), the remainder of this chapter will elucidate what humor meant to Poggio, why it was so essential to a classical scholar, and how proper modes of speech, as well as proper views on moral philosophy, helped to define the distinctive ethos of curial humanism during the reign of Eugenius IV.

Imitating *De oratore*

Although Cicero's fame does not rest on his jokes, *De oratore* includes an extensive digression on the ways in which humor can further an orator's agenda; this part of Cicero's work is the most obvious literary model for Poggio's *Facetiae*. Gerardo Landriani, Bishop of Lodi, rediscovered *De oratore* in 1421 in the library of his own cathedral. Thus, when Poggio wrote his joke collection, Cicero's ideas about humor possessed both the authority of antiquity and the excitement of a novel theory.[46] Caesar Strabo serves as the humor spokesman in Cicero's dialogue, and, following Aristotle, he argues that jokes serve as a way of disgracing another person for one's own amusement or profit.[47] The best way to disgrace a person is to point out his or her faults, but serious vices are not suitable objects of ridicule; they deserve and demand more serious punishment. Instead, the ugly and uncouth aspects of a person's behavior provide the most fitting material for laughter.[48] Although this definition of humor sounds harsh and combative, Caesar devotes much of his discussion of joking to defining the limits of appropriate jests. He reminds his audience not to mock the wretched, not to behave like a mimic or buffoon, and not to use indecent humor. Furthermore, the suitability of jesting depends on the character and status of the joke's object; it is never proper to poke fun at a venerable man.

Given these strictures, what sorts of jokes are appropriate to the orator? Caesar devotes the vast majority of his discussion to raillery, which relies either on words or on facts. For example, when one orator asks another "what are you barking at, Master Puppy?" his addressee responds "I see a thief." When Cato inquires of Lucius Nasica "On your conscience, are you satisfied that you are a married man?" Lucius responds "Married for certain . . . but verily not to my entire satisfaction!" And when Scipio, as praetor, assigns a stupid counsel to a client, the man replies "pray, Mr. Praetor, assign that gentleman as counsel to my opponent, and then I will not ask you to assign any counsel to me."[49] By offering proof of the speaker's acumen and polish, undermining his opponent and lightening the mood of a courtroom, humor serves as an endlessly flexible and useful oratorical tool.

Some of the jokes of the *Facetiae* show how scholars could use witty quips like those of Cicero to negotiate the challenges of the Curia. In one joke, a group of ambassadors comes to Pope Urban V (1362–1370) when he is ill; he agrees to see them but asks them to be brief. The first speaker drones on and on, oblivious to the inappropriateness of his lengthy oration. He finally finishes, and the pope asks if the others have anything to say. A more perceptive member of the party answers, "Most holy father, we have it in our commissions, that if you do not satisfy us immediately on this score, my colleague will present his sermon to you again before we depart."[50] The pope then laughs, and the ambassadors obtain what they are seeking. *De oratore* assumes that an orator will sprinkle jokes throughout his speeches, using them as decorative additions to a powerfully convincing argument, an argument that must unite eloquence with learning. Conversely, in this *facetia*, the learned oration almost ruins the mission, and quick thinking and humor become the essential humanistic skills. Yet, even as Poggio changes *De oratore*'s balance between humor and more serious rhetoric, he retains a Ciceronian vision of how an orator should use jokes. Caesar claims "merriment naturally wins goodwill for its author; and everyone admires acuteness . . . and it shatters or obstructs or makes light of an opponent, or alarms or repulses him; and it shows the orator himself to be a man of finish, accomplishment and taste; and, best of all, it relieves dullness and tones down austerity, and by a jest or a laugh often dispels distasteful suggestions not easily weakened by reasoning."[51] By transforming his colleague into a rhetorical opponent of sorts, the clever ambassador to Urban V uses his joke to win over his audience in a thoroughly oratorical fashion.

While the ambassador employs his quip as a defensive tool to redeem an unfortunate situation and offset the stupidity of his colleague, Poggio also shows how humor can serve as an offensive weapon, especially in the eight jokes that he attributes to the papal secretary Antonio Loschi.[52] Early on in the collection, Loschi repeats two similar stories to make opposing points. When he orders a scribe to correct certain official letters and the scribe fails to do so, Loschi recalls how this trick worked with Giangaleazzo Visconti; by contrasting his consistency with the wavering judgment of the duke of Milan, Loschi emphasizes that no mood or whim will change his rigorous rhetorical standards. In the very next joke, however, Loschi brings a draft letter to the pope's friend, and this friend, who has been drinking heavily, condemns it entirely.[53] Loschi explains that he will follow the example of Giangaleazzo's tailor. The unfortunate tailor had a fitting with the duke just after he had eaten, and the duke complained that his new britches were too tight. When the tailor went back early the next day, the unchanged britches fit perfectly, and Loschi finds the same trick works with the pope's friend. These jokes pick up many of the courtly themes discussed in chapter 2: princes are arbitrary, demanding, and prone to overindulgence; curial servants are duplicitous and lazy. Yet Loschi manages to navigate this dangerous environment with ease, grace, and wit, while staying true to certain standards. His rhetorical prowess preserves him from the corrupting influence of the Curia and allows him to maintain both his good humor and his integrity. As other jokes reveal, Loschi's wit also enables him to pinpoint the failings of those around him. Describing the presumptuous sexual proposition of a Florentine ambassador to Queen Joanna II of Naples (1414–1435), he outlines the dangers of impolitic diplomacy and of an inflated ego. In another joke, he mocks the classical sentimentalism of Cyriac of Ancona and uses a witty story to delineate the limits of acceptable humanist nostalgia.[54]

The last joke attributed to Loschi returns to a favorite humanist theme. An agreeable but unlearned man, Nobilis, is sent by his master to the archbishop of Milan, and asks to be given some great dignity. The archbishop replies that such a position would be beyond his limited abilities. Immediately and confidently, Nobilis responds, "I would act according to native custom. For in Verona they confer no benefices on the learned but on untaught and ignorant men." Loschi concludes the joke by saying that they all laughed at Nobilis. Yet this presumptuous upstart only assumes that standard humanist truism, that princes will always prefer the foolish and corrupt.[55] Some of the same ambivalence occurs in *De oratore*. Caesar repeatedly warns against mocking the infirm and pitiable. He condemns jokes that make fun of a man's short stature and another man's blindness. Yet he praises Crassus' gross pun about a cripple.[56]

The minimal context provided by Cicero and Poggio leaves their audiences without any sure measure by which to assess their jokes. In this way, both authors create a barrier between insiders and outsiders, between the true orator/curial humanist and the presumptuous pretender.[57] Even as these works maintain an aura of mystery, however, they also invite emulation.[58] Loschi is not as fully developed a character as Antonius or Crassus, but he too serves as a professional model, a model who can be admired if never exactly replicated.

More than 2000 years after Cicero penned his dialogue, the sociologist Erving Goffman analyzed the ways in which an individual lays claim to membership in a particular group. Goffman uses the term "front" to refer to "that part of the individual's performance which regularly functions in a general and fixed fashion to define the situation for those who observe the performance."[59] Especially in the case of professions, particular fronts become institutionalized as collective representations, and, the *Facetiae*, albeit less explicitly than *De oratore*, offers a type of collective representation.[60] The properly witty humanist should give off an aura of professional confidence and use his professional authority to manipulate those around him.[61] He should hold, and be ready to discuss, certain opinions on issues like hypocrisy, avarice, and princely policies of preferment. He should never take himself too seriously, never indulge in the kind of exaggerated speech or behavior that could leave him open to criticism or, worse still, ridicule. And he should be as skilled at using jokes and quips in the course of conversation as in dropping Ciceronian allusions. If he does all these things, he can aspire to be another Loschi. The technical expertise required of the curial humanist is not as extensive as that demanded of the orator, but flexibility and sensitivity to circumstances are vital aspects of both of these professional fronts. Thus, even as Poggio and Cicero lament the fact that the social milieus they describe have ceased to exist, they also make their texts into rulebooks, designed to instruct other orators and courtiers.[62]

Ever since its completion, commentators on Poggio's joke collection have compared it to *De oratore,* and they have not tended to do so through a Goffmanesque lens. Instead, they have stressed the differences, rather than the similarities, between the two works. Two of Poggio's humanist critics, Lorenzo Valla and Paolo Cortesi, claimed that the *Facetiae* was simply a bad attempt to imitate the jokes of *De oratore*.[63] More recently, scholars have stressed Poggio's indebtedness to medieval jokes and tales. They have pointed out differences in genre, underscoring the distinction between Cicero's brief quips and Poggio's mini-stories.[64] They have also distinguished between Cicero's concern for decorum and Poggio's inclusion of jokes "not only degrading to a public speaker, but hardly sufferable at a gentleman's dinner-party."[65] Certainly, there are notable differences between the two works. Poggio in no way sets out to rewrite *De oratore,* but he does respond to several of its challenges. In the introduction to book II, Cicero claims that "the art of speaking well, that is to say, of speaking with knowledge, skill and elegance, has no delimited territory."[66] By extending Ciceronian rhetoric into the genre of *facetiae,* Poggio supports Cicero's insistence on rhetoric's universality. By addressing similar themes in his jokes and in his moral dialogues, Poggio affirms Caesar's claim that all subjects of humor can also be treated seriously. And by choosing narrative as opposed to raillery as his principal genre, Poggio embarks on what Caesar describes as "a really difficult subject."[67] In short, Poggio enters into dialogue with his esteemed model, transforming the humanist ideal of civil discussion into a transhistorical debate on the nature of humor and the ways of demarcating a distinctive intellectual elite. The work thus serves as a lively example of how classical sources could inspire humanists to creative, irreverent, and surprising forms of imitation and how they could help scholars like Poggio to craft the professional identity of a new and ambitious avant-garde.[68] This identity demanded a critical, even combative, stance toward both the contemporary environment of the Curia and the literary legacy of ancient Rome.

The Historical Significance of the *Facetiae*

Given the rhetorical focus of early Quattrocento humanism, it is not surprising that Poggio's portrayal of the Curia emphasizes linguistic innovation and linguistic sensitivity. In creating a type of rhetorical "front" for himself and his fellow scholars, however, Poggio comments on action as well as on speech. Because he presents his jokes as acts of primary rhetoric, much of their effect comes from their context and the way in which they are delivered; just as inappropriate comments often elicit jokes at the speaker's expense, so too does inappropriate behavior. Thus, even as Poggio engages with his own works of moral philosophy and those of his fellow scholars, even as he strives to supplement Cicero's commentary on joking as a rhetorical tool, he also contributes—albeit elliptically—to the etiquette literature that became an increasingly important genre as the Renaissance progressed. Comparison of the *Facetiae* with Castiglione's *Il libro del Cortegiano* (set in 1507, first published in 1528) shows how Poggio offered guidance for behavior, as well as speech, and also highlights some of the peculiarities of the curial environment.

Like Poggio, Castiglione took *De oratore* as his model.[69] Like Poggio, he sought to craft both a linguistic and a behavioral ideal, and, again like Poggio, he sought to memorialize the rhetorical and social ambience of a distinctive Renaissance court.[70] This similarity of agenda is matched by a similarity of setting; both the Bugiale and the elite after-dinner discussions presided over by Elisabetta Gonzaga were nominally informal events, which were nevertheless infused with tension and competition. Castiglione's speakers devote much of their time to ridiculing those who do not meet their standards of elegant deportment, so that, as in the *Facetiae*, criticism of others makes up a good portion of the conversation.

The speakers at Urbino, however, are more explicit than the members of the Bugiale about what they see as ideal behavior; they concur on the primary importance of grace, or as Count Lodovico chooses to call it, *sprezzatura*.[71] In part, this grace is a subtle trick. By appearing to do difficult things in a nonchalant manner, the courtier leaves his audience imagining that he could do even greater things if he exhibited real effort. Exhibitions of *sprezzatura* also have a special aesthetic appeal to those courtiers who are in the know.[72] Like the woman who wears such delicate makeup that viewers must guess whether she has makeup on at all, the courtier displaying *sprezzatura* offers an evocative commentary on the play between art and nature and between truth and artifice.[73] The courtier must adapt his gracefulness to different types of activity, from the battlefield to the ballroom, and he must also be sensitive to the wide range of different people he meets. To navigate his ever shifting playing field, he must be endowed with prudence, the attribute that will help him judge how best to speak and act at all times.

If Loschi, the ideal joker of Poggio's collection, does not exactly exhibit grace, he does manage to deliver his quips and stories with a light touch and an air of effortless spontaneity. Loschi's use of the same joke in two different circumstances demonstrates his ability to adapt his repertoire according to the exigencies of the situation at hand, and in all the jokes attributed to him he demonstrates prudence through his constant self-consciousness and careful consideration of every social interaction.[74] The *Facetiae* is not just about Loschi, however. In both Poggio's collection and *Il libro del Cortegiano*, a few speakers enjoy special prominence, but the implicit approval of the audience makes it clear that the ideals established are communal, not just individual. Castiglione and his speakers insist that the discussants at Urbino are experts; like the inner cadre of the Bugiale, they understand a standard of behavior, they judge who does and does not meet this standard, and they decide who deserves mockery or, worse, exclusion.[75] In both works, affectation and presumption consistently provoke mockery. Thus, with Castiglione we find ourselves once again in a Goffmanesque world, where courtiers must struggle to maintain their fronts in the presence of a harsh audience. In fact, this sense of being watched and judged, of being constantly on display is, perhaps, the strongest parallel between the *Facetiae* and *Il libro del Cortegiano*. While Lapo describes the Curia as a theater, these other works illustrate the theatrical, performative behavior of courtly life.[76] Prestige depends on reputation, and reputation is a fragile commodity, to be shielded and defended with obsessive care.[77] Just as Loschi cannot afford to let a scribe return an uncorrected letter to him without advertising his ability to smell out the trick, so the courtier cannot afford to dance in certain ways unless he happens to be masked. Centuries later, La Bruyere described life at court as "a serious, melancholy game, which requires of us that we arrange our pieces and our batteries, have a plan, follow it, foil that of our adversary, sometimes take risks and play on impulse. And after all our measures and meditations we are in check, sometimes check-mate."[78] The *Facetiae* suggests that as early as the mid-1400s, curial humanists engaged in a similar game of careful calculation and used humor as one of the weapons at their disposal. Perhaps the generality of so many humanist anticourtly polemics was appropriate; perhaps once you had seen one medieval or early modern court, you had seen them all.[79]

And yet the *Facetiae* and *Il libro del Cortegiano* are very different texts. As they devise the perfect courtier, the members of the court of Urbino obsessively emphasize the importance of decorum. In his dedication letter, Castiglione claims that the modesty and nobility of the duchess "tempered us all to her own quality and fashion, wherefore each one strove to imitate her style, deriving, as it were, a rule of fine manners from the presence of so great and virtuous a lady."[80] More specifically, the discussion of joking begins with a stern warning from Federico Fregoso that jokes must accord with "soberness and modesty."[81] Bernardo Bibbiena acts as the humor spokesman in the dialogue, and while many of his jokes, like those of Cicero, are combative, he avoids explicit reference to scatological functions or sexual encounters.[82] Furthermore, he insists that the joker must consider the occasion and the position of the person he proposes to mock. Poggio's collection exhibits none of this restraint. Many of the *facetiae* include lewd, even obscene discussions of bodily functions and sexual relations.[83] And bawdiness is not confined to the jokes about nameless peasants. In one joke, a cardinal asks Evardo Lupi, a papal secretary, to fan him; the secretary responds by farting in his face. Instead of arousing indignation, Lupi's impudence is met with laughter.[84] The cardinal has overstepped social boundaries by asking a papal secretary to perform such a menial task, and he is duly punished, to the delight of all.

Thus, while the *facetiae* do not involve a control of bodily functions or a delicacy in discussing those functions, they do idealize foresight, planning, and the ability to control and manipulate one's surroundings.

Whereas prudence and decorum are inseparable in Castiglione's work, in Poggio's they bear little relation to each other. This lack of concern for decorum has social as well as aesthetic implications; Poggio's jokes suggest that courtiers do not enjoy a monopoly on admirable, prudent behavior. A boy offers to sell his goose to a woman in exchange for one round of sex. She agrees but insists that she be on top. When they finish, she wants the goose, but he refuses, saying he has not subdued her. After having sex again, he still refuses to give her the goose, claiming that he has only equalized her unjust action. As they argue, the woman's husband returns home and asks what is wrong. When the woman accuses the boy of raising the price for the goose, the husband says that such a minor detail should not get in the way of dinner and pays the boy the higher price his wife has named.[85] This joke, like all those included in this chapter, suggests Poggio's admiration for control of affect, self-restraint, and calculation. But it also suggests that he believed that some version of Loschi's wit and social mastery could be appropriate and useful outside the confines of the Curia.[86] Whereas Castiglione's courtiers frequently express their disdain for upstarts who try to imitate their behavior and make it clear that courtly behavior should be confined to those at court, Poggio's inclusion of a diverse range of urban characters implies that the *Facetiae* could serve as a behavioral guide to classical scholars in other contexts.[87]

This inclusivity may, in part, explain the lack of political specificity in the work. Poggio presents the members of the Bugiale as models of wit, and he suggests that they are more preoccupied with individual behavior than political counsel.[88] In spite of Martin V's supposed presence in the Bugiale, the *Facetiae* lacks the tense air of princely oversight that permeates Castiglione's Urbino; instead, it evokes the chaotic, peripatetic atmosphere of Eugenius's Curia, a court that was closely engaged with the cities in which it resided, a court whose ruler had no time to concern himself with the jokes of his employees.

The grand arc of Norbert Elias's "civilizing process" makes the similarities and differences between *Il libro del Cortegiano* and the *Facetiae* particularly intriguing. According to Elias, early modern courts served as the nurseries of new "more civilized" manners.[89] As *The Civilizing Process* unfolds, however, it becomes clear that Elias's principal interest is not manners per se but rather the psychological ramifications of increased self-control. Ever more preoccupied with regulating their own affect, courtiers became ever more rigid in policing the behavior of others. Elias gives a definite timeline for these changes: in the sixteenth century, the medieval ideal of *courtoisie* was transformed into the new notion of civility, and in the nineteenth century, civility in turn was replaced by a concept of "civilization."[90] According to this chronology, the *Facetiae* significantly antedates the Renaissance behavioral ideal of civility, but other scholars have questioned Elias's chronology and argued that some of the developments he discusses occurred much earlier than his timeline suggests.[91]

Poggio's *Facetiae* offers a somewhat different commentary on Elias, indicating that the development of modern forms of interdependence and the development of modern manners did not always and everywhere proceed in tandem. At the papal court in the early Quattrocento, natural bodily functions could be used as a way to regulate behavior; Lupi's farts (whether they actually occurred or were simply the subject of primary and/or secondary rhetoric) may have proved as efficacious and as devastating a force of social control as Elisabetta Gonzaga's smiles. The *Facetiae* also undermines Elias's claims about the behavioral gap between court and town. In spite of Poggio's curial career, he remained involved in the politics of republican Florence, and the *Facetiae*, with its many jokes about Italians of different cities, is clearly a product of urban as well as courtly environments. Thus, it indicates that, at least in the Italian context, Becker's arguments about civility as an urban development should be incorporated into Elias's exclusively courtly vision of the driving force behind the civilizing process.[92] Finally, Poggio's reliance on and engagement with Cicero suggests that much of the impetus to civility came from self-conscious imitation of classical ideals.[93] The civilizing process was not just an inevitable force; it was one directed and shaped by men like Poggio and Castiglione as they responded to the agonistic courts and towns of the Quattrocento and Cinquecento.

Agency, inclusiveness, freedom of expression. This sounds strikingly like the traditional, heroic vision of humanism. Certainly, the *Facetiae* lacks the gloom of many of Poggio's other works, and it offers a beguiling vision of open, if combative, conversation. Yet a sense of anxiety and doubt also pervades the work. If the interlocutors in the dialogues of

Cicero and Castiglione offer elusive and contradictory pictures of the perfect orator and perfect courtier, Poggio gives even less guidance about how the curial humanist should behave. The *Facetiae* illustrates a certain type of flexible, pragmatic wit, but it offers no explicit rules as to what this wit entails or how best to achieve it. By providing framing information so rarely, Poggio leaves open the question of how various jokes should be interpreted.

To complicate interpretation of the *Facetiae* further, Poggio includes jokes that seem to contradict each other. For example, in one joke a man is advised not to ask his wife how his penis compares to those of others. He goes home and promptly interrogates her, and she tells him that his is nothing to that of the local priest. Who is the fool here? So many of Poggio's jokes deride ignorant cuckolds and insist on the importance of fully understanding a situation. Yet here, Poggio suggests that the man is worse off for knowing the truth: "Thus, with his wisdom turned to stupidity, he showed that those things which are hurtful should not be disclosed."[94] The wisdom, it seems, was the advice the man received, and his stupidity is revealed by asking the question. But was not the man stupid before, when he did not know that his wife was unfaithful, and is he not now wise? Poggio here extols the benefits of the ignorance he has so often mocked. The joke collection reads like a cross between *Saturday Night Live* and a locker room conversation, but an Escher-like streak also runs through it, troubling and unsettling.

At one level, obfuscating the meaning of the jokes can itself be read as a guide to using humor, as a reminder of the relativity, flux, and indeterminacy of situations and the types of jokes appropriate to them. Because the *facetiae* have no objective value or objective meaning in and of themselves, their value and meaning emerge only when they are put to use.[95] Asking to be made an ass, boasting of one's inability to sleep without turning, farting in a cardinal's face, and taking advantage of a duke's digestive cycle are all highly specific responses to highly specific situations. Poggio makes no attempt to codify principles; he merely exemplifies them, leaving readers to take what they can. Because flexibility, pragmatism, and wit are the virtues extolled, modeling offers the only way to communicate the rules. Furthermore, by leaving it to his readers to consider the context in which certain jokes might be appropriate, Poggio trains them to use humor productively in their own lives. Interpreting the *Facetiae* is analogous to, and serves as practice for, making real decisions about one's own behavior and literary practice.[96]

De oratore and *Il libro del Cortegiano* also challenge their readers to identify a code of speech and behavior that is never explicitly defined.[97] According to the speakers of *De oratore*, oratorical humor is contingent on the persons and situations at hand, and thus no fixed rules can explain it.[98] More generally, Cicero's interlocutors repeatedly insist that rules can offer only limited guidance to the orator. At one point Crassus interjects: "An art of these things which Antonius has been discussing all this time! A practice indeed there is, as he himself told us, of observing sundry conventions serviceable to speakers, but, if this practice could impart eloquence, who would fail to be eloquent? For who could not master these conventions, either readily or at any rate in some measure? However I hold the virtue and benefit of these maxims to lie in this: we do not discover what to say by artificial devices, but, after we have learned a true standard of comparison, they assure us of the soundness, or reveal to us the weakness, of whatever resources we attain by native talent, study, or practice."[99] As a group, the jokes of the *Facetiae* offer a standard of comparison, a set of examples to which humanists can compare their own efforts at wit. Yet Poggio goes much further than Cicero in his refusal to codify any principles of humor. Given Poggio's admiration for Cicero, this may be due to a belief that Cicero's theoretical explanation was more than adequate and that new quips, appropriate to the needs of Quattrocento humanists, could simply fit within Cicero's theory of joking.

By failing to offer any guidance in the interpretation of his jokes, however, and by treating traditional oratorical vices such as deceit as fitting subjects of humor, Poggio depicts an amoral universe strikingly at odds with both *De oratore* and *Il libro del Cortegiano*.[100] In spite of their repeated statements about the impossibility of codifying rules for speech and behavior, both dialogues are, in fact, filled with such rules, and some of these rules insist on the moral rectitude of the professions discussed.[101] While commentators have questioned whether the dialogues in their entirety support these pious protestations, the authors of *De oratore* and *Il libro del Cortegiano* do position themselves as teachers and promoters of virtue, and this emphasis on morality was also at the core of medieval guides to courtly manners. Conversely, while the jokesters of the Bugiale bewail the fact that vice is so regularly rewarded, virtue is not central to the behavioral ideal they create. In fact, they seem to inhabit a world without clear moral standards. Curial humanists can indulge in any witticism that will strengthen their status, readers can interpret these witticisms however they please, and authors can use them to embellish any argument they fancy. Although many of Poggio's jokes are based on medieval *exempla,* his *exempla* no longer provide guides to moral behavior.[102] The *Facetiae* thus serves as a harbinger of the doubts about exemplarity that became increasingly evident in humanist works of the sixteenth and seventeenth centuries.[103] Its moral universe is not that of Cicero or of Castiglione but that of Machiavelli. Even the most prudent of humanists or wisest of rulers may fall prey to the wiles of Fortune.

Life on Olympus

Should we accept the *Facetiae*'s distinctive image of curial life? As Poggio grew older he became increasingly cynical both about the Curia and life more generally, and he is only one witness to a complex environment, which could certainly be interpreted in many ways. Thus, it is interesting to see that several aspects of Poggio's portrait are corroborated by Alberti's *Momus* (1443–1450), an elaborate allegory that is apparently based on events at the Curia in the 1430s and 1440s.[104] Like Poggio, Alberti explicitly dedicates his dialogue to humor, and, again like Poggio, he justifies his project, in part, by the dearth of humorous works in Latin.[105] Alberti was no meek imitator of the older humanist, however. While the two knew each other, there is little evidence that they were particularly close friends, and differences in genre and in classical models make the *Facetiae* and *Momus* dissimilar texts.[106] *Momus,* like Vegio's *Palinurus,* is modeled on the dialogues of Lucian, but it is a far more complex piece. Alberti piles homages to his ancient model on top of each other, leaving the reader discombobulated and uncertain about the overall meaning of the work.[107] Although he claims in his preface that he will write about the prince, in the body of the dialogue Alberti mocks not only princes but women, philosophers, architects, atheists, theater builders and goers, Praise, Virtue, the gods, and makeup.

Much of the dialogue takes place at the court of the gods, where matters are in great disarray. Alberti's portrait of Jupiter as an inept ruler resonates with humanist writings about courts. Dependent on the advice of those around him, tyrannical but also inept, subject to vagaries of fortune and mood, ungrateful, foolish and arbitrary, Jupiter is a thoroughly humanistic prince. Modern scholars have equated him with Nicholas V or Eugenius IV, but, in terms of the *Facetiae,* what is perhaps more interesting than Jupiter's allegorical significance is the nature of his court.[108] Even more than most dialogues, *Momus,* like Poggio's joke collection, comments on modes of conversation, and as Momus changes from an arrogant courtier to an exile to a jester to a counselor to an exile once again, his methods of communication shift repeatedly. In the beginning of the dialogue, he follows a conversational mode that ensures that he will run into trouble; he boasts of his own achievements, criticizes those of others, and devotes special care to attacking Jupiter himself. As a result, he is exiled from heaven, and he quickly begins to rethink his "front." Momus advises himself "keep the real you, the man you want to be, deep inside your heart, while using your appearance, expression and words to pretend and feign that you are the person whom the occasion demands." In other words, Momus undertakes to become a model of prudence, albeit a deceptive type of prudence. Soon thereafter, he also urges himself to be "a friendly fellow . . . easygoing and affable" and to devote himself to discovering what other men think and desire, while hiding his own motivations completely.[109] Thus, Momus sets as his standard of behavior an ideal very like that illustrated by Loschi; the only difference is that he puts more explicit emphasis on the importance of hiding, of masking his true self.[110]

As long as Momus maintains this attitude, his efforts meet with unqualified success. He becomes Jupiter's favorite and the approbation of all the other gods soon follows. Unfortunately, his aspirations increase, and he wants to be treated as a serious counselor rather than a mere toady. He begins to put faith in his "brilliant observations on kingship," and when he is deputed by Jupiter to preside over the council of the gods, he scolds them fiercely.[111] This combination of arrogance, self-righteousness, and ambition gives his enemies the perfect opportunity to strike. Momus explains his own understanding of his fall:

> What caused my destruction was being loaded with great honors. Thanks to this, I thought it would be better for me to set aside those wicked arts and reclaim my former freedom of spirit, casting off the

servility of a yes-man and a flatterer. I'm fully aware of what I've done,
how I've studied to benefit the gods. Passing over everything else, I was
so concerned for the gods that when Jupiter was contemplating renovations to the world, I spent many sleepless nights gathering together
those old systems of governing gods and men I used to discuss with you,
my dear Gelastus. I wrote them down in notebooks and gave them to
him, but events have shown how much value he set on them. As you
can see, that honest and useful advice did not suit Jupiter, but it did suit
him to drive me out into this wretched state.[112]

In other words, when Momus stopped being a courtier and became a
humanist scholar, when he stopped looking out for himself and instead
devoted himself to moral philosophy for the instruction of others, he
ran into trouble. According to Alberti, there is no place for the true
humanist at court; his advice is unwelcome and his skills make those
around him suspicious.

And yet, in *Momus* even more than in the *Facetiae*, there is always a
catch. The dialogue ends with a brief account of the contents of Momus's
notebooks:

The prince should be instructed that he must neither do everything nor
do nothing. What he does he should not do alone, or with everyone
else. He should make sure that no one individual has too many things,
or that men have nothing and have no power. He should reward the
good even when they don't want rewards, and he should visit evils
upon the wicked only when he is unwilling. He should take notice of
people for their less obvious qualities rather than for their immediately
apparent ones. He should refrain from making changes, unless com-
pelled to do so for the sake of maintaining his authority, or unless he
has some guarantee of increasing his glory.[113]

The advice continues, but from this excerpt, the tenor of Momus's
instructions should be clear. Like a good humanist, he writes *in utramque
partem*.[114] As a result, his notebooks demand that the prince must engage
in a constant balancing act, simultaneously doing and not doing the
same thing. And when the advice is not contradictory, it is so obvious
as to be banal. Momus neatly outlines a program of rule that will allow
Jupiter to be as ineffectual and powerless as ever. Thus, it is not clear if
Alberti is bewailing princes' unwillingness to listen to the humanists at
their courts or if he is mocking humanist moral philosophy. Probably
he is doing both.

How then does this relate to the *Facetiae?* Clearly, Alberti does not present a figure like Loschi, a figure who can combine humanist talents with a successful curial tenure. He presents these two personae as essentially at odds. But in doing so, he acknowledges that someone who *behaves* like Loschi can succeed at court and suggests that this figure is well known to him. Some scholars have argued that Momus is supposed to represent Alberti himself, and if this is true, then Alberti implies that he has adopted this courtly persona.[115] Throughout his life, Alberti presented himself as embattled, and he derided those whom he felt were blocking his path to success; the character Momus nicely represents this outsider status.[116] Whereas Poggio, the quintessential curial insider, associates himself with the witty humanist Loschi, Alberti, the cynic, argues that a humanist can never succeed at court.

But if Poggio's work can be seen as more optimistic about the prospects for curial success, the works share two important traits. First, both Poggio and Alberti suggest that courts are not and should not be isolated from urban realities. Momus attributes much of his newfound cunning to his experience on earth, and his tales of earth win him Jupiter's favor and appreciation. In other words, in *Momus,* as in the *Facetiae,* wit and success at court are associated with knowledge of the city; this, as much as knowledge of court, instills urbanity. Second, both works are deeply ambivalent. Just as it is difficult to determine how any individual joke of the *Facetiae* should be understood, so too, as the copious scholarship on *Momus* shows, no single interpretive frame can make sense of Alberti's entire work. Although *Momus* reads as a narrative, Alberti continually switches gears, moving into new realms and new topics. Thus he, like Poggio, makes his work more ambiguous and destabilizing than the ancient dialogues on which it is modeled. Even as he honors his ancient exemplars, Alberti also tries to craft a more complex text, one that will engage not simply with a single Lucianic dialogue but with the entire corpus and with other ancient authors as well.

It is possible that humanists chose to destabilize their readers as an intellectual exercise. But this is not what the *Facetiae* and *Momus* suggest. Instead, both works, in their different ways, relate flux, ambivalence, and moral uncertainty to the environment of the Curia in the 1430s and 1440s. Whereas Elias saw early modern courts as exerting ever greater constraints on the individual, both Burckhardt and Greenblatt insist that the rules of Renaissance society created their own sort of

freedom.[117] This freedom brought with it a new sense of the possibility
of self-fashioning, of an author's right and ability to craft a unique persona. But for Poggio and Alberti self-fashioning was not an independent exercise; it was inextricably linked to the fashioning of others, of
fronts, of professions, of institutions.[118] Both *Momus* and the *Facetiae*
present the curial humanist as an elegant tightrope walker, constantly
under siege, lacking a clear moral standard, dependent on others and
yet strikingly isolated in a world of flux and uncertainty.[119] With this
image in mind, the efforts of curial humanists to diagnose the evils of
the court they inhabit seem more than exercises in classical imitation
or reworkings of medieval themes. Instead, they appear as heartfelt
efforts to use moral philosophy to make sense of a courtly environment
that was itself in the midst of major transformations.

4

⊰⊱

Curial Plans for the Reform of the Church

A T ONE point in *De curiae commodis,* the character Angelo da Recanate, a longstanding member of the papal court, asks: "What can be more alien to the curia than religion?"[1] Although the character Lapo comes to the Curia's defense, Angelo's rhetorical question reflects contemporary skepticism about the religious mission of the Curia, and this skepticism only increased in the following decades and centuries. The profane nature of the Renaissance papacy is legendary, immortalized by writers like Luther, Erasmus, and Machiavelli and more recently reinterpreted in the Showtime series "The Borgias." Without describing Borgian excess, the first three chapters of this book have done nothing to suggest that spiritual concerns were a driving force in the early Quattrocento Curia. Martin worked to revive his native city, Eugenius struggled to best the conciliarists of Basel, and the humanists in their employ sought to market their distinctive skills and to craft an intellectual identity suitable to the Curia. In all these efforts, popes and scholars appear more like members of secular courts than like the leaders of Christendom. They may not have been pimps and poisoners, but they were certainly preoccupied with the challenges of managing an Italian State. Nevertheless, in spite of their practical, political problems Martin, and, even more, Eugenius, were eager to lead the Church, and members of their Curias also sought prescriptions for the ills of contemporary religion.

According to a range of witnesses, these ills were legion. In Boccaccio's *Decameron,* Sacchetti's *Trecentonovelle,* Poggio's *Facetiae,* and other literary texts, clerics appear ignorant, irreligious, and obsessed with sex and money.[2] Dominicans and Franciscans make a particularly inglorious showing, but monks, popes, members of the Curia, bishops, and priests demonstrate the same tendencies. With Boccaccio's story of the hermit who taught a young woman to enjoy putting the "devil" back in "hell" fresh in one's mind, it is difficult to accept the old stereotype of the Middle Ages as the "Age of Faith."[3] While these stories are beguiling, however, Van Engen warns that it is far from clear how late medieval Europeans interpreted them or how they viewed the contemporary Church.[4] Precise historical contextualization is an important prerequisite to deciphering anticlerical texts, but the conflicting pictures sketched by historians of fifteenth century religion (and the phantom of the Reformation) frustrate such an undertaking.[5]

The majority of modern scholars do, however, agree on one point: many late medieval Europeans expressed dissatisfaction with the behavior of the clergy, if not necessarily with Catholicism per se or with their personal religious experiences.[6] Early Quattrocento Italy and Rome, more specifically, offer plentiful testimonies, besides mocking jokes and stories, of the sorry state of the clergy. Members of the secular clergy received inadequate training, and there was a dearth of seminaries equipped to train them. Bishops examined ordinands in a perfunctory manner, if at all, and certain families automatically enjoyed the proceeds of certain churches.[7] Most curial ordinations involved simony.[8] Not surprisingly, the clergy that emerged from this process lacked a clear incentive to maintain religious standards, and ample evidence suggests that the state of the regular clergy was no better.[9]

At the same time that these problems threatened the availability, efficacy, and validity of religious services, monks, friars, and priests also indulged in more quotidian forms of bad behavior, which undermined their position in society. A bull from early in Eugenius IV's pontificate attests to pervasive problems with the deportment of Rome's clergy.[10] The bull stipulates that no clerics should keep concubines and that even a priest's legitimized sons should not be allowed to serve in the mass.[11] It forbids clergymen to play at dice or other games of chance, either in public or private places, especially if money or wine is to be given to the winner. Clerical gloves must be narrow; clerics should not wear crowns or carry weapons and should be tonsured.[12] In taking aim at the sexual, sartorial, and entertainment choices of Rome's clergy, the bull affirms many of the stereotypes of anticlerical literature, portraying clerics as lascivious, greedy, vain, bellicose, lazy, ambitious, and more inclined to pleasure than to their priestly duties. Of late, there has been a tendency to focus on the positive, as opposed to the negative, aspects of Quattrocento religious life, and several scholars have presented the Italian clergy as vital members of society rather than as corrupt hangers-on.[13] But these recent studies, while offering critical new perspectives on the functions of the Quattrocento Church, do not drown the anguished protests of fifteenth-century clerical authorities and social commentators.

Problems with the education, deportment, and level of commitment of the clergy were hardly new in the early fifteenth century. Because of the frequency of calls for *reformatio* in pre-modern European history, modern scholars have worked to clarify the meaning and significance of the term, coming up with a range of sometimes complementary and sometimes conflicting definitions.[14] Giles Constable offers an expansive reading of the term: when medieval Europeans wrote about Church reform they referred "either to restoration and revival in a backwards-looking sense, or to rebirth and re-formation, as a forwards-looking change."[15] With the Schism, demands for both types of reform reached a fever pitch.[16] Radical conciliarists envisioned a new structure of authority within the Church, and religious figures like Catherine of Sienna and Margery Kempe sought to return to the religious ideals of the apostles and the martyrs. Furthermore, institutions as well as individuals issued clarion calls for reform. The Council of Constance was charged with three major tasks: ending the Schism, combating heresy, and reformation of the Church "in capite et membris."[17] Thus, cardinals and theologians, as well as saints and mystics, sought restorative and/or innovative changes.

Because of the looming shadow of the Reformation, modern scholars of the late fourteenth and early fifteenth centuries have worked extensively on the issue of reform, but in doing so they have tended to focus either on reform as a personal endeavor or on reform of the Catholic Church as a whole. Studies of individual religious ideals look for precursors to Lutheran theology and spirituality.[18] Conversely, most studies of conciliarism focus on the inability of conciliarists to check curial corruption and papal autocracy, some of the characteristics of the early sixteenth-century Church that drove Luther and his followers to open revolt.[19] Although most discussions of reform at the councils have argued that their members failed to enact and implement major improvements, councils and conciliarists still appear as the institutional leaders of Church reform in the early fifteenth century.[20] Because questions of papal authority and questions of reform were tightly intertwined in this period, the popes, as enemies of the councils, have also appeared as enemies of reform.

Conversely, this chapter argues that in the early Quattrocento the popes (especially Eugenius IV) and their Curias were keenly aware that they needed to improve the quality of the clergy and the public face of the Church.[21] Eugenius had specific, well-developed ideas about what religious reform should look like, and members of his Curia, including humanist scholars, also sketched out reform programs.[22] These plans were not as sweeping as those promoted by the Councils of Constance or Basel, but they show sensitivity to environment, to individual psychology, and to the balance between the spiritual concerns and practical duties of the Quattrocento religious. Both as a cardinal and as pope, Eugenius supported the Congregation of Santa Giustina, which broke with the hierarchical tendencies of Benedictine monasticism in favor of an egalitarian system of government.

Although members of Eugenius's Curia did not necessarily share the pope's enthusiasm for Santa Giustina, they did pursue Church reform in other ways. Even as he wrote scurrilous stories, Poggio, who was one of Eugenius's secretaries, also composed two dialogues that dissected clerical vice and several orations that offered images of exemplary religious figures. Alberti, while working as a papal abbreviator, parsed the duties of a busy bishop, arguing that he should embody many of the same virtues as a wealthy Florentine merchant, and Cardinal Domenico Capranica (1400–1458) sought to create an ideal environment in which to prepare poor young men for the challenges of the priesthood.[23]

This rudimentary sketch makes clear that popes, cardinals, and humanists addressed the issue of reform from different perspectives and in different ways. They did, however, share a common approach, an approach already apparent in the speech that Poggio gave at the Council of Constance in 1417. In spite of the fact that the council was supposed to institute reformation in "the head and members" of the Church, conciliar reformers at Constance (and later at Basel) focused on reform *in capite* (in other words, reform of the papacy and Curia), confident that reform *in membris* (reform of other clerics and the laity) would follow.[24] Poggio takes aim at this agenda. Change, he argues, must start from below, not from above; the bad morals of the clergy, more than the excesses of the antipopes, are fueling the crisis of the Schism.

> For it is easy to speak beautifully and elegantly in public in the guise of a lamb, striving after the notice of men and the esteem of the vulgar; but unless, through your actions, you confirm those things which you advocate in your speeches, you will have accomplished nothing for yourself or others. Virtue is a greater thing, greater I say, than can be shown with empty words or a vain display of speaking. It requires action and exercise, otherwise it will be subjected to ridicule. First, men believe what they see more than words. Second, the way to virtue via precepts is long, but through examples it is brief, efficacious and open. To see the life of a good man, to pay attention to his mores, to consider his mode of living is a great incitement to imitate his virtue.[25]

Here, Poggio, the great exponent of eloquent language, argues for the weakness of rhetoric alone. Only by becoming exemplars of virtue can conciliarists and clerics hope to improve the state of religion and morality.

Over the next thirty years, members of the Curia continued to focus on reform of the Church's *membra,* and in doing so they raised issues that had long been central to discussions of reform. Like the reformers of the eleventh and twelfth centuries, Eugenius, Poggio, Alberti, and Capranica sought to define the relative merits of the secular versus the spiritual life and the extent to which religious figures should take an active role in the world.[26] They bewailed the misuse of Church funds and argued that clerics should devote their wealth to the care of their flocks, not to luxury and personal aggrandizement. Finally, they believed that reform should be personal or focused on specific institutions; the Church and society were to be improved man by man and monastery by monastery, not through sweeping conciliar edicts.[27] Thus, even as the religious programs of Eugenius, Capranica, Poggio, and Alberti reveal the conflicting ideals of classical scholars and their employers, they also speak to a common engagement in the religious debates of the High Middle Ages. Humanists positioned themselves as irreverent critics of the institution for which they worked, but they also thought carefully and critically about how the Curia could take the lead in religious reform.

Eugenius IV and the Observant Movement

While Eugenius IV's political abilities as pontiff have not been rated highly, his contemporaries recognized his personal austerity and piety. According to Vespasiano, "in his private lodgings he kept at his call four ecclesiastics, two of the order of Santa Giustina, who occupied the Badia of Florence, and two of the Blue Friars—Pope Eugenius's own order— besides a secular priest. With these four he did the services day and night and never failed to arise to say matins."[28] As pope, Gabriele Condulmer thus maintained the religious rigor of his youth, when he lived as a secular canon at the Augustinian community of San Giorgio in Alga; among his companions were his cousin Antonio Correr, Lorenzo Giustiniani (the future bishop, patriarch, and saint), and the prior of the canons, Ludovico Barbo (1381–1443). Along with a few priests and deacons, this small group of Venetian patricians was deter- mined to start a new religious society in which they would hold all material goods in common, eat and sleep together, wear the simplest of clothes, and be subject in all things to the prior's will.[29] Questions remain about the inspiration for and driving force behind the reforms at San Giorgio, but the ascetic, communal religious experience bound its members for life.[30] San Giorgio also shaped the young Condulmer's ideas about how Church reform could best be accomplished; as pope, he worked to promote austere religious communities like the one that he himself had experienced.

Most notably, Eugenius played an important role in promoting the Congregation of Santa Giustina, which was founded by his former com- panion, Ludovico Barbo, and which, thanks to its copious records, offers greater insight into the religious priorities of Barbo and his papal patron than the solitary experiment at San Giorgio. In 1408, Gregory XII (Angelo Condulmer, Gabriele's uncle) nominated Barbo to take charge of the Benedictine house of Santa Giustina, located in Padua.[31] Barbo agreed to do so on the condition that the monastery be removed from the system of *commenda*.[32] This practice (in which popes chose and installed abbots in a monastery rather than allowing them to be elected by the monastery's monks) was introduced to promote reform, but by the fifteenth century it had become one of the most harmful abuses of the Benedictine order.[33] Soon other Benedictine monasteries joined into a congregation with Santa Giustina; they too were allowed to elect their own abbots.[34] The congregation led the effort to reform the Benedictine order in Italy, and it was thus an important branch of the Observant Movement, a collection of initiatives by reformers of various orders to improve the quality of fifteenth-century regular life.[35] By 1447, the congregation of Santa Giustina included more than seventeen Benedictine houses, and between three and four hundred monks; twenty-five years later, it included twenty-nine houses.[36]

As both cardinal and pope, Gabriele Condulmer was closely connected with the congregation's growth. In 1425, the papal basilica San Paolo fuori le Mura became part of the congregation, and Condulmer, its cardinal protector, took an active role in restoring the dilapidated basilica, as well as the church's monastery.[37] After his election as pope, Condulmer did more than lend architectural support to the congregation; he also furthered its structural and governmental reforms. Although several of the original monasteries withdrew over the issue of whether monks or abbots should be the true arbiters of the general chapter, the remainder of the congregation refused to give special powers to the abbots. The final innovation of the congregation's rules was that abbots were to be elected for only one year, rather than for life, an innovation that was pioneered at San Paolo under Condulmer's leadership.[38] Soon after his election as pope, in a bull of 1432, Eugenius confirmed this highly democratic vision of the congregation:

> Even if, according to our duty of pastoral care, it is fitting that we be equally favorable and benign to each regular cleric fighting for the Most High . . . nevertheless, even before we rose to the seat of the Highest Apostle through the favor of divine clemency, we bore a special feeling of charity in the Lord to the excellent congregation of the cherished monks, our sons, of the Benedictine order under the observance of Santa Giustina. We observe their life and conversation blessed with spiritual joy, by which they profit themselves and others and offer salutary examples to the pious minds of the faithful. Insofar as, through our promotion to the pontificate, greater means have been given to us, by so much we have determined assiduously and very shrewdly to establish and pursue those things by which the state of the congregation can be

happily improved and made more solid. We hope that from this greater
health will come continually to Christians. Knowing that our predecessor Pope Martin V of happy memory gave some privileges to these
monks (which were not fully adequate for the greater strength or
growth of the congregation), we, on account of the laudable life and
exemplary habits of the said monks (which we have known for a long
time), following our aforementioned predecessor, and also changing
and increasing some things where it was opportune, with proper affection, Apostolic authority and certain knowledge ratify these privileges
with an indisputable and perpetual constitution.[39] We have earnestly
established these privileges for the present, and we equally wish and
ordain that all those who profess the order of this congregation, both
now and in the future (although they may stay in diverse monasteries
or places for a time), shall still exist as one body and one congregation.
We approve this congregation with similar authority and knowledge,
and we urge that it may be held in reverence and devotion by faithful
Christians. We declare and establish that the congregation is under the
order and rule of St. Benedict.[40]

In this bull, the pope repeatedly emphasizes his intimate bonds with
the congregation. His general duty of pastoral care for all regulars binds
him to its members, but so too does his long-standing feelings of charity
for them and his knowledge of their rich spirituality and exemplary
behavior. Here, Eugenius is simultaneously pope and simple monk,
acting both from his apostolic authority and from personal affection
and experience. In the body of the bull, he goes into considerable detail
about the proper governance of the congregation, but in the proemium
what he emphasizes instead is the unity of the congregation, a unity
that he hopes will be perpetual. And even as Eugenius privileges the
close relationship between himself and the congregation, he insists
repeatedly on the ways in which it will benefit other Christians. This
new institution, this conclave of reformed Benedictine monasteries will
provide laypeople with examples of virtue and thus improve their spiritual and moral life.

   Eugenius's support of Santa Giustina did not stop with the 1432
bull. The pope's enthusiasm for an organization that strove so rigor-
ously to be democratic may seem surprising in light of his fierce opposition to the Council of Basel. Nevertheless, more than sixty-one official
papal documents attest to his enduring concern for the congregation.[41]
In 1436, he made the congregation independent of the authority of the

Benedictine order and placed it under the special care of the papacy. The congregation and Barbo's efforts at reform are regularly cited as the one bright light in the gloomy story of Benedictine monasticism in Quattrocento Italy, and most discussions argue that Eugenius's support was essential.[42] Moreover, the relationship between pope and congregation was mutually beneficial; while Eugenius showered favors on the congregation, he also depended on its members. The pope sent Barbo on two trips to Basel in the tense year of 1433, and the abbot of Santa Giustina worked to convince the council not to break with the pope. At Basel, Barbo also took an active part in discussions about Church reform and, in spite of his well-known intimacy with Eugenius, was chosen by the council as a visitor of Benedictine abbeys. In 1437, Eugenius made Barbo bishop of Treviso, and he continued to be a visitor of monasteries in Aquilea until his death.[43] One of Barbo's greatest successes as bishop was the establishment of a seminary for poor clerics, and Eugenius himself established a similar seminary in Florence during his sojourn there.[44]

Barbo was not the only member of the Congregation of Santa Giustina on whom Eugenius relied. He also chose Giovanni De Primis, abbot of San Paolo fuori le Mura, to help him in both diplomatic and spiritual matters.[45] He made the abbot visitor in Sicily and gave him broad powers to improve the state of religious life there; part of De Primis's charge was to establish a Sicilian branch of the Congregation of Santa Giustina, as well as a seminary for aspiring priests. Although Eugenius also sought other assistants (who were not associated with Santa Giustina) to help him in his efforts to reform the secular clergy, his old associates were some of his most trusted collaborators. Martin V relied on his relatives and family clients to carry out his agenda in Rome and the Papal States, but his successor preferred to enlist members of his spiritual family and to focus on widening his religious, rather than his political, dominion.

Eugenius's bulls attest to his support of the governmental and organizational innovations of the congregation, but they say less about its spiritual outlook. What type of life and religious experience prepared Barbo's Benedictines to serve as virtuous exemplars to laypeople? What sort of spirituality did Eugenius seek to promote? The various monasteries of Santa Giustina maintained scrupulous uniformity in their performance of the divine office, but the prayers stipulated by Saint

Benedict were only one part of the monks' devotional life. In a 1440 letter to the monks of the congregation, Barbo gives detailed instructions on both oral prayer and meditation; this letter serves as a rudimentary guide to the mental prayer that distinguished the congregation's spirituality.[46] In it, Barbo recalls the early Christian idea of *reformatio*, which related, first and foremost, to an individual's experience of Christ. Because men are made in the image of God, through personal renewal, they can bring themselves closer to their Maker, especially when they enjoy the support of a monastic community.[47] At the same time that Barbo evokes this late antique understanding of *reformatio*, he also offers a vision of spiritual life that looks forward, sometimes in surprising ways, to the ethos of the Counter-Reformation. The letter thus suggests that Barbo and his papal patron envisioned reform as both a conservative and a transformative process.

Barbo begins his letter by saying that, during oral prayer, the monks should imagine that they are addressing God and should admit their foulness. However, they should go on to claim that their intercessors are worthy to be heard. The first of these intercessors is Mary, and the monks should ask her to intercede with God so that they may be His faithful servants. Then, each monk should choose twelve saints with whom he feels a special affinity. Starting with the first, he should say:

> "Most dear one" (say his name) "on account of the love which you had in this miserable age for our lord Jesus Christ," (if he is a martyr say) "on account of the passion which you suffered bravely for love of Him," (if he is a confessor say) "on account of the care and love which you had for God, for whom you sustained many labors, ask God on my behalf that He may make me His faithful servant and that I may persevere in this to death." Praying to the second saint with the same most sweet words, beg him to intercede for you, so that you may be constant and patient in all tribulations, misfortunes, troubles and temptations. Request the third to ask on your behalf that God may infuse the grace of obedience in you not so much towards your elders but towards all the brothers, even those lesser or inferior or junior to you. Beseech the fourth to pray for you so that you may be humble, pious, peaceful and benign to all; entreat the fifth that God may give you the grace of abstinence from superfluous things and make you cherish fasting, vigils, silence and other holy works of religion which are gates to the sweetness of contemplation. Ask the sixth to pray for you so that God will give you more grace of not sinning, at least not mortally, and give to

you true contrition for things you neglected and satisfaction before death according to what shall please Him.[48]

Few passages offer a clearer statement of the importance of intercession in the late medieval Church. Each saint functions as a spiritual intermediary, petitioning God for a particular favor, and most of these favors apply to the individual monk at prayer; only after eight saints have focused on the monk's behavior and mental state does Barbo turn to larger issues of the monastery and the world. With the help of additional intercessory saints, the monk then goes on to ask for assistance for the abbot, charity for his fellow monks and the whole congregation, and defense of the Church. In spite of these nods in the direction of general well-being, however, the passage focuses on prayer as a way of improving the internal state of the individual monk.

Barbo's rules for oral prayer are thus considerably more personal than the standard schedule of prayers instituted by Saint Benedict, and they echo the concerns of twelfth-century mystics like Bernard of Clairvaux and of Franciscan spirituality. For example, whereas Benedict instructs the monk to behave humbly, Barbo tells him to pray that "God will infuse the grace of obedience in you not so much towards your father but towards all the brothers even those lesser or inferior or junior to you." Thus, like Saint Bernard, he sees humility as a state of being rather than a way of performing specific actions.[49] Similarly, Barbo's ideas about holy living as a prerequisite to contemplation recall the writings of Bonaventure.[50] According to Barbo, "fasting, vigils, silence and other holy works of religion . . . are gates to the sweetness of contemplation." In short, Barbo agrees with the great Franciscan that control of the senses prepares the soul for closer association with God. Mystical authors found inspiration in earlier works, and many of them seem to have shared similar experiences; thus it is impossible to attribute specific aspects of Barbo's thought to a particular source.[51] Rather than defining the origin of Barbo's ideas, the preceding parallels demonstrate his general affinity with earlier spiritual writers. Even as Barbo follows Bernard in infusing psychology and spirituality into Benedictine life, he continues to affirm the same virtues of poverty, chastity, and obedience that were so important to the author of the *Rule*.

In its rigorous vision of Christian virtue, Barbo's letter also brings to mind contemporary works, most particularly those associated with the *Devotio Moderna*.[52] Members of this lay reform initiative, which was centered in the Low Countries, sought a simple, communal life of piety. They tended to be skeptical of the Church but continued to attend parish services, while also reading the Bible and other spiritual texts in the vernacular. One of the most popular of these texts was Thomas à Kempis's *Imitation of Christ*.[53] Acting as God's faithful servant, having patience in tribulation, being obedient and humble, practicing abstinence and charity, and feeling true repentance are all, to greater or lesser extents, emphasized by Thomas, and several scholars have argued that the *Imitation of Christ* served as an important inspiration for Barbo's ideas of spirituality.[54] But rather than presenting Christian virtue as the product of a monk's own efforts, Barbo presents it as a communal activity, communal not in the context of the monastery but in the much broader congregation of all the saints. Whereas Thomas says "Let the learned be still, let all creatures be silent before You; do You alone speak to me," Barbo calls on a whole bevy of spiritual spokesman.[55] The writings of the *Devotio* insist that intermediaries to God are not necessary, that the individual can speak directly to Him. Barbo, conversely, revels in the number of intermediaries on whom he can draw. His list of requests reads like that of a secular client who is proud to show off the number of his patrons.[56]

After his discussion of oral prayer, Barbo next turns to the question of how monks should meditate. He claims that during meditation, one prays not with words but with the heart, intellect, and affect. The intellect rejoices when it surveys God's works; the spirit burns to serve and honor the Creator and to despise the world.[57] Evoking the nature mysticism of Saint Francis, Barbo waxes eloquent about the beauties of creation and the awe and gratitude they should inspire. As Barbo's guidance on meditation continues, however, it takes on a different tone and focuses on a strict schedule of topics. On Monday, the monk should meditate on the fall of Adam, the evils of the world and his own misdeeds. On Tuesday, he should contemplate the nativity and on Wednesday the flight into Egypt. During this contemplation, Christ addresses the monk directly, telling him to abandon himself. If he does so, Christ in turn will give Himself wholly to the monk and will often visit and console him. From this point on, the meditation becomes ever more personal as the monk directly experiences the Last Supper and then the agonies of Good Friday. He sees Judas going to betray Jesus. He goes with the Apostles to pray with Jesus at the Mount of Olives; there, he begs Jesus to let him die as well. Again and again, Jesus tells the monk that his time has not yet come and that his duty is, instead, to pray. The monk weeps for the anguish of Jesus when he is abandoned by all his disciples. He speaks to Jesus while He is in jail, asking Him why he suffers and begging to be allowed to suffer with Him. Again he is told to go and pray, but he still sees Jesus, judged, crowned with thorns, carrying the cross. He hears Jesus speaking to Mary and to the thief crucified with Him. He listens to Jesus's last words to God, sees his death, sees Mary's collapse, and goes with the Magdalene to weep over Jesus's feet. The next day, Saturday, he accompanies Christ to hell.

A focus on the human Christ, and particularly on his sufferings, was not only characteristic of the *Devotio Moderna* but of late medieval spirituality more generally. Thus, Barbo's Christocentric piety is not distinctive, but the immediacy of his description is. For example, Thomas à Kempis instructs his readers that they should devote all their efforts to studying the life of Christ and tells them to love the cross of Jesus.[58] But while he includes numerous conversations between the disciple and Christ, the conversations are impersonal. They deal with the proper attitude of true Christians during their imprisonment on earth and occur in a neutral zone of "internal consolation." Barbo's depiction of the interaction between Christ and the monk is instead histrionic, operatic, and decidedly macabre; his account of Good Friday reads almost like a movie script. Through meditation one can personally "be there," can see Christ's life and death with an immediacy to which Mel Gibson can only aspire. This sense of immediacy accords more closely with the extravagant writings of certain female mystics such as Catherine of Siena, Margery Kempe, and Teresa of Avila than with the somber admonitions of Thomas à Kempis. Furthermore, Barbo's concern with a schedule, his neat designation of what the monk should do each day presages the well-ordered program of Loyola's *Spiritual Exercises*. Barbo calls for a spirituality that is not just internal but also individualistic (after all, even the choice of saints is personal), and in doing so, he looks back to the twelfth century and forward to the sixteenth century.

In making these comparisons between the advice of Barbo and that of better known spiritual writers, I do not mean to exaggerate the importance of the Venetian reformer. The parallels between his discussion of prayer and the works of earlier and later writers speak to the stability of spiritual writings and experiences rather than to any special influence that Barbo's work exerted. But if Barbo's letter does not represent a major causeway between late medieval and Counter-Reformation thought, it does offer some insights into the reform agenda of a select group of early Quattrocento figures, many of whom were closely associated with the Curia.

Santa Giustina represented a centripetal force, drawing in various reformers. Like Barbo, the Camaldolese monk and humanist Ambrogio Traversari (1386–1439) believed that personal spiritual renewal was the essential precondition to reform of the Church; in fact, his modern biographer suggests that if Traversari had been able to tackle the problem of *commenda* with the same success as Barbo, he might have been able to revive the Camaldoli just as Barbo revived the Benedictines.[59] In the 1430s, the canonist and theologian Johannes de Turrecremata (Juan de Torquemada, 1388–1468) contributed to reform efforts at Basel and thus seemed to share a conciliarist vision of reform. In 1439, however, he split from the council over the issue of papal authority and was made a cardinal. Thereafter, Turrecramata focused his reforming zeal on the reorganization of various religious communities; among his other activities, he wrote a commentary on the Benedictine rule to help Arsenius, Barbo's successor as leader of the Congregation of Santa Giustina.[60] In short, many of those closest to Eugenius and some of the key supporters of his claims of papal authority were involved in the congregation that was dear to his heart.

Eugenius's close collaboration with members of the Congregation of Santa Giustina also served as a foundation for his more general efforts to support the Observant Movement. The Observants sought to respond to the most glaring problems that threatened the integrity of the regular clergy: closed houses, low numbers of monks and nuns in each house, failure to observe the traditional vows (especially that of poverty), lack of concern for studies, and regulars living secular lives outside of the monastery.[61] In the face of these problems, Observants tried to regain the original austerity of their rules, sometimes, as at Santa Giustina, by changing their governmental structure, sometimes, as in the case of the mendicants, by setting up their own independent governing bodies. Whereas the Fraticelli threatened both the hierarchy of the Church and the unity of their own order, the Observants, at least in theory, did not intend to impose their reforms on all their brethren.[62] In spite of this, tensions abounded between the Observant and Conventual branches of various orders. The Conventuals wished to maintain control over their orders and were unwilling to accept the innovations proposed by the Observants. The Observants, in their turn, wanted to pursue and expand their revitalized spiritual mission, and if they could not do so within the traditional structures of their orders, they called for autonomy. The Council of Constance attempted to guarantee peace between the two wings of the especially cantankerous Franciscan Order, but it clearly favored the reforming element and established, at best, an uneasy truce.[63] Martin V continued this tradition and was a definite, if moderate, supporter of the Observants throughout his pontificate.

If Martin demonstrated appreciation of the Observant Movement, his successor was passionately attached to it. In his "Life" of Eugenius, Vespasiano claimed that Eugenius "imposed it [the Observant rule] in lieu of the Conventual rule wherever he could: indeed he would say that, if God would give him grace enough, he would bring all religious persons under the Observantists."[64] The pope's support of [the Observant groups began immediately; twelve days after his election, Eugenius revoked some the concessions that Martin had made to the Conventual Franciscans, and seven years later, he confirmed the popular and influential Bernadino of Siena as the vicar general of the Observant Franciscans. Throughout his pontificate, Eugenius sought to increase the authority of Observant vicars general, creating an Observant branch of the Franciscans that was almost completely independent of the Minister General and the rest of the order. The number of Observant Franciscans increased thanks to papal support.[65] Although Eugenius's plans for the Franciscans were not all implemented, he offered a vision of reform that looked forward to the definitive split of the order in 1517.[66] Furthermore, Eugenius's support of the Observants was not confined to the Franciscan and Benedictine orders. It was Eugenius who insisted on the meeting of the General Chapter Camaldolese that led to the election of Ambrogio Traversari as General of the Order and that prompted his visitations and efforts at reform. In the 1440s, Eugenius also gave papal approval and a measure of autonomy to reformist congregations of the Carmelites and the Servites of Saint Mary.[67]

In an article about the limitations of the phrase "Catholic Reform and Counter-Reformation," O'Malley argues that Ignatius Loyola should not be described primarily as a reformer. "For reform, some intentionality is required, some self-conscious intention not merely to reanimate existing institutions but to reorganize them according to some clear pattern or to displace them with new ones."[68] Eugenius's efforts to promote the Congregation of Santa Giustina and Observant groups more generally fit into this definition of reform. Like the reformers of the eleventh, twelfth, and thirteenth centuries, the pope believed that the Church should be improved and strengthened through institutions, especially religious orders, and that the organization of those orders needed to be rethought in new and imaginative ways. Barbo saw his task at Santa Giustina as one of *reformatio* in the sense of looking back.[69] He was determined to return the monastery and other members of the congregation to the original purity of the Benedictine rule, and he was willing to introduce major institutional innovations, such as democratization of the general chapter and radical transformation of the role of abbots, in order to achieve his goal.[70] In supporting Barbo and other Observants, Eugenius not only looked back to the original purity of monastic and mendicant rules but also to the example and approach of some of his greatest papal predecessors, such as Gregory VII and Innocent III.[71] As a political thinker and an intellectual, Eugenius could not compete with either of these pontiffs; personal sympathy and inclination shaped his reform agenda as much as strategic thinking. Eugenius was no Celestine V, but he was a pope who advanced an introspective, personal, mystic style of spirituality that he himself may well have continued to practice throughout his life in spite of his secular status. If he failed to communicate effectively with councils and princes about the *reformatio* of the church, this may have been, in part, because *reformatio* was for him, first and foremost, a personal, spiritual revival, a revival that no council could effect, a revival dependent on the example of Christ, the Apostles, the early Fathers, and the saints, a revival that used institutions only insofar as they shaped and improved individuals. Papal authority did not challenge or obscure this ideal of reform; in fact, a well-intentioned pope with adequate resources might have been the perfect leader of such an initiative.

Poggio Bracciolini and the Ideal of the Secular Cleric

Although the reforms championed by Eugenius resonate with the spirituality of late medieval and Counter-Reformation saints, they did not meet with unalloyed enthusiasm among his own employees. Poggio Bracciolini's penchant for excoriating clerical vice was expressed in works ranging from his oration at Constance, to personal letters, to the *Facetiae,* to anticlerical dialogues; this taste for vituperation led Burckhardt to characterize Poggio as a leader of a pagan Renaissance.[72] Poggio did not just criticize religion or clerics in the abstract, however; many of his attacks were aimed directly at Eugenius and his Curia. As discussed in chapter 3, Poggio offered a scathing account of his employer's political dealings in *De varietate fortunae,* and, in *Contra Hypocritas* (1447–1449), he presents an equally negative assessment of those with whom Eugenius chose to surround himself. Marsuppini, Poggio's interlocutor in the dialogue, begins by asking about how things are at the Curia:

> In the pontificate of our pope Nicholas, is the Roman Curia surrounded or rather besieged by cohorts of hypocrites as it was under Eugenius? I remember that superfluous crowd, from all places and of all orders, swarming within the walls of the palace, like ants from an ant hill; it was hateful to many.[73] Indeed (for it is permitted to speak the truth since he is dead) Eugenius was truly a good pope in many ways, but in this, either he thought according to the judgment of the vulgar or he believed that they were good men. In my opinion, he deviated a little from the right path, because he indulged hypocrites excessively, favoring them so much that his indulgence revealed the faults of many. They had easy access to the pope, they consumed much of his time on the most frivolous matters, and they filled his ears. Some seduced his mind with dreams, others with revelations of the future, yet others with new miracles; indeed they deceived him with an aura of holiness. Thus they very often obtained the things which they wanted or sought (and they asked for many things).[74]

In *De curiae commodis,* Lapo describes the crowd of eager hangers-on at the Curia, but his picture of bustle and excitement is far removed from Poggio's grotesque image of an infestation of ants. The hypocrites around Eugenius appear not only as subhuman but also as hacks, two-bit magicians and sorcerers clouding the mind of the credulous pope. Thus, Poggio presents the Curia as a theater of deceit and self-promotion, and he insists that hypocrisy hurts not just the hypocrite but all those around him; when someone is deceived by a hypocrite, he ceases to trust in virtuous individuals.[75] Insincerity keeps people from admiring the noble behavior of others, and it thus destroys the exemplary potential of virtue, the potential that, thirty years earlier at Constance, Poggio had described as the surest means of reforming the Church.

Lest the reader wonder about the identity of the Curia's hypocrites, Poggio takes care to name at least some of the worst culprits. The speakers condemn the hypocrisy of Bernardino of Siena, Gregory XII, Giovanni Dominici,[76] and Bartolomeo Malatesta.[77] Thus, while they include the most famous Franciscan of his day, Poggio and his interlocutors focus on the upper echelons of the church hierarchy: bishops, archbishops, cardinals, and popes. They also take aim at Barbo, whom Marsuppini says should rightly be called Atticus because of his pomp, arrogance, and pride.[78] The comparison to Atticus suggests that Barbo belongs in another one of Poggio's anticlerical dialogues, *De avaritia*.[79] In fact, the original version of *De avaritia* began with a polemic against the Observants.[80] Thus, even as Poggio's view of the clergy's central failing changed, even as he came to see hypocrisy as worse than avarice, his opposition to the Observants continued unabated.

While Poggio is better known for his criticisms of contemporary religion than for his positive religious program, in fact the two facets of his thought were intertwined. Both by excoriating the vices of Quattrocento clerics and by praising those clerics who were admirable, Poggio sought to persuade the religious community to adopt his vision of virtuous, exemplary behavior. This vision appears most clearly in Poggio's funeral orations, and these orations also reveal the extent to which even the most scrupulously honest of Observant reformers would have met with his scorn. Poggio shows no interest in the internal spirituality advocated by Barbo; instead, he emphasizes the importance of active, engaged clergymen who can set an example of useful service to others. Demonstrative oratory has long been seen as vapid and insincere, and it is not usually the place where scholars look for a well-developed religious or philosophical program.[81] When read together, however, Poggio's funeral orations offer a clerical ideal, an ideal that prioritizes charity and good works over contemplation and that thus opposes many of the key values of Observant reformers.

Poggio delivered his first funeral oration for a cardinal in 1417 and his last almost thirty years later; while his orations cover a broad chronological swathe they also describe three different types of cleric. Cardinal Zabarella (d. 1417) was a great legal scholar and one of the key players at the Council of Constance.[82] Niccolò Albergati (d. 1443) was a Carthusian monk who unwillingly became bishop of Bologna, and Giuliano Cesarini (d. 1444) was the President of the Council of Basel, spokesman for the Latins at the Council of Florence and a martyr of the Battle of Varna.[83] In spite of these diverse *vitae*, Poggio insists that all three cardinals were admirable, and in his orations in their honor, he reiterates the thesis of his speech at Constance: exemplary religious figures serve as the surest means of improving Quattrocento morals. In Poggio's funeral orations, the same virtues recur, but he emphasizes them to different extents with each figure, crafting three distinctive portraits.

Poggio presents Zabarella as the cardinal most in keeping with humanist ideals and refers repeatedly to the canonist's eloquence and knowledge of moral philosophy. Zabarella's speech, like that of Nestor, was sweeter than honey, and this was nowhere more apparent than at the Council of Constance, where the Cardinal gave a speech that struck everyone dumb.[84] In "pouring out his spirit" for the Church, he became a type of martyr, literally overwhelmed by the strength of his own beliefs. He was a true orator, according to the exacting standards of Cicero and Quintilian. Eloquence and virtue were not Zabarella's only talents, however. He was a skilled legal scholar and an excellent teacher, who sent forth students eager to imitate his personal example as well as his juridical knowledge.[85] Zabarella was also noteworthy for prudence, "the one virtue which is most necessary in the society of men" and the virtue that Poggio mentions most often in his speech.[86] Poggio dwells on Zabarella's liberality (especially toward those who display virtue) and his detestation of avarice. In short, throughout the oration, the papal secretary emphasizes Zabarella's active, civically minded virtues rather than his spiritual purity or otherworldliness. Poggio delivered this funeral oration around the same time as his 1417 speech at Constance.[87] In describing Zabarella, Poggio provides the very type of virtuous role model whose efficacy he had emphasized and whose absence he had lamented. At the same time, his speech also advances another, more self-interested agenda. The Cardinal, as presented by Poggio, demonstrates that even a modicum of classical learning can supplement and heighten other forms of knowledge and authority. To achieve this modicum of learning, however, men like Zabarella needed the help of professionals; Poggio's oration thus advertises the advantages of supporting scholars like himself.[88]

The benefits of humanist learning play a smaller role in Poggio's orations for Albergati and Cesarini, but Poggio is equally enthusiastic in his celebration of these figures. In his oration for his friend Cesarini, Poggio demonstrates his sensitivity to the political problems shaking the Church through two digressions.[89] First, he offers an extended paean to the city of Rome, Cesarini's birthplace as well as the home to which the Curia has finally returned after more than ten years in Florence. Second, he devotes several minutes to excoriating the members of the Council of Basel. In the context of Basel, Cesarini appears as a zealous crusader, so blinded by his own desire for reform that he cannot see the faults of others. Even as Poggio criticizes Cesarini's conduct vis-à-vis Basel, he still presents him as an exemplary religious leader; in fact, he claims that the Cardinal was single-handedly able to bear the whole burden of the Church.

> Wise men have argued correctly that one day lived well and virtuously is to be preferred to an eternal life of sin. Believing this and inspired by the teachings of wise men through his whole life, Giuliano made virtue the leader of his life in everything. He directed all his actions according to the rules of wisdom. He thought nothing must ever be sought in life except true praise and eternal glory. He always acted so that his words, plans, and deeds were esteemed by everyone.[90]

In short, by leading his own life in imitation of others, Cesarini made himself into an ideal role model. Poggio here offers a clear vision of how imitation could not only infuse the Quattrocento Curia with virtue and morality but could also serve as a link between past, present, and future.

There are significant parallels between the rhetorical portraits of Zabarella and Cesarini. While Poggio chooses to highlight slightly different attributes (prudence and knowledge versus wisdom and probity), he emphasizes the importance of learning and virtue and deemphasizes the importance of spirituality in both orations. Yet in spite of these similarities, the cardinals appear as distinctive individuals. Cesarini seems to have little of Zabarella's eloquence; Zabarella's death pales in comparison with Cesarini's gory martyrdom. Zabarella's virtue is consistent, whereas that of Cesarini is episodic and operatic. Most basically, Zabarella is a lawyer and teacher, whereas Cesarini is a diplomat and Church spokesman. In both instances, Poggio was praising men with whom he was on friendly terms, men who were his patrons and supporters. Yet these orations do more than offer enthusiastic praise—they map out two overlapping but different clerical ideals, and in the second oration especially Poggio highlights the importance of imitation. Because of his skill at imitating virtuous men, Cesarini himself becomes the perfect exemplar for other clerics. Thus, like the authors of humanist dedications, Poggio endorses the ancient theory of history as *magister vitae*. Whereas dedicators strove to make antiquity relevant to the present, however, Poggio focuses on the ways in which contemporary figures within the Church can instruct and improve each other.

Poggio's oration for Cardinal Albergati differs yet again from his eulogies for Zabarella and Cesarini. The acerbic humanist did not have any special relationship with the Carthusian monk, but he still presents Albergati as a model of imitable virtue. In fact, Poggio begins his oration by saying that the ancients extolled the virtues of great men principally because they wanted to spur the living to imitation; honoring the dead was only a secondary motivation. Having suggested his reasons for speaking, Poggio goes on to detail Albergati's merits. As Bishop of Bologna, the former monk demonstrated his attentive, selfless, pastoral concern, and, in spite of the unruliness of his flock, Albergati's virtue soon transformed the city. Albergati interested himself in the quotidian concerns of his flock, ordering Jews to wear a special badge, compelling a wayward cleric of minor orders to marry, helping the poor, giving dowries to virgins, and enlarging the public food supply. Poggio also discusses Albergati's involvement in extra-Bolognese affairs, briefly cataloguing the many missions on which Martin and Eugenius sent the cardinal and praising his refusal to accept any gifts. To explain why Albergati was repeatedly chosen, in spite of the plethora of available prelates, Poggio writes:

> First, he was most holy, most blameless, most pure, and he could not be reproved for anything. Throughout his whole life, he was blessed with singular temperance, moderation, learning and knowledge of all things, so that he equaled the most learned men. He was accustomed to action and this endowed him with the greatest prudence. He offered weighty advice, a spirit free of all partisanship and as much authority as could exist in any man due to virtue and behaving well. Furthermore, he had the most estimable personal habits and reached a very advanced age with no little blemish seen at any time. . . . To these virtues he added a certain humanity and gentleness, which made him most beloved by all. Therefore the popes worthily employed him in especially difficult

matters, for everyone believed that he supported himself not with personal gain but with useful labor, and not for his own aggrandizement but for the good of all.[91]

Integrity, learning, experience, and gentleness define the portrait. Albergati's authority stems from his inner goodness and virtuous actions rather than from force of personality. While Poggio mentions some familiar classical virtues such as *prudentia,* Albergati's Christian virtues form the essential part of his character. Poggio only refers to Albergati's *religio* briefly here, but he returns to it at three other points in the oration. Along with this devotion to religion, *integritas* (mentioned five times) and *continentia* (mentioned seven times) represent Albergati's defining qualities.

In short, Poggio does not present three identical cardinals but men who embody a range of virtues, which they manifested in the very different circumstances in which they found themselves. Just as Plutarch tells his readers to consider many *Lives,* so too Poggio implies that imitation should be selective and individual, and here, he finds some common purpose with Eugenius and Barbo. For members of the Congregation of Santa Giustina, the process of reform involved a personal commitment to following Christ and the saints and walking—at least spiritually—in their footsteps. Conversely, Poggio preferred more immediate and tangible role models. Trinkaus argues that the humanists' main justification for their optimistic individualism was their recognition that they were made "in the image and likeness" of God and could, through their own efforts, increase this likeness.[92] Trinkaus's thesis applies more aptly to Barbo than to Poggio, but Poggio's plan for *reformatio* entails its own sort of optimism, an optimism that men can help each other simply by example and that individuals can reform themselves by looking not up to heaven but at those around them. Even as Poggio disagrees with Barbo (and thus, presumably, Eugenius) on the nature of clerical virtue, he suggests that *reformatio* is both possible and, in large part, an exercise in *imitatio.*[93]

If Poggio and Eugenius shared some ideas about how reform could happen, however, they disagreed on what the end result of reform should be. Poggio's portraits of virtuous cardinals eschew the ideals of spiritual manuals, hagiographic *vitae,* and thematic sermons.[94] He praises religious individuals for the same active, socially useful virtues that he lauded in civic and scholarly figures. Thus, he seeks to impose his secular values on the clergy. In Poggio's funeral orations, the implications of this transposition do not seem drastic. A faithful, if irascible, papal servant, he praises other faithful (if not always docile) papal servants and affirms, rather than challenges, the Church hierarchy.

In Poggio's interactions with fellow scholars, however, the radical potential of his program becomes more apparent. Poggio penned an evocative and sympathetic portrait of the heretic Jerome of Prague in a 1416 letter to Bruni, and Poggio's Jerome has many of the same characteristics that he would attribute to Zabarella a year and a half later.[95] Like the cardinal, Jerome combines spellbinding eloquence and deep moral probity. In his oration, Poggio briefly suggests that Zabarella is a martyr, but, in describing Jerome's trial and death, he fully develops the martyr analogy. Poggio's Jerome compares his own predicament with that of Socrates, Plato, Anaxagoras, Zeno, Rutilius, Boethius, Moses, Joseph, Isaiah, Daniel, Susannah, John the Baptist, Christ, Stephen, and the Apostles, and the longest speech that Poggio attributes to Jerome reads like a paraphrase of Plato's *Apology*. Poggio thus drives a sharp wedge between the authority of the council and the authority of the ancients, the Patriarchs, Jesus, and the Apostles; in doing so he offers a serious ethical challenge to the ecclesiastical order.[96] According to the young humanist, exemplars of truth and wisdom do not have to be accepted members of the Quattrocento Church; heretics, Jews, and pagans may be more virtuous, and thus more akin to Christ, than members of the Church hierarchy. True religion is synonymous with adherence to a personal moral code, and adherence to established doctrine is less important, in part because it cannot be proven by erring judges. Thus, in his letter on Jerome, as in the *Facetiae*, Poggio reminds his readers that morality is not and never will be a measurable, absolute quality. Since there are no fixed rules as to how to achieve virtue, imitation of a range of worthy exemplars offers a sensible, if not a foolproof, means of self-improvement.

Poggio did not limit his theory of emulation to contemporary figures; in his speech to the members of the Council of Constance, Poggio extols the example of the Apostles, presenting them as ideal role models. He also demonstrates how, in his mind, praise and blame were inextricably intertwined rhetorical (and thus educational) tools. Having discussed the worldly aspirations of contemporary clerics, he says:

But if they examine these things according to correct judgment, they will understand that they pile up eternal ruin for themselves and the destruction of their spirits. These are not the divine precepts of the Gospels. These are not the footsteps of the Apostles and other sacred Fathers, whose inheritance you take by force. The Apostles and Fathers created the Church with their blood for our sake; you drain the blood of others. They sustained physical torture to strengthen the faith; you inflict torments on many men to the detriment of faith. They lived in want; you seek gain. They rejoiced in poverty, you wealth. They spurned worldly power, seeking humility; dominion and exaltation delight you. They sought to be cherished and loved; you wish to be feared, not realizing that fear is never mixed with affection or charity. Finally, they contributed to our health; you seem to have been put here for our destruction. How then is it wonderful that with so much difference of life and mores, so much wickedness, so much perversity, ecclesiastics are hated by men, since whoever speaks well lives badly?[97]

Here, Poggio offers a stark series of oppositions between the Church that was and the Church that is. Whereas the Apostles and Fathers suffered and sacrificed, the Quattrocento clergy take from others and seek to exalt rather than abase themselves. Not surprisingly they are feared rather than loved and undermine rather than support the faith of their contemporaries. Antithesis was a favorite rhetorical ploy of Cicero and other ancient authors admired by Poggio, but it was also a key element in a much more radical contemporary work, Valla's *On the Donation of Constantine*. In particular, Sylvester, in his speech to Constantine, presents a series of strong antitheses, contrasting Christ's poverty with the wealth Constantine offers and earthly dominion over the Western part of the Empire with the spiritual dominion that is a priest's true and proper sphere.[98] He ends his speech by saying "'Render to Caesar the things that are Caesar's and to God the things that are God's.' Wherefore it turns out that neither you, Caesar, should give up what is yours nor should I accept what is Caesar's." Thus, just as Poggio sets up a clear contrast between Apostolic ideals and the behavior of Quattrocento clerics, so Valla sets up a sharp distinction between secular and spiritual authority.[99]

Most scholarship has argued that Valla and Poggio represent two opposing camps, camps that perceived rhetoric, theology, and the reforms necessary for each in very different ways.[100] Conversely, Fubini claims that the invective war waged between the two humanists should be "understood in the terms of a rivalry between members of the same cultural context."[101] Valla and Poggio shared a conviction that contemporary religion was corrupt and a hope that reform could be effected by returning to the ideals of the early Church. Poggio's early works, most particularly the oration at Constance and the first draft of *De avaritia*, attest to the careful study of the Church Fathers that he described in a 1420 letter to Niccolò Niccoli.[102] Like Valla, he used quintessentially humanistic ingredients (including exploratory forays into primary rhetoric) as he mapped out his plans for religious reform, but whereas Valla focused more on patristic austerity Poggio emphasized the value of ancient, secular ideals. In order to understand the significance of this distinction, it is necessary to look at a work that explores, far more closely and carefully than Poggio's funeral orations, what it would mean to insert secular ideals into clerical life. Chapter 3 argued that Alberti's *Momus* affirmed the picture of curial life that Poggio sketched so elliptically in his *Facetiae*. The next section argues that Alberti's *Pontifex* takes the prescriptions of Poggio's funeral orations and explores how they would play out in practice.

Alberti's Bishop

Alberti's preference for the secular clergy is more pronounced than Poggio's; this is particularly apparent in his *Pontifex* (1437), one of the last works Alberti wrote before shifting his patronage focus from the Roman Curia to secular princes. As discussed in chapter 3, much recent scholarship on Alberti draws parallels between his various works, often to the end of uncovering a core of cynicism and ambivalence in Burckhardt's posterchild for confident Renaissance individualism.[103] Rather than accepting that the dark, ironic vision of *Momus* and the *Intercenales* pervades all Alberti's writings, the following analysis, at least at first, assumes that Alberti is sincere in offering proactive solutions to the problems of the clergy. Comparing Alberti's discussion of a bishop's duties in *Pontifex* and his advice for mercantile patriarchs in *I libri della famiglia* suggests that the humanist believed the same virtues were essential for both secular and religious leaders. Such a comparison highlights the consistency of Alberti's thought and his desire to incorporate ancient values into all spheres of Quattrocento life.[104]

Pontifex, which Alberti wrote in just four days in October 1437, records a supposed conversation between Alberto di Giovanni Alberti and Paolo di Jacopo Alberti about the challenges of the episcopate. Paolo was a Franciscan, but he was also a bishop, holding consecutively the sees of Orte, Aiaccio, and Ascoli. Alberto was a doctor of law who held many offices for the popes; eventually, he was made bishop of Camerino and then cardinal deacon of Sant' Eustacio. In the dialogue, which is set just after Alberto's consecration as bishop, he claims to find the duties of the priesthood overwhelming:

> Who is continually so thoughtless that he can approach this tribunal of God without terror? God said that whoever performs this sacrifice unworthily brings judgment on himself (Corinthians 11:27 and 29): shall we touch the altar of God with impious hands? But I scarcely dare to speak about this, because I understand that the Lord of Lords established that this sacrifice should be made not for the most incorrupt angels but for mortal men, among whom even those who are just are not altogether lacking in vice. I remember that, according to the judgment of the saints, this sacrifice is the medicine of spirits, which a sick man may take not unprofitably every day, provided that he perseveres enough in other things. Indeed perhaps I have reflected for too long about myself; I do not, as they say, sin seven times, but I feel I am not as completely constant in the path of the Lord as is suitable for a priest because of human stupidity. For this reason too, my father, I judge the priesthood to be the most serious thing: I feel that along with the duty of sacrificing (which I understand is common to a bishop like me and to some vagrant priest with no flock) the care has been entrusted to me of curing the multitude of vice, instilling virtue and promoting worth in the people. Even if I am somewhat tinged with letters, nevertheless because I understand that leadership is required, not less than knowledge of good arts, I, new and inexpert and eager to do these things correctly, think that all this is beyond my abilities, as is fitting.[105]

Although Alberto does speak briefly about his terror in approaching God, he focuses on a bishop's responsibilities for his flock. If the Eucharist is medicine, then the bishop—and in fact anyone who has been ordained—is a doctor, healing the sick through the rite he practices. Thus, Alberto, at least initially, offers a definition of the priesthood that looks back to the ideas of Gregory the Great: the priest is a "physician of souls" and his duties appear similar to those of a good Benedictine abbot.[106] In writing *Pontifex*, Alberti drew heavily on works by Ambrose and Jerome, and many of his other writings also speak to his engagement with the Fathers of the Church.[107]

Paolo encourages his friend, saying that he feels confident that Alberto will prove more than equal to the challenges of the episcopacy. But when Alberto begins to explain his definition of a good bishop, Paolo does not agree with his view. Dropping the doctor analogy, Alberto argues that bishops are, in fact, fathers, magistrates, leaders, and kings, and the rest of the dialogue consists of a Socratic discussion between the interlocutors. Paolo insists that it is only the worst of bishops—those who want to live a luxurious life and be worshipped as gods—who have anything in common with leaders and kings, but he is gently led by Alberto through an extended discussion of these secular roles and shown the strong similarities between them and his own Episcopal duties. By the end Paolo declares that he is convinced, and he says, "I am grateful to you, Alberto, for ornamenting me with so many offices today. You have made me the best *paterfamilias*, the best magistrate, the best leader and finally a king."[108] In short, by the end of the dialogue, Gregory the Great's definition of priestly responsibility has fallen by the wayside, and the two members of the Alberti family agree that the best way to understand a bishop's role is through secular concepts and secular roles that emphasize leadership over the care of souls. The central premise of the dialogue calls to mind Luther, who famously declared in the *Freedom of a Christian* that all Christians are priests and kings. Just as Luther rearranged the traditional order of society and played with some of its most familiar positions, so too did Alberti. But rather than attempting to sacralize the laity, Alberti, far more explicitly than Poggio, sought to secularize the clergy. Thus, in spite of his apparent prescience of some of the core controversies of the Reformation, Alberti's dialogue is, in fact, antithetical to Luther's ideas; rather than focusing on faith and spiritual duties, he works to make high clerics more attuned to ancient morality and virtuous leadership.

If *Pontifex* does not foreshadow Reformation thought, it does evoke many of the themes of Alberti's other works. The use of secular categories is just one of the textual ties connecting *Pontifex* with Alberti's longer and better-known dialogue *Della famiglia*. Close reading reveals numerous textual ties between the two works, ties suggesting that Alberti intended that they should be read together.[109] In both dialogues,

Alberti uses august older members of his family as interlocutors. Alberti's choice of characters speaks to his desire for familial acceptance, but it also gives both *Della famiglia* and *Pontifex* a type of *gravitas*.[110] Like Cicero who, in *De oratore*, chose respected orators of an earlier age as his speakers, Alberti instructs his readers not just through the content of his dialogues but through the character and demeanor of his speakers. Thus, as with Poggio, exemplary role models are an essential component of his argument.

Furthermore, while, *Della famiglia* is a longer and considerably more complex dialogue than *Pontifex*, both works deal with some of the same topics: wealth and the proper use of it, household management, and the importance of virtue and continuous activity.[111] In *Pontifex*, Alberto argues that it is both fitting and necessary for a highly placed cleric to have a good-sized *familia* (and thus considerable wealth) and says that it is more difficult for him to maintain a sober, honest household than it is for a layman.[112] Yet *Della famiglia* suggests that the construction of a well-run secular home is no mean feat; Uncle Giannozzo insists on the necessity of ruling not just the nuclear family but the entire household with moderation and wisdom and of instilling order and discipline.[113] Other speakers describe the father's duty to watch over his sons, teaching them to follow his example and paying attention to their aptitudes.[114] The good father, it seems, should guide his children, servants, and even his wife with the same vigilance that the high prelate must observe toward his household. Yet even more than similar passages and terms, it is the tone of tense, arachnid watchfulness and faint air of suspicion that shows the similarity between the duties of a good father and a good bishop. Just as Giannozzo keeps his record books from the prying eyes of everyone, including his wife, so Paolo admits that there are certain things he never tells even his most trusted servants.[115]

The parallels between the duties of a father/head of household and a bishop represent the most striking similarities between *Pontifex* and *Della famiglia*, but the two dialogues continue to share thematic ties even after Paolo and Alberto move on to analyze a bishop's other roles. While Paolo says that judicial matters should be left to those who are trained in law, Alberto pushes him to agree that when these matters deal with the health of spirits, the observance of religion, the care of sacred things, and divine matters more generally, it is a bishop who is the most effective arbiter; more than a secular judge, he can convert vice-ridden individuals back to a good life by using the weapons of virtue and religion.[116] In fact, all vices can be combated by virtue—not virtue in the abstract but virtue practiced on a regular, faithful schedule. Discussing his own habits, Paolo says:

> Indeed, only one thing comes to my mind which is that we should approach the best and greatest God before other business, so that we may pray with most sincere vows, that He may wish to keep us safe from the noxious and deadly number of our enemies. I profess this thing about myself. Since I turned twenty, at which point I recovered a little from the fervor of youth to a more worthy and mature knowledge of myself, there has not been a day on which I have not neglected other things and been zealous to take part in mass, and I have prayed to the highest God that he would defend me from all adverse chance and from all evil. I commend this as habit for all other priests, so that their first duty may be celebrating mass, and I judge that it is necessary for everyone and especially for priests.[117]

At one level, this mass-centered routine seems far removed from Uncle Giannozzo's Franklinesque days of thrift. But Giannozzo, like Paolo, attends mass daily and other speakers in *Della famiglia* discuss the importance of giving thanks to God.[118] More generally, an Aristotelian definition of virtue as a type of habit stands at the very core of *Della famiglia*.[119] According to Lionardo, it is habit, more than anything, which instills virtue or its opposite, and Giannozzo's entire discourse serves as a clarion call to using time well, not just occasionally but day after day.[120]

Thus even though Alberti does not make the practice of religion his central topic in either *Della famiglia* or *Pontifex*, he presents it as an important duty for both clerics and laymen.[121] In focusing on priests' interpersonal responsibilities rather than their spiritual lives, he suggests that the former is the area in which they are most in need of reform. He may also recognize that the social failings of clerics are the ones most amenable to a humanistic solution, the solution of looking for noble exemplars who embody and illustrate ancient virtues. A brief but significant vignette in *Della famiglia* highlights Alberti's vision of how clerics can contribute to society; Giannozzo mentions a modest and gentle old priest who used to visit the house of Niccolaio Alberti. This priest reminded his listeners of the gratitude they should feel for God's gifts and their duty to make good use of said gifts. He also argued that "nothing properly belongs to us except a certain power of will and reason."[122] Thus, in a dialogue that can be seen as a harbinger of Weber's Protestant Ethic, a priest serves as one of the spokesmen for the importance of rational thought. In *Pontifex,* Paolo and Alberto develop this topic and, more particularly, the relationship between virtue and reason. While virtues offer a potent challenge to vice, they alone cannot lead a bishop through all the challenges that beset him; instead, he must look to reason, which can rouse the daughters of virtue—justice, fortitude, prudence, and temperance.[123]

Both temperance and reason are especially important when it comes to money. Most of Alberti's complaints against the high clergy in *Pontifex* relate to their desire for and misuse of wealth, and Giannozzo devotes his memorable discourse to explaining the idea of thrift, of using one's "possessions as the need arises and spend[ing] enough, but not more than enough."[124] According to Alberto, bishops should live according to a somewhat different economic ethic. He argues that, like a good king, a bishop needs to be wealthy so that he can benefit his flock and help its members in calamities.[125] In short, while there are subtle differences of emphasis, Alberti's bishop and his merchant patriarch share an ethical code, a code based on vigilance, good habits, reason, and the careful use of money.[126] Poggio attributes secular virtues to clerics, but Alberti takes another step, creating parallel figures to demonstrate that, in the exigencies of daily life, episcopal and mercantile virtue are practically interchangeable.

Like all of Alberti's writings, *Pontifex* is open to a broad range of interpretations.[127] Piccardi, the modern editor of the dialogue, emphasizes different aspects of Alberti's thought than those just discussed, highlighting Alberti's condemnations of clerical behavior rather than any positive reform program. This argument is compelling, both when one considers *Pontifex* in isolation and even more so when one considers it in the context of Alberti's other writings. As discussed in chapter 2, Alberti painted a critical portrait of the Curia in his *Momus,* and some of his other works are equally disparaging in their descriptions of priests.[128] In "The Cynic" (which is part of the book of the *Intercenales* that Alberti dedicated to Poggio) Mercury and Apollo are trying to judge the souls who have died with the help of their self-appointed amanuensis, the Cynic. The Priests claim to have "interpreted the will of the gods, celebrated their rites, and practiced piety." The Cynic responds:

Phoebus, they are lying, as they often do, for in their entire lives they cleverly strove to dissemble their real natures. Dishonest, shameless, and fouled with every vice, they made a pretense of seeming virtuous men. They impudently claim that they spend entire nights communing with celestial powers, and conversing with the gods of heaven and hell. By this deception, they have managed to live in lazy indolence, getting drunk at the expense of others. . . . Phoebus, do you hear the sound of arms, the groans of wounded men, and the din of collapsing buildings and cities with which the seas and mountains resound? These depraved men have wrought this woe through their fraud and treachery, inciting one faction to violence and another to revenge. Let me briefly describe this entire baneful race. They are idle and indolent, and sunk in debauchery and drowsiness. Their gullets are immense, their tongues impudent, their brows brazen, and their greed and avarice implacable. They contend among themselves in hatred, foment discord between men at peace and stir up war and destruction. In short, they are the principal instigators and architects of all crimes and sins.[129]

Although the Cynic uses particular rhetorical force in his attack on priests, most of the dialogue's complaints against clerics also appear in *Pontifex*. Alberto and Paolo accuse contemporary clerics of being deceitful, wicked, lazy, drunken, greedy, and bellicose. Thus, even as Alberti offers the possibility of improvement and virtue among the clergy, he also excoriates most of the clerics he sees around him. In his writings, as in Poggio's, praise and blame are often intertwined, as they are in *Pontifex*. The curial abbreviator, like his senior colleague, may have offered secular solutions to the Church's woes for rhetorical or ironical or political or professional reasons.[130] Perhaps the irony and the cynicism of book 4 of the *Intercenales* demonstrate the true convictions of the two scholars; perhaps pessimism was the most fundamental component of their religious programs.

Yet by choosing to focus on more or less contemporary figures in his discussion of the secular clergy, Alberti, like Poggio, suggests that elements within the Quattrocento Church can promote reform. The fact that the pagan priests of the *Intercenales* are guilty of the same sins as the clerics described by Paolo and Alberto implies that the Church of the fifteenth century is not extraordinarily corrupt; instead, the tendency of priests to grow wealthy, powerful, and then decadent is a transhistorical problem. In spite of this tendency, Poggio and Alberti recognized (or at least could create and bring to rhetorical life) virtuous clerics who improved the Church by their loyal, practical, activist work in the Curia, the secular courts of Europe, Church councils, and their own sees. At one level, the worn-out Plutarchan idea that men would become more virtuous by reading or hearing about these moral role models seems romantic and naïve. Did Poggio and Alberti really believe that the example of clerics they admired, or rather the image of those clerics in their writings, would effect a *reformatio in capite e membris?* Unlike Barbo and Eugenius, they had no institutional tools or practical means to implement their ideas of reform; they relied solely on the power of rhetoric, power that Poggio denigrated in his speech at the Council of Constance. Furthermore, many of their ideals directly challenged those of the clerics for whom they worked. Eugenius and Barbo believed that reform should come from the regular clergy, and Poggio and Alberti strenuously opposed this approach. For the two humanists, the secular clergy was preferable to the regular because they took an active role in the world and contributed to society in important ways, much like their lay brethren.

Disagreements about the special place of the regular clergy and the importance of activist versus internal religiosity might seem unbridgeable; after all, these were some of the key points of contention during the Reformation. Yet in spite of this critical divide, all of these curialists saw reform as an individual undertaking, dependent on the action of individuals and/or the creation of relatively small institutions. One such institution, the college founded by Cardinal Domenico Capranica in 1457, suggests that the reforming ideals of Eugenius IV and his humanist employees were not completely incompatible and that an institution could draw on both these strains of thought.

Capranica's College

Chapter 5 describes some of the bumps in Domenico Capranica's early career as cardinal, but by the time of his death in 1458, he had been an active, respected member of the College for at least twenty-three years. Capranica held several important positions under Eugenius, and Nicholas V entrusted him with delicate diplomatic missions, most notably the negotiations that ended the conflict between Genoa and

Naples and brought relative peace to the Italian peninsula.[131] Even as he pursued this active schedule, Capranica devised a project for the reform of the church, attacking absenteeism, pluralism, simony, and annates with particular ferocity.[132] Toward the end of his life, however, Capranica's focus became more local; he personally composed the constitutions for the college for poor students that was to be housed in his palazzo, the Collegio Capranica.[133] Capranica begins the constitutions by explaining that he is founding the college for the praise of God, the propagation of the faith, and the benefit of the republic.[134] More specifically, the college is designed for poor secular clerics attending the *Studium Romanum* (University of Rome) in the faculties of art, law, or theology; the majority of these students must either come from one of Rome's rioni or be nominated by local secular and religious leaders "so that the city of Rome may gain greater utility from the said college than other places."[135] Throughout the rulebook, Capranica's devotion to Rome is clear; he does not ever claim that he is attempting a general reform of the Church but instead looks to "the honor and utility of our sweet city."[136]

Along with this localism, Capranica evinces striking attention to detail. His statutes begin with rules about the chapel, which should be manned by two chaplains, neither of whom may hold a benefice, and "who are of good fame and honest and laudable conversation and life and likewise lettered and well learned in the divine office."[137] At least one of these chaplains should celebrate mass in the chapel every day, and on the anniversary of the cardinal's death they should celebrate masses for him and the members of his family, unless the anniversary falls on a holiday, in which case the masses should be performed on a later, suitable day. On Sundays and feast days, the students should go to services at Santa Maria in Aquiro, walking two by two, and they should either sing with the clerics or sit modestly, attending to the office and not talking. "They should behave themselves in all things so that, as the Apostle said, their modesty may be known to all men (Philippians 4:5), and their light should shine so that all give praise, seeing in them their Father who is in heaven (Matthew 5:16)."[138] From Capranica's detailed instructions, it is clear not only that he knows his New Testament but that he has experienced the ills of Quattrocento religion: untrained chaplains, absenteeism, scheduling problems, straggling processions, and whispering in Church. The antidote to these problems is detailed instructions, and the result of following such instructions is glory both for the members of the college and for God.

Capranica does not limit his attention to detail to liturgical contexts, however. He explains how masters should balance reading and disputing in their daily lessons, and forbids students from gambling because "even if very little money is lost in a game, fraternal love tends to be diminished."[139] Capranica establishes the length of each student's tenure and of the academic year, acknowledging that students may need to return later than the October eighth starting date if the plague is particularly bad. Diet, clothing, care for the sick, servants, morning wake-up calls, punishments, and the college's accounting are all delineated in a spartan, practical, and thoughtful fashion. The rulebook makes clear that Capranica, like Alberti, believed that virtue is a habit. Unlike Alberti, however, he was not content to leave the formation of good habits to the individual. Convinced that the success or failure of his college would lie in the details, he strove to legislate against every malefaction he had witnessed during his long career. Inherent in the constitutions is a faith in the power of institutions to shape and improve individuals, a faith much like the one that inspired Barbo and Eugenius; all three men believed that following a clear, strict rule could create truly devout clerics. The Collegio Capranica follows in the tradition of the seminaries founded by Barbo, De Primis, and Eugenius himself, suggesting coherence in the reforming program of this group of curialists.[140]

How then does the college reflect humanist ideals of reform? The Cardinal specifies that the college's students should follow a traditional scholastic curriculum. The theology students will focus on the works of Aquinas, Bonaventure, Alexander of Hales, Egidius Romanus, and Albertus Magnus, and, because Capranica is not satisfied with the quality of theological instruction at the University of Rome, he makes a provision for the college to have its own master of theology. Meanwhile, the canonists will devote themselves to the works of Innocent IV, Johannes Andreae, and Antonio de Butrio. This reading list hardly sounds humanistic, and the biographical evidence for Capranica's interest in the *studia humanitatis* is minimal.[141] For example, Poggio wrote frequently and warmly to the cardinal, whom he seems to have regarded as an essential advocate at the Curia once he left it for Florence, but in these letters he discusses classical studies rarely and in the most general of terms, and he does not ever mention the cardinal's plans for his seminary.[142]

In spite of the fact that Poggio and his colleagues did not attribute great classical learning to Capranica, the cardinal's library did include a humanist's essential reading list. An inventory of Capranica's library from the 1480s lists 386 volumes, and there is good reason to think that this inventory is almost identical to the collection that the cardinal bequeathed.[143] The collection was divided among twenty-two desks, and three of these were devoted almost exclusively to classical or humanist works.[144] The cardinal left the college texts by Cicero, Quintilian, Caesar, Virgil, Plautus, Ovid, Valerius Maximus, Gellius, Apuleius, Livy, and Seneca, as well as writings of Petrarch, Boccaccio, Bruni, Giustiniani, Loschi, Vegio, Poggio, Biondo, Barbaro, and others. In all, about sixty-five volumes were filled with classical and/or humanist texts. Antonovics speaks of the "generally conventional content of the classical sections of [the library]," but it is still surprising that someone whose humanist interests were relatively minor took the trouble to amass such a collection—especially if his goal was a library that would serve the needs of traditional seminarians.[145] The library bears the personal stamp that characterizes better known Renaissance collections, and, a striking feature of the collection is the prevalence of patristic texts, especially works by Augustine.[146] In this arena, Capranica appears to be not just a follower of humanist trends but an active and noteworthy leader, showing an enthusiasm for the venerable Church Father like that of Niccolò Niccoli or Nicholas V.[147]

Just as Capranica shared in Nicholas's love of patristic texts, he also shared in the pope's meticulous concern for the proper management of his library.[148] Given the expense of books at this time and his own limited resources, Capranica must have worked slowly and carefully to amass what was, by the standards of the day, a major collection.[149] Not content simply to leave his books to the college, Capranica laid out precise rules for their preservation.[150] Each year, two of the college's students were to be chosen as librarians. Whereas most monastic rules stipulated that library collections should be checked once a year, Capranica instructs the librarians of the college to check the books every Saturday against their detailed inventory "lest at the strong persuasion of the devil one of the students should furtively take some book or part of a book."[151] As the librarians perform their inventory, they must also dust and check on the condition of the library "lest with bad custodianship, the roof should leak or wind should come through the windows or mice should settle in the walls, or some other thing of this sort, for in these ways books are easily destroyed."[152]

Care of the library is not solely the responsibility of the librarians; according to Capranica all students should see this as one of their principal duties. Candles are strictly forbidden and so too are scribes from outside the college. Students are responsible for ensuring that they have closed all books consulted (as well as the windows and door) before leaving the library. The punishments for breaking these rules are severe. If anyone enters the library at night or with a candle or leaves some outsider unattended in the library or gives his key to someone, he is to be deprived of his key and his right to enter the library until he has performed some special satisfaction. (Even then his key will not be restored except by the consent of two thirds of the college.) If a student steals all or part of a book, he will be expelled from the college with no hope of readmission. And lest anyone claim ignorance of these rules, they are to be posted in several places throughout the library.[153]

Many if not most of these rules have earlier equivalents in rules for monastic libraries.[154] Only the frequency with which the collection is to be checked and the cardinal's aversion to having books removed from the library distinguish it from earlier institutions. But if the rules are not innovative, Capranica's detailed compendium of them evinces a concern for books as physical objects that is in keeping with the new ethos of the Renaissance library. The collection thus speaks to Capranica's own participation in the revival of Rome's classical and late antique legacy.

Having books in a library does not mean that they are read, but Capranica did more than give students access to humanistic works; he also made study of moral philosophy part of the college's curriculum:

> And because moral philosophy, from which laws have their origin, is truly useful to both theologians and canonists, we wish that on each Sunday and holiday on which there is no lecture at the university, either the master of theology who must be hired by the college or some suitable scholar who is present should lecture on the *Ethics* of Aristotle and when this is done, he should lecture on Aristotle's *Economics* and *Politics*. All students must come to this lecture and if outsiders wish to come, they shall be admitted as long as the honor of the college is safe.[155]

Although students received some exposure to moral philosophy in Italian secondary schools of the mid-Quattrocento, it was not a standard part of the university curriculum.[156] Thus, Capranica inserted a new, humanistic subject into a plan of study which was, for the most part, highly traditional. The fact that the master of theology was usually responsible for the lectures in moral philosophy suggests that Aristotle's ethical works were most likely taught in a scholastic manner, but the library's inclusion of Bruni's translations of some of Aristotle's ethical works (along with scholastic translations and commentaries) serves as yet another example of how Capranica supported the new learning in spite of the ire of university philosophers.[157] Alberti and Poggio might have preferred to balance the writings of Aristotle with those of Cicero; Capranica hardly designed a humanist school. But quietly, and without fanfare, he nevertheless acknowledged the importance of humanist philosophical concerns. Clearly he saw them as complementary to, rather than incompatible with, the traditional university topics of law and theology. Scholars writing about the Congregation of Santa Giustina herald it as a harbinger of the reforms of the Reformation and Counter-Reformation. The Collegio Capranica looks forward in another way, to the humanist schools that were founded by the Jesuits in order to educate "youth in letters, learning and Christian life."[158] This was a mission which both Poggio and Alberti could enthusiastically support.

The Curial Vision of Reform

Van Engen warns that, for historians of the fifteenth-century Church, there is "a temptation to reduce everything to 'reform,'" even when the relevant evidence comes from very different types of sources.[159] Certainly, a papal bull, a meditation manual, three funeral orations, a humanist dialogue, and the constitutions of a college offer disparate witnesses to an interest in religious revival. Because of differences in genre, as well as differences of agenda, the elements of coherence between the reform plans of Eugenius, Barbo, Poggio, Alberti, and Capranica appear most clearly when their plans are contrasted with better-known contemporary projects. Members of the Councils of Constance and Basel believed that reform would come from specific measures on annates, provisions, episcopal appointments, and the size and geographical makeup of the

College of Cardinals. They "thought big" and tried to handle systemic abuses that affected all of Christendom; they called for change and refused to accept the abuses of the last several centuries, abuses that favored rich clerics at the expense of both their poorer brethren and the laity. Although specific members of the councils, such as Bishop Pierre D'Ailly, tried to investigate and improve the ethics of individual clerics, the councils were not in the business of legislating virtue.[160] Most of their members argued that reform of the Church's members would naturally follow from reform of the head.

If the councils were the primary adversary of Eugenius, Lorenzo Valla proposed an extension and radicalization of the ideas of Poggio and Alberti. In his *De professione religiosorum,* Valla breaks down the barriers between the secular and religious state. Rather than simply suggesting an importation of secular values into existing religious institutions, he questions the very validity of those institutions, and he proposes a new Christianity in which personal autonomy is the basis of an ethical life.[161] Valla's *On the Donation of Constantine,* calls repeatedly for a return to apostolic standards. In his eyes, the corruption of the contemporary Church makes it impossible that any contemporary figure could be a fitting subject for *imitatio.* Instead, Quattrocento Christians should imitate the Apostles and the early leaders of the Church.[162] Contemporary Catholicism, according to Valla, did not need reform; it needed a total makeover. In arguing that ancient secular virtues could reform religion as well as other aspects of life, Poggio and Alberti called for change, but they did so in a conservative fashion. Ideals that were already infiltrating secular life could be used to improve the clergy, and thus reform did not demand a break with the existing order but rather a shift in emphasis. If Poggio and Alberti were religious insurrectionists, Valla was a full-scale revolutionary.[163]

In light of what occurred in the 1520s, the councils' calls for sweeping institutional reforms and Valla's demand for a revived patristic spirit appear prescient. Perhaps, if the Council of Basel had bested Eugenius and if other reformers (before and besides Erasmus) had pursued Valla's initiatives, the Reformation could have been less divisive, less bloody, and less destructive of Catholic authority.

The wisdom of hindsight was obviously not available to reformers of the early Quattrocento, however, and local initiatives in Rome suggest that the Curia's preference for small-scale reformation was both appropriate and in keeping with the spirit of the age. It was only in the 1400s that Roman confraternities became well organized, developing their own constitutions and laying claim to distinct spiritual sites and duties.[164] For example, members of the Gonfalone, one of the most powerful of Rome's confraternities, composed their book of protocols between 1436 and 1457. While these protocols focus on behavior rather than personal spirituality, confraternity members, like reformers associated with the Curia, believed that religious revival involved personal striving to attain an ideal of perfection. In fact, the confraternities can be seen as small experiments in how to find a religious life capable of transcending the divide between the laity and the clergy.[165] Even as the adherents of these small institutions tried to legislate a more satisfying religious experience, Francesca Romana made a similar journey by leaps and bounds.[166] The austerity of her life was only matched by the profusion of her tears as she contemplated the sufferings of Christ during his Passion. When she thought of his hands, she could not hold anything; when she thought of his feet, she could not walk.[167] While the women who knew and lived with her at Tor de' Specchi also gave marvelous accounts of her piety, charity, ability to work miracles, obedience, self-mortification, and hatred of the world, it was her passionate devotion to Christ that bound her to Barbo and the ethos of Santa Giustina. Yet Francesca and the other inhabitants of Tor de' Specchi were not nuns; they chose a semi-religious status in order that they could continue to perform works of charity outside of their own community.[168]

In short, there are some interesting parallels between the initiatives of the Roman confraternities, Santa Francesca, Eugenius IV, Capranica, Alberti, and Poggio. Whereas the councils and Valla called for sweeping reforms, reformers in Rome preferred to focus on the small scale. Whereas the councils failed to address tensions between the laity and the clergy, these tensions were at the heart of humanist writings, confraternal protocols and the lives of women like Francesca Romana. And whereas Valla argued that the contemporary Church needed to change completely, Roman citizens and curialists were more interested in promoting active virtue and personal spirituality along familiar lines. It is arguably the Curia's failure to recognize and join with confraternities and new religious organizations like that at Tor de' Specchi, rather than its opposition to conciliarism, which prevented the sort of wide-scale reform that might truly have changed the nature of fifteenth-century religion.[169] Both humanists and curialists focused on certain subsections of Latinate culture and directed their ideas to this elite audience; this meant that the secularism of humanist scholars and the spiritual immediacy of the Congregation of Santa Giustina did not infiltrate the population at large.[170] Members of the Curia in the early fifteenth century focused on some of the ideas that would become central to the Reformation—and it can be argued that they did so with care, thoughtfulness, and sincere commitment. They were, however, incapable of or unwilling to extend these ideas beyond their various small, coterie subcultures. The limitations of curial reform programs in the early Quattrocento were not due to narrow scope or lukewarm enthusiasm; instead, these programs failed to diminish anticlericalism and improve lay satisfaction with the Church because they did not reach outside the sacred confines of monasteries, colleges, humanist séances, and the Roman Curia.

5

$$\Longrightarrow\!\cdot\!\Longleftarrow$$

Acting as the One True Pope:
Eugenius IV and Papal Ceremonial

EVEN as they condemned the wealth and display of many Quattrocento clerics, Eugenius IV and members of his Curia did not eschew splendor in their public appearances. Instead, they reveled in ceremonial magnificence, such as that characterizing Eugenius's consecration of Florence's Duomo (Santa Maria del Fiore) on March 25, 1436. In many ways, the period from 1433 to 1436 was the low point of a chronically beleaguered pontificate. Yet none of this weakness appears in Giannozzo Manetti's enthusiastic description of the consecration. Manetti says that he will tell of a "parade of papal magnificence, unparalleled in modern times and absolutely unbelievable."[1] He describes the basilica itself, comparing its form to that of a human body and suggesting that it should be mentioned among the Seven Wonders of the World. He enumerates the special decorations prepared for the consecration, including banners, shields with the papal arms, papal tiaras, splendid vestments, and jeweled reliquaries. A special walkway, built for the occasion by Brunelleschi, stretched from the pope's residence at Santa Maria Novella to the Duomo and was decorated with the papal coat of arms and canopies making it "the very pinnacle of ornamentation."[2] Having recounted the splendor of his stage set, Manetti then turns to the procession on the day of the consecration, a procession led by trumpeters and lutists, richly clothed young men, ambassadors and city officials "so adorned with ankle-length togas woven with purple and gold that they seem to the spectators to be kings—and justifiably so, because of their regal trappings." Next come the "far more wondrous pontifical dignitaries"—lawyers, chamberlains, bishops, archbishops, patriarchs and cardinals.[3] And finally:

At the end [of the procession], the supreme pontiff, between two apostles, most gravely processed, so wonderfully adorned with purple, gold,
and gems of every sort interwoven that truly to those who looked on
the pope he seemed more than a man, God Himself. His toga, reaching
to his ankles, was most lavishly ornate with purple, gold, and gems; a
distinguished prelate of the church carried its train, lifting it slightly off
the ground. And gloves, wonderfully encircled with every type of ring
and gem, most attractively adorned his most sacred hands. Then his
holy head was divinely covered by the most wonderful pontifical miter
ever seen. It truly seemed to have been endowed with so much ornamentation of gems, pearls, pearl solitaires, and other similar stones that
it made everyone's eyes turn towards it to see. Once their eyes were
turned, it held them so firmly fixed and absorbed in their admiring gaze
that they seem completely unable to look at anything else.[4]

According to Manetti, what makes the pope seem like more than a man
is not the authority of his office, not his personal piety, but, instead, his
exceptional splendor. The pope appears godlike but also imperial, and
Manetti goes on to claim that none of the triumphs of the Romans can
be compared with this splendid procession. In his account, poor, embattled Eugenius sounds like one of the absolutist monarchs of a later age,
glorified by a truly Baroque spectacle.[5]

"Reading" Papal Ceremonies of the Early Quattrocento

As with the other humanist texts discussed in this book, it would be a
mistake to take Manetti's description at face value, as a factual account
of an event. Manetti sought to use his rhetorical skills to celebrate the
city on the Arno, and the piece may have had the more specific purpose
of masking the tensions of the period just after the Medici restoration.[6]
In spite of its propagandistic intent, however, Manetti's text highlights
several important points about papal ceremonial of the early
Quattrocento. First, rituals mattered, especially in the later Middle Ages
and the Renaissance as public performances became ever more elaborate.[7] Ceremony and ritual were a part of statecraft but, thanks to their
ties to myth and religion, they were more than simply political propaganda.[8] Second, Manetti's account of the consecration serves as a
reminder that individuals experienced the same ceremonies in different
ways.[9] As a diplomat, Manetti probably took part in the procession, and
he indicates that he was inside the cathedral during the consecration.

Although his description emphasizes the effect of the pope's presence on the crowd, most people would have seen very little of the parade (because of the platform) and none of the consecration. If an individual's role in a ceremony impacted his experience, then his political, cultural, intellectual, social, and religious commitments played an even more important part in shaping his "reading" of the event.[10] Manetti saw the consecration as a celebration of Florence's greatness, but a Siennese ambassador might have focused on the prodigality of the Florentines, whereas a conciliarist might have emphasized the autocratic attitude of the pope.

Even as individuals responded to ceremonies in different ways, their responses were shaped by the religious and political environment in which a specific rite occurred.[11] Discussions of papal ceremonial have tended to describe it as unchanging.[12] This attitude gains credence from much of the anthropological literature on ritual, which assumes that rituals continue to have the same meaning as long as they have the same form.[13] From a liturgical perspective, the consecration of Santa Maria del Fiore did not differ from consecrations performed by earlier and later pontiffs.[14] Yet, because of its religiopolitical context, this event, in addition to sacralizing a particular space, also symbolized Eugenius's reliance on Florence, his support of the Medici regime upon its return from exile, Cosimo de' Medici's willingness and ability to help finance curial projects, and the pope's refusal to change his monarchical self-representation, even as he maintained a temporary truce with the Council of Basel.[15]

According to historians of ritual, formal rites and ceremonies have proved particularly necessary in times of political or social unrest; they mask disconnects between the image a regime wants to display and the actual political workings of that regime, while offering a comforting appearance of stability.[16] Papal ceremonial was no exception. Most of the ceremonial protocols followed by Eugenius IV dated from the fourteenth century, a time when the papacy faced some of its greatest pre-Reformation challenges. The popes of Avignon and of the Schism era used ceremony to establish their authority in the face of dislocation (i.e., removal from the stational world of Rome) and threats to their authority (i.e., rival popes).[17] They also used it to demonstrate their superiority to secular rulers. Although the papal court at Avignon was criticized for its luxury and Petrarch and others referred to the period as the Babylonian captivity, the Avignon popes presented themselves as glorious monarchs and enlisted ceremony to affirm this image.

If the fourteenth century was a challenging time for the papacy, the early fifteenth century was little better. One scholar claims that "after the Schism, just as after World War I, normalcy was an illusion, because the underlying reality had changed so dramatically."[18] Yet this illusion of normalcy was just what Martin and Eugenius wanted to create. Unlike Martin, Eugenius had no power base in Rome; as an ascetic Venetian aristocrat, he could not rely on his family or clients to help affirm his authority. Thus, ceremony offered an alternative form of legitimation, and throughout his pontificate Eugenius used it to assert and clarify his role as the leader of Christendom. Most accounts of Eugenius's reign portray the pope as lacking agency or control in his dealings with his political and conciliar opponents. Analysis of his use of ceremony (like analysis of his plans for religious reform) suggests instead that Eugenius thought carefully about how to surmount the challenges he faced. Since he did not have the baronial powers of his Colonna adversaries or the legal expertise of his opponents at Basel, he relied on the traditional symbols of papal authority and the pope's traditional role as leader of the clergy. By the end of his reign, Eugenius regained the political power that he had enacted throughout his pontificate; while this success was due to a variety of factors, including the aggressive campaigns of cardinals Vitelleschi and Scarampo and the political triumph of the Council of Ferrara-Florence, this chapter argues that ceremonial events helped to assert and establish, as well as display, Eugenius's claims to authority.[19]

The chapter begins by exploring the ways in which urban townspeople experienced papal ceremony. It then moves to a discussion of what papal ceremony communicated to its participants, the lay elite, members of the College of Cardinals and, finally, the Holy Roman Emperor Sigismundo. But this analysis does more than make an argument about the role ceremony played in Eugenius's political dealings. By tracing his Curia's use of earlier ceremonial forms and later popes' employment of the protocols of the mid-Quattrocento, the chapter argues that traditional demarcations between the medieval, Avignon, Renaissance, and Baroque papacies ignore significant elements of continuity.[20] One of the most important and lasting legacies of Martin V and Eugenius IV was the fourteenth-century ceremonials that they brought back to Rome and passed on to their successors. The Curia used these manuals (or rather an updated, fifteenth-century version of them) to guide ceremonial behavior well into the twentieth century. Thus, in addition to returning the Curia to Rome, Martin and Eugenius also established the ways in which the papal court would perform its relationship to the seat of Saint Peter throughout the early modern and modern eras.

Papal Ceremony as Public Performance

The average Florentine or Roman would not have known about all the political machinations of Eugenius's pontificate, but citizens of both cities understood that Eugenius's position as pontiff was far from secure. Partly because of the political dangers he faced, the pope seldom appeared on the streets of Rome or Florence. According to Vespasiano, when Eugenius did show himself "the reverence felt by them [the Florentines] was so great that they stood astonished at the sight of him, silent and turning towards the spot where he stood."[21] Other documents suggest that, at least once the Council of Florence opened, Eugenius's appearances were rare but splendid. On January 16, 1439, the pope left Ferrara on a horse with crimson trapping, dressed as if for mass and giving blessings to those who flocked around him while his servants threw coins; upon his arrival in Florence twelve days later, Cosimo de' Medici marched beside Eugenius and held the bridle of the pope's horse.[22]

On March 3, 1439, the Florentines celebrated the eighth anniversary of Eugenius's election.[23] The pope came out into the piazza in front of Santa Maria Novella (his residence in Florence) to give out twigs of olives on Palm Sunday; on Maundy Thursday, he gave his benediction to the crowds assembled outside the church's loggia. At the end of April, Eugenius officiated at the translation of the relics of Saints Zenobius, Eugenius, and Crescentius from the crypt of the Duomo to a specially prepared chapel; on this occasion, he was assisted by six cardinals as well as both Greek and Latin bishops and archbishops.[24] In June, he attended the greatest civic event of the Florentine year, the feast of Saint John the Baptist (June 24), complete with pageants and processions, and on July 6, he led the grand celebration of union between the Western and Eastern Churches, which was also a holiday for the city of

Florence.[25] Even when the commune was not the focus of attention, Florentine officials played an important and sometimes a guiding role in the ceremonial events of the council. Although Eugenius seems to have appreciated the importance of ceremony from the beginning of his reign, the exceptional grandeur of Florentine civic events would have enriched his understanding of how rituals could advertise and promote an image of power.[26]

If Eugenius exposed himself to public scrutiny relatively rarely while in Florence, he made even fewer public appearances in Rome. The Romans presumably recognized that they had precipitated Eugenius's departure from the seat of Saint Peter, but the pope's absence would not have seemed unusual. For more than a century prior to Martin's arrival in 1420, it was the exception, rather than norm, for popes to be resident in Rome, and even when fourteenth-century pontiffs visited their bishopric, they were increasingly removed from its urban landscape. For most of the Middle Ages, popes performed liturgical ceremonies throughout the city of Rome, following the stational system that was established in late antiquity. On Candlemas, for example, the pope and Curia processed from Sant' Adriano in the Forum to Santa Maria Maggiore, where the ceremonial presentation of candles occurred.[27] Boniface VIII (1294–1303) began to ignore the stational calendar, however, and conducted liturgical ceremonies within the exclusive confines of the papal chapel.[28]

The papacy's sojourn at Avignon accelerated the tendency to remove papal ceremony from public view; parts of the Avignon palace were given the same name as significant ceremonial sites in Rome, but this did not indicate any particular allegiance to the stational system.[29] The extent to which Martin and (when he was in Rome) Eugenius followed the stational routes is not clear, but it seems that, in the early 1400s, papal ceremonial was concentrated in the papal chapel.[30] Thus, the average Roman, like the average Florentine, saw only a small part of papal ceremony, and while urban dwellers participated in urban and neighborhood festivals, they were generally spectators for the grand rituals of the Church.

Given their increasing exclusion from papal ceremonies, how did Florentines and Romans interpret these events? What messages did they glean from the processions they saw and the rare appearance of the pope on loggias and in piazzas? The diary of the Florentine vintner Bartolomeo del Corazza offers some insights on the Florentine perspective. While Corazza enjoyed a successful career as a wine merchant, he did not take a leading part in government and thus did not have the complex political or rhetorical agenda of Manetti.[31] He did, however, make careful notes on papal ceremony; his diary records who performed mass on major feast days during Eugenius's sojourn in Florence, and he also offers some detailed accounts of papal ceremonies and processions:

> Wednesday, April 18, 1436, Pope Eugenius left Florence in this manner. The Signori made a grand invitation to citizens and representatives of the Palace, with the colleges and six of the merchant guilds and officials of the Monte, summoning a great company and the standard of Florence and fifty youths with torches to accompany the most sacred sacrament. They went to Santa Maria Novella to meet the pope. They dismounted near the pope, who mounted on a horse, and the Signori went on foot, accompanying the horse, with the Gonfaloniere taking the bridle on one side, and the Proposto taking it on the other side. Before the pope were many citizens, ambassadors and other noble foreigners. They went in groups of four, with four hats before them, the cloth bunched into three bunches, and an umbrella of yellow and red cloth. The podestà carried the flag with the arms of the church, the captain carried the flag of the pope and a friar (who was accompanied by two friars on horses, dressed in red cloth with a white cross) carried another flag. This flag was red with the keys, the symbols of the church, in every corner. Six cardinals followed: Piacenza, Tricarico, San Marco, Conti, Colonna and the pope's nephew, the Chamberlain.[32] The holiest sacrament was in a case covered in red taffeta, which was placed on a white horse with a red covering, and around the horse were the aforementioned young men with their torches lit. Before the horse went seven white horses and one white mule, with saddles of velvet and cloth, their rears covered with red cloth, and bearing richly adorned reins and bridles. Then came 100 citizens and the officials. Then came the pope with the Standard and the Signori around him. Then came the patriarch with a great number of bishops and other prelates and foreigners.[33]

Corazza goes on to describe the pope's parting from the Signori after protracted conversation and a brief visit to San Gallo (where Eugenius changed his clothes.) Only then does the pope proceed on his journey.

Corazza's description lacks the ekphrastic richness of Manetti's account of the consecration of the Florentine cathedral, but it emphasizes many of the same aspects of papal ceremonial that were important to Manetti. Like his fellow-citizen, Corazza notes the relative position of participants in the procession with care. He recognizes that proximity to the pope is an essential source of status, and he also recognizes that the clothing and ceremonial accoutrements of participants reinforce the procession's hierarchy. While Corazza does not describe Eugenius's outfit in any detail, he offers vivid accounts of the banners and trappings of the horses, especially the horse bearing the Sacrament, and he displays his appreciation of rich ceremonial props and fine fabrics. His diary shows that average Florentines did not trouble themselves with parallels between the pope and ancient emperors. Instead, they enjoyed papal ceremony as a performance, a performance that flaunted the wealth and magnificence of both the Church and their own city.[34]

Those who staged papal ceremonies were not simply interested in providing entertainment, however. One of the primary purposes of papal ceremony in Florence was to transform the pope's presence from a financial burden into a spiritual blessing; ceremonies showed the Curia and civic leaders in harmony and made Eugenius into a symbol of divine support for the Florentine state.[35] Such a transformation did not come cheaply. Neither Manetti nor Corazza is explicit about the financing of papal ceremonies, but both suggest that Florentine largesse was a necessary prerequisite to the performances they describe. Nevertheless, considering his limited income, Eugenius spent considerable sums of money to create an aura of ceremonial splendor. Like his predecessor, he commissioned a grand tiara from Lorenzo Ghiberti, better known for his work on the doors of the Florentine baptistery, and this tiara was one part of a more general pattern of expenditure on liturgical garments.[36] Corbo contrasts the relative sobriety of Martin V's taste with the "esplosione di fantasia" that occurred under Eugenius.[37] For his coronation, the pope spent more than seventy-three florins on embroidery; this included red silk for his own mantle, four different types of hat, bridles for horses, fourteen banners, hats for the two newly appointed cardinals, and a cloth with Eugenius's coat of arms, which was to be used when he gave the benediction. Two years later, he spent twenty-one florins for a hat, perhaps in honor of the emperor Sigismundo's coronation. Although the most lavish of these garments would only have appeared on special occasions, proper garb was an essential element of all papal ceremony. The brilliant tints of liturgical vestments marked the major feasts of the Church calendar, but they also brought texture and color to the dirty streets of Rome and Florence.

Eugenius took the same care with ceremonial paraphernalia that he did with ceremonial costumes. For example, in May of 1437, the Camera spent more than two hundred and thirty-five florins on candles.[38] As Corazzo notes, candles and torches were important components of papal ceremonies and processions, and the Curia also financed more splendid props. Eugenius kept jewelers on hand to create lavishly decorated swords (which were given on Christmas night) and golden roses (which were given on the Feast of the Rose, the Fourth Sunday of Lent.)[39] Each year on the Feast of the Rose, the pope performed mass while holding a golden rose, which was scented with musk and balsam.[40] When the mass was over, the pope bestowed the rose on one of the dignitaries present, as a mark of his particular favor, and it seems that he calibrated his choice in accordance with his political agenda.[41] For example, the week before the consecration of Santa Maria del Fiore, Eugenius presented the cathedral with a rose. It cost one hundred forty-one florins and included a large sapphire, and Manetti took care to note that it lay on the main altar during the cathedral's consecration.[42] In general, however, Eugenius gave the rose to an individual not an institution, and the honored recipient carried it through the city in which the pope was residing, advertising the Church's largesse.[43]

Papal ceremony was not simply a visual and olfactory performance. Although Corazzo does not describe any music in his account of the papal procession, he does mention that the pope stopped to talk to civic officials before leaving the city. In his longer account of a more spectacular event, Manetti discusses music in some detail, and less sophisticated urban dwellers were also attuned to the music of processions and ceremonies.[44] Their attention reflected pontifical care for and investment in music. Eugenius, like his predecessor, gave special privileges to his musicians, and while the *Apostolica Camera* tended to be erratic in most of its payments, it paid the salaries of the singers of the papal chapel at the beginning of each month with great regularity.[45] These singers, who were mostly French and Flemish, were hired to sing polyphonic music; Martin V brought six men back with him after the Council of Constance, and for most of the period between 1420 and 1447 there were between eight and twelve papal singers. France and Burgundy were not the sole source of musical influence; at Constance, the English delegation made a notable impression on the whole company with their cyclic masses, and it was probably in the early

Quattrocento that the cyclic mass (which was also shaped by German liturgical norms) became part of the papal musical tradition. The need to provide appropriate and impressive music for the Council of Florence may have prompted interest in and use of this new musical form. The Curia and its grand ceremonies provided occasions for musical innovation, even as older practices also persisted.[46]

The limited survival of early Quattrocento music makes it difficult to recreate the musical experience of ordinary papal ceremonial.[47] The music performed at the consecration of Santa Maria del Fiore has received special attention, however, from Quattrocento as well as modern scholars. According to Manetti: "Melodies were raised by so many and varied singing voices, alternating with songs made with such symphony lifted up to heaven, that to the audience they appeared for sure angelic and divine. The ears of the hearers were so titillated by the wonderful sweetness of the varied voices that they seemed exceedingly awestruck, as if enchanted by the Sirens' songs."[48] Later, Manetti waxes still more eloquent, claiming that when the host was elevated, the music was such that he "seemed to be enjoying the blessed life here on earth."[49]

Even as the music performed at the consecration delighted and inspired its listeners, the words sung offered pointed messages about papal authority. Guillaume Dufay, who was a member of the papal chapel in 1436, wrote a number of works for the event, including "Nuper rosarum flores."[50] The work's first stanza refers to Eugenius's gift of the rose, and the second stanza reads "Today the vicar / Of Jesus Christ and successor / Of Peter, Eugenius, / This same most enormous Temple / With sacred hands / and holy oils / Has deigned to consecrate."[51] Thus, the very beginning of Dufay's piece emphasizes the Petrine succession and Eugenius's role as vicar of Christ. Another piece written by Dufay for the consecration begins by describing Eugenius as "homo regens celi fores" and goes on the say that he fills the church with the eternal word.[52] Scholars have elucidated the ways in which Dufay's music for the consecration, especially "Nuper rosarum flores," affirms Florentine pride in the cathedral and in Florence as a New Jerusalem.[53] Dufay's praise of Eugenius does not undermine this praise of Florence; his music, like the consecration as a whole, was intended to exalt both pope and city. Music was one of the many ways in which the Curia sought to present a triumphant image of the Church Militant.[54]

In short, papal ceremonies, including those that did not merit special descriptions by urban viewers, were rich, multimedia displays. Although they did not boast original motets, processional walkways, or cornucopias of flowers and banners, ordinary ceremonies still featured professional singers, splendid vestments, and a complicated interplay of curial figures. But what did these events mean to Romans who, unlike the Florentines, were unaccustomed to ceremonial splendor? Unfortunately, Romans were not as apt to write chronicles as their Florentine counterparts. But the diary of Stefano Caffari offers one account of how Eugenius was greeted when he returned to Rome in 1443. Caffari, who was a canon of the Lateran and Sant'Eustacio and may have had some connection with the papal court, notes that, before his entrance into the city, the pope spent the night at Santa Maria del Popolo:

> On Sunday which was the twenty-ninth day of the said month [September], at the nineteenth hour, Eugenius rode processionally and honorably with all the people. I was dressed and present in the capacity of my office. The pope went to St. Peter's along the way of the Colonna and San Marco. . . . [Caffari elaborates the pope's route, noting the various houses at which he turned as well as street names.] He entered the church of Saint Peter and he gave an oration and blessing at the altar, and the Veronica was displayed. Then he entered his room with peace and tranquility.[55]

Caffari's description lacks the ebullient excitement of Manetti or Corazzo. He is more concerned with the pope's route through familiar streets than he is with the order of the procession or the richness of the participants' garments. Papal ceremonies may have lost some of their splendor once the pope returned to Rome and gave up the ritual resources of Florence, but given the poverty of Rome even a relatively staid procession would have seemed like a miracle of light, color, and wealth. Furthermore, upon Eugenius's return, papal ceremonies took on a new meaning; they signaled the Romans' acceptance of the pope's presence. Caffari's emphasis on Eugenius's peaceful withdrawal to his own apartments is notable. This minor civic official, like many both inside and outside the Curia, may have worried whether the pope's ceremonial presence was sufficient to calm the impoverished and recalcitrant Romans. In reading Caffari's description, there is a sense that the papal performance might be interrupted at any minute by a

Neapolitan attack or a sudden outbreak of popular hostility. After all, ceremonial events often served as occasions for, rather than antidotes to, popular violence in early modern Europe.[56]

Ceremonial and the Communication of Papal Authority

Much of the scholarship on papal ceremony has focused on spectacular ceremonies such as coronations, triumphal entries, and funerals.[57] As adherence to the stational liturgy of Rome crumbled in the fourteenth century, these were the only events that urban populations were likely to witness, and they were undoubtedly important in expressing the political and cultural agendas of particular pontiffs. These special events, however, were constructed on a single foundation: the papal mass. Celebration of the mass varied in subtle but significant ways throughout the liturgical calendar; the annual cycle of festivals emphasized the unchanging nature of the Church and served as the inspiration for special ceremonies, both secular and religious.[58] Ceremonial manuals provide valuable insights into what happened (or what was supposed to happen) during both annual and extraordinary events. With their minute focus on the interactions of the pope and his cardinals, they suggest that many of the messages of papal ceremonial were aimed not at an urban populace but at the performers themselves—in other words, members of the Curia and their visitors. Anthropological work on performance theory can offer assistance in reading ceremonial manuals, just as it helps in interpreting the experiences of urban spectators.[59]

As bishop of Rome, the pope originally performed the same religious services as all other bishops.[60] Over the course of the Middle Ages, interest in the behavioral, as opposed to the doctrinal, aspects of the liturgy increased, and the thirteenth and fourteenth centuries witnessed extensive elaboration of correct ceremonial behavior. During this period, protocols appropriate for and unique to the papal court were codified in pontificals.[61] Rome, MS Biblioteca Corsiniana, 41 E 22 (hereafter referred to as "the Corsiniana manuscript") provides the curial protocols for both annual liturgical ceremonies and special events, such as consecrations and coronations.[62] The manuscript and two others just like it were written for Pietro del Monte, bishop of Brescia, who was closely associated with the Curia from 1434 until his death in 1457.[63] The Corsiniana manuscript shows how the various pontificals of the last one hundred and fifty years were combined and fused into a fairly coherent program in the early-mid Quattrocento; in particular, it indicates the Curia's reliance on fourteenth-century ceremonial, as the ceremonials of Jacopo Stefaneschi (1270–1343) and Pierre Amiel (1330–1401) are its major sources.[64]

In spite of this use of Trecento protocols, the Corsiniana manuscript is more than a copy of earlier works. In the text, the latest precedent cited is that of Martin V, and the marginalia written by Pietro del Monte mention events that occurred during the pontificates of Eugenius IV and Nicholas V.[65] Although marginalia of this sort are not extensive, they indicate that the bishop wanted to connect his rubrics to actual ceremonial performance.[66] The Corsiniana manuscript thus provides a ceremonial snapshot of the early-mid Quattrocento, and this is especially valuable because there are only a few fragmentary records from the papal ceremonial clerks of this period.[67]

After an introductory section on the papal mass, the Corsiniana manuscript begins the liturgical year with the Candlemas service, a service that displays many of the priorities and preoccupations of papal ceremonial.[68] On Candlemas, the pope enters the chapel where the cardinals are gathered. He prays before the altar and goes to sit while they receive their copes. The service then continues:

> A cloth is prepared and extended over the knees of the pope by two chaplains, who assist him from the side and, kneeling, hold the said cloth, one on the right and one on the left. Two senior cardinal deacons assist the lord pope in the accustomed fashion. Then the first of the cardinal bishops, with his miter removed, standing while the mitered pope sits, gives an unlit candle to the pope. He says "he who is greater than others is nothing" and kisses the pope's hand.[69] The first or the second of the cardinal bishops kneels there, receives an unlit candle from the hand of the pope, and kisses his right knee. Then all the cardinals, first the cardinal bishops, then the cardinal priests, then the cardinal deacons, and all the bishops who are wearing the vestments of the day take off their miters and receive a candle from the hand of the pope and kiss his knee. Prelates who are not in vestments after they receive the candle kiss the pope's foot not his knee. (It must be noted that if the cardinal bishop or priest who celebrates before the pope on this day comes dressed before the service to receive the candle, he does not take off his *planeta* but fully robed he receives the candle from the

hand of the pope in the aforementioned manner.) Even if the treasurer, any of the notaries, the auditor of appeals or the corrector is an arch-bishop or bishop he kisses the pope's foot because these officials are not accustomed to come in formal vestments but wearing woolen caps. The chaplains (both those of the table who ought to be in a surplice and other chaplains) and similar men even penitentiaries and, in short, all the other familiars of the pope, even laymen, and any others who are not familiars, even if one of them is a king, receive candles from the pope while kneeling and then kiss the pope's foot not his knee.[70]

While ceremonial props are important to the service, the Candlemas protocol focuses on the actors and their interrelationships. The pope's four assistants highlight his actions, and their presence also underscores his special status. Like all others who participate in the Candlemas ser-vice, the pope receives a candle, but he does so sitting while the first of the cardinal bishops kneels to him and kisses his hand. From then on it is the pope who gives; the presentation of the candles reminds their recipients that the pope acts as the liaison between them and "the light of the world." He is practicing largesse, and the proper response is to kneel before him and kiss him reverently. Each of the cardinals expresses his subservience to the pope, and each of them is reminded that he has a specific niche in the hierarchy of the College. Then, bishops and arch-bishops proceed in the same manner, and their right to kiss the pope's knee instead of his foot depends on what they are wearing; status is not something that is entirely secure, and one individual can occupy mul-tiple positions in the hierarchy. Only then do other members of the Curia and laypeople receive the candle, and they do so again in a rigid hierarchical order, an order that was sometimes contested. In 1421 and 1422, envoys from the kings of Castille and England each argued that they should receive a taper in the Candlemas ceremony before the rival ambassador. To avoid a diplomatic fracas, Martin V gave a taper pri-vately to the ambassador to Castille while, in another room, the papal confessor gave a taper to the English ambassador.[71]

Participants in papal ceremonies understood that these events affirmed the structure of society, a structure in which proximity to the pope was the ultimate mark of status. Such affirmations were not neu-tral or pro forma, as papal secretaries (see chapter 2) and foreign ambas-sadors recognized. Sensitivity to rules of precedence suggests that the deference that laypeople showed to clerics served as an admission that, at least in liturgical contexts, they were inferior to the curial elite; a king, unlike a cardinal or even a bishop, had to kiss the pope's foot.

Those scholars who discuss ritual as a type of performance emphasize its bodily nature.[72] Participants in a liturgical act signal their support of it; it is impossible, or at least very difficult, to participate in such an act and simultaneously challenge it.[73] This does not mean that everyone who knelt to kiss the pope's foot believed that he had the keys to the kingdom of heaven, the power to bind and loose. Nor does it mean that a participant in the ceremony might not decide to attack the pope the next day. Within the special space created by this liturgical act, however, there was conformity to a particular code of conduct, which emphasized the pope's special role.[74] This code of conduct (especially when reinforced on other occasions) encouraged those participating in a liturgy to behave in a similar manner in other contexts as well, even though it could not compel them to do so.[75]

While performance theory offers a helpful lens through which to read protocols like the Corsiniana manuscript, there are several reasons why it cannot fully elucidate what papal ceremonies meant to members of the clerical elite or to their honored visitors. The first is that the notion of performance implies a division between actors and audience, and members of the Curia and their visitors were both the actors in and audience for curial ceremonial. The second reason is that anthropological works comparing ritual and performance have tended to isolate the ritual event from the society in which it occurs; implicit in the performance analogy is the idea that rituals are special, separate activities that can be considered in isolation.[76] While this may have been true for men like Corazzo and Caffari, ceremony was simply one aspect of life in the Curia. As Poggio's anguished letter about precedence in processions suggests, ceremony played an integral role in the general struggle for position. A third problem with the performance perspective is its very emphasis on activity. Performance theorists of ritual tend to devote most of their attention to action, and action is indeed what would have been apparent to urban viewers of processions. But those participating in papal ceremonies would have taken part in the performance of the liturgy even as they read or sang it; together, these two components of papal ceremonies would have communicated hybrid messages.[77] Since communication always depends on a shared cultural code, thinking about ritual as a form of communication explicitly embeds it in a social framework.[78]

Like the ceremonial blocking of the Candlemas mass, the prayers offered before the distribution of candles emphasize the pope's special status. One prayer petitions God to bless and sanctify the candles for the good of the worshippers and the health of their bodies and spirits. Another prayer claims that the sacred fire represents God's glory, and a third asks that the invisible internal fire of the Holy Spirit dispel all vices in the heart, just as the candles dispel shadows.[79] In short, before the pope distributes the candles, the words of the service establish them as mystical intermediaries between man and God, capable both of reaching Him and of bringing Him into His People. While the actions of the participants emphasize physical abasement to the pope, the accompanying prayers present him as the essential mediator between heaven and earth, and other ceremonies in the liturgical calendar reaffirmed similar messages. Members of the Curia and visiting nobles bowed to the pope, and received holy objects from him, in a similar way on Ash Wednesday, Palm Sunday, and the first Saturday after Easter.[80] All of these events demonstrated the Curia's deference to the pope's person and a carefully demarcated, hierarchically organized vision of the social order. Thus, papal ceremonials, with their focus on the minutiae of personal interactions, superimposed a pronounced concern with hierarchy and power on the religious messages of the Roman Rite.[81]

Such deference to the pope was not confined to liturgical contexts; the Corsiniana manuscript includes both liturgical and nonliturgical ceremonies without making any distinction between them.[82] In general, the nonliturgical events include only the curial elite and honored visitors, but they communicate messages similar to those of the Candlemas ceremony. On Maundy Thursday, the night of the Last Supper, the pope invites his cardinals and other honored guests to a dinner after mass. At dinner, a set protocol unfolds:

> The pope sits at one eminent table with diverse large gold and silver dishes placed on it. At another table which is to the right of the pope . . . sit the cardinal bishops according to order of their election (for those elected earlier sit first) and among them sit the four patriarchs of the principal patriarchal churches (if they are present).[83] After the tables of the cardinals come the tables of the prelates and nobles. Of the laymen

who are present, those who are greater in birth and nobler serve the pope in the duties that are assigned to them. It must be noted that one of the more prominent nobles, even if he is a king, places the first dish before the pope. If he is a king, he then goes to sit at the table to the left between the first two cardinal deacons. Karolus, first king of Sicily and the kings descending from him did this. The emperor of Constantinople who was at the Curia at the time sat to the right between the first two cardinal bishops.[84] Probably he placed the first dish before the pope and the king of Sicily carried the second dish. Other great nobles, even if they are sons of the emperor or of kings, also serve the pope at table.[85]

As in the protocol for the Candlemas ceremony, the description of the Maundy Thursday dinner focuses on the relationship between the pope and the other individuals present. Although the ranking of each cardinal was determined from the moment of his election, the seating arrangement at dinner reinforces that order. Cardinal bishops always outrank cardinal priests and deacons, and, beyond that, seniority serves as the principal determinant of status.[86] For the secular attendees, this occasion involves a mixing of honor and subservience. Princes have to serve the pope, but they also sit among the cardinals, something that would never occur in a liturgical context. Repeatedly, but in slightly different ways, the papal ceremonial of the early Quattrocento established a hierarchical vision of society, a hierarchy with the pope at the top. Both the annual cycle of ceremonial displays and special events like the consecration of a cathedral disseminated similar messages about the nature of authority.[87]

Affirmations of the superiority of religious to secular authority were hardly new in the fifteenth century, but they were especially pregnant. Many secular rulers hoped to take advantage of the papacy's weakened position in the aftermath of the Schism and during the struggle with the Council of Basel; they sought to manipulate the crisis between Church and council in order to increase the independence of their national churches. In one of the more famous examples of princely propaganda against Eugenius, Valla's *On the Donation of Constantine* called for a simple, frugal church, led by a modest bishop who avoided all political concerns.[88] Francesco Sforza was more direct in his attacks on papal rapacity: "We will not be deprived of rights, nor damaged, nor be trampled on by these clerical bosses with their insatiable appetite which is not satisfied with spiritual income only but demands also the temporal.

We have never accepted such practices but have continued in the way of the Visconti our predecessors; and so have done and still do many princes big and little everywhere in Italy."[89] Eugenius and his Curia responded to such ideas by insisting on the ceremonial abasement of secular rulers in the face of spiritual power.

In presenting the pope as a grand monarch, the ceremony of the Corsiniana manuscript follows the example of the most extravagant fourteenth- and early fifteenth-century pontiffs. The manuscript repeatedly mentions precedents to justify certain practices or to explain what to do in emergencies. For example, at the end of the discussion of Candlemas, the manuscript notes that in 1356 Innocent VI had gout and was not able to leave his room; thus, the cardinals were not called to vespers, there was no mass, and candles were not given out. In the third year of Clement VI's pontificate, the pope presented the ceremonial candles from the tower of the papal palace, and then the procession proceeded to the chapel, through the window of which he gave candles to the people.[90] Clement VI is the pope most often cited in the Corsiniana manuscript; fifteen of the text's precedents relate to ceremonial behavior during his pontificate.[91] This reliance on the rules established during the reign of one particular Avignon pope is far from neutral. Clement allegedly said that his predecessors did not know how to be pope and strove to reform their errors by hosting ever more lavish displays.[92]

The use of precedents accords with other versions of ceremonial texts. The ceremonials of Stefaneschi and Amiel, which are the sources for most of the Corsiniana manuscript, frequently cite the example of the Avignon pontiffs. The Corsiniana manuscript includes more of these precedents than do other versions of the same texts, however, and, more significantly, it repeatedly cites the example of Benedict XIII, one of the most prodigal and ceremonially minded antipopes of the Schism.[93] At times, he is included in a laundry list and so the significance of his ceremonial predilections is not clear, but some of the references to him suggest ways in which he increased the pomp of papal ceremonial. For example, during Benedict's pontificate, the cardinals accompanied the recipient of the papal rose as he carried it around the city. The splendor of Benedict's garb is repeatedly mentioned, and the references also suggest that the antipope minimized his own role in certain ceremonies, preferring to sit in regal inactivity while cardinals performed the service. In addition to the precedents that explicitly cite Benedict, some of his ceremonial protocols are included as part of the Corsiniana manuscript. Thus, rather than shunning the innovations of two unpopular chapters in papal history, Eugenius, like his predecessor, embraced them.[94] This was one of the many ways in which the two popes demonstrated their lack of interest in reforming the perceived abuses of the last hundred years, and because papal ceremonial put not just the pope but the Curia on display, it actually highlighted one of those abuses— the substantial growth of the Curia over the course of the fourteenth and early fifteenth centuries. The ceremony of the early 1400s responded to challenges from secular rules by affirming a monarchical vision of the papacy.[95]

Ceremony and Eugenius's Relations with the College of Cardinals

Eugenius's love of splendid ecclesiastical garments suggests that he appreciated the show and drama of papal ceremonies, but there is also other evidence that this was a pope who took the ritual of his court seriously. In a bull of 1432, Eugenius begins a long list of rules for Rome's clerics with directions about processions.[96] As discussed in chapter 4, Eugenius was deeply concerned with the morals and behavior of the clergy, especially the clergy of Rome. The fact that he commences his stipulations for their reform with ceremonial protocol indicates that ceremony represented, in his opinion, an essential measure of the Church's order.

This section explores the ways in which papal ceremony not only affirmed Eugenius's position as a papal monarch but also helped to establish and confirm the hierarchical organization of the rest of the Church. In particular, it examines the role ceremony played in Eugenius's fraught relations with his cardinals. At the beginning of the pope's reign, the Council of Basel and the College of Cardinals were challenging the traditional model of Church power, a model with the pope at the top, a model in which both councils and cardinals derived their authority from the successor of Peter. The representatives at Basel and the College agreed that the Church should instead be an oligarchy, with the cardinals sharing in papal power and participating in all papal decisions. Eugenius's success in convincing his cardinals that they had more to lose than to gain from their support of conciliarism played a vital role in his eventual triumph over the Council of Basel. Charting the vicissitudes of his relations with the College elucidates the ways in which the pope used the demarcation and enactment of the Church's hierarchy as a diplomatic tool.

From the beginning of his pontificate, Eugenius did not have cordial relations with the College. Because the cardinals had objected to the nepotism and high-handedness of Martin V, in the consistory after his death, they signed an election capitulation. During the previous eighty years, election capitulations had become routine, but this particular capitulation demanded that the pope observe the decrees of the Council of Constance and articulated the rights of cardinals more fully than earlier capitulations.[97] Eugenius IV not only signed this capitulation but issued a bull to ratify it. Although he did not adhere to the capitulation for long, in theory, it obligated him to move ahead with the Council of Basel and to include the Sacred College in his decisions. Making promises he did not intend to fulfill did not endear Eugenius to his cardinals, and one more particular tension quickly arose. In 1426, Martin V had secretly made Domenico Capranica a cardinal, although he did not announce the appointment until November 1430. Because of his absence from Rome, Capranica was not given a red hat before Martin's death, and his fellow cardinals, led by Giordano Orsini, used this as an excuse to ban the Colonna client from consistory.[98] Capranica fled, first to Siena, then to Milan, and finally to Basel, where he added important ammunition to the Father's ire against Eugenius, claiming that Eugenius's election was invalid because of his own exclusion from the consistory.[99]

Capranica was not alone in his opposition to the pope. When Eugenius arrived in Florence on June 23, 1434, he had no cardinals with him and thus did not celebrate mass on the feast of Saint John.[100] The situation began to improve relatively quickly; by the end of 1434, seven cardinals had come to Florence, and throughout 1435, others joined them, including Capranica (whom Eugenius had recognized in 1433 thanks to the reconciliation efforts of Cardinal Albergati.)[101] Not all of the cardinals who hesitated to join the pope had played an active role at Basel, but Eugenius's initial position in Florence underscored his political weakness and his shaky relations with the College. Cardinal Cesarini remained at Basel until 1437, and his authority and reputation contributed greatly to the council's prestige. Thus, rather than standing with Eugenius to defend a curial vision of the Church, members of the

College, including the Italian cardinals who should have been Eugenius's natural allies, demonstrated their independent agendas and their ability to undermine his fragile authority.[102]

Like his predecessor, Eugenius did not respond to the challenges he faced by immediately filling the College with a host of friends and relatives.[103] While this would have been an obvious way to strengthen his position, the Council of Constance had limited the number of cardinals to twenty-four and stipulated that they must be from all parts of Christendom. Upon his election, Eugenius promoted his nephew Francesco Condulmer and another Italian, Angelotto Foschi. In 1437, the notorious Giovanni Vitelleschi was made a cardinal. But the vast majority of Eugenius's promotions occurred in 1439, when, on December 18, he created seventeen new cardinals, including Isidore of Kiev and Bessarion. These creations reflected a new confidence on the part of Eugenius, a confidence that was largely due to his success at the Council of Florence. In September 1439, the pope had issued the bull, *Moyses vir,* condemning the Council of Basel and denying the supreme authority of general councils as defined in *Haec sancta.*

But why did Eugenius's strengthened position induce him to make new cardinals, given the problems that the College had created for him? Certainly red hats were a way of thanking Bessarion and Isidore for their staunch support of the Catholic position in spite of the resistance of other Orthodox prelates. Many of Eugenius's other promotions went to representatives of European powers as a way of rewarding or securing their support against the Council of Basel.[104] From Eugenius's perspective, however, red hats were more than a thank-you present or a tool to create or strengthen diplomatic channels. The pope saw the naming of cardinals and the existence of a large College as a way of affirming his own authority, as he made clear in an important bull of late 1440 or early 1441. This bull, *Non mediocri dolore,* was the first papal document to fix the status of the cardinals officially, and it became the foundation of all later writings on the cardinalate.[105] It was prompted by a specific political problem, the battle for precedence between the Archbishop of Canterbury, Henry Chichele, and Cardinal John Kemp (formerly Archbishop of York).[106] Chichele claimed that noncurial cardinals did not have the same rights as curial cardinals and that, in royally convoked assemblies, Kemp was not a cardinal but merely Archbishop of York and thus inferior to him. Writing to Chichele, Eugenius assures him that he is mistaken and discusses the historical position of the cardinalate.

Since recent discussions of the cardinalate had tended to argue for an oligarchical model of Church government, Eugenius had to find a way of affirming the unique position of the cardinals without in any way undermining his vision of papal monarchy.[107] To do this, he argued that the cardinalate was modeled on biblical precedents but was not, in fact, divinely ordained. The title *cardinal* did not exist in the primitive Church, although the cardinals were the true heirs of the priests of the house of Leviticus (Deuteronomy 17:8–12).[108] The office was formally instituted by Peter, and Peter established not a group of his equals but a group of men who would help him. Since Peter and his successors represent the person of Christ, the cardinals represent the Apostles and support the pope as the Apostles supported Christ. "Thus from the origin of the Church so too today the cardinals assist the highest pontiffs in ruling and governing the universal Church."[109]

It is not surprising that Eugenius defines the office of cardinal largely in relationship to that of the papacy. Since the eleventh century, cardinals had been expected to take an active role in the government of the Church, and Eugenius cites several precepts from canon law to prove the superiority of cardinals to bishops.[110] The bull, however, also uses analysis of the cardinalate as a way of emphasizing the preeminence of the bishop of Rome. The successor of Christ as well as Peter, God on Earth, he is not simply the head of the Roman church, Eugenius *is* the Roman church. As the bull proceeds, Eugenius devotes more and more energy to defending the primacy of Rome, the "head, standard and teacher" of the other churches.[111] The Church of Rome has determined that certain churches should have greater authority than others, and this hierarchy cannot be altered, even by Eugenius himself (although he has the right to bestow the office of cardinal on whomever he chooses). Thus, if the Church is inseparable from the person of the pope, it is also inseparable from an *ordo* that was laid down long ago. "It is against public honor and the government of the universal Church." and verges on a scandal to church discipline if by any action a deacon precedes a priest or a priest a bishop or a bishop a patriarch."[112] Eugenius goes on to say that challenging the hierarchy ordained by the Church is a threat to the dignity of magistrates and is likely to upset the state. In other words, the bull recalls the warnings of the *libellus apologeticus*.

In crafting his bull, Eugenius relies on an impressive array of authorities in addition to those mentioned in the preceding paragraphs. He starts his substantive discussion by citing "the statutes of the holy fathers and your custom for this office, which was always observed at general councils."[113] But Eugenius's conception of the Church is not based solely on textual sources, and he is not simply concerned with the practical matter of more powerful and less powerful offices. In his eyes the order of the Church mirrors the celestial hierarchy, and throughout the bull, he offers an image of harmony, an image that is closely connected to the physical ideal of the Church as a body. The practical representation of this order was nowhere more apparent than in papal ceremonies, and the immediate impetus for the bull was an argument about precedence. Thus, the bull is closely, though indirectly, linked to liturgical protocols, and the protocol for the creation of cardinals complements Eugenius's vision of the cardinalate in important ways. It makes clear that the cardinals are subservient to the pope and that they depend on him (and to a much lesser extent their colleagues) for their position.

According to Stefaneschi's protocol, the creation of cardinals is a multistep process.[114] First, the cardinals meet in consistory, and the pope asks them whether it will be beneficial to add to the College and how many members should be added. On the following Friday, the pope returns with a list of names, and the cardinals "respond with their opinion to the [pope's] candidates, according to how God directs them."[115] Then the pope creates the new cardinals, saying "by the authority of God, the omnipotent Father, of the holy apostles Peter and Paul and of ourself, we absolve this man, if he is a prelate, from the chain which was holding him to his church and we receive him as a cardinal priest of the Roman Church."[116] Thus, as in so many rites of initiation, the first step in the creation of new cardinals involves their detachment from their earlier place in the Church structure.[117] On Saturday, the pope repeats the statements of the previous day, freeing the new cardinals from their earlier duties before the whole Curia.

The new cardinals are then summoned to the papal chapel, according to the order in which the pope named them. Two senior cardinal deacons receive the first new cardinal whom the pope named, and after that, other cardinal deacons pair up with the new cardinals according to their seniority. The escorts lead the new cardinals to kiss the pope's foot and then lead them to the altar, where they lie prostrate. After kissing the altar, the new cardinals kiss the senior cardinal bishops, then the senior cardinal priests, then the senior cardinal deacons, and the group retires to consistory. The senior cardinal deacons lead the new cardinals to kiss the foot and the mouth of the pope and then show them to their proper seats in consistory.

Even in this initial phase of the creation, it is possible to trace many, sometimes conflicting modes of legitimation. The cardinals are supposed to choose whether to add members to their body and how many members to appoint, but they may only vote *yes* or *no* on particular names. Thus, while the College participates in the election of its members, its participation is minimal and firmly constrained. The second day of ceremony adds several additional layers of complexity to the cardinal-papal division of authority. Initially, it emphasizes the importance of the Curia. Even before the cardinals are formally invested, they must be presented to the papal court and seen functioning within the fixed ceremonial order. The repetition of the formulas from the preceding day ensures that no one can claim that a new cardinal is still only a bishop. But the ceremony also begins the elaborate chain of bodily interactions that characterizes papal ceremonial as a whole. Again and again, the order of the new creations is stressed; from the first, the new cardinals are taught to occupy a set position in the clerical hierarchy. They do kiss all their fellow cardinals on the mouth, however, whereas they kiss the pope's foot and his mouth. Thus, even as the hierarchy of the College is stressed, so too is its collegiality. The sharp divide is not between particular cardinals but between all cardinals and the pope. He alone can instruct them publicly. It is to him alone that they must kneel. The cardinals are not welcomed as members of an oligarchy; they are created by and owe their position to a monarch.

The remainder of the cardinals' investiture occurs in private. The pope begins by imposing silence on the new cardinals. He then gives them instructions about how they should speak prudently and with reverence in consistory and how they ought to honor their fellow cardinals. After these admonitions, all the cardinals go for lunch at the pope's palace, where they sit according to their freshly established order. Following lunch, the new cardinals receive their red hats from the pope, again kissing his foot and then being received to the kiss of the mouth. Thus, again and again, each new cardinal is reminded of his abasement before and his proximity to the supreme pontiff. At the next consistory, with the approval of the senior cardinals, the pope "opens the mouths" of the new cardinals; thus as in the initial election, the cardinals participate but the pope is clearly in control. On the same day, the pope gives rings to the new cardinals and assigns them their churches, and this leads to another round of hand, foot, and mouth kissing. At this point, the new cardinals, having received their hats, rings, and titles, are fully established as part of the College.

The investiture ceremony emphasizes the cardinals' positioning in the curial hierarchy more than it emphasizes their receipt of a particular church.[118] If power is "a matter of techniques and discursive practices," the cardinals are instructed in both.[119] They are physically trained in the ceremonial behavior that should accompany their new duties, and they are also instructed as to how to participate in the discourse of the College. Given this, Eugenius could hope that the cardinals he created would support him; at the very least, the ceremonial rules of the Corsiniana manuscript constrain them, albeit briefly, to act in accordance with the papal vision of their office.[120] In the creation of cardinals, the most important relationship is that between the pope and the new cardinal. The cycle of mouth, hand, and foot kissing puts the cardinals in the place of Apostles—below their Lord, but also welcomed by him as sons and brothers. The giving of rings, hats, and titles emphasizes the flow of power from head to members. The ritual does not simply affirm a hierarchy; it emphasizes that all authority emanates from the pope, the true and sole head of the Roman Church.

Yet Eugenius was no creator of a Panopticon or a mental institution; clearly, his ability to constrain his cardinals was never very considerable. The gap between the power he claimed and the power he had is hinted at in the Corsiniana manuscript. It contains a section on how cardinals should perform services in their own chapels, and in this rubric, the cardinals assume the central role that the pope himself enjoys in most of the ceremonial.[121] Even the initiation process, focused as it seems to be on the relationship between the new cardinals and their pontiff, hints at freedoms cardinals can enjoy.

A separate initiation process occurs in tandem with that described in the preceding paragraphs. The new cardinals are supposed to visit the older cardinals, not following the usual strict order but in whatever order they choose.[122] During these visits, the senior cardinals should secretly instruct the initiates how they ought to honor and revere the pope and cardinals and how to speak in consistory. One can imagine that the lessons exchanged were not always so bland and that this was an important opportunity for scheming and the creation of allegiances, especially as the senior cardinals were expected to reciprocate these visits. By making individuals into cardinals, Eugenius endowed them with certain rights. The ceremony for the investiture of cardinals ensured these men an exalted place in the Church hierarchy, and, because of this, it also gave them the power to be as harmful to Eugenius as Cesarini and Capranica had proved to be. Ceremonial did more than express papal aspirations. It also reflected the amorphous, contested nature of authority in the Church of the early Quattrocento.

If Eugenius could not always enforce his own authority, however, he could enact it through bulls and through ceremonies. For all his political vacillation, Eugenius (or at least members of his Curia) had a coherent, traditional vision of papal authority that was reiterated in a variety of circumstances. By affirming the vision of the Church laid out in *Non mediocri dolore,* the protocol for the creation of cardinals demonstrates how papal ceremonial expressed and elaborated the ideological and political agenda of Eugenius's Curia.

Eugenius, Sigismundo, and the Legacy of the Early Quattrocento Papacy

As this chapter began with a humanist's description of papal ceremonial, it is fitting that it should end in the same way. In May 1433, Eugenius IV crowned Sigismundo as Holy Roman Emperor, and Poggio Bracciolini enthusiastically described the event. The emperor marched into the city preceded by an impressive procession of provisions, ambassadors, boys in colorful costumes, trumpet players, flutists, city magistrates, and Roman citizens, many of whom were ringing bells. At Saint Peter's, Sigismundo was met by the pope, and they advanced together to the altar, where a solemn Mass was performed. On the actual day of the coronation, Sigismundo entered the porch of Saint Peter's and made his oath to the pope.

> Then he went further into the church behind the high altar and stood at the right, dressed like a deacon, and was anointed by the Bishop of Ostia with the sacred oil; I think that the name of Augustus must have

come down from this. For you know that the ancients called places that
were consecrated to augury "augusta," and this name, considered as
holy, was given by the Senate to Octavian. In observance of this even
our emperors are called Augustus after consecration. After this, he
[Sigismundo] came to the Pope, who was celebrating mass at the altar,
and who received him with a kiss; and during the ceremony the Pope
first put a white miter on his head, so that the horns rose above his
temples, and then on top of this he placed a golden crown. Then the
pope gave him a golden orb and scepter and a naked sword, as if he
were a soldier of Christ, who would take up arms if necessary to defend
the Church of Rome and the faith of Christ. After these ceremonies
were finished, according to custom, he put on a cope; and then the Pope
and Emperor mounted their horses and started together toward the
Bridge of Hadrian. Emperors used at one time to travel on foot as far as
this place, holding the Pope's bridle; this Emperor was prevented by his
gout from keeping the custom.[123]

While Poggio's description is evocative, it raises more questions than it
answers, partly because it bears so little relation to the protocols laid out
in the Corsiniana manuscript.[124] According to the rubric for the coronation of an emperor, which comes from Stefaneschi's ceremonial, when
the soon-to-be-emperor first meets the pope at the doors of Saint Peter's,
he reverently kisses the pope's foot, promises to be a protector and
defender of the papacy and the Roman church, and presents the pope
with gold. Poggio merely notes that Sigismundo was received by
Eugenius. During the coronation itself, according to the Corsiniana
manuscript, the emperor-to-be prostrates himself on the ground so that
he can be blessed by the bishop of Ostia. Again and again, he is reminded
that he receives his position not from any earthly electors but from God
and Christ and that his duty is to protect the Church. He is also reminded
of the superiority of papal authority. When the pope presents him with
the imperial sword, he says "Here above the body of the Blessed Peter,
receive the sword from our hands; although they are unworthy, nevertheless they are consecrated by the authority of the blessed apostles.
This sword is conceded to you imperially with our blessing, and it is
divinely ordained for the defense of the holy mother Church for the
punishment of all evildoers and the praise of the virtuous."[125] Just after
this, the emperor receives his crown and kisses the pope's feet.

   At the end of the ceremony, the emperor again puts gold at the feet
of the pope and then acts like his subdeacon, giving him the cup and

salver. Finally, the emperor holds the pope's bridle but then he too rides to Santa Maria in Transpontina where the two part. In other words, the one place where Poggio suggests the emperor should have presented himself as subject to the pope (were it not for the imperial gout) is the one place, according to the Corsiniana manuscript, where the two traditionally rode side by side. What precedent or protocol did Poggio have in mind? The fact that Poggio says the two went all the way to the Ponte Sant' Angelo and the Corsiniana manuscript claims that the pope should turn around at Santa Maria in Transpontina adds a final element of disjunction to the two sources; the degree of disagreement between them offers almost comic proof of Schimmelpfennig's claim that it is difficult to recreate what happened in papal ceremonies in the earlier part of the Quattrocento.[126]

But even more intriguing than the question of what happened on May 31, 1433, is the question of how the coronation was arranged. Did Sigismundo negotiate to have the rules changed? Or did Poggio, who clearly wants to emphasize the parallels between ancient and modern emperors, simply choose to describe a ceremony of relative equality? Either is possible, indeed probable. Eugenius's position at this time was certainly very weak. Sigismundo made the trip to Rome, in part, to stave off a disastrous showdown between the pope and the Council of Basel. He was successful in doing so largely because Eugenius, who was facing a revolt in the Papal States, realized that he could not afford to make an open rupture with an ecumenical council.[127] Needing Sigismundo's support, Eugenius was in no position to demand gold or obeisances. Most of the prayers and orations included in the protocol for an emperor's election focus on the emperor's duties, not his inferiority to the pope. Thus, simply changing how Sigismundo moved through the coronation would have altered the tenor of the event and potentially made the interactions between pope and emperor as equitable as Poggio's description suggests. But if Eugenius's political weakness is undeniable, so too is Poggio's rhetorical agenda. He begins the letter, which is addressed to the acerbic Niccolò Niccoli, by complaining about how the present age despises history and fails to record illustrious deeds. "If it occasionally happens that some image of former glory is manifested to us. . . . I enjoy double happiness, on the one hand seeing these things which delight the eye, since they are far from usual with us, and on the other hand, enjoying with my mind those historical events which we admire when we read about them."[128] Thus, Poggio readily admits to his comparative perspective; he is more interested in tracing the intersections between past and present than he is in recording the present accurately.

At first, an account of the next imperial coronation (that of Frederick III in 1452) by Petrus Burgensis seems to undermine the reliability of Poggio's account still further.[129] Burgensis was Nicholas V's master of ceremonies, so he would have had a keen eye for details, and he says that the emperor kissed Nicholas's feet and gave him gold at their first meeting. In the description of the coronation itself, which occurred on Rose Sunday, Burgensis notes how Frederick acted as a deacon to the pope and describes the humble genuflections of the emperor and empress. There is no mention of a final horse ride, but the physical deference highlighted in the Corsiniana manuscript appears here in an abbreviated form. And yet it is not quite that simple. Burgensis notes that the College of Cardinals was rightly displeased that the empress received the peace before the cardinals themselves, and he bewails the fact that, on another Feast of the Rose, the Marchess of Brandenburg was allowed to sit between two cardinals, even though he was not a king or emperor.[130] In short Burgensis's account of ceremony under Nicholas V suggests that Poggio may have exaggerated the physical equality of emperor and pope in his description of Sigismundo's coronation, but it also serves as yet another reminder that ceremony was an important playing field for competing claims of religious and secular authorities. Although Nicholas V's hold on the papacy was stronger than that of his predecessor, he too may have had to compromise in the staging of specific events.[131] Based on Manetti's biography, Nicholas V has been seen as an important figure in the development of Renaissance ritual.[132] But the concern for ritual that Manetti ascribes to Nicholas was already present in his two predecessors, and here as elsewhere it seems that scholars may have put too much weight on Manetti's dramatic claims for Nicholas's originality.[133]

Poggio's letter is a harbinger of things to come, not so much in the years immediately following but in the High Renaissance. The ceremonial that was codified in the fourteenth century and adopted by Martin and Eugenius had remarkable staying power, but only after it enjoyed a humanist makeover. In 1488, Agostino Patrizi Piccolomini presented a new ceremonial compendium to Innocent VIII. Although it was more substantial than MS Biblioteca Corsiniana 41 E 22, it too collated the protocols of Stefaneschi, Amiel, Gregory X, and Benedict XIII.[134] It too tried to divide the annual and the special services of the papal chapel. What Patrizi claimed to add to papal ceremonial was not a distinctive ritual vision but rather a humanist Latinity, a humanist sense of order, a humanist concern with collating and studying his sources, and a great team of fellow scholars to assist him in his mighty task.[135] His preface recalls the arguments of Poggio in his introduction to the *Facetiae*; he defends his use of words that "censors of the Latin language" may criticize and insists that such neologisms help make his explanations clearer.

It was not just humanistic language that permeated ceremonial protocols, however; like Poggio and Manetti, the popes of the High Renaissance and Baroque took the ancient triumph as their model and performed ever more extravagant and more explicitly classicizing rites.[136] Julius II entered Bologna like a victorious *imperator*, and, throughout his pontificate, he claimed that he was a second Julius Caesar, destined to increase the *imperium* of the Church.[137] Leo X chose a more pacific role model; his *possesso*, probably the most elaborate to date, portrayed him as a new Augustus, the bringer of peace and culture.[138] While some of the early Counter-Reformation popes eschewed such extravagant ceremonies, ritual in Rome reached its peak in the seventeenth century under popes like Urban VIII; these rulers too looked to the past, not only comparing themselves to specific ancient figures, but also littering their ceremonies with elaborate classical allegories.[139] Thus, in their enthusiasm for antiquity, Poggio and Manetti gave their accounts of early Quattrocento papal ceremonial an overly classicizing tinge (or, arguably, a full dye job). By looking to the past, however, they unknowingly looked forward and foretold, with surprising prescience, the ceremonial ideals of the High Renaissance and Baroque.

Much changed in the two hundred fifty years after the writings of Poggio and Manetti. Yet if the trappings of papal ceremony adapted to humanist ideals and Baroque excess, its fundamental substance remained the same up until Vatican II; no new ceremonial manual ever really challenged Patrizi's.[140] The ceremonial vision of the Curia that was first recorded and preserved at Avignon and then brought back to Rome by Martin V, Eugenius IV, and their antipope predecessors saw the papacy through the glories of the High Renaissance, the devastation of the Sack, the tumultuous years of the sixteenth century, the triumph of the Baroque, and beyond. Historians have tended to emphasize the innate conservatism of the Curia or to tease out relatively minor variations from one pontificate to another. But ceremonial consistency was not simply due to a lack of creativity on the part of curialists, who could and did change rites to suit their purposes.[141] For example, in the consecration of the Florentine cathedral, the freeing of captives and the knighting of the standard-bearer of justice were special one-time additions to the thirteenth-century rules for consecrating a cathedral.[142] If the popes of the High Renaissance had wanted to make more substantive changes to papal ceremonial, they would have done so. But they did not. This implies that they were content with the Avignon vision of papal power.

Some theorists have argued that ritual does not simply represent power but is itself a form of power.[143] If this is the case, then the continuity of curial ceremony suggests that papal power did not fundamentally change between the mid-fourteenth century and the 1960s. The evidence presented in this chapter does not support such a radical conclusion. The late medieval, Renaissance, and Baroque papacy (to say nothing of the papacy of the eighteenth and nineteenth centuries) was not a theater state in which court ceremonialism was the driving force of court politics.[144] The amount of papal power clearly fluctuated with specific political developments. However, the *nature* of papal power may not have changed as much as has often been argued, at least between the thirteenth and the early sixteenth centuries.[145] Historians have tended to draw a firm line between the papal monarchy of the late Middle Ages and the papal principate of the Renaissance. The upheavals of Avignon, the Schism, and the early Quattrocento have facilitated this sharp demarcation. But if the years from 1309 to 1447 are viewed not as an unmitigated disaster but instead as an important period in the codification of an image of the papacy, the distinction between the medieval papal monarch and the Renaissance papal prince seems far less clear. While the verdure of the Renaissance principate may have had its richest efflorescence in the early Cinquecento, its roots date back to the thirteenth century, and they were nurtured, cultivated, and pruned in the ceremonies of the fourteenth and early fifteenth centuries.

6

Eugenius IV, Biondo Flavio,
Filarete, and the Rebuilding of Rome

CHAPTERS 4 and 5 explored some of the principal preoccupations of Eugenius IV. A pope who loved splendid ceremony, he was also a zealous reformer, determined to ameliorate the religious life of the clergy. In neither of these chapters does Eugenius appear as a particularly Roman pope, however. His program for Church reform had its origins in Venice's lagoon, and most of the splendid ceremonies of his pontificate—and, indeed, the majority of that pontificate—occurred in Florence. In contrast, Martin V's ties to the Eternal City are obvious; he was from a Roman clan and responsible for returning the papacy to the seat of Saint Peter. After being ignominiously chased out of Rome, Eugenius, a Venetian nobleman, had little reason to feel particular interest for or sympathy with the *caput mundi*.

Yet in spite of the inauspicious beginning to his career as pope, Eugenius spent much of his reign trying to return to Rome, and there are other signs of his commitment to the city. For a pope who sought to improve the quality of religious life, Rome was a natural place to begin, and for a pope who loved ceremony, Rome, even in its dilapidated state, remained the most fitting stage. Registers in the Archivio di Stato di Roma demonstrate that both before Eugenius's departure from Rome in 1434 and during his sojourn in Florence, curial funds were used to repair the Lateran, Santa Maria Maggiore, Saint Peter's, and several of the city's other major churches, and Eugenius paired these architectural initiatives with his promotion of Observant religious communities in Rome.[1] The pope also commissioned Antonio Averlino, called Filarete (c. 1400–c. 1469) to complete a splendid set of doors for the central portal of Saint Peter's, the *Porta Argentea*. These doors, which were (most likely) commissioned in 1433 and installed in 1445, are arguably the first surviving monument of the Roman Renaissance.[2] While the major figures on the doors are Christ, Mary, Peter, and Paul, in between these large panels are small reliefs depicting the successes of Eugenius's reign, all in terms of ceremonial events. Thus, in spite of limited resources and political problems, Eugenius sought to revive Rome's urban fabric, and, in doing so, he continued to promote the reformist and ceremonial agendas discussed in the previous two chapters.

Eugenius's pontificate also left memorials "more lasting than bronze"; if Rome did not yet look like a Renaissance capital in the 1430s and 1440s, it was the center for some important Renaissance scholarship.[3] Poggio drafted the antiquarian section of *De varietate fortunae* between 1432 and 1435, and Biondo Flavio (1392–1463) wrote *Roma instaurata* in the mid-1440s.[4] While Martin's aspirations for Rome are frequently linked with Signorili's *Descriptio*, scholars tend to relate the works of Biondo and Poggio to earlier and later antiquarian studies rather than to the goals of the pontiff who employed them.[5] Yet, as papal secretaries, both Poggio and Biondo worked closely with Eugenius. Biondo dedicated *Roma instaurata* to his papal patron, and the body of the treatise, as well as the dedication, includes effusive praise for Eugenius's efforts to rebuild the city; the treatise is a product of early Quattrocento curial patronage as well as a monument of innovative scholarship. While Poggio maintained a more critical attitude to his monkish employer (as discussed in chapters 3 and 4), his reading of Rome's ruins was also shaped by his experience of Eugenius's reign. Modern scholars have traditionally dated the beginning of the Roman Renaissance to Nicholas V's election, but the writings of Poggio and Biondo suggest that, before 1447, members of the Curia were striving to create dialogues between ancient and modern Rome, dialogues that could highlight the failures of the papacy but could also contextualize and promote papal efforts at rebuilding. Whether humanists focused on the inferiority of modern Rome or on her potential, they saw a city that transcended the exigencies of the early Quattrocento, and they utilized the glories of the past to interpret the culture and significance of the *caput mundi*.

Signorili and the chroniclists who were his predecessors also hoped that a revival of Rome's ancient legacy would strengthen the political and cultural capital of their city. In describing Rome's past, however, Signorili offered a story of continuity; Martin had only to continue the agenda of his papal predecessors (which was, itself, a natural outgrowth of ancient imperial practices) to return Rome to her former glory. By contrast, Poggio and Biondo saw Rome's past as a series of peaks and valleys, with a divide between antiquity and the Christian era. This chapter begins by parsing the political and cultural messages of *Roma instaurata,* and, more particularly, Biondo's understanding of revival.[6] The crises of Eugenius's pontificate pushed Biondo to go beyond the admiring nostalgia of Petrarch and to urge his papal master to build on the greatness of antiquity, while also acknowledging the differences between a pagan and a Christian society. Next, as in chapter 1, analysis moves from author to patron and to the reasons why Eugenius IV devoted some of his limited energy and resources to restoring parts of Rome. In addition to using architecture and monumental art to further his ceremonial agenda and plans for religious reform, the pope also, through his building endeavors, worked to remake the Rome of his predecessor, moving the city's center from the baronial fortress of the Colonna toward the Vatican and the Borgo. Thus, Eugenius and Biondo sought to recreate and reimagine Rome physically and ideologically. The similarities and differences in their agendas reflect the important but still liminal role of humanism in the Curia of the 1440s.

Biondo's Ideal of Urban Revival

In an influential article of 1950, Arnaldo Momigliano lauded Biondo's antiquarian work (particularly *Roma triumphans,* 1459) as the reawakening of Varronian antiquarianism, a style of scholarship that Biondo's immediate successors ignored but that went on to flourish in the sixteenth and seventeenth centuries.[7] According to Momigliano, one of the hallmarks of antiquarian scholarship is that it seeks to construct precise information about antiquity as an end in itself, and in the body of *Roma instaurata,* Biondo offers a systematic account of the material remains of the classical city. His goal is to understand the topography and, to a lesser extent, the culture of ancient and late antique Rome.[8] *Roma instaurata* is divided into short chapters, like a humanist notebook.[9] Biondo devotes some of these to particular buildings, some to a type of structure, some to a specific area, and some to a Roman institution or custom. Physical evidence plays a subsidiary role in his work; instead, *Roma instaurata* represents an impressive example of textual archeology.[10] Biondo relies most extensively on Livy, Pliny the Elder, Suetonius, and Varro, but he also cites a range of other classical and medieval authors.[11] Painstakingly piecing together quotations and citations from these sources, he parses the names and histories of various Roman monuments.[12]

The techniques of citation developed in *Roma instaurata* are equally characteristic of Biondo's later works, and modern scholars argue that his modes of reading vary considerably; at times he is a passive intermediary, at other times an active interpreter. Plausibility and probability play important roles in his argument and do not always produce correct conclusions.[13] Nevertheless, modern studies of Biondo's scholarship tend to follow their specific criticisms of his lapses in historical and archeological judgment with praise of his overall method. The claims of Momigliano and Weiss that Biondo was a revolutionary figure have not been fundamentally challenged.[14]

Comparing Biondo's description of the Capitol with that of Signorili highlights Biondo's innovations. In spite of Signorili's antiquarian interest in inscriptions, his text differs dramatically from Biondo's in organization, use of sources, and weighing of evidence. Signorili seeks to craft a continuous story of Rome's greatness in which inscriptions, like relics, offer tangible proof of the city's role as the center of both secular and spiritual authority. While he does not explicitly discuss Rome's hills, he does describe the medieval rioni that contain them; Campitelli, the tenth rione, includes both the Palatine and the Capitoline. In his section on Campitelli, Signorili mentions specific structures like the houses of Romulus and Augustus, the place where auguries were taken, the old Curia, and the Septizonium of Septimius Severus. Then, he says that the region contains twenty streets, twenty temples, forty-eight long streets, two offices, 2742 apartments, eighty-nine houses, forty-eight barns, twenty cisterns, twenty tanks, and an area of 11,210 square feet.[15] There is no indication in Signorili's brief account of Campitelli that the area served as the center of ancient Rome's religious and political authority; for him, it is a part of the modern city, a place where his fellow-citizens live, drink, store grain, and go to church. Signorili also fails to identify his sources. He suggests that Rome's ruins serve as useful landmarks but have little practical or historical interest.

Thus, the architectural parts of his text read like an inventory—a less detailed version of the sort of inventory he made as the secretary of a rich confraternity. It is only when Signorili moves to Rome's relics that he engages in detailed description.

   Biondo's approach could hardly be more different, especially in his description of the Capitol. This is one of the more emotional passages of *Roma instaurata;* here, Biondo's precision and concern for detail give way to some nostalgia, but, in spite of this, the method that he uses in this section is indicative of his mode of proceeding throughout his account of Rome.

>   It is shameful and grievous to speak of the depredation of Rome, beginning at the Capitol. Cicero often calls this hill the home of the gods (most of all in the *Oratio ad Quirites* which he gave the day before he went into exile) and Vergil calls it golden. In his *Res gestae*, discussing Constantius II, son of the great Constantine, Ammianus Marcellinus shows what the Capitol was even three hundred years after the death of Cicero and Virgil. Constantius, coming for the first time from Constantinople (where he was born and educated) to Rome was stupefied when he inspected the city. These are the words of Ammianus in book 16: "then inside the peaks of the seven hills, surveying the various parts of the city and the suburbs, both the high areas and the low, he looked for what stood out among all the other structures—the temple of Tarpeian Jove, which surpasses divine things as much as earthly ones." [Biondo then includes another quotation from Marcellinus in which he says that the wonders of Egypt are the most splendid structures in the world after Rome's Capitol.] . . . . Sharing the same judgment, the most learned and best man Cassiodorus in an edict of Theodoric, the first king of the Ostrogoths in which he ordered the aqueducts of the city be repaired, said the following ". . . to ascend the lofty Capitol, this is to see human ingenuity surpassed." Now, in truth, except for the brick house built on the ruins by Boniface IX for the use of the Senate and the deputy of causes (a house that an ordinary Roman citizen would once have despised), except for the Franciscan church of the Aracoeli, built on the foundations of the temple of Jove the Subduer of Enemies, the Capitol (or Tarpeian hill), once ornamented by so many buildings, now is bare. We judge it superfluous to write what was on the Capitol. For since it was designated first and foremost as a holy space, it had more than sixty altars, chapels, shrines, sanctuaries, and temples, the names of which (if we judged they would contribute to our work) it would be easy to enumerate from ancient writers.[16]

Here, Biondo strives to give the reader a transhistorical experience of the Capitol. He starts out by emphasizing its current decay and then brings a variety of witnesses to attest to its former grandeur. Only one of these witnesses, however, saw the Capitol in its heyday. Biondo ends his discussion of the famous hill with a passage from Valerius Maximus (which explains that no patrician could have a house on the Capitol), but his other quotations highlight the reactions of fourth- and sixth-century authors, authors who themselves experienced nostalgia and displacement, who saw the Capitol as a museum not a bustling religious center.[17] Biondo thus presents a hill that is more legendary than real, a symbol of greatness rather than an active civic arena.[18] While Biondo is as careful in his approach to sources here as in the rest of *Roma instaurata*, in this instance, he uses these sources to create a mood, an ethos of glory and loss, rather than to identify ancient structures. In this passage, he seems to share Petrarch's conviction of the deep divide separating ancient and contemporary Rome; Biondo's discussion of the Capitol creates longing veneration in his readers.[19] Signorili, for whom the Capitol is a geographical site in a familiar urban space, is incapable of this longing because he lacks Biondo's sense of decay and change.

Yet Biondo was not content to wallow in Petrarchan nostalgia; instead, he sought to use his knowledge of ancient Rome to strengthen and revive the Quattrocento city. But how did he balance his presentist agenda and his occasional bouts of wistfulness with the focus and precision of an antiquarian scholar? Fubini has argued that Biondo was not, in fact, a Varronian antiquarian, eager to recover ancient civilization as an end in itself; he valued Rome's ruins primarily because of their contemporary relevance and meaning.[20] Biondo's focus on change and development over time was no accident and was in fact an essential component of his interest in revival. Although other scholars have not gone as far as Fubini in challenging the traditional reading of Biondo's scholarship, they too have emphasized the humanist secretary's preoccupation with renewal and restoration. Their studies, however, do not explore in any detail the ways in which Biondo's idea of revival intersected with that of his papal patron.[21] Biondo was one of the pope's most trusted servants; he was sent on delicate diplomatic missions and was recognized as a powerful broker by those seeking Eugenius's patronage.[22] Thus, at the same time that Biondo describes Rome's architectural past in all its richness, he also celebrates the initiatives of his papal patron and spurs him on to future action. Whereas Signorili urged Martin simply to follow tradition, Biondo offered Eugenius specific historical role models as he instructed the pope on how best to reenergize contemporary Rome.

Roma instaurata begins with a dedication to Eugenius IV, in which Biondo laments the ignorance of earlier generations and predicts the devastating effects of this ignorance:

> It appears that soon Rome, the parent of genius, the nurse of virtues, the model of fame, the summit of praise and glory and the school of all good things which the earth possesses, will suffer a great diminution of her fame and glory. Her buildings have become unknown, just as her affairs and power were obscured long ago. Your return of the papacy to this seat, an act so useful and necessary to Rome's conservation, confirmed my plan to describe the city. She was so worn out by decay and calamities that if you had been absent another ten years, she would have been completely destroyed. And you are helping the Romans not only by the presence of the Curia, which always contributed greatly to the wealth of the city, but throughout the city you are also restoring and rebuilding collapsed and ruined buildings at great expense. . . . Thus since I owe all things which I have to your Holiness, why should I not strive so that you may continue to restore Rome with the literary monuments of my little intellect, as you do with the work of masons, smiths and carpenters? Restoration of our city commemorates the work of the Roman popes who were your predecessors, which is fitting to the sanctimony of your dignity and adds to your glory most of all. In describing parts of the city by old and new names, I will make known basilicas and also temples and holy sites, which we call churches, places founded or increased or restored by popes and other Christians.[23]

As discussed in chapter 2, dedications tend to be highly formulaic, so it is not surprising that Biondo's dedication recalls that of Signorili. But this similarity also makes the differences in emphasis instructive. Biondo praises Rome with all the enthusiasm of his predecessor, but he does so briefly, taking Rome's position as the "parent of genius" almost for granted. More than Signorili, he chooses to focus on the dangers that face the city and on Eugenius's essential role as Rome's protector. He simultaneously emphasizes the importance of understanding the physical structure of the city, insisting that such knowledge—his knowledge—is an essential part of preservation and renovation. At first, by comparing his work to that of masons and carpenters, Biondo seems to be placing himself in a subordinate position, but when he promises to commemorate Christian places in honor of earlier popes and of Eugenius, Biondo suggests that he is the pope's partner in the project of restoration rather than a simple laborer. His work can grant a type of glory that no building, in and of itself, can create. Biondo thus argues forcefully for the efficacy of papally funded rebuilding when advertised and contextualized by antiquarian research.

Once he finishes his dedication, Biondo follows the customary order of Roman guidebooks and starts his examination at the city's walls.[24] He discusses Rome's size and the names of the various gates, relying solely on ancient sources and making no mention of later building. Biondo then breaks with tradition, however, moving his reading of Rome to the Vatican side of the Tiber. This implies a shift in the city's center, a translation of authority from the seven ancient hills to the Vatican. It also allows Biondo to focus on papal as opposed to imperial or republican building, and he devotes twenty-one of the thirty-three chapters on the Vatican side of the Tiber to papal constructions. He notes that Calixtus I built Santa Maria in Trastevere "which is now famous" where the temple of the Ravennati used to be. Pope Honorius I richly ornamented San Pancrazio, although in the 1440s the church is close to ruin.[25] Ecclesiastical structures serve as the most obvious evidence of papal largesse, but Biondo does not limit his discussion to religious projects; he also praises the aqueduct work of Hadrian I and the defensive towers of Leo IV.[26] In fact, Leo IV is the main protagonist of Book I. Biondo describes the defensive wall the pope built around the Leonine city to protect Saint Peter's from attacks by the Turks.[27] Most importantly, Leo gave rich gifts to the church itself, along with silver doors, and an extraordinary bell tower.

> In his great care for this (the Leonine wall) and for the basilica of the blessed Peter, Pope Leo carried out many building projects, but so many things have happened recently that his improvements, which stood for six hundred years, have deteriorated and would have soon disappeared entirely were it not for your efforts, most blessed father Eugenius. Now, seeing these things restored, we may rejoice. For where Leo ornamented the church with gifts, you made his donation better with an outfit of sacred furnishings, with repairs to a large part of the roof, and with new chambers for the sacristy. In one thing alone you seem to be surpassed by Leo, for he commissioned silver doors for Saint Peter's and

you commissioned bronze ones. But there is equal magnificence in having replaced silver gates made with no special skills with bronze ones, gilded and decorated with many scenes of the union of the Greeks, Armenians, Ethiopians, Jacobites, and other peoples who were reconciled to the church thanks to your efforts and your expenditure. In fact, the price for the work on the doors was more than four times that for the bronze and the gold. And where Leo built a campanile which was the greatest in the entire world, you built a workshop for bronze-making and, nearby, a most beautiful door for the palace. The covered court of the palace and the road which leads into many parts of the city, after it divides, are so decorated that by these things the city of Rome seems to be restored to what she was many centuries ago.[28]

In his analysis of the doors, Biondo, like his friend Alberti, emphasizes the way in which artistic skill adds value to an object.[29] He suggests that Eugenius's ability to appreciate this added value separates him from the vulgar crowd, which might categorically prefer silver to bronze. In mentioning the small panels that depict scenes from the Council of Florence, Biondo also highlights some of the most notable triumphs of Eugenius's pontificate. Yet rather than presenting the decrees of union as a sign of Eugenius's prowess as a religious leader, Biondo suggests that these triumphs and Eugenius's architectural commissions are all part of a coherent, successful policy based on painstaking, intelligent expenditure. Thus, Biondo celebrates Eugenius's pontificate in a decidedly secular fashion, and he simultaneously demonstrates how his research can exalt the pope through historical associations.

There is, however, another side to Biondo's comparison of Eugenius and Leo IV. Just as dedicators of Plutarchan *Lives* subtly pressured their dedicatees to live up to the standards of ancient heroes, so too does Biondo offer Leo to Eugenius as a model for emulation. The humanist raises Eugenius's stature by equating him with one of the popes credited with "saving Rome," but by carefully explaining how Eugenius's doors are as impressive as the doors they replace, Biondo underlines the fact that the pope's other building efforts at the Vatican are mostly decorative. They certainly do not equal the creation of the Leonine city, and Biondo thus indirectly encourages Eugenius to continue his efforts.[30] Throughout *Roma instaurata*, Biondo gives special attention to the renovation of ancient buildings; he is as interested in identifying the individuals who restored structures as he is in identifying the original patron. Thus, even as Biondo emphasizes the distance separating antiquity from the Quattrocento, he tells a story of minirevivals, not a story of continuous decay. Although Biondo mentions building projects and repairs funded by popes or cardinals less often once he moves away from the Vatican area, such references appear throughout *Roma instaurata*.[31]

This emphasis on postclassical revivals of Rome's ancient legacy leads to an interesting parallel between the texts of Biondo and Signorili. Like the municipal official, the papal secretary shows a special fondness for Theodoric. Biondo praises Theodoric's efforts to repair the aqueducts, the theater of Pompey, and the city's walls at some length, but he also makes briefer mention of Theodoric's restoration of the city's amphitheaters, palaces, baths, sewers, and aqueducts.[32] In fact, Biondo says that during Theodoric's reign, the Romans did not long for Augustus, Trajan, Hadrian, Antoninus Pius, or Severus—they had found a good emperor.[33] Biondo does not just describe Theodoric's achievements; he repeatedly quotes from the *Variae* to illustrate Theodoric's concern for and appreciation of Rome's great ancient structures.[34] In discussing the theater of Pompey, he includes an excerpt from Theodoric's letter to the patrician Symmachus, to whom the emperor entrusted repair of the building.

> And therefore, I have decided that the fabric of the theater [of Pompey], yielding to the pressure of its vast weight, should be strengthened by your counsel. Thus, what your ancestors evidently bestowed for the glory of their country will not seem to decay under their nobler descendants. What can old age not disintegrate, when it has shaken so strong a work? You might think it would be easier for the mountains to fall than to shake that solidity. For that very mass is so entirely formed from vast blocks that, but for the added craftsmanship, it too might be thought the work of nature. I might perhaps have neglected the building, if I had not happened to see it: those arched vaults, with their overhanging stonework and invisible jointing, are so beautifully shaped that you would suppose them the caverns of a lofty mountain, rather than anything made by hands. The ancients made the site equal to so great a population, intending those who held the lordship of the world to enjoy a unique building of entertainment.[35]

In discussing the theater of Pompey, Biondo also quotes Pliny, Tacitus, and Ovid, but it is only Cassiodorus who expatiates at length on the beauty of the structure. By including quotations like this one, Biondo turns Theodoric into more than just a restorer. Through the elegant words of his amanuensis, the fierce Gothic king becomes an aesthete, a true lover of Rome. He, like Leo IV, is a figure to whom Eugenius is implicitly compared, or at least a model to whom the pope can aspire. By introducing characters like Leo and Theodoric and by using long quotations from the *Variae* to make the Ostrogothic emperor a three-dimensional figure, Biondo reminds his readers, including Eugenius, that Rome's ancient grandeur is not an irrevocably distant reality but something that has been revived before and can be revived again. Throughout *Roma instaurata*, Biondo suggests that Rome's past and her present are in dialogue and that it is possible for his contemporaries to learn from this dialogue, to make it more fruitful.[36]

If discussion of past restorations helps to emphasize the potential for a Quattrocento revival, discussion of decline can also bridge the apparently vast gap between ancient and modern Rome. Throughout *Roma instaurata*, Biondo laments and condemns the Romans' attitude toward the remains of the ancient city, their endless thirst for lime. He claims that the vulgar blame the cruelty of the Goths and old age for the destruction of the aqueducts. Having warmly defended Theodoric, Biondo goes on to show that old age did not destroy the aqueducts either.

> We judge that old age was not in truth the cause of such an evil because during the more than one thousand year period that has passed since the downfall of the Goths such solid structures (parts of which are still seen intact in fields that are far from the convenience of the multitude) could not have fallen and wholly disappeared. Only those wicked men, with their blameworthy and detestable hands, who erected private and most squalid buildings or cooked stones for lime or used them for the sides of houses have not scrupled to despoil the majesty of the city's walls. Nevertheless, so that we may accuse old age in some way, we say that the structures of the aqueducts were demolished for no greater reason than that, as the city aged, certain branches of the government no longer took care to preserve them.[37]

Biondo then quotes from Frontinus to emphasize how assiduously the aqueducts were maintained during the empire. He thus contrasts the selfishness and self-interest of medieval Romans with the civic commitment of their predecessors. Furthermore, Biondo does not let the issue of destruction rest here; he returns to it repeatedly, bewailing the depredations of certain marbles on the Aventine, of the Colosseum, and of the amphitheater of Titus.[38] In condemning modern Romans' use of their city, Biondo suggests that a whole change in attitude is necessary. Rome's restored greatness depends on Eugenius IV, but it also depends, as Petrarch insisted, on the devotion of the city's citizens. They must cease treating Rome as a quarry of riches and look at her with the admiration and respect of a humanist scholar. If Biondo's perspective is decidedly scholarly, his ire is not unlike that expressed by Martin V in his 1425 bull; both men insist that Rome is more than just a city and that its inhabitants must treat it like the seat of the Apostles and of *imperium*. But whereas Martin demonstrated at least some interest in supporting the city's communal officers, Biondo only mentions municipal government to disparage it as a form of tyranny; in his opinion, there should be no civic government distinct from the papacy.[39]

In spite of his undeniable admiration for ancient Rome, Biondo does not praise it unequivocally, and he does blame some of Rome's collapse on the ancient city's spiritual and moral decline.[40] In his discussion of the baths, he details imperial Roman bathing habits—in particular the bathing habits of various emperors—and condemns their lack of modesty and sobriety.[41] While acknowledging that the entertainments of the baths lessened public unrest, he nevertheless judges their luxury to have been excessive. Biondo offers a more historical, and more admiring, account of the development of Roman theater, noting that Cicero himself was friends with actors, but he then goes on to cite Cassiodorus, Anneus Seneca, and Valerius Maximus on the dangerous influence of the mimes.[42] If theater under the emperors became corrupt, the games at the Colosseum and other amphitheaters were even worse. To emphasize the horror of the games (and, indirectly, to excuse Theodoric for allowing the Romans to use stones from the Colosseum for building), Biondo cites a long letter written by Cassiodorus that describes the agony of men and beasts in grotesque detail.[43] He also devotes considerable space to the deleterious effects of bringing the camps of the praetorian guards into the city.[44]

All of these sections serve as harbingers of *Roma triumphans*, the companion piece to *Roma instaurata* and the work in which Biondo proves himself to be a true historical anthropologist of ancient Rome. They also show that, in spite of his support of Eugenius IV and his skepticism of municipal authority, Biondo equates Rome's republican era with virtue and nobility and sees imperial rule as a source of moral and political corruption. This bias accords with the general preference of early humanists for republican regimes, but it also serves as another way in which Biondo can make the current, dilapidated state of the city seem logical and explicable.[45]

In *Roma instaurata*, Biondo presents the city's classical and medieval legacies as combining to create the Rome of his own day, but he also assumes a break between pagan and Christian Rome, a break that Signorili studiously denied. This break becomes most explicit at the end of Biondo's work. Having lamented the fact that there are still structures in the city that he cannot identify, Biondo claims to love Rome more than anything except religion. He admits that Rome's glory is much diminished since antiquity but disagrees with those who say that contemporary Rome is a mere ruin. "The glory and majesty of Rome still and certainly flourish, and although they are spread throughout a smaller portion of the world, they rest on a more solid foundation."[46] This more solid foundation is religion, and Biondo contrasts the willing religious veneration of Quattrocento Europeans with the hard-won subjugation of people conquered by the Romans. At the same time, he employs military terminology, describing Christ as the *summus imperator* and Rome as the *arx* of religion. In spite of his claim to love the city less than religion, the two appear inseparable, locked in a marvelous and mutually beneficial codependency. The popes now take the place of ancient dictators; the cardinals make up the senate, and, just as in the past, tribute and visitors flow to Rome from all of Europe and (thanks to Eugenius) from parts of Asia. For Biondo, Rome is still the head and mistress of the world, but only through understanding of the past can the Quattrocento city be restored to her full, former glory.

Certainly the majority of *Roma instaurata* is devoted to an antiquarian reconstruction of the city, not to a discussion of revival. In spite of his fondness for Cassiodorus, Biondo relies principally on ancient authors, and he painstakingly patches together their testimony to locate ancient structures and explain their functions. But if examination of scholars' methodologies reveals important information about their intellectual programs, so too does looking at what they hoped their research would accomplish.[47] Biondo believed that Quattrocento society could be improved by a preferential revival of antiquity, and this was his avowed rationale for composing *Roma instaurata*. The treatise serves as a rallying call to a distinctively Roman Renaissance and offers one of the most explicit early examples of a humanist composing an independent scholarly work that is intended to bolster the prestige and authority of the papacy. Like Biondo, later Quattrocento popes were involved in picking and choosing, reviving ancient Roman culture preferentially and in a way that would support their own political agendas.

Eugenius's Building Projects in Rome

In spite of Biondo's accolades, art historians have not celebrated Eugenius IV as one of the great papal patrons of Rome. The pope's secretary had ample reason to exaggerate the importance of Eugenius's restoration work; he wanted to praise his employer, to spur him on to further efforts at rebuilding, and to create a role for himself as an interpreter of Rome's ruins. In both his dedication and his conclusion, Biondo sounds more like a panegyrist than a careful chronicler of architectural work. If the bookends of Biondo's work suggest reasons for skepticism, the body of *Roma instaurata* presents a different challenge. Eugenius's restoration projects are a recurrent theme, but Biondo's references to contemporary projects (with the exception of the Filarete doors) are brief. He mentions that Eugenius repaired the bridge of Valentinian.[48] He writes that "the stupendous vault of the Pantheon, broken by old age and earthquakes and facing ruin was restored with your care and at your expense, pope Eugenius."[49] But descriptions like these do not clarify the extent or nature of the work performed.

Sometimes, other surviving records can supplement Biondo's brief accounts. For example, Biondo claims that the piazza in front of the Pantheon was paved and cleared of merchants' stalls during Eugenius's reign, and a license from 1457 notes that Eugenius's Chamberlain, Cardinal Scarampo, established where and to what extent both stalls and roofs could reach into the Piazza.[50] By combining the two sources, it becomes apparent that Eugenius (or at least his Chamberlain) was interested in the cleanliness and openness of this important public space, as well as the integrity of the Pantheon itself.[51] Furthermore, curial interest in the urban fabric of the city was not confined to the Pantheon. In his 1446 decree, Scarampo stipulated that part of the Senator's salary had to go to repairs on the Capitol. He decreed that butchers could not sell their wares in major markets and he forbade vehicular traffic, "quantum fieri potest," on some of the most crowded of Rome's streets.[52] While decrees by later popes suggest that Scarampo's orders were not enforced, his legislation nevertheless shows that Eugenius's Curia, like Martin's, was concerned with the condition and cleanliness of Rome's streets.[53] In fact, Modigliani argues that it was during Eugenius's pontificate that the Curia began to differentiate Rome's various urban spaces according to their functions.[54]

How did Eugenius and members of his Curia strive to designate certain parts of Rome for certain purposes? And what sort of evidence of their efforts remains? The areas and buildings on which repair work was completed have been the subject of multiple architectural interventions since 1447, and Eugenius did not share his successors' predilection for leaving coats-of-arms and other visual reminders of his patronage. Thus, there is almost no surviving physical evidence of the pope's restoration projects. Muntz and Corbo have painstakingly sifted through papal expense accounts and found records of substantial work on the Lateran and the Castel Sant'Angelo between 1433 and 1434.[55] The one archival source devoted to architectural work during Eugenius's pontificate— Archivio di Stato di Roma, Camerale I, Fabbriche 1501—covers only 1437 and 1438.[56] Fabbriche 1501 details the amounts spent by the Curia on some of Rome's major religious spaces; more than 200 ducats were spent on Santo Spirito, 830 went to Santa Maria Maggiore,[57] repairs to the Lateran cost more than 930 ducats, and 580 ducats were devoted to Saint Peter's.[58] (Fabbriche 1501 also includes lesser sums for a few other churches and wood for unspecified locations.) The total amount expended in a twenty-month period came to more than 3,000 ducats, thus demonstrating the Curia's engagement, even *in absentia,* with Rome's urban fabric.[59]

By the standards of the great building projects of the Renaissance, 3,000 ducats is hardly a princely sum, but given the political problems facing Eugenius, it is far from insignificant. Partner estimates that in 1436, Eugenius's entire income amounted to 59,000 ducats; by comparison, Martin V's income ten years earlier was almost twice as great.[60] In fact, on average, Martin spent close to 100,000 ducats on his mercenary army alone. Thus, even if Eugenius had devoted his entire income to condottieri, his military expenditures could not have approached those of his predecessor, although his military needs were considerable. At the same time that he had to try to win the Papal States back for the papacy and combat the Council of Basel, Eugenius also staged the costly Council of Florence. In short, this was hardly a pope with 3,000 ducats to spare. The Fabbriche records, like many of the other financial records for Eugenius's reign, are incomplete. Thus, it is impossible to know if Eugenius's spending on urban repairs in 1433, 1434, 1437, and 1438 was atypical or if he maintained a similar focus on rebuilding throughout his pontificate.[61] In 1434, the Curia spent a great deal of money trying to win back Rome, and in 1438, it was heavily encumbered by the cost of the Greeks' journey to and sojourn in Ferrara and Florence; perhaps Eugenius's largesse in years when he had fewer financial commitments was even more extensive.[62]

If it is not clear how the expenses of the Fabbriche records fit into Eugenius's pattern of expenditure, it is equally uncertain what projects were financed by these sums.[63] Some of the money was spent on wood and the transportation of materials and lime, but the majority went to workers' salaries. Although Rome was certainly less prosperous than Florence at this time, wages for the 1437–1438 projects were roughly in keeping with those of the larger city; in fact manual workers were somewhat better paid in Rome than in Florence.[64] Corbo identifies a labor pool of almost one hundred and fifty individuals, many of whom were from outside of Rome and even outside Italy.[65] A labor pool of this size suggests that there was more building in Rome at this time than is generally believed, but it reveals almost nothing about what this labor pool did. Furthermore, given Biondo's tendency to describe rebuilding in general terms, reading *Roma instaurata* and the Fabbriche records in tandem still does not permit a detailed account of Eugenius's projects. When these sources are brought together with the material presented in chapters 4 and 5, however, they do suggest some insights into what is perhaps a more interesting question—why, given its poverty and the plethora of pressing political problems, did Eugenius's Curia choose to spend money rebuilding Rome's churches? The following sections will argue that the Curia used building projects to further the pope's ceremonial, religious, and political agendas, remaking Rome in accordance with his needs and interests. While many of these plans did not reach fruition, the Eugenian Curia had a considerably more sophisticated ideological agenda for the city of Rome than has often been suggested.

Building and the Spiritual State of Rome

At first glance, there is nothing remarkable in Eugenius's decision to focus his repairs on the city's major basilicas; after all, many of the popes of the Middle Ages sponsored work on Saint Peter's, the Lateran, and/ or Santa Maria Maggiore. In 1433, 1434, 1437, and 1438, Eugenius's largest expenditure was for the Lateran, and in *Roma instaurata*, Biondo devotes particular care to discussing Eugenius's work at his Episcopal seat and his erection of a monastery there.[66] The Lateran palace was once the main residence of the Roman popes, but prior to Eugenius's reign it had become all but uninhabitable, prompting Biondo to say, "But you most blessed father Eugenius, first repaired the remains of the palace and then you continued to restore other parts around it at great expense." Biondo goes on to note that Eugenius added a monastery, and, while digging its foundations, that pavements, columns, and statues were found "which surpass the buildings erected not only in our age but in many ages in various parts of Italy."[67] Here, the two parts of Biondo's agenda seem to be in direct competition; at one level, he wants to celebrate his patron but, at the same time, he cannot resist the opportunity to praise the ancient discoveries that seem more miraculous than any modern construction. (In his enthusiasm for ancient statuary, he fails to mention that Eugenius commissioned Pisanello to continue working on the frescoes for the basilica's interior, which had been begun by Gentile da Fabriano.[68]) If Biondo gets temporarily diverted, however, he still presents Eugenius's project at the Lateran as a major architectural endeavor.

The Colonna family's strong connections with the Lateran might seem to be a reason for Eugenius to ignore the basilica, but his vision for the site clearly differed from Martin's. As discussed in chapter 4, Eugenius was concerned with the reform of religious orders, and the Lateran was one of the sites he hoped to transform. Almost as soon as he became pope, Eugenius asked the Observant Congregation of Canons Regular of Santa Maria di Fregionaia (which followed the rule of Saint Augustine) to undertake responsibility for the basilica.[69] His forced departure from Rome interrupted these plans, but in February 1439 he issued a bull, praising the observant life of the congregation and entrusting the Lateran to thirty of its canons; he threatened the secular canons who had traditionally been in charge of the basilica with excommunication if they did not give way to the new authority.[70] In spite of this threat, the established clergy of the Lateran, who profited handsomely from their position, refused to yield. Although they did allow the Augustinians to enter the Lateran (probably in the early fall of 1439), on Corpus Domini of the next year, they chased the newcomers from the area and forced them to seek refuge in the Castel Sant' Angelo and the palace of Saint Peter's.[71] The regular canons soon returned to the Lateran, accompanied by the city's municipal officials, but the secular canons continued their persecution, and the regulars finally received papal permission to leave the city. Even after Eugenius's return to Rome in 1443, the Observants remained fearful and hesitant, but, at the pope's prodding (and after a meeting in which cardinals and other prelates agreed that the Lateran could not be reformed by the secular canons), the regular canons finally agreed to take over the running of the church in 1444. In 1446, Eugenius favored the Lateran branch of the congregation again, praising their way of life and conceding to them the monastery and cloister that had been built "at great expense."[72]

Neither Biondo nor the building records of 1501 make clear what proportion of the rebuilding effort at the Lateran was devoted to the church, what to the palace, and what to the new monastery, but Eugenius's aspirations for the Lateran canons and his focus on the Lateran complex demonstrate that the pope was no Saint Francis. He was keenly aware that the Observants he supported needed practical resources if they were to survive. As a cardinal, he had restored San Paolo fuori le Mura, which became a member of his beloved Congregation of Santa Giustina. In 1439, Eugenius ordered that the convent at Santa Bibiana should be closed and joined with Santa Maria Maggiore; apparently, the nuns were misbehaving, but their convent was also in ruins.[73] Eugenius settled a community of Celestine monks, known for their austerity, at Sant' Eusebio and probably did some restoration work on the Church.[74] There is no indication that the pope sponsored work at Santa Maria in Aracoeli, but he entrusted it to a group of Observant Franciscans, and he personally attended the chapter meeting that took place there in 1446, thus providing personal if not architectural support for the new chapter.[75] In short, Eugenius sought to install reformed communities throughout Rome and to break the entrenched privilege that characterized many of the city's ecclesiastical institutions. Where possible and/or necessary, he was willing to use some of his scarce resources to support this endeavor.

Given the disasters of Eugenius's early reign and, in particular, his problems with the Colonna and the Roman commune, he could not afford to think only of religious reform as he planned projects of restoration. In order to return to Rome and to maintain papal control over the city, he needed to consider the strategic meaning and potential of various sites. While Eugenius's religious agenda at the Lateran is clear, his political motivations are less so. Was he trying to diminish the rights of the *Raccomandati,* the favored Colonna confraternity, by his ardent support of the Canons of Santa Maria di Fregonaia? Or was he, like his predecessor, intervening at the Lateran in order to disrupt older links between the secular canons and Rome's baronial families? Given the dense web of connected interests at the Lateran, it is difficult to say, but another one of Eugenius's projects demonstrates his determination to reconfigure the Colonna map of the city. As discussed in chapter 1, in supporting the *Raccomandati,* Martin also supported the hospitals under their care, which were near the Lateran. Eugenius instead chose to patronize the hospital of Santo Spirito, which was founded by Innocent III. The compound, which is located far from the Lateran, on the Vatican side of the Tiber, remains one of Rome's major hospitals today.[76]

During the thirteenth and much of the fourteenth century, the Ospedale di Santo Spirito was the most organized and comprehensive hospital in Rome.[77] In addition to caring for pilgrims, it also helped sickly, indigent, and elderly Romans of all classes, with particular attention to prostitutes and orphans. Each week, the lay brothers and sisters in charge of the hospital went out looking for those in need, and they brought these patients to Santo Spirito for spiritual comfort, absolution, and the Eucharist, as well as for medical care.[78] From its inception, the hospital was closely associated with the papacy, and even during the Avignon era, popes supported it both with monetary gifts and with a variety of exemptions and privileges.[79] During the Schism, however, its fortunes rapidly declined, and by 1414, due in large part to the sacks of Ladislaus, it had to suspend all activity.

Eugenius was determined to revive the hospital and to make it, once again, a purveyor of practical charity and spiritual assistance; he made his nephew, Pietro Barbo, the preceptor of the *Fraternitas Sancti*

Spiritus et Sanctae Mariae in Saxia in urbe and gave its members, who followed the Augustinian rule, their own constitution.[80] Together, Eugenius and Barbo sponsored major work on the main building by the Tiber, built a hospital for women (and a dormitory for the sisters who cared for them) closer to Saint Peter's, and, thanks to generous donations, gave the hospital a degree of financial autonomy.[81] By turning the attention of sick Romans and pilgrims from the Lateran to the Vatican, the Venetian pope was challenging his predecessor's vision of the city, and, by emphasizing papal charity, he was competing with communal charity without actively discouraging it. In the fourteenth century, the Orsini had used their patronage of Santo Spirito and the Colonna had used their patronage of the *Raccomandati*'s hospitals to showcase their generosity and thus to further their ongoing political rivalry. In the later Quattrocento, Sixtus IV, known as the second founder of Santo Spirito, would use his support of the hospital to challenge but not obstruct the charitable work of Rome's communal confraternities.[82] Thus, Eugenius, like his predecessors and successors, used charity as a weapon in the contest between baronial, papal, and communal interests. Restoration of the church and hospital of Santo Spirito indicates that, by the later 1430s, Eugenius was learning to assert papal authority by more subtle means than those he had used in the early part of his pontificate.

Filarete's Doors and Papal Ceremony

The revival of Santo Spirito was not the only project with which Eugenius challenged Colonna geography. Through his work on the Lateran, Santa Maria Maggiore, and Saint Peter's, Eugenius was moving the center of papal power from Rome's ancient center (and the Colonna palace at Santi Apostoli) back to its traditional strongholds. More particularly, he was crafting a papal center in the Vatican area, presaging the later initiatives of Nicholas V. Biondo's organization of *Roma instaurata* may have been intended to promote his patron's reorientation of the city, even as it declared his own independence from the traditional order of the *Mirabilia*. While surviving expense accounts suggest that Eugenius spent more on the Lateran than on Saint Peter's, his commissioning of Filarete's bronze doors serves as a spectacular indication of his interest in the basilica of his most illustrious predecessor.

Today, Filarete is best known for the architectural treatise he wrote in the 1460s, but he also worked for decades as a sculptor. The huge bronze doors that still hang in the central portal of Saint Peter's represent his most significant project. (Figure 7, each door is 6.5 m × 1.8 m). With various interruptions, Filarete worked on the doors throughout much of Eugenius's reign, and their program was changed sometime after 1439 so that they could celebrate the pope's religio–political successes.[83] Because they represent a different aesthetic than the roughly contemporary doors of Ghiberti and because of Vasari's withering indictment of them, the doors have not received as much scholarly attention as other major commissions of the period.[84] Furthermore, interpretations of the decorative program differ, with some scholars describing it as thoroughly medieval and others emphasizing its ancient and thus humanistic elements.[85]

There are, however, two points on which scholars agree. First, the program of the doors is eclectic both in style and subject matter. Second, the purpose of the doors is to celebrate and affirm the power and authority of the Roman papacy. The program includes six main panels, which are surrounded by additional scenes and elaborate decorations. At the top left sits the figure of Christ, enthroned on a stool of flowers, acanthus leaves, and lions' feet (Figure 8a). To his right is the Virgin, enthroned on an equally elaborate throne (Figure 8b). Below Christ is a larger panel of Saint Paul, with his sword held proudly aloft (Figure 9a). To Paul's right (and below the Virgin) is a stately Saint Peter, who passes his famous keys to a kneeling (and smaller) Eugenius IV (Figure 9b). Below the two apostles are square scenes of their martyrdoms (Figures 10 and 11). Whereas the four larger panels are simple, each consisting of one major personage, the martyrdom scenes are complex, depicting unfolding story lines and including numerous figures, horses, and ancient structures.

The doors record the lineage of power in the Church. Christ and Mary appear not in the humble and domestic forms that began to gain favor in the fourteenth and fifteenth centuries; instead, they are as proudly monarchical (if not as splendidly dressed) as the Christ and Mary of the apse mosaics of Santa Maria in Trastevere or Santa Maria Maggiore. Below them, Peter and Paul both stand with rocklike authority. Their facial types had appeared on papal bulls with little variation for several centuries.[86] The small figure of Eugenius, which is modeled after the Lateran monument to Boniface VIII, not only indicates humility but also accords with the medieval tendency to use size to indicate the importance of those portrayed.[87] If Peter and Paul (and thus, indirectly, Eugenius) receive authority from Christ and Mary, they also obtain it from their martyrdoms, which are depicted with a wealth of topographic detail and recall the decorative program of ancient monuments, especially the columns of Trajan and Marcus Aurelius. To further emphasize that ancient Rome, as well as the Church, contributes to the power and strength of the papacy, the cornices of the door contain an array of mythical figures. It seems that Filarete's choice of scenes was inspired by Ovid (the *Metamophoses* and *Fasti*), Livy, Vergil, and ancient coins, as well as various medieval collections of myths.[88] Yet even though the doors display Filarete's antiquarian knowledge and attest to his conversations with humanist scholars, they recall the spirit of Signorili more than that of Biondo. In the doors, the ages of Rome are intermingled to augment the authority of the papacy.

Among the periods that contribute to the papacy's prestige, Eugenius's reign has a small but noteworthy place. Originally, Filarete intended to use the same decorative motifs that appear in the cornices below the four large panels, but, sometime after 1439, the plan was changed, and four scenes from Eugenius's pontificate were cast. Below the figure of Christ, a panel depicts the departure of the Greek deputation from Constantinople (Figure 12a) and the Emperor Giovanni Palaeologus's meeting with the pope at Ferrara (Figure 12b). Although, in fact, both men stood when they met, in Filarete's depiction, the emperor kneels to Eugenius. Below Mary is a panel with the pope presiding at the Council of Florence (Figure 13a) and the Greeks embarking to return to Constantinople (Figure 13b). Below Peter, the Copts agree to union with the Catholic Church (Figure 14a) and then tour Rome (Figure 14b). Finally, below Paul, the emperor Sigismundo is crowned by the pope (Figure 15a), and is accompanied by him to the Castel Sant'Angelo (Figure 15b).[89] While both men are on horseback (in accordance with ceremonial protocol and with the testimony of Poggio), the depiction of the coronation itself emphasizes the emperor's abasement before the pope. While Eugenius sits in regal splendor, Sigismundo kneels before him. Thus, twice in these panels Filarete presents temporal authority bowing down to religious authority and, more particularly, the Western and Eastern emperors united in their acknowledgement of Eugenius and thus of papal power.

Filarete's small scenes thus illustrate the ceremonies that marked some of the great successes of Eugenius's reign—his winning over of Sigismundo to the papal as opposed to conciliarist cause (at least briefly) and his supposed triumph in uniting the Eastern and Western churches. The reliefs also reflect Eugenius's interest in and concern for papal ceremony. Just as he used ceremony throughout his pontificate as a way of asserting his position, so too he chose to be immortalized by and through ceremony. Eugenius's projects, and his efforts to shape his own image and legacy, serve as a harbinger of the more splendid projects of Sixtus IV; both pontiffs mixed self-aggrandizement, defense of papal monarchy, antiquarian elements, charitable goals, and a clear religious agenda as they sought to rebuild Rome.[90] Eugenius still presides in ceremonial splendor over the flocks of visitors—and the liturgical events—that flow in and out of the newer doors on either side of Filarete's bronze monument.

The Later History of Filarete's Doors and the Renaissance Papacy

The fact that Filarete's doors were one of the few parts of the Old Saint Peter's incorporated into the new basilica suggests that they continued to appeal to the Curia's vision of the papal office as proud, triumphant, and quintessentially Roman. (The doors were hung in the new Saint Peter's in 1619.)[91] Given this, they serve as a good place to end this book's discussion of the papacy in the first half of the fifteenth century. Less than two years after the doors were erected, Eugenius died, and in spite of all the tumult of his reign, by its end, the authority of the papacy was in the ascendant. Eugenius's successor, Nicholas V, was able to enjoy the exalted position for which Eugenius had struggled.[92] On April 7, 1449, antipope Felix V finally resigned, signaling the end of the Council of Basel, and while conciliarism continued to threaten papal authority, the threat was never again so strong as it had been in the first half of the Quattrocento. Nicholas devoted his pontificate to being not just a strong pope but one who promoted humanist scholarship and the city of Rome. Even the disastrous fall of Constantinople in 1453, an event deeply lamented in Rome and throughout Europe, added to the importance and prestige of his pontificate; it made his sponsorship of

Greek studies not simply an intellectual program but an essential task of cultural preservation.

In the following seventy years, Rome grew and prospered economically and demographically as well as culturally and artistically.[93] The popes who followed Nicholas continued his program of work on Saint Peter's, his efforts to instill some order on the city, and his commissions of art by the masters of the Renaissance. But whereas Nicholas appears to have thought carefully and sometimes critically about his own program of cultural patronage, men like Alexander VI, Julius II, and Leo X indulged in more grandiose, less nuanced programs of personal and papal publicity. The pontificates of Martin V and Eugenius IV laid the foundation for many of their efforts; in the aftermath of the Schism, the papacy's sorry predicament pushed popes, bureaucrats, scholars, and artists to experiment, to reimagine their roles and the meaning of Rome, and the pontiffs of the next seventy years profited from this experimentation. Like Martin and Eugenius, later popes used strategies of familial aggrandizement, charitable investment, infrastructural repair, and political manipulation to cement their hold on the city and employed ceremonies and art to instill pride in their Roman subjects and to celebrate their own glory.[94] The High Renaissance popes did not, however, adopt the example of their predecessors wholesale. None of them had the local ties that would have enabled them to rule as Roman barons and none of them had Eugenius's personal commitment to religious austerity. Thus, the monarchical aspects of the early Quattrocento papacy were embellished and developed, making the pope more like the secular princes of Italy: The feudal and monastic elements of the Curias of Martin and Eugenius gradually died away, and each new pope continued to bring with him a personal style and personal priorities.

Curial Humanism After 1447

While there was considerable continuity between the later part of Eugenius's pontificate and that of Nicholas V, the role of humanism at the Curia changed in some important ways in the years around 1450. Biondo's response to Filarete's doors attests to the independence that scholars enjoyed under Eugenius and shows that even the pope's most loyal propagandist had a clear sense of his own intellectual identity.

The site of Peter's martyrdom was a particularly contentious topic among mid-Quattrocento antiquarian scholars, and, as Huskinson has deftly shown, Filarete chose to locate the martyrdom on the Janiculum. In doing so, he followed Maffeo Vegio's explanation of the event, directly refuting Biondo's argument.[95] In spite of his reverence for the pope, Biondo could not resist using *Roma instaurata* to criticize Filarete's panel. Biondo acknowledges that "There are not lacking those who falsely seek to ornament the Janiculum with this glory (i.e., Peter's martyrdom)," and in response he explains and defends his own interpretation, implicitly criticizing Filarete's design.[96] Suggesting that Christian sources are more concerned with adulation than with facts, he argues that Tacitus's evidence is credible because it comes from an enemy of the true faith. According to Tacitus, Nero built his gardens in the Vatican valley and, after the great fire, he devoted them to the slaughter of Christians; thus, Biondo reasons, Peter must have been crucified in this area. In his discussion, Biondo is instructing his readers not only on how to imagine the ancient city but also on the skeptical approach they should take toward hagiographical sources and antiquarian research. Modern Romans—most especially popes and artists who want to depict historical scenes—cannot read books or view artistic works uncritically, and they must compare and contrast various accounts to determine which are most authoritative; in short, they must view the city through the classicizing lens of a humanist notebook. If they fail to do so, then great works of papal largesse like the doors will be marred by historical inaccuracies.

Biondo raises no complaint about the doors except in regard to the location of Peter's martyrdom. Both his effusive praise of the work as a whole and his criticism of one panel may indicate that he was consulted about their program. But his abrupt shift from praise to criticism suggests that he could not completely reconcile his roles as papal propagandist and antiquarian scholar—and also that he did not have to do so. An anecdote from one of Biondo's letters (dated February 1446) offers further proof that the duties of and expectations for humanist secretaries were still in flux at the end of Eugenius's reign. Writing to the humanistically inclined Leonello D'Este, Biondo describes a recent banquet:

> In recent days, our Prospero Colonna, a man whose humanity and virtue are even greater than the nobility of his family and the exalted rank of the cardinalate, called and invited to dinner Sigismundo Malatesta, Prince of Rimini. I was invited to go to the gardens of Maecenas, not

indeed, as I believed, to dinner but for the indulgence of my most loving prince Colonna.[97] After he had reclined, I understand from Sigismundo that the dinner was prepared and organized in the first place so that he would be filled more by my uninterrupted discussion of Roman things (as much as the brevity of the time allowed) than by the wealth of food and delicacies provided by the master of the feast. When thus asked about many matters, I responded, and I heard a great deal from the group of most learned men who were gathered, things which are most pleasing and worthy of your ears and which cannot be explained in a letter but in a volume of a rather long book. Mention was made of the Romans' treasure and Malatesta told the cardinal and me a most pleasing thing about you: you have overseen the forging of ten thousand bronze coins, according to the custom of the old princes of the Romans, on one side of which the image of your head is inscribed with your name. When Malatesta wanted to say what was on the other side, he could not recall. Colonna praised your inclination, he praised the imitation of ancient practice which seems to have inspired you. Thus you pursue the path of the ancients, whose love of fame and glory you emulate, also in these artistic enterprises, which will bring true and solid glory.[98]

Although Biondo suggests that he was somewhat dismayed not to be treated as an ordinary guest, pride and satisfaction pervade his letter. The topics dear to his heart, not the elegant banquet, turned out to be the real focus of the evening. Biondo says that he learned many things, but he also makes clear that his knowledge was the pivot around which the conversation moved.

This letter suggests an important change from the patronage environment discussed in chapters 1 and 2: Rather than offering occasional support to humanist scholars, patrons like Colonna expressed a deep interest in their studies. In a 1435 letter to Bruni on the subject of what language the ancient Romans spoke, Biondo suggested that curial discussions of antiquity were confined to a small coterie of secretaries and a few stolen moments outside the papal bedchamber.[99] Conversely, by 1446, scholars, cardinals, and other learned dignitaries arranged elegant séances in classical settings so that they might enjoy exchanging ideas and designing new projects.[100] Even if artists like Filarete and patrons like Eugenius did not always listen to a specific scholar, the works they crafted and commissioned were nevertheless influenced by the new learning.

Because neither artists nor patrons had the leisure or skills to pursue the sort of research recorded in *Roma instaurata*, such research was a valuable commodity. In his letter, Biondo goes on to say that Colonna instructed him to send the section of *Roma instaurata* on bronze coins to Leonello. In other words, rather than crafting a pleading dedication letter and a translation that might be ignored, Biondo could send his original work as part of Colonna's effort to reach out to another Italian prince. Shared cultural interests were used to promote political ties, and the fact that humanists like Biondo could offer antiquarian scholarship to the patrons of their choice increased their status and influence. Interest in antiquity was still ad hoc and unpredictable; a humanist secretary never knew which hat he might be called upon to wear, and individual scholars were still subject to the vagaries of political events and the triumphs of influential rivals. Nevertheless, even before the election of Nicholas V, humanism was recognized as an important component of curial and, more generally, of Italian culture, and humanists associated with the papal court enjoyed a new prestige.

The Renaissance, however, was not all about the triumph of humanism, and the classical scholars of Eugenius's court presaged the gloom, as well as the optimism, that infected their successors. At the beginning of Book I of *De varietate fortunae*, Poggio recalls how he and his friend and fellow secretary Antonio Loschi explored the city's ruins.[101] The conceit of a perambulation with one learned friend links Poggio's ramble with Petrarch's letter to Giovanni Colonna about the ruins of Rome; it also, if less exactly, recalls the famous stroll of Aeneas and Evander in book VIII of the *Aeneid*.[102] Like Petrarch and Colonna, Loschi and Poggio pause in their perambulations to rest and converse, but whereas Petrarch suggests that the day's conversation is as irrevocable as Rome herself, Poggio claims to remember and record the discussion verbatim. Loschi is the first speaker.

O how much, Poggio, this Capitoline differs from that which our Vergil celebrated "Golden now, once bristling with overgrown brambles." Indeed this verse serves as a worthy response: "Golden once, now rough with thorns and full of brambles." That Marius comes to mind, who once upheld the military might of the city. They assert that, driven from his fatherland as a poor fugitive, when he reached Africa, he sat before the ruins of Carthage, wondering at his own fate and that of Carthage, considering the fortune of each and doubting whether the spectacle of either fortune was more remarkable. I, in truth, am able to consider the immense ruin of this city in no other way. She has surpassed the ruin of all other things, both those which nature created and those which the hands of men raised. Even if you should peruse all histories, explore all literary monuments, examine all annals of great deeds, fortune has offered no greater example of her changeful nature than the city of Rome, once the most beautiful and magnificent of all cities which ever were or would be. Libanius, the most learned Greek author, wrote to a friend eager to see Rome that it was not a city but like some part of heaven.[103] With this saying in mind, it is more wonderful and bitter to see that the cruelty of fortune has changed the beauty and the form of the city, so that now she lies prostrate and stripped of all honor, the image of a giant corpse, corrupt and utterly destroyed.[104]

For Loschi as for Petrarch, the ideas conjured up by the city are more significant than its physical reality; just as Petrarch weaves a tapestry of lost political grandeur, so too Loschi insists that the discerning observer should see specific messages, not just stones or columns, when he looks at Rome. But if Loschi's response to the Capitol is reminiscent of Petrarch's, it is even more closely tied to Biondo's account. Whereas Biondo focuses on the responses of Constantius II and Theodoric, who saw the Capitol well after its prime, Loschi compares his own experience to that of Marius looking at Carthage. Thus, even as they describe the ancient Capitol, both Poggio and Biondo emphasize displacement, be it chronological or geographical. Instead of focusing on the physical realities of the ancient hill, they highlight its mythical status.[105]

For Poggio the Capitol is a mirage that evokes the power of fortune rather than a historical reality. Except when he vaunts his own skill at retrieving inscriptions, Poggio's equation of ancient and modern Rome is not about revival; the two are linked not by their grandeur but by their fragility. *De varietate fortunae* suggests that Poggio's experience of Eugenius's reign heightened his frustration with those who are guided by others, but it also suggests that it instilled in him a belief in the inescapable workings of fate, a belief that was supported by many of the classical texts he read. While Rome might be revived temporarily, through the inscription reading of devoted scholars or the political successes of an atypically sagacious pontiff, she, like all human creations, will succumb to the caprice of Fortune. At the end of *The Prince*, Machiavelli optimistically argues that a great ruler can adapt his behavior in order to respond to Fortune's constant contortions; Poggio offers no such hope. *De varietate fortunae* portrays a world of endless

struggle in which the "insanity of men confers authority on fortune
and makes her frightful."[106] If Biondo's *Roma instaurata* looks forward to
the rebuilding of Saint Peter's and the other architectural and artistic
triumphs of the late fifteenth and early sixteenth centuries, Poggio
presages the city's sack in 1527 and the inability of its pontiffs to maintain the glittering union of classical and Christian culture, the union
that made Rome, for eighty years, the cultural capital of Europe and the
epicenter of Renaissance optimism.[107]

While the writings of Poggio and Biondo presage later developments, they also represent the end of an era. Nicholas V was himself a
skilled classical scholar, eager to promote humanist studies, but neither
Poggio nor Biondo prospered under his rule. In 1448, Poggio dedicated
De varietate fortunae to the new pontiff, who may well have been offended
by Poggio's reminder that, in spite of God's intent, the papacy had not
proven itself beyond the power of fortune.[108] Poggio still had enough
intellectual and social capital at the Curia to engineer the departure of
his enemy, George of Trebizond, in 1452, but a year later the elderly
humanist, dismayed by Valla's rising star, decided to leave the Curia for
the Florentine chancery.[109] Biondo claimed that his own loss of status
was due to an unnamed enemy, but Aeneas Silvius Piccolomini suggests that Biondo, like other former favorites, was naturally disliked by
the new pontiff.[110]

The fact that Poggio and Biondo did not succeed in Nicholas's Curia
was, however, due to more than personal antipathies. It is not necessary to suggest that Nicholas was a cruel and arbitrary tyrant to explain
why the milieu of his Curia was inhospitable to the two scholars.[111]
Nicholas spearheaded the systematic translation of Greek works into
Latin, an effort that left older humanists behind.[112] While he sponsored
translations of a wide range of Greek works, Nicholas, like Capranica,
was particularly devoted to patristic authors, authors who were not at
the center of the classical revival proposed by Poggio and Biondo.[113]
Furthermore, Manetti's laudatory biography has often been presented
as the paradigmatic work of his regime; whereas Biondo seeks to promote his patron in *Roma instaurata* when it fits with his scholarly program, Manetti devotes his entire text to celebration of the Parentucelli
pope. Under Nicolas's successors, if not the learned pontiff himself,
curial humanists spent their time crafting works of classicizing propaganda; in extreme cases, pontiffs fired, imprisoned, and even executed

scholars like Porcari, Leto, Platina, and Callimachus who vaunted the intellectual freedom and critical stance enjoyed by Poggio.[114]

The crises of the early Quattrocento Church had encouraged humanists to question tradition and to take a skeptical attitude toward their society. Perhaps just as importantly, these crises had distracted popes and cardinals, allowing Poggio, Biondo, and their colleagues an unusual degree of independence. As the position of the papacy improved, the Curia ceased to be a hotbed of political and social criticism; while intellectual debate flourished, the debate tended to be between scholars competing for the attention of popes and other involved patrons rather than the free-for-all that Poggio and Biondo celebrate in their descriptions of curial conversations.[115] The end of Poggio's *Facetiae* offers a melancholy, but fitting, farewell to Rome and the Curia as they have been described in *Reviving the Eternal City*.[116] "Today, these men are dead, and the Bugiale has ceased to exist. All the custom of joking and conversing has ended, the fault of men and of the times."[117] Like so many avant-garde movements, curial humanism was taken over by a ruling elite that turned it into a potent cultural tool but also robbed it of its early spontaneity and fluidity.

Figure 7: Filarete, Porta Argentea, St. Peter's, Vatican City

Per gentile concessione della Fabbrica di San Pietro in Vaticano

Figures 8a (left) and 8b (right): Filarete, *Christ and Mary,* detail of Porta
Argentea, St. Peter's, Vatican City

Per gentile concessione della Fabbrica di San Pietro in Vaticano

Figures 9a (left) and 9b (right): Filarete, *Saints Peter and Paul,* detail of Porta
Argentea, St. Peter's, Vatican City

Figure 10: Filarete, *Martyrdom of St. Paul,* detail of Porta Argentea, St. Peter's, Vatican City

Per gentile concessione della Fabbrica di San Pietro in Vaticano

Figure 11: Filarete, *Martyrdom of St. Peter,* detail of Porta Argentea, St. Peter's, Vatican City

Per gentile concessione della Fabbrica di San Pietro in Vaticano

Figures 12a (top) and 12b (bottom): Filarete, *Greeks leave Constantinople and Meeting of Emperor Giovanni Palaeologus and Eugenius IV,* detail of Porta Argentea, St. Peter's, Vatican City
Per gentile concessione della Fabbrica di San Pietro in Vaticano

Figures 13a (top) and 13b (bottom): Filarete, *Council of Florence and Greeks depart for Constantinople,* detail of Porta Argentea, St. Peter's, Vatican City

Per gentile concessione della Fabbrica di San Pietro in Vaticano

Figures 14a (top) and 14b (bottom): Filarete, *Union of the Copts and the Copts visit Rome,* detail of Porta Argentea, St. Peter's, Vatican City

Per gentile concessione della Fabbrica di San Pietro in Vaticano

Figures 15a (top): Coronation of the Emperor Sigismundo and 15b (bottom): Eugenius and Sigismundo Process to the Castel Sant'Angelo

Per gentile concessione della Fabbrica di San Pietro in Vaticano

Abbreviations

AHR — *American Historical Review*

Alle Origini — Chiabò, Maria, Giusi D'Alessandro, Paola Piacentini, and Concetta Ranieri, eds. *Alle Origini Della Nuova Roma, Martin V (1417–1431)* (Roma, 1992).

ASRSP — *Archivio della Società Romana di storia patria*

DBDI — *Dizionario biografico degli italiani* (Rome, 1960–)

JHI — *Journal of the History of Ideas*

JWCI — *Journal of the Warburg and Courtauld Institutes*

Martino V — Piatti, Pierantonio, and Rocco Ronzani, eds. *Martino V: Genazzano, Il Pontifice, Le Idealità*. Roma, 2009.

RQ — *Renaissance Quarterly*

Notes

Author's Note: I have used English translations of Latin and Italian texts, where available. In all other instances, the translations are my own.

Introduction: Rome ca. 1420

1. Carol Richardson, *Reclaiming Rome: Cardinals in the Fifteenth Century* (Leiden, 2009), 30–34.

2. On the challenges and delights of writing about Rome, see Robert Brentano, *Rome Before Avignon: A Social History of Thirteenth Century Rome* (Berkeley, 1990), 3–8; Leonard Barkan, *Unearthing the Past: Archaeology and Aesthetics in the Making of Renaissance Culture* (New Haven, 1999), xxvii–xxxii.

3. Many thanks to Katherine Parks for an illuminating discussion on this point. For analyses of the enduring importance of Burckhardt's project, see William Kerrigan and Gordon Braden, *The Idea of the Renaissance* (Baltimore, 1989), 3–35; Randolph Starn, "A Postmodern Renaissance?," *RQ* 60, (2007), 1–24.

4. On the election of Martin, see Walter Brandmüller, "L'elezione di Martino V," in *Martino V,* 3–9. From Constance, Martin proceeded to Geneva, Pavia, Milan, Mantua, and then Florence, where he remained from February 1419 to September 1420. Concetta Bianca, "Martino V," in *DBDI,* vol. 71, 278–282.

5. Peter Partner, *The Papal State under Martin V: The Administration and Government of the Temporal Power in the Early 15th century* (London, 1958), 42–63.

6. For general studies of the Avignon papacy, see Guillaume Mollat, *The Popes at Avignon (1305–1378)* (New York, 1963); Edwin Mullins, *The Popes of Avignon: A Century in Exile* (New York, 2008). In 1378, the Great Schism began, and while there was a Roman line of popes (as well as an Avignonese and, later, a Pisan line), they rarely lived in Rome.

7. Torgil Magnuson, *The Urban Transformation of Medieval Rome, 312–1420* (Stockholm, 2004), 127–128.

8. On the tumultuous political situation in Rome during the Schism, see Ferdinand Gregorovius, *History of the City of Rome in the Middle Ages,* trans. Anne Hamilton (London, 1900–1909), vol. 6, part 2.

9. Sandro Carocci, "Baroni in città: Considerazioni sull'insediamento e i diritti urbani della grande nobilità," in *Roma nei secoli XIII e XIV,* ed. Étienne Hubert (Rome, 1993), 137–173.

10. Ronald Musto, *Apocalypse in Rome: Cola di Rienzo and the Politics of the New Age* (Berkeley, 2003), 84.

11. Bruni offers eloquent accounts of the chaos in Rome in the early 1400s. Leonardo Bruni, *Epistolarum libri VIII,* ed. James Hankins (Roma, 2007), vol. 1, 21–43. The most frequently cited description of Rome in 1420 is that of Platina. *Platynae historici Liber de vita Christi ac omnium pontificum* (Città di Castello, 1933), 309–310. See also Stefano Infessura, *Diario della città di Roma di Stefano Infessura scribasenato,* ed. Oreste Tommasini (Roma, 1890), 23–24.

12. Antonio di Pietro dello Schiavo, "Il diario di Antonio di Pietro dello Schiavo: 19 ottobre 1404–25 settembre 1417," in *Rerum Italicarum Scriptores,* ed. Ludovico Muratori (Bologna, 1917), vol. 24, part 5, 3–165.

13. Maria Blasio, "Immagini di un condottiero: Braccio da Montone e l'occupazione di Roma del 1417," in *Condottieri e uomini d'arme nell' Italia del Rinascimento,* ed. Mario Del Treppo (Napoli, 2001), 215–226.

14. Manuel Chrysoloras, "Comparison of Old and New Rome," in *Architecture in the Culture of Early Humanism: Ethics, Aesthetics, and Eloquence, 1400–1470,* ed. Christine Smith (Oxford, 1992), 200. On the ways in which Chrysoloras's letter on Rome shaped the responses of Quattrocento humanists, see Giuseppe Lombardi, "La città, libro di pietra: Immagini umanistiche di Roma prima e dopo Costanza," in *Alle Origini,* 17–45; Smith, *Architecture in the Culture of Early Humanism,* 150–170, 199–215.

15. Anna Esposito, "La popolazione romana dalla fine del secolo XIV al Sacco: caratteri e forme di un'evoluzione demografica," in *Popolazione e società a Roma dal Medioevo all'età contemporanea,* ed. Eugenio Sonnino (Roma, 1998), 38–39. Other estimates tend to be lower: 25,000: Magnuson, *Urban Transformation,* 146; 17,000: Carroll Westfall, *In This Most Perfect Paradise: Alberti, Nicholas V, and the Invention of Conscious Urban Planning in Rome, 1447–55* (University Park, PA, 1974), 63; Richard Krautheimer, *Rome: Profile of a City, 312–1308* (Princeton, NJ, 1980), 231–232.

16. The city was divided into twelve rioni in the twelfth century, and sometime in the thirteenth century Trastevere began to be considered as a thirteenth rione. Brentano, *Rome Before Avignon,* 17–19.

17. Infessura, *Diario della città di Roma,* 23.

18. In the early 1400s, Rome was theoretically ruled by a foreign-born Senator, who would serve for six months, helped by the three Conservators (each

of whom served three-month terms). Peter Partner, *The Lands of St. Peter: The Papal States in the Middle Ages and the Early Renaissance* (London, 1972), 162; Westfall, *In This Most Perfect Paradise*, 71–72. The Caporioni were originally militia leaders who represented Rome's thirteen districts. Amanda Collins, *Greater than Emperor: Cola di Rienzo (1313–1354) and the World of Fourteenth-Century Rome* (Ann Arbor, 2002), 195.

19. Ludwig Pastor, *The History of the Popes from the Close of the Middle Ages*, trans. Frederick Antrobus (London, 1906), vol. 1, 214.

20. The population of Milan was 90,000 and that of Florence was 55,000. Paul Bairoch, Jean Batou, and Pierre Chèvre, *The Population of European Cities, 800–1850: Data Bank and Short Summary of Results* (Genève, 1988), 43–47.

21. Anna Modigliani, *Disegni sulla città nel primo Rinascimento Romano: Paolo II* (Roma, 2009), 1–8.

22. Franco Astolfi, "La Piazza del Popolo dall'antichità al *Medioevo* in *Santa Maria del Popolo: Storia e restauri*, ed. Ilaria Mariani and Maria Richiello (Roma, 2009), 13–30.

23. See the map following the introduction to this book. For a description of the *disabitato* around 1300, see Krautheimer, *Rome*, 311–326.

24. On the papal palace prior to the renovations of Nicholas V, see Torgil Magnuson, *Studies in Roman Quattrocento Architecture* (Stockholm, 1958), 98–115.

25. Philine Helas and Gerhard Wolf, "'E fece uno granni bene alla città di Roma:' Considerazioni sulle opere di Martino V per la città di Roma," in *Martino V*, 233.

26. For descriptions and images of St. Peter's in the Middle Ages, see Alberto Carpiceci, *La fabbrica di San Pietro: venti secoli di storia e progetti* (Città del Vaticano, 1983), 14–41; Alessandro Tomei, "La basilica dalla tarda antichità al secolo XIV," in *La basilica di San Pietro*, ed. Carlo Pietrangeli (Firenze, 1989), 66–89; Antonio Pinelli, "The Old Basilica," in *The Basilica of St. Peter in the Vatican*, ed. Antonio Pinelli (Modena, 2000), 191–218; Herbert Kessler, *Old St. Peter's and Church Decoration in Medieval Italy* (Spoleto, 2002), 1–13. For a description of St. Peter's at the time of Martin's return, see Hannes Roser, *St. Peter in Rom in 15. Jahrhundert: Studien zu Architektur und skulturaler Ausstattung* (Munchen, 2005), 29–56.

27. Sible De Blaauw, *Cultus et Decor: Liturgia e architettura nella Roma tardoantica e medievale* (Città del Vaticano, 1994), vol. 2, 632–638.

28. Krautheimer, *Rome*, 260–269. For an overview of the experience of late medieval pilgrims, see Massimo Miglio, "Romei a Roma," in *La storia dei giubilei, 1300–1423*, ed. Jacques Le Goff (Firenze, 1997), 90–103.

29. Anna Modigliani, *Mercati, botteghe e spazi di commercio a Roma tra Medioevo ed età moderna* (Roma, 1998), 269–274.

30. On accomodations for pilgrims, see *Taverne, locande e stufe a Roma nel Rinascimento* (Roma, 1999).

31. Mario Romani, *Pellegrini e viaggiatori nell'economia di Roma dal XIV al XVII secolo* (Milano, 1948), 14. Compare Richardson, *Reclaiming Rome*, 148.

32. Magnuson, *Studies in Roman Quattrocento Architecture*, 4. On Santo Spirito, see chapter 4.

33. Cesare D'Onofrio, *Castel Sant'Angelo e Borgo tra Roma e Papato* (Roma, 1978), 227–236. See also Enrico Guidoni, *L'urbanistica di Roma tra miti e progetti* (Roma, 1990), 98–101.

34. The Orsini also had strongholds near S. Angelo in Pescheria, the 16th-century S. Carlo ai Catinari, and the Theater of Pompey. Francesca Bosman, "Incastellamento urbano a Roma: il caso degli Orsini," in *Settlement and Economy in Italy, 1500 BC–1500 AD: Papers of the Fifth Conference of Italian Archaeology*, ed. Neil Christie (Oxford, 1995), 499–507.

35. The other two streets were the Via dei Coronari and the Via Mercatoria, which ran near the banks of the Tiber and connected the major markets of the city. Modigliani, *Mercati*, 11.

36. Platina, *Liber*, 310; Krautheimer, *Rome*, 237.

37. Magnuson, *Studies in Roman Quattrocento Architecture*, 11. On the benefits of proximity to the Tiber, see Luciano Palermo, "Sviluppo economico e organizzazione degli spazi urbani a Roma nel primo Rinascimento," in *Spazio urbano e organizzazione economica nell'Europa medievale: Eleventh International Economic History Congress*, ed. A. Grohmann (Napoli, 1995), 421–422.

38. Cum itaque (sicut rei evidentia palam edocet) Urbs districtusque praedicti, quos paterno amplectimur affectu, ex defectu officii magistrorum, quod antiquitus pro viarum, stratarum, platearum et locorum aliorum tam publicorum quam privatorum, necnon aedificiorum lapideorum et ligneorum, parietum tignorum, banchorum, tectorum, tabulatuum, mignanorum, apothecarum et pontium, portarum, passorum, aquarum decursuum, canalium et meatuum, necnon urbanorum et rusticorum praediorum, pratorum, hortorum atque vinearum, finium, restaurationum, servitutum et libertatum administratione, institutum et ordinatum extitit, in praemissis et eorum singulis grandem deformitatem seu ruinam potius abhominabilem patiantur et iacturam. Et (sicut accepimus) nonnulli ex civibus, habitatoribus et incolis Urbis et districtus praedicti, macellarii videlicet, piscarii, sutores, pelamentellarii, diversisque artifices, loca ac etiam ergasteria Urbis inhabitantes, suasque inibi artes exercentes, viscera, intestina, capita, pedes, ossa, cruores, necon pelles, carnes et pisces corruptos, resque alias foetidas atque corruptas in viis, stratis, plateis et locis publicis atque privatis huiusmodi proiicere atque occultare. Martino V, "Etsi in cunctarum, 31 marzo 1425," in *Visitiamo Roma nel Quattrocento: La città degli umanisti,* ed. Cesare D'Onofrio (Roma, 1989), 17–18.

39. Anna Modigliani, "Artigiani e botteghe nella città," in *Alle origini,* 455–477.

40. Modigliani, *Mercati,* 62–64, 76–84. The main area for selling fish was S. Angelo in Pescheria, just a few blocks northeast of the Tiber Island.

41. Magnuson, *Urban Transformation,* 106–112, 134–139.

42. On the early Quattrocento fear that the conditions of Roman housing had reached a crisis point, see Giovanna Curcio, *"'Nisi celeriter repararetur totaliter est ruitura': Notazioni* su struttura urbana e rinnovamento edilizio in Roma al tempo di Martino V," in *Alle origini,* 537–554.

43. Magnuson, *Urban Transformation,* 102.

44. Biondo Flavio, *Scritti inediti e rari di Biondo Flavio,* ed. Bartolomeo Nogara (Roma, 1927), 156.

45. Some notable recent works on Cola include Collins, *Greater than Emperor;* Tommaso di Carpegna Falconieri, *Cola di Rienzo* (Roma, 2002); Musto, *Apocalypse in Rome;* Anna Modigliani and Andreas Rehberg, *Cola di Rienzo e il Comune di Roma* (Roma, 2004).

46. Magnuson, *Urban Transformation,* 130–134.

47. Modigliani, *Mercati,* 29–55.

48. Lorenzo Finocchi Ghersi, "Le residenze dei Colonna ai Santi Apostoli," in *Alle origini,* 61–75.

49. Modigliani, *Disegni sulla città.*

50. Aldo Olivio, "Il Luogo," in *Il complesso dei SS Apostoli: Interventi di restauro,* ed. Cosima Arcieri (Roma, 1992), 34–39.

51. Gregorovius, *History of the City of Rome,* vol. 6, part 2, 505. Compare Pastor, *The History of the Popes,* vol. 1, 57–73.

52. For brief accounts of the Avignon Exile and Western Schism that emphasize the impact of these crises on ordinary Europeans, see Walter Ullmann, *A Short History of the Papacy in the Middle Ages* (London, 1972), 279–305; Giuseppe Alberigo, *Chiesa conciliare: Identità e significato del conciliarismo* (Brescia, 1981), 68–71. Compare Daniel Bornstein, *The Bianchi of 1399: Popular Devotion in Late Medieval Italy* (Ithaca, 1993), 200–202.

53 Aldo Landi, *Il Papa Deposto (Pisa 1409): L'idea conciliare nel Grande Scisma* (Torino, 1985); Walter Brandmüller, *Papst und Konzil im Grossen Schisma, 1378–1431: Studien und Quellen* (Paderborn, 1990).

54. For some important modern studies of the Council, see Universität Freiburg im Breisgau Theologische Fakultät, *Das Konzil von Konstanz: Beiträge zu seiner Geschichte und Theologie* (Freiburg, 1964); Alberigo, *Chiesa conciliare;* Walter Brandmüller, *Das Konzil von Konstanz, 1414–1418* (Paderborn, 1991–1997); Philip Stump, *The Reforms of the Council of Constance, 1414–1418* (Leiden, 1994).

55. The five nations that voted at the Council were France, Spain, Germany, England, and Italy. Ullmann, *Short History,* 298–301.

56. Fillastre's chronicle provides a vivid picture of the deadlock created by the national organization of the Council. Guillaume Fillastre, "The Council as seen by a Cardinal," in *The Council of Constance: The Unification of the Church,* ed. Louise Loomis (New York, 1961), 200–465.

57. Stump, *Reforms,* 3–21, 270–272.

58. Andreas Rehberg, "'Etsi prudens paterfamilias . . . pro pace suorum

sapienter providet': Le ripercussioni del nepotismo di Martino V a Roma e nel Lazio," in *Alle origini*, 41–42.

59. On Martin's reclamation and rule of the Papal States, see Peter Partner, *The Papal State*; Mario Caravale and Alberto Caracciolo, *Lo Stato pontificio da Martino V a Pio IX* (Torino, 1978), 3–49.

60. Peter Partner, "The 'Budget' of the Roman Church in the Renaissance Period," in *Italian Renaissance Studies*, ed. E. F. Jacob (London, 1960), 263.

61. Giannozzo Manetti, *Vita Nicolai V summi pontificis*, ed. and trans. Anna Modigliani (Roma, 2005); ———. "On the Achievements of Nicholas V, Supreme Pontiff," in *Building the Kingdom: Giannozzo Manetti on the Material and Spiritual Edifice*, ed. Christine Smith and Joseph O'Connor (Tempe, AZ, 2006), 362–429. See also Vespasiano da Bisticci, *Renaissance Princes, Popes, and Prelates: The Vespasiano Memoirs, Lives of Illustrious Men of the XVth Century*, trans. William George and Emily Waters (New York, 1963), 31–58; ———. *Le Vite*, ed. Aulo Greco (Firenze, 1970–76), vol. 1, 35–81.

62. Studies of Renaissance Rome that present Nicholas as the first Renaissance pope include John D'Amico, *Renaissance Humanism in Papal Rome: Humanists and Churchmen on the Eve of the Reformation* (Baltimore, 1983); Charles Stinger, *The Renaissance in Rome* (Bloomington, 1985); Paolo Prodi, *The Papal Prince: One Body and Two Souls: The Papal Monarchy in Early Modern Europe* (Cambridge, 1987).

63. See chapter 1 of this book.

64. Joachim Stieber, *Pope Eugenius IV, the Council of Basel and the Secular and Ecclesiastical Authorities in the Empire: The Conflict over Supreme Authority in the Church* (Leiden, 1978); Johannes Helmrath, *Das Basler Konzil, 1431–1449: Forschungsstand und Probleme* (Cologne, 1987). While Gill and, more recently, Decaluwue, offer important insights on the papal position, they still focus almost exclusively on the Councils. Joseph Gill, *The Council of Florence* (Cambridge, 1959); ———, *Eugenius IV, Pope of Christian Union* (London, 1961); ———, *Personalities of the Council of Florence* (Oxford, 1964); Michiel Decaluwe, *A Successful Defeat: Eugene IV's Struggle with the Council of Basel for Ultimate Authority in the Church, 1431–1449* (Bruxelles, 2009).

65. George Holmes, *The Florentine Enlightenment, 1400–1450* (Oxford, 1992), 1–35, 106–136; Christopher Celenza, *The Lost Italian Renaissance: Humanists, Historians, and Latin's Legacy* (Baltimore, 2004), 80–114.

66. Paul O. Kristeller, "Humanism and Scholasticism in Renaissance Italy," *Byzantion* 17 (1944–45): 346–374; Augusto Campana, "The Origin of the Word 'Humanist'," *JWCI* 9 (1946): 60–73.

67. On the evocative power of the ruined city, see Massimo Miglio, "Materiali e ipotesi," in *Scritture, scrittori e storia: Città e corte a Roma nel Quattrocento* (Roma, 1993), vol. 2, 19–32; Barkan, *Unearthing the Past*, 17–63.

68. Gualdo's studies offer an important exception to this rule. Germano Gualdo, *"Francesco Filelfo e la curia pontifica: Una carriera mancata," ASRSP* 102 (1979): 189–236; ———. "Umanesimo e segretari apostolici all' inizio del Quattrocento:

Alcuni casi esemplari," in *Cancelleria e cultura nel Medio Evo*, ed. German Gualdo (Città del Vaticano, 1990), 307–318; ———. *Diplomatica pontifica e umanesimo curiale: Con altri saggi sull'Archivio Vaticano, tra medieovo ed età moderna* (Roma, 2005).

69. Christopher Celenza, *Renaissance Humanism and the Papal Curia: Lapo da Castiglionchio the Younger's* De curiae commodis (Ann Arbor, 1999).

70. For some significant responses to Baron's thesis, see Jerrold Seigel, "'Civic Humanism' or Ciceronian Rhetoric: The Culture of Petrarch and Bruni," *Past and Present* 34 (1966): 3–48; James Hankins, "The 'Baron Thesis' after Forty Years and Some Recent Studies of Leonardo Bruni," *JHI* 56 (1995): 309–338; Ronald Witt, "'The Crisis' after Forty Years," *AHR* 101 (1996): 110–118; James Hankins, ed. *Renaissance Civic Humanism: Reappraisals and Reflections* (Cambridge, 2000).

71. Studies of humanism outside of Florence have mapped scholars' engagement with the political and social life of Italy's other major cities. Margaret King, *Venetian Humanism in an Age of Patrician Dominance* (Princeton, NJ, 1986); Jerry Bentley, *Politics and Culture in Renaissance Naples* (Princeton, NJ, 1987); Gary Ianziti, *Humanistic Historiography Under the Sforza: Politics and Propaganda in Fifteenth Century Milan* (Oxford, 1988); Diana Robin, *Filelfo in Milan: Writings, 1451–1477* (Princeton, NJ, 1991); Patricia F. Brown, *Venice and Antiquity: The Venetian Sense of the Past* (New Haven, 1996); Marcello Simonetta, *Rinascimento Segreto: Il mondo del segretario da Petrarca a Machiavelli* (Milano, 2004).

72. *Alle origini; Martino V.*

73. Stephen Greenblatt, *The Swerve: How the World Became Modern* (New York, 2011), 13.

1. Rome's Third Founder? Martin V, Niccolò Signorilli, and Roman Revival, 1420–1431

1. Francesco Petrarca, *Familiarium rerum libri,* ed. Vittorio Rossi and Umberto Bosco, trans. Ugo Dotti (Racconigi, 2004–2009), vol. 2, 774–795. (Translations of all Petrarch's letters can be found in Francesco Petrarca, *Rerum familiarium libri,* trans. Aldo Bernardo (Albany, 1975–1985). On Petrarch's letter to Colonna, see Angelo Mazzocco, "Petrarca, Poggio, and Biondo: Humanism's Foremost Interpreters of Roman Ruins," in *Francis Petrarch, Six Centuries Later: A Symposium,* ed. Aldo Scaglione (Chapel Hill, 1975), 353–363; Philip Jacks, *The Antiquarian and the Myth of Antiquity: The Origins of Rome in Renaissance Thought* (Cambridge, 1993), 35–40; David Galbraith, "Petrarch and the Broken City," in *Antiquity and Its Interpreters,* ed. Alina Payne, Ann Kuttner, and Rebekah Smick (Cambridge, 2000), 17–26; Jennifer Summit, "Topography as Historiography: Petrarch, Chaucer, and the Making of Medieval Rome," *Journal of Medieval and Early Modern Studies* 30 (2000): 215–223.

2. The topographical sections of the text are edited in Nicolo Signorili, "Descriptio urbis Romae eiusque excellentiae," in *Codice topografico della città di Roma,* ed. Roberto Valentini and Giuseppe Zucchetti (Roma, 1940–1953), vol. IV,

151–208. I cite Valentini and Zucchetti where possible and MS Vatican City, Vat. Lat. 3536 in other instances.

3. Ab hoc incipiens, Pater sancte, unum esse firmum, et probabili argumento, ac sine dubitatione verissimum, ymo adeo cunctis nationibus manifestum, quod probatione non indiget, Romam scilicet solam esse, quae in spiritualibus et temporalibus, in terris de iure praecipua dignitate refulget, cum ibi summi apostolatus et excelsi imperii solia sint locata. Et ob hoc sequitur, haud mirum, quod urbs ipsa tam sublimibus decorari muneribus, talibus insigniri titulis, et tam grandi excellentia, divina permittente clementia meruit sublimari, ut caput orbis, caputque fidei, mater legum, et communis patria ac domina gentium, et magistra, tam ex dispositione legum, quam universo sermonis eloquio nuncupatur; de quo Sanctitas vestra perhibere potest testimonium veritatis. Nam Te, qui per eam orbis dominus reputaris, ut Romanum Praesulem magnorum Regum et Principum munificentia reveretur, et ideo eam teneris, et debes caripendere, et in suis honoribus et dignitatibus conservare, nec illam permittere a suis subditis vilipendi, quae debet ab omnibus rationabiliter honorari. Signorili,"Descriptio," 163–164.

4. Ibid., 164–165. The combination of admiration and grief was also characteristic of earlier medieval responses to Rome. Arturo Graf, *Roma nella memoria e nelle immaginazioni del Medio Evo* (Sala Bolognese, 1987), 1–33.

5. Peter Burke, *The Renaissance Sense of the Past* (New York, 1969); Eric Cochrane, *Historians and Historiography in the Italian Renaissance* (Chicago, 1981), 3–20; Thomas Greene, *The Light in Troy: Imitation and Discovery in Renaissance Poetry* (New Haven, 1982). Compare Janet Coleman, *Ancient and Medieval Memories: Studies in the Reconstruction of the Past* (Cambridge, 1992), 558–583.

6. Patricia F. Brown, *Venice and Antiquity: The Venetian Sense of the Past* (New Haven, 1996), 49–141.

7. Pero Tafur, *Travels and Adventures, 1435–1439*, trans. Malcolm Letts (London, 1926), 34–35; ———. "Cosa singolare: Roma nelle Andanças e viajes por diversas partes del mondo avidos di Pero Tafur," in *Viaggiatori spagnoli a Roma nel Rinascimento*, ed. Manuel Pineiro Bologna, 2001, 26–31. On the legend of Gregory, see Tilmann Buddensieg, "Gregory the Great, the Destroyer of Pagan Idols: The History of a Medieval Legend concerning the Decline of Ancient Art and Literature," *JWCI* 28 (1965): 44–65.

8. Viewing Rome in a "humanistic" manner was not the sole prerogative of Quattrocento viewers, any more than it was of humanists. Christina Nardella, "La Roma dei visatori colti: Dalla mentalità umanistica di Maestro Gregorio (XII–XIII secolo) a quella medioevale di John Capgrave (XV secolo)," *ASRSP* 119 (1996): 49–64.

9. Charles Dickens, *Pictures from Italy* (London, 1846), 167–169, 215–216, 231; Edward Gibbon, *Autobiography* (New York, 1846), 167–169; Henry James, *Italian Hours* (Boston and New York, 1909), 189–213.

10. On the adaptability of Rome's legacy, see Carrie Beneš, *Urban Legends:*

Civic Identity and the Classical Past in Northern Italy, 1250–1350 (University Park, PA, 2011), 15–36.

11. The *Bandaresi* were the two heads of the Roman militia, the *Felice Società dei Balstrieri e Pavesati*. Amanda Collins, *Greater than Emperor: Cola di Rienzo (1313–1354) and the World of Fourteenth-Century Rome* (Ann Arbor, 2002), 137–138, 190–197. For more on the government of Rome's commune, see Laura Moscati, *Alle origini del comune Romano: economia, società, istituzioni* (Roma, 1980); Jean-Claude Marie Vigeur, "Il comune romano," in *Roma medievale*, ed. Andre Vauchez (Roma, 2001), 117–157; Ronald Musto, *Apocalypse in Rome: Cola di Rienzo and the Politics of the New Age* (Berkeley, CA, 2003), 143–159.

12. Arnold Esch, *Bonifaz IX und der Kirchenstaat* (Tubingen, 1969), 209–276; ———. "Dalla Roma comunale alla Roma Papale: La fine del libero comune," *ASRSP* 130 (2007): 1–16.

13. Anthony D'Elia, *A Sudden Terror: The Plot to Murder the Pope in Renaissance Rome* (Cambridge, MA, 2009); Anna Modigliani, *Disegni sulla città nel primo Rinascimento Romano: Paolo II* (Roma, 2009).

14. Max Lehnerdt, "Cencio und Agapito de' Rustici: Neue Beitrage zur Geschichte des Humanismus in Italien, mitgeteilt," *Zeitschrift fur vergleichende Litteraturgeschichte* 14 (1900): 165–167. For the rhetorical context of the oration that describes Martin as a third Romulus, see Wouter Bracke, "Le orazioni al pontifice," in *Alle origini*, 125–142.

15. Maria Blasio, "Radici di un mito storiografico: il ritratto umanistico di Martino V," in *Alle origini*, 111–124.

16. *Alle origini; Martino V.*

17. Andreas Rehberg, "Etsi prudens paterfamilias . . . pro pace suorum sapienter providet": Le ripercussioni del nepotismo di Martino V a Roma e nel Lazio," in *Alle origini*, 225–282.

18. Compare Sandro Carocci, *Il nepotismo nel medioevo: Papi, cardinali e famiglie nobili* (Roma, 1999), 136–138.

19. Orietta Verdi, *Maestri di edifici e di strade a Roma nel secolo XV* (Roma, 1997), 21, ftn. 18.

20. Louis Aleman, Benedetto Guadalotti, and Oddia Poccia were Martin's three Vice-Chamberlains. Peter Partner, *The Papal State Under Martin V: The Administration and Government of the Temporal Power in the Early 15th Century* (London, 1958), 132. Compare Mario Caravale, "Per una premessa storiografica," in *Alle origini*, 1–15.

21. Arnold Esch, "Nobilità, comune e papato nel prima metà del Quattrocento: Le conseguenze della fine del libero comune nel 1398," in *La nobiltà Romano nel medioevo*, ed. Sandro Carocci (Roma, 2006), 495–513.

22. On the economic unrest of Rome and the *campagna* in the 14th century, see Sante Polica, "La crisi del XIV secolo," in *La nobiltà Romana*, 461–493.

23. Anna Modigliani, "L'aristocrazia municipale romana nel XV secolo:

identità politica e autorappresentazione," in *Vecchia e nuova aristocrazia a Roma e nel Lazio in età moderna: Strategie economiche e del consenso,* ed. Daniela Cavallero (Roma, 2006), 13. For the financial dealing of one of these new nobles, see Giuseppe Coletti, "Dai diari di Stefano Caffari," *ASRSP* 8 (1885): 555–575.

24. Paolo della Valle (d. 1440), the doctor to Alexander V and Martin V, employed all of these social strategies. Anna Esposito, "'Li nobili huomini di Roma': Strategie familiari tra città, Curia e municipio," in *Roma capitale: 1447–1527,* ed. Sergio Gensini (S. Miniato, 1994), 375–376.

25. Paola Pavan, " *'Inclitae Urbis Romae iura, iurisdictiones et honores':* Un caso di damnatio memoriae?," in *Alle origini,* 305–309.

26. On the added value of commercial and residential property when the pope and Curia were in the city, see Luciano Palermo, "Sviluppo economico e organizzazione degli spazi urbani a Roma nel primo Rinascimento," in *Spazio urbano e organizzazione economica nell'Europa medievale: Eleventh International Economic History Congress,* ed. A. Grohmann (Napoli, 1995), 432–435; Anna Modigliani, "Taverne e osterie a Roma nel tardo Medioevo: Tipologia, uso degli spazi, arredo e distribuzione nella città," in *Taverne, locande e stufe a Roma nel Rinascimento* (Roma, 1999), 24–26.

27. Rehberg, "'Etsi prudens paterfamilias,'" 248–249.

28. Carroll Westfall, *In this Most Perfect Paradise; Alberti, Nicholas V, and the Invention of Conscious Urban Planning in Rome, 1447–55* (University Park, PA, 1974), 72; Giovanna Curcio, "'Nisi celeriter repararetur totaliter est ruitura': notazioni su struttura urbana e rinnovamento edilizio in Roma al tempo di Martino V," in *Alle origini,* 552; Esch, "Nobilità, comune e papato," 502.

29. Vat. Lat. 3536, f. 4–5.

30. On attribution of Rome's founding by Noah to Hescodius/ Escodius/ Estodius/ Eustodius, see Graf, *Roma nella memoria,* 61–72. As late as 1547, the story that Rome was founded by Noah was included by Pierfrancesco Giambullari in *Il Gello.*

31. *The Marvels of Rome,* trans. Francis Morgan Nichols (New York, 1986), 3–4. This description of the city's early origins was added to the earliest version of the *Mirabilia* sometime after 1154 and is not included in the most recent Latin and Italian editions. Maria Lanzillotta, *Contributi sui* Mirabilia urbis Romae (Genova, 1996), 16–19.

32. Denys Hay, *Annalists and Historians: Western Historiography from the Eighth to the Eighteenth Centuries* (London, 1977), 63–86; Augusto Vasina, "Medieval Urban Historiography in Western Europe (1100–1500)," in *Historiography in the Middle Ages,* ed. Deborah Deliyannis (Leiden, 2003), 317–352; Sharon Dale, Alison Lewin, and Duane Osheim, eds., *Chronicling History: Chroniclers and Historians in Medieval and Renaissance Italy* (University Park, PA, 2007); Beneš, *Urban Legends.*

33. John Melville-Jones, "Venetian History and Patrician Chroniclers," in *Chronicling History,* 199–201.

34. Giovanni Villani, "Chronica," in *Chroniche storiche di Giovanni, Matteo e Filippo Villani,* ed. Francesco Dragomanni (Milano, 1848), 15–31. See Francesco Salvestrini, "Giovanni Villani and the Aetiological Myth of Tuscan Cities" in *The Medieval Chronicle II: Proceedings of the 2nd International Conference on the Medieval Chronicle,* ed. Erik Kooper (Amsterdam, 2002), 199–211.

35. On the lack of Roman chronicles, see Cochrane, *Historians and Historiography,* 41. One exception to this trend was the Roman *Cronica* of Bartolomeo di Jacopo da Valmontone. Vasina, "Medieval Urban Historiography," 339–340.

36. Vat. Lat. 3536, f. 5.

37. Ibid., f. 8–9.

38. Twenty-nine books of Livy's *Ab urbe condita* were known in the Middle Ages, but "the Middle Ages took relatively little interest in Livy." B. L. Ullman, "The Post-Mortem Adventures of Livy," in *Studies in the Italian Renaissance* (Roma, 1973), 53–60. For a study of Bruni's complex use of Livy, see Gary Ianziti, *Writing History in Renaissance Italy: Leonardo Bruni and the Uses of the Past* (Cambridge, MA, 2012), 61–88.

39. Vat. Lat. 3536, f. 9–11.

40. Three paraphrases come from Saint Augustine, *Concerning the City of God Against the Pagans,* trans. Henry Bettenson (New York, 1984), book 5, chaps. 12 and 15.

41. Ibid., book 5, chaps. 16 and 18.

42. Dominus noster Jesus Christus hanc urbem voluntate sua factam, ampliatam et defensam in hoc culmine rerum produxit cuius maxime cum venit Romanus voluit esse civis census professione Romani. O felix secundum legem Romanorum genus cunctis aliis nationibus anteponendum. O felix Roma quam mundi creator excelsus deus te in tam grandi fastigio tantarum sublimitatum erexit, qui sub toto imperio eius filium constituit incarnari, qui Romano imperio censum dedit et pro salute humani generis sub eodem imperio voluit crucifigi et inquantum mori dignatus est teque sanctorum apostolorum et martyrum infinitorum suorum demum sanguine rubricari. Vat. Lat. 3536, f. 11v.

43. Peter Brown, *Augustine of Hippo: A Biography* (Berkeley, CA, 2000), 312–329.

44. John A. Burrow, *A History of Histories: Epics, Chronicles, Romances, and Inquiries from Herodotus and Thucydides to the Twentieth Century* (New York, 2008), 260–261.

45. Compare Hans-Werner Goetz, "The Concept of Time in the Historiography of the Eleventh and Twelfth Centuries," in *Medieval Concepts of the Past,* ed. Gerd Althoff, Johannes Fried, and Patrick Geary (Cambridge, 2002), 139–166.

46. Vat. Lat. 3536, f. 12–20. Much of this material can be found in Signorili, "Descriptio," 166–169, 192–194.

47. Roberto Weiss, *The Renaissance Discovery of Classical Antiquity* (Oxford, 1988), 62; Jacks, *The Antiquarian*, 94. By editing only Signorili's descriptions of Rome's urban fabric, Valentini and Zucchetti present a coherent version of the eclectic *Descriptio*. The tendency to focus on the antiquarian sections of the text began as early as the 15th century, as evidenced by MSS Vatican City, Vat. Lat. 10687 and Chig. J V 168, which include Signorili's descriptions of Rome's rioni along with earlier compendia of epitaphs but do not include the religious or historical elements of the *Descriptio*.

48. On medieval interpretations of Rome's ancient statues, see Chiara Frugoni, "L'antichità: dai *Mirabilia* alla propaganda politica," in *Memoria dell'antico nell'arte italiana: Tomo Primo, L'uso dei classici,* ed. Salvatore Settis (Torino, 1984), 32–53.

49. Cassiodorus, *The Letters of Cassiodorus, Being a Condensed Translation of the* Variae Epistolae *of Magnus Aurelius Cassiodorus Senator,* trans. Thomas Hodgkin (London, 1886), 331.

50. Cassiodorus, *The* Variae *of Magnus Aurelius Cassiodorus Senator,* trans. S. J. B. Barnish (Liverpool, 1992), 61.

51. Harold Stone, "The Polemics of Toleration: The Scholars and Publishers of Cassiodorus' *Variae,*" *JHI* 46 (1985): 157.

52. Vat. Lat. 3536, 24–30. For the Donation, see Lorenzo Valla, *On the Donation of Constantine,* trans. G. W. Bowersock (Cambridge, MA, 2007), 162–183. For the Donation of Pippin and Charlemagne, see Emil Reich, *Select Documents Illustrating Mediaeval and Modern History* (London, 1905), 141–143. For the confirmation of Louis the Pious, see Alfredus Boretius, ed. *Capitularia regum francorum* (Hannoverae, 1883–1897), vol. 1, 353–355. For the confirmation of Otto I and Henry I and for the confirmation of Henry II, see J. E. T. Wiltsch, *Handbook of the Geography and Statistics of the Church,* trans. John Leitch (London, 1868), vol. 1, 270–272.

53. Valla, *On the Donation of Constantine,* 2–161. On medieval responses to the Donation, see Robert Black, "The Donation of Constantine: A New Source for the Concept of the Renaissance?," in *Language and Images of Renaissance Italy,* ed. Alison Brown (Oxford, 1995), 51–85. On the use of the Donation by Renaissance popes, see Massimo Miglio, Il ritorno a Roma: Varianti di una costante nella tradizione dell'Antico: le scelte pontificie," in *Roma centro ideale della cultura dell'Antico nei secoli XV e XVI: da Martino V al sacco di Roma, 1417–1527,* ed. Silvia Squarzina (Milano, 1989), 216–220; Modigliani, *Disegni sulla città,* 20–60.

54. Haec est enim illa felicissima Roma quam ipse deus omnipotens totius orbis ac orthodoxae fidei voluit esse caput. Haec est illa Roma sanctissima quam in fidei firmamentum elegit et beatorum apostolrum ac martyrum et sanctorum suorum sanguine consecravit. Haec est illa civitas gloriosa quae tot et tantis divinis dotari muneribus totque mirabilium rerum splendoribus illustrari et tot ornamentorum fulgoribus meruit decorari quod in stuporem inducitur animus intuentis. Vat. Lat. 3536, f. 31.

55. The list of Christian kings is at Ibid., f. 34. The list of bishops is at f. 35–46v.

56. Signorili, "Descriptio," 170–187.

57. Vat. Lat. 3536, f. 54–84.

58. Bonvesin della Riva's *De Magnalibus urbis Mediolani* offers one of the closest parallels to Signorili's *Descriptio.* J. K. Hyde, "Medieval Descriptions of Cities," *Bulletin of the John Rylands Library* 48 (1966): 308–340.

59. Compare Green's assessment of Giovanni Villani as betraying "an unconscious sense of the possible contradiction between the world of his experience and the overriding order within which he sought to place it." Louis Green, *Chronicle into History: An Essay on the Interpretation of History in Florentine Fourteenth-Century Chronicles* (Cambridge, 1972), 6.

60. Vat. Lat 3536, f. 3–4. On the uses of the phrase *translatio imperii* in the High Middle Ages, see Andrea Giardina, *Il mito di Roma: da Carlo Magno a Mussolini* (Roma, 2000), 37–43.

61. On Cola di Rienzo's claims to restore *imperium* to the Roman people, see Carrie Beneš, "Cola di Rienzo and the Lex Regia," *Viator* 30 (1999): 245–250; Collins, *Greater than Emperor,* 41–47.

62. On late medieval Italians' belief in the superiority of republics, see John Mundy, "In Praise of Italy: The Italian Republics," *Speculum* 64 (1989): 815–834.

63. Pavan, "'Inclitae Urbis Romae iura,'" 304–305.

64. On Stefano Porcari, see Massimo Miglio, "'Viva la libertà et popolo de Roma': Oratoria e politica, Stefano Porcari," *ASRSP* 97 (1974): 5–37; Anna Modigliani, *I Porcari: storie di una famiglia romana tra Medioevo e Rinascimento* (Roma, 1994), esp. 477–498; Arjo Vanderjagt, "Civic Humanism in Practice: The Case of Stefano Porcari and the Christian Tradition," in *Antiquity Renewed: Late Classical and Early Modern Themes,* ed. Zweder von Martels and Victor Schmidt (Leuven, 2003), 63–78; Anthony D'Elia, "Stefano Porcari's Conspiracy against Pope Nicholas V in 1453 and Republican Culture in Papal Rome," *JHI* 68 (2007): 207–231.

65. Massimo Miglio, "Marco Antonio Altieri e la nostalgia della Roma municipale," in *Effetti Roma: Nostalgia e rimpianto,* ed. Massimo Miglio et al. (Roma, 1993), 11–23.

66. Compare Edward Muir, *Civic Ritual in Renaissance Venice* (Princeton, 1981), 3–8, 299–305; Richard Trexler, *Public Life in Renaissance Florence* (Ithaca, 1980), 365–553.

67. On the implications of Martin's decision to live in Rome's historic center see Giorgio Simoncini, *Roma: Le trasformazioni urbane nel Quattrocento,* vol. I, *Topografia e urbanistica da Bonifacio IX ad Alessando VI* (Firenze, 2004), 74–76.

68. Vat. Lat. 3536, f. 12.

69. Nos igitur praemissas deformitates et excessus huiusmodi sub dissimulatione ulterius praeterire non valentes, attendentes propterea, quod in eadem Urbe, multo temporis decursu, neglectum fuit, in usum plurimum pullulasse,

et praemissis incommodis possetenus occurrere cupientes: officium magistratus huiusmodi, iuxta illius antiquam institutionem, auctoritate apostolica renovamus, suscitamus et reintegramus atque restituimus. Martino V, "Etsi in cunctarum, 31 marzo 1425," in *Visitiamo Roma nel Quattrocento: La città degli umanisti,* ed. Cesare D'Onofrio (Roma, 1989), 17.

70. Luigi Schiaparelli, "Alcuni documenti dei *Magistri aedificiorum urbis:* secoli xiii e xiv," *ASRSP* 25 (1902): 5–60; Cristina Vendittelli "Documentazione inedita riguardante i *magistri edificiorum urbis* e l' attività della loro curia nei secoli XIII e XIV," *ASRSP* 113 (1990): 169–188.

71. Camillo Re, ed. *Statuti della città di Roma* (Roma, 1880), 217–220.

72. Camillo Scaccia-Scarafoni, "L'antico statuto di *Magistri stratarum* e altri document relativi a quella Magistratura," *ASRSP* 50 (1927): 268–280.

73. Verdi, *Maestri di edifici,* 177–178.

74. Westfall, *In this Most Perfect Paradise,* 80.

75. For more on how Martin sought to preserve Rome's ancient monuments see David Karmon, *The Ruin of the Eternal City: Antiquity and Preservation in Renaissance Rome* (New York, 2011), 58–63.

76. Ibid., 52–58.

77. On Martin's efforts to make Rome more accessible to pilgrims, see Concetta Bianca, "Martino V e le orgini dello Stato della Chiesa," in *Martino V,* 15–16.

78. For discussion of later papal initiatives regarding the *Maestri,* see Scarafoni, "L'antico statuto," 250–266; Westfall, *In this Most Perfect Paradise,* 79–84; P. Cherubini et al., "Un libro di multe per la pulizia delle strade sotto Paolo II" *ASRSP* 107 (1984): 51–274; Orietta Verdi, "Da ufficiali capitolini a commissari apostolici: I maestri delle strade e degli edifici di Roma tra XIII e XVI secolo," in *Il Campidoglio e Sisto V,* ed. L. Spessaferro and M. E. Tittoni (Roma, 1991), 44–86; Verdi, *Maestri di edifici,* 38–86; Manfredo Tafuri, *Interpreting the Renaissance: Princes, Cities, Architects,* trans. Daniel Sherer (New Haven, 2006), 31–37.

79. Lorenzo Finocchi Ghersi, "Le residenze dei Colonna ai Santi Apostoli," in *Alle origini,* 61–75. Consistory records indicate that between 1420 and 1424, Martin split his time between St. Peter's and Santa Maria Maggiore. After that, he was usually at Santi Apostoli when he was in Rome. MS Vatican City, Vat. Lat. 12,126, f. 51v–63v.

80. Eugène Muntz, *Les arts à la cour des papes pendant le xve et le xvie siècle* (Paris, 1878), 9–14.

81. On the Lateran frescoes, see Marina Tosti-Croce, "Pisanello a S. Giovanni in Laterano," in *Da Pisanello alla nascita dei musei capitolini: L'Antico a Roma alla viglia del Rinascimento,* ed. Anna Cavallaro and Enrico Parlato (Milano, 1988), 107–108; Andrea De Marchi, "Gentile da Fabriano et Pisanello à Saint-Jean de Latran," in *Pisanello: Actes du colloque organisé au Musée du Louvre par le Service culturel,* ed. Dominique Cordellier and Bernadette Py (Paris, 1998),

161–213; Maria Bernardini, "Il ciclo perduto in San Giovanni in Laterano: un problema ancora aperto," in *Il '400 a Roma: la rinascita delle arti da Donatello a Perugino*, ed. Maria Bernardini and Marco Bussagli (Milano, 2008), 119–125.

82. Martin was the first pope in about 150 years to be buried at the Lateran. Joachim Poeschke, "Still a Problem of Attribution: The Tomb Slab of Pope Martin V in San Giovanni in Laterano," in *Large Bronzes in the Renaissance*, ed. Peta Motture (New Haven, 2003), 59.

83. Hellmut Wohl, "Martin V and the Revival of the Arts in Rome," in *Rome in the Renaissance: The City and the Myth* ed. P. A. Ramsey (Binghamton, NY, 1982), 171.

84. On the 1425 project, see Simonetta Valtieri, "Il ruolo dell'area compresa nell'ansa del Tevere nelle strategie Papali dal Medioevo fino al XV secolo," in *Saggi in onore di Renato Bonelli*, ed. Corrado Bozzoni, Giovanni Carbonara, and Gabriella Viletti (Roma, 1992), 338. On Martin's encouragement of his cardinals' building projects, see Carol Richardson, *Reclaiming Rome: Cardinals in the Fifteenth Century* (Leiden, 2009), 157–168.

85. Muntz, *Les arts à la cour des papes*, 16–17; Bianca, "Martino V e le orgini dello Stato della Chiesa," 16. For the work Martin sponsored on the Ponte Santa Maria see Karmon, *Ruin of the Eternal City*, 182–184.

86. Simoncini, *Topografia e urbanistica*, 76–80.

87. Ruth Kennedy, "The Contribution of Martin V to the Rebuilding of Rome," in *The Renaissance Reconsidered: A Symposium*, ed. Leona Gabel (Northhampton, 1964), 27. See also Philine Helas and Gerhard Wolf, "'E fece uno granni,'" in *Martino V*, 219–240.

88. Palermo, "Sviluppo economico." See also Curcio, "'Nisi celeriter repararetur,'" 553–554.

89. Eduard Safarik, *Palazzo Colonna* (Roma, 1999), 48–50.

90. On the likely patrons of the altarpiece, see Paul Joannides, "Catalogue 23, Masolino and Masaccio, the Colonna Altarpiece," in *Masaccio and Masolino: A Compete Catalogue* (London, 1993), 416–417; Ria O'Fughludha, "Roma Nova: The Santa Maria Maggiore Altarpiece and the Rome of Martin V" (Ph.D. diss., Columbia University, 1998), 240–262; Carl Strehlke, *The Panel Paintings of Masaccio and Masolino: The Role of Technique* (Milano, 2002), 124–126.

91. On the history of the triptych and its division into three parts (now in Naples, London, and Philadelphia), see Fabrizio Mancinelli, "La Basilica nel Quattrocento," in *La basilica Romana di Santa Maria Maggiore*, ed. Carlo Pietrangeli (Firenze, 1987), 191–193. For arguments about the dating of the triptych, see Paul Joannides, "The Colonna Triptych by Masolino and Masaccio: Collaboration and Chronology," *Arte cristiana* 76 (1988): 339–346; Perri Roberts, *Masolino da Panicale* (Oxford, 1993), 96–98.

92. Kenneth Clark, "An Early Quattrocento Triptych from Santa Maria Maggiore," *Burlington Magazine* 93 (1951): 339–347. On the difficulties of attributing works to Masaccio, Masolino, and/or their assistants, see Stefano L'

Occaso, "Osservazioni sulla pittura a Roma sotto Martino V," *ASRSP* 125 (2002): 43–51; Mauoko Ikuta, "Gli affreschi della Cappella di S. Caterina nella chiesa di S. Clemente a Roma," *Annuario VIII* (1970/1971): 73–99.

93. Helas and Wolf, "'E fece uno granni,'" 231.

94. Giorgio Vasari, *Le opere di Giorgio Vasari con nuove annotazioni e commenti di Gaetano Milanesi* (Firenze, 1998), vol. 2, 293–294.

95. On Martin's preference for the Gothic style, see Silvia Maddalo, "Identità di una cultura figurativa," in *Alle origini,* 47–60.

96. In the 13th-century mosaic of Rusuti, which was the closest model for Masolino's design, the pope holds a pointer, not a hoe.

97. On Masolino's attention to the details of Rome's topography, see Silvia Maddalo, *In figura Romae: Immagini di Roma nel libro medioevale* (Roma, 1990), 170–183.

98. On the changing location of the triptych in the 15th and 16th centuries, see Anna Cavallaro, *La pittura Rinascimentale a Roma da Martin V ad Alessandro VI (1420–1503)* (Roma, 2001), 19–20.

99. On the ways in which the original plan of the triptych was changed in the midst of its composition, see M. Meiss, "The Altered Program of the Santa Maria Altarpiece," in *Studien zur toskanischen Kunst. Festschrift für Ludwig Heinrich Heydenreich* (München, 1964), 169–190. Meiss's study has been updated thanks to new technologies. Carl Strehlke and Mark Tucker, "The Santa Maria Maggiore Altarpiece: New Observations," *Arte cristiana* 75 (1987): 105–124; Strehlke, *The Panel Paintings,* 111–129, 220–243; ———, "Sul polittico di Santa Maria Maggiore," in *Masaccio e Masolino, pittori e frescanti: dalla tecnica allo stile,* ed. Cecilia Frosini (Milano, 2004), 223–235.

100. Ulrich Richental, "Chronicle," in *The Council of Constance: The Unification of the Church,* trans. Louise Loomis (New York, 1961), 166–168.

101. Cardinals Giacomo (cardinal from 1278–1318) and Pietro (cardinal from 1288–1326) Colonna commissioned some of the basilica's mosaics, and both Pietro and Cardinal Agapito (cardinal from 1278–1280) were buried there. Cardinal Sirleto, "Brevis Tractatus di Basilica Sancta Mariae Maioris," in MS Vatican City, Chigiani G III 79, f. 22–22v, 27–27v. The Colonna were also important in the late medieval revival of the area around Santa Maria Maggiore. Charles Burroughs, *From Signs to Design: Environmental Process and Reform in Early Renaissance Rome* (Cambridge, MA, 1990), 140–141.

102. For a vivid account of the Assumption Eve procession, see Herbert Kessler and Johanna Zacharias, *Rome 1300: On the Path of the Pilgrim* (New Haven, 2000), 65–157. This procession was one of the most enduring elements of the stational liturgy; the last record of it dates from 1509. Sible De Blaauw, *Cultus et Decor: Liturgia e architettura nella Roma tardoantica e medievale* (Città del Vaticano, 1994), vol. 1, 420–421. For more on Rome's holy images and the confraternities to which they were entrusted, see Barbara Wisch, "Keys to Success: Propriety and Promotion of Miraculous Images by Roman

Confraternities," in *The Miraculous Image in the Late Middle Ages and Renaissance*, ed. Erik Thuno and Gerhard Wolf (Rome, 2004), 161–184. Gerhard Wolf "Per uno studio delle immagini devozionali e del culto delle immagini a Roma tra medio evo e Rinascimento," ASRSP 132 (2009): 109–132.

103. Blaauw, *Cultus et Decor,* vol. 1, 398–400.

104. L. Vayer, "Analecta iconographica masoliniana," *Acta Historiae Artium* (1965): 219–224.

105. Meiss, "The Altered Program," 178. On the ways in which Raphael's Stanze construct a distinctively Julian image of papal authority, see Bram Kempers, *Painting, Power and Patronage: The Rise of the Professional Artist in the Italian Renaissance,* trans. Beverley Jackson (London, 1992), 254–263.

106. Wisch, "Keys to Success," 165–166.

107. Paola Pavan, "Gli statuti della Società dei Raccomandati del Salvatore *ad Sancta Sanctorum* (1331–1496)" ASRSP 101 (1978): 35–96; ———. "La confraternita del Salvatore nella società Romana del Tre-Quattrocento," *Ricerche per la storia religiosa di Roma* 5 (1984): 81–90.

108. Anna Esposito, "Gli ospedali romani tra iniziative laicali e politica pontificia (sec. XIII–XV)," in *Ospedali e città: Italia del Centro-Nord: XIII–XVI secolo,* ed. Allen Greico and Lucia Sanrdi (Firenze, 1997), 235–242.

109. O'Fughludha, "Roma Nova," 120–121.

110. Verdi, *Maestri di edifici,* 24–27.

111. For an elegant study of Cinquecento propaganda, see Loren Partridge and Randolph Starn, *A Renaissance Likeness: Art and Culture in Raphael's* Julius II (Berkeley, CA, 1980).

112. On Renaissance Rome as the precursor to modern states, see Paolo Prodi, *The Papal Prince: One Body and Two Souls: The Papal Monarchy in Early Modern Europe* (Cambridge, 1987).

113. On the sophisticated propaganda programs of Augustus and Louis XIV, see Paul Zanker, *The Power of Images in the Age of Augustus,* trans. Alan Shapiro (Ann Arbor, 1988); Peter Burke, *The Fabrication of Louis XIV* (New Haven, 1994).

2. In the Theater of Lies: Curial Humanists on the Benefits and Evils of Courtly Life

1. Concetta Bianca, "Dopo Constanza: Classici e umanisti," in *Alle origini,* 108. Loschi was a papal secretary from 1406 to 1436. On his writings and career, see Giovanni da Schio, *Sulla vita e sugli scritti di Antonio Loschi* (Padova, 1858); Paolo Viti, "Loschi, Antonio," in *DBDI,* vol. 66, 154–166.

2. George Holmes, *The Florentine Enlightenment, 1400–1450* (Oxford, 1992), 63–69.

3. Eugenius did study Greek. Giovanni Mercati, "Intorno a Eugenio IV, Lorenzo Valla and Fra Ludovico di Strassoldo," *Rivista di storia della Chiesa in Italia* 5 (1951): 43–47.

4. Poggio Bracciolini, "In Funere D. Francisci Cardinalis Florentini," in *Opera Omnia*, ed. Riccardo Fubini (Torino, 1964–1969), vol. 1; ———, *Lettere*, ed. Helene Harth (Firenze, 1984–1987), vol. 2, 157–163.

5. Compare James Hankins, "Cosimo de' Medici as a Patron of Humanistic Literature," in *Cosimo 'il Vecchio' de' Medici, 1389–1464*, ed. Francis Ames-Lewis (Oxford, 1992), 69–94.

6. John D'Amico, *Renaissance Humanism in Papal Rome: Humanists and Churchmen on the Eve of the Reformation* (Baltimore, 1983), 9.

7. On Manuel Chrysoloras (1355–1415) and his influence in Italy see: Michael Baxandall, *Giotto and the Orators: Humanist Observers of Painting in Italy and the Discovery of Pictorial Composition, 1350–1450* (Oxford, 1971), 78–97; Christine Smith, *Architecture in the Culture of Early Humanism: Ethics, Aesthetics, and Eloquence, 1400–1470* (Oxford, 1992), 150–170; James Hankins, "Manuel Chrysoloras and the Greek Studies of Leonardo Bruni," in *Humanism and Platonism in the Italian Renaissance: vol. I Humanism* (Roma, 2003), 243–271.

8. On the income and expenses of the Avignon popes, see Fausto Caselli, "L'espasione delle fonti finanziarie della Chiesa nel XIV secolo," *ASRSP* 110 (1987): 63–97.

9. On Innocent VII (1404–1406) as a patron of humanists, see Germano Gualdo, "Antonio Loschi, Segretario Apostolico (1406–1436)," in *Diplomatica pontificia e umanesimo curiale: Con altri saggi sull'Archivio Vaticano, tra Medioevo ed età moderna*, ed. Rita Cosma (Roma, 2005), 372–373.

10. Between 1418 and 1423 Poggio lived in England, in the employment of Henry Beaufort, Bishop of Winchester. Bracciolini, *Lettere*, vol.1, 10–59. English translations of Poggio's letters to Niccolò Niccoli (vol. 1 of the Harth edition) can be found in Poggio Bracciolini, *Two Renaissance Book Hunters: The Letters of Poggius Bracciolini to Nicolaus de Niccolis*, trans. Phyllis Gordan (New York, 1974). For Poggio's biography, see Ernst Walser, *Poggius Florentinus: Leben und Werke* (Leipzig, 1914); Armando Petrucci, "Bracciolini, Poggio," in *DBDI*, vol. 13, 640–646.

11. Est dissensio imo lis et fere iurgium inter secretarios et advocatos utri sint digniori gradu ponendi penes pontificem, velut in coronatione, in missa, in processione. Atque hoc inde processit, quod cum pontifex nuper processionem faceret, nos petivimus ab episcopo Electensi quo loco iremus. At ille dixit: "Post advocatos propinquiores domino nostro." Hoc cum fecissemus, illi egre tulerunt, reclamantes nos debere preire. Denique post eo deventum est clamoribus eorum qui semper lites et iurgia tractant, ut committeretur cardinalibus Sancti Eustachii et Sancti Marci, qui nos audirent et referrent. Papa nobiscum est. Sed nosti eius humanitatem; nescit contraire importunitati eorum. Dicunt enim in coronationibus summorum pontificum secretarios semper preisse et se esse loco digniori penes papam. Episcopus Aretinus negat; nam is solus est quem habeamus ex iis qui interfuerunt coronationibus pontificum. Ideo tu, cuius est

dignitatem officii nostri tueri, adversus istos foraneos declamatores, assiste nobis et scribe quid observari vidisti et quid tibi videatur. Deinde scribe pontifici, ut dignitatem familiarium suorum tueatur. Nullum est enim dubium eos, qui secreta principum tractant, dignioris esse officii illis, qui tanquam publicani latrant propter questum ad unius etiam lenonis voluntatem. . . . Nam si ita est, ut olim secretarii propinquiores fuerint pape, nunc vero negligantur, ignominia erit officii sempiterna. Bracciolini, *Lettere,* vol. 2, 70.

12. Robert Darnton, *The Great Cat Massacre and Other Episodes in French Cultural History* (New York, 1985), 107–144.

13. The fight for precedence between the secretaries and lawyers continued into the 1470s. D'Amico, *Renaissance Humanism in Papal Rome,* 29–32.

14. Brigide Schwarz, "L'organizzazione curiale di Martin V ed i problemi derivanti dallo Scisma," in *Alle origini,* 329–345.

15. John A. F. Thomson, *Popes and Princes 1417–1517: Politics and Polity in the Late Medieval Church* (London, 1980), 95–113.

16. For lists of Martin V's curialists, see Francois-Charles Uginet, ed., *Le liber officialium de Martin V* (Roma, 1975). A total of approximately 6,000 people worked in and around the Curia during the sixteen-year reign of Eugenius IV. Hermann Diener, "Gli officiali della Cancelleria pontificia nel secolo XV e la loro attività nelle arti e nelle lettere," in *Cancelleria e cultura nel Medio Evo,* ed. Germano Gualdo (Città del Vaticano, 1990), 324.

17. The average curial career was twenty–four years. Peter Partner, *The Pope's Men: The Papal Civil Service in the Renaissance* (Oxford, 1990), 93.

18. The Curia also included the *Rota* (a court), the Penitentiary, and the Camera; for helpful summaries of its structure, see D'Amico, *Renaissance Humanism in Papal Rome,* 19–35; Walter Ullmann, *A Short History of the Papacy in the Middle Ages* (London, 1972), 527–550.

19. Hofmann's study remains the most authoritative account of the early Renaissance chancery. Walther von Hofmann, *Forschungen zur Geschichte der Kurialen Behorden vom Schisma bis zur Reformation* (Rom, 1914). See also Harry Bresslau, *Handbuch der Urkundenlehre für Deutschland und Italien* (Leipzig, 1912), vol. 1, 287–352; Paulius Rabikauskas, *Diplomatica Ponticifia: Praelectionum lineamenta* (Rome, 1972), 75–140. On the form and paleography of documents produced by the chancery, see ———, *Die römische Kuriale in der Päpstlichen Kanzlei* (Rome, 1958); Thomas Frenz, *Papsturkunden des Mittelalters und der Neuzeit* (Stuttgart, 1986).

20. Secretaries first emerged in the pontificate of Benedict XII (1334–1342). Hofmann, *Forschungen zur Geschichte der Kurialen,* vol. 1, 142–150.

21. On the workings of the Camera, see William Lunt, *Papal Revenues in the Middle Ages* (New York, 1934), vol. 1, 3–136; Peter Partner, *The Papal State under Martin V: The Administration and Government of the Temporal Power in the early Fifteenth Century* (London, 1958); ———. "The 'Budget' of the Roman Church in the Renaissance Period," in *Italian Renaissance Studies,* ed. E. F. Jacob (London,

1960), 256–278; ———. "Papal Financial Policy in the Renaissance and Counter-Reformation," *Past and Present* 88 (1980): 17–62; Maria Ruggiero, *La reverenda camera apostolica e i suoi archivi, secoli xv–xviii* (Roma, 1984); Luciano Palermo, "Capitali pubblici e investimenti privati nell'amministrazione finanziaria della città di Roma all' epoca di Martino V," in *Alle origini,* 501–535.

22. On the collaboration of popes and individual secretaries, see Germano Gualdo, "Umanesimo e segretari apostolici all' inizio del Quattrocento: Alcuni casi esemplari," in *Cancelleria e Cultura,* 308.

23. The number of humanist secretaries gradually increased, especially under Pius II. Andreas Kraus, "Die Sekretäre Pius' II: Ein Beitrag zur Entwicklungsgeschichte des päpstlichen Sekretariats," *Römische Quartalschrift für christliche Altertumskunde und Kirchengeschichte* 53 (1958): 25–80.

24. In addition to the works already cited, see John O'Malley, *Praise and Blame in Renaissance Rome: Rhetoric, Doctrine, and Reform in the Sacred Orators of the Papal Court, c. 1450–1521* (Durham, 1979).

25. On the importance of personal relations in a patronage-based society, see Ronald Weissman, "Taking Patronage Seriously: Mediterranean Values and Renaissance Society," in *Patronage, Art, and Society in Renaissance Italy,* ed. F. W. Kent and Patricia Simons (Oxford, 1987), 25–45.

26. Jerry Bentley, *Politics and Culture in Renaissance Naples* (Princeton, 1987), 84–137.

27. Marcel Mauss, *The Gift: The Form and Reason for Exchange in Archaic Societies,* trans. W.D. Halls (New York and London, 1990); Natalie Zemon Davis, *The Gift in Sixteenth-Century France* (Madison, 2000), 3–22, 34–66.

28. Christopher Celenza, "Parallel Lives: Plutarch's 'Lives,' Lapo da Castiglionchio the Younger (1405–1438) and the Art of Italian Renaissance Translation," *Illinois Classical Studies* 22 (1997): 121–155.

29. On Chrysoloras's preference for Plutarch, see Manuel Chrysoloras, "Letter to Salutati," in *Epistolario di Coluccio Salutati,* ed. Franceso Novati (Roma, 1891–1911), vol. 4, 341–343; Ernesto Berti, "Manuele Crisolora, Plutarco e l' avviamento delle traduzioni umanistiche," *Fontes* 1 (1998): 81–99.

30. Little is known about Antonio Pacini (often called Tudertino because he was from Todi), who studied under Filelfo and translated six of Plutarch's *Lives.* For bibliography on Pacini see Simona Iaria, "Un discepolo di Ambrogio Traversari: Fra Michele di Giovanni Camaldolese" *Italia medievale e umanistica* 45 (2004) note 45.

31. Quis enim est qui iustitiae amore non ardescat si Aristidem Atheniensem legat? Quis est qui animi libidinem non extingueret atque castitatem coleret, si Alexandrum Darii filias mira et singulari pulchritudine ornatas accuratissime intactas seruauisse audiuerit? Quis legendo Fabricii fortitudinem non admiraretur et coleret, qui neque auro neque terrore ingentis bestiae a feroci Pirro sua animi magnitudine dimoueri potuit? Nescio profecto quid sit, quod magis animos nostros ad colendas uirtutes trahere possit, quam ipsa rerum gestarum cognitio. Quis

est qui se omnino litterarum studiis non deuoueret si aut Platonem in Egiptum proficiscentem studiorum gratia legeret, aut Apollonium Arabiam Syriam Persas, Medos disciplinae causa petentem audiret? Marianne Pade, *The Reception of Plutarch's* Lives *in Fifteenth-Century Italy* (Copenhagen, 2007), vol. 2, 64–65.

32. Although examples play a significant role in Aristotelian rhetorical theory, it was the Romans and Hellenistic Greeks who insisted upon the exemplary value of history. Donald Kelley, *Faces of History: Historical Inquiry from Herodotus to Herder* (New Haven, 1998), 48–74; Reinhart Kosselleck, "*Historia Magistra Vitae:* The Dissolution of the Topos into the Perspective of a Modernized Historical Process," in *Futures Past: On the Semantics of Historical Time,* trans. Keith Tribe (New York, 2004), 26–42. On Petrarch's revival of this understanding of history, see Benjamin Kohl, "Petrarch's Prefaces to *De viris illustribus,*" *History and Theory* 13 (1974): 132–144.

33. For the influence of Plutarch on Bruni's historical method, see Gary Ianziti, *Writing History in Renaissance Italy: Leonardo Bruni and the Uses of the Past* (Cambridge, MA, 2012), 7–60. On other early Quattrocento humanists who did not simply regurgitate the exemplar theory of history, see Robert Black, "The New Laws of History," *Renaissance Studies* 1 (1987): 126–156; Anthony Grafton, "Historia and *Istoria:* Alberti's Terminology in Context," *I Tatti Studies: Essays in the Renaissance* 8 (1999): 37–68; ———. "The Identities of History in Early Modern Europe: Prelude to a Study of the *Artes Historicae,*" in *Historia: Empiricism and Erudition in Early Modern Europe,* ed. Nancy Siraisi and Gianna Pomata (Cambridge, MA, 2005), 41–74; ———. *What Was History? The Art of History in Early Modern Europe* (Cambridge, 2007), 49–61.

34. Max Lehnerdt, "Cencio und Agapito de' Rustici: Neue Beitrage zur Geschichte des Humanismus in Italien, mitgeteilt," *Zeitschrift für vergleichende literatur-geschichte und renaissance-litteratur* 14 (1900): 164. On this dedication, see James Hankins, *Plato in the Italian Renaissance* (Leiden, 1991), 81–84. Cencio (1390–1445) became a scriptor in 1411 and a papal secretary in 1417.

35. See, for example, Traversari's dedication of the *Life of Athanasius* to Cesarini, Lorenzo Mehus, ed. *Ambrosii Traversarii Generalis Camaldulensium aliorumque ad ipsum et ad alios de eodem Ambrosio Latinae epistolae* (Forni, 1968), vol. 2, cols. 960–961.

36. Ibid., col. 958.

37. On Traversari's devotion to patristic studies and his dedications to Eugenius IV, see Charles Stinger, *Humanism and the Church Fathers: Ambrogio Traversari (1386–1439) and Christian Antiquity in the Italian Renaissance* (Albany, 1977), 83–166.

38. Quia cognitione dignam putavi et ad rei publicae regimen utilissimam tuo in nomine perscripsi, qui rei publicae ecclesiasticae gubernaculis diu versatus es ac continuo versaris. Hanc si Dominatio tua pro sua egregia huius dicendi facultatis eruditione ac ingenio singulari paulo diligentius legerit, comperiet ex parte quibus studiis quibusque artibus rerum publicarum status

pereat et quibus servetur augeaturque. Dean Lockwood, "De Rinuccio Aretino Graecarum litterarum interprete," *Harvard Studies in Classical Philology* 24 (1913): 87. Condulmer (1390–1453) was made a cardinal immediately after the ascension of his uncle, Eugenius IV, and served as the pope's Chamberlain. A. Olivieri, "Condulmer, Francesco," in *DBDI*, vol. 27, 761–765. In the 1410s, Rinuccio (c. 1395–1450) traveled to Constantinople, where he collected many Greek manuscripts. Under Eugenius, he became a scriptor and a guard of the apostolic chancery; he was made a secretary by Nicholas V or Calixtus III (1455–1458). Hankins, *Plato in the Italian Renaissance*, 85–89; Partner, *The Pope's Men*, 47–51.

39. Mehus, ed. *Ambrosii Traversarii . . . epistolae*, vol. 2, cols 955–957.

40. Quapropter cum cuperem et ipse non privato aliquo abs te officio sed communi beneficio affectus tibi, quantum mea fert facultas, gratias agere et in alicuius excellentissimi philosophi vita tuas virtutes divinas atque admirabiles collaudare, et si neminem ex omni antiquitatis memoria reperire possem, qui tecum illa ex parte comparandus foret, attamen Solonis Atheniensis res gestae mihi ex omnibus maxime cum tuis convenire visae sunt, qui et sapiens fuit unus ex septem et legumlator solus ex septem. Atqui huic tu non virtute solum, sed fortuna etiam antecellis, nam ille Croesi opulentissimi regis Lydorum thesauros contempsit, quod saepe superbia et insolentia fit, tu proprios effudisti. Ille unam urbem suis legibus non potuit continere, tuis vero populi pene infiniti obtemperant. Ille patriam, quam liberam, et magnae parti Greciae imperantem acceperat, tyranno oppressam et seruientem reliquit, tu Romanae ecclesiae spoliatae, et sub iugum pene missae libertatem suam imperiumque reddidisti. Quare quod pridem tibi polliciti sumus, beatissime pater, Solonem ipsum ad sanctitatem tuam attulimus, non ut imiteris, nec enim tibi opus est, sed ut quam longe superasse laetere. Cuius instituta vitae, si tibi probabilia in legendo videbuntur, debebunt te admonere, ut eos homines, qui spe tuae humanitatis erecti ad eius doctrinam et sapientiam, quoad possunt suis studiis pervenire, contendunt, ut consuesti, et confirmes et adiuves. Pade, *Reception*, vol. 2, 34–35.

41. For another interpretation of this dedication, see Ibid., vol. 1, 275–280.

42. Compare Margaret Meserve, *Empires of Islam in Renaissance Historical Thought* (Cambridge, MA, 2008), 117–154.

43. Lehnerdt, "Cencio und Agapito de' Rustici," 160.

44. Lockwood, "De Rinuccio Aretino," 96.

45. Lapo, dedication of translation of Plutarch's *Life of Theseus* to Prospero Colonna, in Pade, *Reception*, vol. 2, 17–20.

46. Priscos philosophos tam Graecos quam Latinos, praestantissime domine, siquid laude dignum eorum industria uigilando litterarum monumentis quandoque mandassent, consueuisse legimus uel amicissimis suis uel

regiis uiris illud dedicasse, ut et illos laude gloriaque immortali afficerent et libros eorum auctoritate quadam illustrarent. Quod non modo Platonem et Aristotelem ac Homerum et Virgilium, uerumetiam diuinarum rerum scriptores Hieronymum et Augustinum fecisse reperimus. . . . Nam et res egregie gestas in lucem ad exemplum aliorum expromebant, et virtutem illorum, quibus libros suos dedicarant, claram et laudibus celebratam efficiebant. Dedication of a translation of Plutarch's *Life of Theseus* to Cardinal Acciapaccio, in Pade, *Reception,* vol. 2, 21. Written between 1439 and 1447.

47. Ludwig Pastor, *The History of the Popes from the Close of the Middle Ages,* trans. Frederick Antrobus (London, 1906), vol. 1, 256–259, 303–307.

48. Charles Trinkaus, *Adversity's Noblemen* (New York, 1940); Anthony Grafton, *Leon Battista Alberti: Master Builder of the Italian Renaissance* (New York, 2000), 31–70; Christopher Celenza, *The Lost Italian Renaissance: Humanists, Historians, and Latin's Legacy* (Baltimore, 2004), 115–133.

49. On Lapo's epistolary collection, see Elizabeth McCahill, "Finding a Job as a Humanist: The Epistolary Collection of Lapo da Castiglionchio the Younger," *Renaissance Quarterly* 57 (2004): 303–323.

50. For historical works on brokers, see Sharon Kettering, *Patrons, Brokers, and Clients in Seventeenth Century France* (1986); Mario Biagioli, *Galileo, Courtier: The Practice of Science in the Culture of Absolutism* (Chicago, 1993), 1–101; Sharon Kettering, "Brokerage at the Court of Louis XIV," *Historical Journal* 36 (1993): 69–87; Anne Goldgar, *Impolite Learning: Conduct and Community in the Republic of Letters 1680–1750* (New Haven, 1995), 12–53; Susanne Saygin, *Humphrey, Duke of Gloucester (1390–1447) and the Italian Humanists* (Leiden, 2002), 144–200.

51. Verum insperato quodam et inopinato eventu atque exitu sic perturbatus sum, ut haec nostra studia, quae semper coluissem et in quibus bonam aetatis meae partem versatus essem, et a quibus omnia praesidia ornamenta decus dignitatem quietem denique petenda esse statuissem, odisse iam coeperim. Etenim quamquam ab initio nulla honoris et gloriae cupiditate, sed tantum voluntate et delectatione adductus et spe quadam excolendae vitae, contemptis abiectisque ceteris rebus omnibus, me ad harum ingenuarum et humanarum artium studia contulissem; attamen paulo in his provectus, cum et legissem saepissime et audissem quanto ea in honore apud maiores extitissent, quanta et quam amplissima praemia splendorem dignitatem a clarissimis eius aetatis principibus earum studiosi homines assequi consuessent, non immutata quidem priori sententia sed mehercule labefactata parumper, ad ea ipsa sic animum intendere coepi non ut prae illis honestatem abiiciendam putarem sed cum illis coniunctam appetere. Itaque veterum exemplis propositis, horum temporum horum hominum horum morum, totius denique rationis ignarus, fore existimabam ut, cum his litteris non dico imbutus et ornatus sed leviter tinctus prodirem, ad omnes vel amplissimos honores et dignitatis gradus facilis pateret aditus; nec eos petendos esse aut desiderandos, sed

ultro vel invito recusanti deferendos esse. . . . In quo longe aliter evenit atque eram opinatus. Incidimus enim in ea tempora, in quibus nullus non modo rectis studiis bonis[que] artibus honos propositus, sed nec virtuti quidem et probitati locus relictus esse videatur. Lapo da Castiglionchio, "Studi su l'epistolario e le traduzioni di Lapo da Castiglionchio Juniore," ed. F. P. Luiso, *Studi Italiani di filologia classica* 8 (1899): 235.

52. On Petrarch's interrogation of the patronage system, see William Kennedy, "Versions of a Career: Petrarch and His Renaissance Commentators," in *European Literary Careers: The Author from Antiquity to the Renaissance*, ed. Patrick Cheney and Frederick de Armas (Toronto, 2002), 146–164.

53. See, for example, Castiglionchio, "Studi su l'epistolario," 225.

54. Compare Paul McLean, "A Frame Analysis of Favor Seeking in the Renaissance: Agency, Networks and Political Culture," *American Journal of Sociology* 104 (1998): 51–91; ———, *The Art of the Network: Strategic Interaction and Patronage in Renaissance Florence* (Durham, 2007).

55. When writing to younger scholars, Lapo indulges in exaggerated praise of the *studia humanitatis*. MS Vatican City, Ott. Lat. 1677, f. 154v–156v, 218v–226v.

56. Leonardo Bruni, *Epistolarum libri VIII*, ed. James Hankins (Roma, 2007), 1–6.

57. On the humanist job market in the 1430s, see Germano Gualdo, "Francesco Filelfo e la curia pontificia: Una carriera mancata" e la curia pontificia," *ASRSP* 102 (1979): 189–236; Saygin, *Humphrey, Duke of Gloucester*, 205–217.

58. On the European-wide popularity of the *Facetiae*, see Lionello Sozzi, "Le 'Facezie' di Poggio nel Quattrocento francese," in *Miscellanea di studi e ricerche sul Quattrocento francese*, ed. Franco Simone (Torino, 1967), 412–516; Joanna Lipking, "The Traditions of the *Facetiae* and their Influence in Tudor England" (Ph.D. diss., Columbia University, 1970), 119–448; Lionello Sozzi, "Le *Facezie* e la loro fortuna Europea," in *Poggio Bracciolini 1380–1980: Nel VI centenario della nascita* (Firenze, 1982), 235–259.

59. Grafton, *Leon Battista Alberti*, 51.

60. For another analysis of how the *Facetiae* reflects and responds to the curial milieu, see Stephen Greenblatt, *The Swerve: How the World Became Modern* (New York, 2011), 135–154.

61. On recurrent character types in medieval and Renaissance stories, see Lauro Martines, *Strong Words: Writing and Social Strain in the Italian Renaissance* (Baltimore, 2001), 199–231. On Poggio's adaptation of ancient stories and medieval tales, see Armando Bisanti, "I temi del 'doppio' e del 'morto che parla': vitale di Blois, Giocanni Sercambi, Poggio Bracciolini," *Quaderni medievali* 29 (1990); ———, "Notorelle braccioliniane," *Maia* 44 (1992); ———, "La tradizione favolistica mediolatina nella letteratura italiana dei secoli XIV e XV," *Schede Medievali* 24–25 (1993); ———, "Dall' exemplum alla facezia: l'apologo dell'asino," *Esperienze letterarie* 22 (1994). These articles are revised in ———. *Tradizione retoriche e letterarie nelle* Facezie *di Poggio Bracciolini* (Cosenza, 2011).

62. The *Facetiae* was soon translated, and translations began to be published in 1483. Olimpia Cirelli, "I primi volgarizzamenti italiani delle 'Facezie' di Poggio," *Annali della facoltà lettere e filosofia dell Università di Bari* 25–26 (1982–1983):, 201–290. For contemporary joke collections, see Barbara Bowen, "Renaissance Collections of *Facetiae* 1344–1490: A New Listing," *Renaissance Quarterly* 39 (1986): 1–15.

63. Riccardo Fubini, *Humanism and Secularization from Petrarch to Valla,* trans. Martha King (Durham, NC, 2003), 1–8.

64. Germano Gualdo, "Leonardo Bruni Segretario Papale (1405–1415)," in *Diplomatica pontificia e umanesimo curiale,* 405–429.

65. Poggio Bracciolini, *Facezie,* trans. Marcello Ciccuto (Milano, 1983), 138–139, 174–175, 168–169.

66. Ibid., 132–133.

67. See Poggio Bracciolini, "De miseria conditionis humanae," in *Opera Omnia,* vol. 1; Bracciolini, *Lettere,* vol. 1, 45–59; vol. 2, 386–388, 393–395, 408–411.

68. Hans Baron, *In Search of Florentine Civic Humanism: Essays on the Transition from Medieval to Modern Thought* (Princeton, NJ, 1988), vol. 1, 3–23, 134–288.

69. Renaissance humanists inherited Stoicism secondhand in its Roman form. Brian Copenhaver and Charles B. Schmitt, *Renaissance Philosophy* (Oxford, 1992), 16–18; Jill Kraye, "The Revival of Hellenistic Philosophies" in *The Cambridge Companion to Renaissance Philosophy,* ed. James Hankins (Cambridge, 2007), 99–100.

70. Aeneas Silvius Piccolomini, *De curialium miseriis epistola,* ed. Wilfred Mustard (Baltimore, 1928). Piccolomini lived from 1405–1464 and became pope in 1458. On Piccolomini's career and influence in Northern Europe, see Thomas Mauro, "Praeceptor Austriae: Aeneas Sylvius Piccolomini (Pius II) and the Transalpine Diffusion of Italian Humanism Before Erasmus" (Ph.D. diss., University of Chicago, 2003), 1–29.

71. Juvenal, "Satire V," in *Juvenal and Persius* (Cambridge, Ma, 1940), 70–71.

72. Qualis coena tamen? Vinum quod succida nollet lana pati?' ut Iuvenalis ait, affertur quod cum biberis, insanus fias, acetosum, aquaticum, corruptum, pendulum, acerbum, aut frigidum nimis aut tepidum, colore saporeque malo. Taceo illos principes qui tantum ceruisiam in potu praebent, quae cum ubique amara sit, in curiis tamen et amarissima et stomachosissima est. Nec tibi vel in argento vel in vitro dari pocula credas; nanque in uno furtum timetur, in altero fractura. Potabis igitur ex ligneo scipho, nigro, antiquo, foetido, in cuius fundo faex concreta est, in quo saepe minxisse domini consueuerunt. Nec tibi uni sciphus dabitur ut, si velis, vel aquam misceas vel purum bibas, sed in communi potabis; atque ibi mordebis ubi nunc vel pediculosa barba vel salivosa labia vel immundissimi dentes fuerunt. Interea vinum antiquum in tua praesentia regi propinabitur, cuius tanta fragrantia est, ut eius odore tota

domus impleatur. Bibet ille muscatellum, aut maluaticum, ex Galliis, ex Matrigali, ex Riparia Ianuensi, ex Ungaria atque ex ipsa Graecia sibi afferri vina iubebit; nec unquam tibi vel minimum cyathum communicabit, quamvis cardiaca passione crucieris. Quod si bonum vinum ante te sit, non tamen iocunde sapiet, cum melioris frangrantiam tuae hauserint nares. Velles nonnunquam bibere, sed non audes, nisi maiores incipiant. Nec famuli vinum apponunt nisi post medium mensae; quod si ante petieris, et importunus et petulans et ebriosus indicaberis; nec cum hac ignominia quod postulas obtinebis, nec ad tuam, sed ad maiorum sitim potabis. Vinum postquam in mensa fuerit, per multas manus transibit, antequam ad te veniat. Nec speres mundari sciphum, dum pincernae remiscent, quamvis in fundo faex haereat, vel intus aliquis ructaverit; nam sicut in templis aquae benedictae superinfunditur, sic in curiis principum vinaria vasa, quibus familiae potant, in anno semel evacuata mundantur. Piccolomini, *De curialium miseriis,* 43–44.

73. Claus Uhlig, *Hofkritik im England des Mittelalters und der Renaissance* (Berlin, 1973), 27–136; C. Stephen Jaeger, *The Origins of Courtliness: Civilizing Trends and the Formation of Courtly Ideals 939–1210* (Philadelphia, 1985), 54–66; ———. "Courtliness and Social Change," in *Cultures of Power: Lordship, Status, and Process in Twelfth Century Europe,* ed. Thomas Bisson (Philadelphia, 1995), 287–309.

74. William of Malmesbury, *Gesta Regum Anglorum* trans. R. A. B. Mynors (Oxford, 1998–1999), vol. 1, 560–561.

75. Peter of Blois, "Epistola XIV," in *Patrologia Latina,* ed. Jacques-Paul Migne (Paris, 1844–1864), vol. 207, col. 44–48. On Peter's letter as a source for Piccolomini, see Uhlig, *Hofkritik im England,* 182–185.

76. Walter Map, *De nugis curialium: Courtiers' Trifles,* trans. M. R. James (Oxford, 1983), 8–9.

77. Jaeger, *The Origins of Courtliness,* 54–66.

78. On Vegio's career and oeuvre, see Luigi Raffaele, *Maffeo Vegio: Elenco delle Opere* (Bologna, 1909).

79. On the limitations of Vegio's borrowing from Lucian, see David Marsh, *Lucian and the Latins* (Ann Arbor, 1998), 67–71.

80. Maffeo Vegio, *Maphei Vegii, sua aetate oratorum principis, Inter inferiora corpora, scilicet terram, aurum, & superiora, praesertim solem, elegantissima disputatio; eiusdem De miseria & felicitate dialogus* (Basileae, 1518), 45–46.

81. Tunc cernes eos pallere, tristari, consumi, expavere omnia, torqueri scelerum suorum conscientia, quae prima est poenarum omnium, timere hostium insidias, civium conspirationes, domesticorum perditiones, oppressorum vindi ctas. Tunc securum nihil existimare, nisi quod vi ac ferro tueantur. Propterea non credunt se tuto cuiquam non ministris, non necessariis, non germanis, quorum maiorem etiam quam aliorum autoritatem magis formidant. Arcent se ab aspectu et praesentia omnium, cingunt se fossis et aggeribus, claudunt se arcibus, quasi ad perpetuous damnati carceres. Ibid., 52.

82. Jacob Burckhardt, *The Civilization of the Renaissance in Italy*, trans. S. G. C. Middlemore (New York, 1990), 19–97.

83. Compare Virginia Cox, *The Renaissance Dialogue: Literary Dialogue in its Social and Political Contexts, Castiglione to Galileo* (Cambridge, 1992), 10–11.

84. Bracciolini, *Facezie*, 130–131.

85. Poggio Bracciolini, *De infelicitate principum*, ed. Davide Canfora (Roma, 1998). On Piccolimini's debt to Poggio, see Keith Sidwell, "Il *De curialium miseriis* di Enea Silvio Piccolomini e il *De mercede conductis* di Luciano," in *Pio II e la cultura del suo tempo: Atti del I convegno internazionale* (Milano, 1991), 329–341.

86. Compare Bracciolini, *Lettere*, vol. 2, 29–30, 181–188, 215–219.

87. Bracciolini, *De infelicitate principum*, 18.

88. Poggio Bracciolini, *De varietate fortunae*, ed. Outi Merisalo (Helsinki, 1993), 107.

89. On Poggio's claim that modern events equal those of antiquity, see Iiro Kajanto, *Poggio Bracciolini and Classicism: A Study in Early Italian Humanism* (Helsinki, 1987), 28–39; Fubini, *Humanism and Secularization*, 114–117. Compare Frederick Krantz, "Between Bruni and Machiavelli: History, Law and Historicism in Poggio Bracciolini," in *Politics and Culture in Early Modern Europe: Essays in Honor of H.G. Koenigsberger* ed. Phyllis Mack and Margaret C. Jacob (Cambridge 1987), 119–151.

90. Bracciolini, *De varietate fortunae*, 118. On Scaligeri, 121–122; on Trinci, 144; on Guidantonio, 149–150.

91. Some individuals whom the humanists do not condemn include Francesco il Vecchio and Ludovico Alidosi. Ibid., 122, 124–125.

92. Lapo da Castiglionchio, "De curiae commodis," in *Renaissance Humanism and the Papal Curia: Lapo da Castiglionchio the Younger's* De curiae commodis, ed. Christopher Celenza (Ann Arbor, 1999), 110–111.

93. Ibid., 136–137.

94. Ibid, 148–151.

95. For analyses of how Lapo balances praise and condemnation of the Curia in his work, see D'Amico, *Renaissance Humanism in Papal Rome*, 117–118; Partner, *The Pope's Men*, 114–118.

96. Celenza, *Renaissance Humanism and the Papal Curia*, 30–85.

97. Ibid., 36–45.

98. Bracciolini, *Facezie*, 138–141, 262–263, 322–323.

99. Ibid., 148–151, 348–349. The jokes on 144–145 and 364–367 further emphasize Foschi's unsuitability. Foschi became a cardinal on the election of Eugenius and remained a favorite of the pope until his death in 1444. Partner, *The Pope's Men*, 48–51.

100. Poggio's fiercest political commentary is directed at the rival popes of the period just prior to the Council of Constance. Bracciolini, *Facezie*, 142–143, 170–173, 214–217.

101. On the fortune Poggio made while working for the Curia, see Lauro

Martines, *The Social World of the Florentine Humanists 1390–1460* (Princeton, 1963), 123–127.

102. Ibid., 267.

103. Non enim quia placeat mihi curia, ideo versor in curia, sed ne levitatis accuser, qui genus vitae receptum nesciverim persequi. Idem et te arbitror retinere. Accidit enim nobis sicut et coniugatis. Sunt enim admodum multi qui vivente coniuge matrimonium damnant et uxoris obitum cupiunt libertatis amore . . . at hi postquam libertatem sunt assecuti, mox alteram ducunt coniugem, ut vix quidem exequias defunctae valeant expectare. Sic enim est hominum cacetes [cacoethes], ut vitam quam vivunt diuque vixerunt, etsi malam sciunt, mutare tamen aut nesciant aut nequeant. Piccolomini, *De curialium miseriis*, 25.

104. See, for example, Bracciolini, *Lettere*, vol. 1, 34–37.

105. Francesco Petrarca, *Le familiari*, ed. Vittorio Rossi and Umberto Bosco, trans. Ugo Dotti (Racconigi, 2004–2009), vol. 5, 3494–3511.

106. For discussion of Petrarch's Stoicism, see Giuseppe Mazzotta, *The Worlds of Petrarch* (Durham, 1993), 87–91. See also Ronald Witt, *Hercules at the Crossroads: The Life, Works, and Thought of Coluccio Salutati* (Durham, 1983), 355–367; George McClure, *Sorrow and Consolation in Italian Humanism* (Princeton, NJ, 1991), 3–98.

107. Burckhardt, *Civilization*, 136.

3. A Reign Subject to Fortune: Guides to Survival at the Court of Eugenius IV

1. Nam raro tantam provinciis Romanae ecclesiae vastitatem, tantam calamitatem hominibus alterius attulit pontificatus. Bellis quassatae atque afflictae regiones, vastatae urbes, disiecta oppida, populati agri, itinera latrociniis infesta, multa ferro igneque assumpta, ad quinquaginta amplius loca aut diruta aut foede a militibus direpta, nullum genus saevitiae effugerunt. Plures dirutis opidis pro servis venundati, nonnulli carceribus enecti fame, Romam ipsam diutino bello afflictam amissis fortunis, omni spe subsidii destitutam novas res moliri et a pontifice desciscere desperatio coegit . . . satis constat nullo superiorum pontificatu adeo malam fortunam subditos ecclesiae Romanae fuisse expertos. Poggio Bracciolini, *De varietate fortunae*, ed. Outi Merisalo (Helsinki, 1993), 133–134.

2. Ibid., 152.

3. On the conclave that elected Eugenius, see Walter Brandmüller, "Der Ubergang von Pontifikat Martins V zu Eugen IV," *Quellen und Forschungen aus Italienischen Archiven und Bibliotheken* 47 (1967): 596–629.

4. For the financial conflict between Eugenius and the Colonna, see Andreas Rehberg, "'Etsi prudens paterfamilias . . . pro pace suorum sapienter providet': Le ripercussioni del nepotismo di Martino V a Roma e nel Lazio," in *Alle origini*, 265–269.

5. Stefano Infessura, *Diario della città di Roma di Stefano Infessura scribasenato,* ed. Oreste Tommasini (Roma, 1890), 26–28. On the rebellions of Eugenius's reign, see Anthony D'Elia, *A Sudden Terror: The Plot to Murder the Pope in Renaissance Rome* (Cambridge, MA, 2009), 40–51.

6. Ferdinand Gregorovius, *History of the City of Rome in the Middle Ages,* trans. Anne Hamilton (London, 1900–1909), vol. 7, part 1, 42–47.

7. For some new approaches to Quattrocento conciliarism, see Johannes Helmrath and Heribert Müller, *Die Konzilien von Pisa (1409), Konstanz (1414–1418) und Basel (1431–1449): Institution und Personen* (Ostfildern, 2007); Gerald Christianson, Thomas Izbicki, and Christopher Bellitto, eds., *The Church, the Councils, and Reform: The Legacy of the Fifteenth Century* (Washington, DC, 2008).

8. A council did meet at Pavia in 1423, but Martin V soon closed it due to poor attendance. See Walter Brandmüller, *Das Konzil von Pavia-Siena, 1423–1424* (Paderborn, 2002).

9. On the place of *Haec sancta* within the conciliarist tradition, see Brian Tierney, "Hermeneutics and History: the Problem of *Haec sancta,*" in *Essays in Medieval History Presented to Bertie Wilkinson,* ed. T. A. Sandquist and M. R. Powicke (Toronto, 1969), 354–370; ———, *Foundations of the Conciliar Theory: The Contribution of the Medieval Canonists from Gratian to the Great Schism* (Leiden, 1998), ix–xxix. See also Giuseppe Alberigo, *Chiesa conciliare: identità e significato del conciliarismo* (Brescia, 1981), 187–205, 340–354; Francis Oakley, *The Conciliarist Tradition: Constitutionalism in the Catholic Church, 1300–1870* (Oxford, 2003), 81–99; Michiel Decaluwe, "Three Ways to Read the Constance Decree *Haec sancta* (1415): Francis Zabarella, Jean Gerson and the Traditional Papal View of General Councils," in *The Church, the Councils, and Reform.* 122–139.

10. Et primo declarat, quod ipsa Synodus in spiritu sancto legitime congregata, generale concilium faciens, et ecclesiam militantem repraesentans, potestatem a Christo immediate habet, cui quilibet cuiuscumque status vel dignitatis, etiam si papalis exsistat, obedire tenetur in his quae pertinent ad fidem et exstirpationem dicti schismatis et ad generalem reformationem ecclesiae Dei in capite et in membris. Joachim Stieber, *Pope Eugenius IV, the Council of Basel and the Secular and Ecclesiastical Authorities in the Empire* (Leiden, 1978), 405–406.

11. Loy Bilderback, "Eugene IV and the First Dissolution of the Council of Basle," *Church History* 36 (1967), 243–253.

12. For a summary of national responses to the Councils, see John A. F. Thomson, *Popes and Princes 1417–1517: Politics and Polity in the Late Medieval Church* (London, 1980), 29–53.

13. Georg Hofmann, ed. *Epistolae pontificiae ad Concilium Florentinum spectantes* (Roma, 1940–1946), part 1, 21–22 and 24–25.

14. Michiel Decaluwe, *A Successful Defeat: Eugene IV's Struggle with the Council of Basel for Ultimate Authority in the Church, 1431–1449* (Bruxelles, 2009), 66–99.

15. Johannes Dominicus Mansi, ed. *Sacrorum conciliorum nova et amplissima collectio* (Venice, 1788), vol. 29, cols 48–52.

16. Alan Ryder, *Alfonso the Magnanimous, King of Aragon, Naples and Sicily 1396–1458* (Oxford, 1990), 214–241.

17. Nihil aliud est, quam potestatem summi Pontificis Christique vicarii in terris totaliter annihilare et supremam potestatem ipsi a Christo datam in manibus multitudinis ponere, quod est non tam erroneum, quam etiam ab omni doctrina sanctorum patrum totaliter alienum, immo toto statu catholicorum principum valde pernicosum, quoniam pari modo possent eorum populi si congregarentur, supra eos praetendere potestatem et sic episcoporum statum et politiam Christianam evertere, quod minime est dicendum aut tolerandum. Odoricus Raynaldus, *Annales Ecclesiastici* (Lucae, 1752), vol. 9, 203–204.

18. For the Council of Basel's ruling on annates and the role of the College of Cardinals, see Mansi, ed. *Sacrorum conciliorum nova et amplissima collectio*, vol. 9, cols. 104–108, 110–121.

19. On the protracted arguments about the location of the council with the Greeks, see Joseph Gill, *The Council of Florence* (Cambridge, 1959), 46–84. On the Greeks' limited understanding of the struggle between the pope and the Council of Basel, see John Meyendorff, "Was There an Encounter Between East and West at Florence?," in *Christian Unity: The Council of Ferrara-Florence 1438/39–1989*, ed. Giuseppe Alberigo (Leuven, 1991), 153–175.

20. Stieber, *Pope Eugenius IV*, 190–202.

21. For a speech that emphasizes the military problems of the Greeks, see Georgius Scholarius, *Orationes Georgii Scholarii in Concilio Florentino habitae*, trans. Joseph Gill, (Roma, 1964), 5–20. For a gloomy account of the Greeks' sojourn in Italy, see Silvester Syropoulus, *Vera historia unionis non verae inter Graecos et Latinos*, trans. R. Creyghton (Hagae-Comitis, 1660).

22. On the response to the decree in Constantinople, see Gill, *The Council of Florence*, 349–388.

23. According to Chadwick, "The Pope gained everything that he could imaginably have hoped to achieve." Henry Chadwick, "The Theological Ethos of the Council of Florence," in *Christian Unity*, 230.

24. Hofmann, *Epistolae pontificiae*, part 2, 101–106. See also ibid., "Etsi non dubitemus," part 3, 24–35.

25. Ibid., part 2, 123–138. Union with the Copts was announced in February 1442, while Eugenius was still in Florence. Ibid., part 3, 45–65.

26. Peter Partner, *The Lands of St. Peter: The Papal States in the Middle Ages and the Early Renaissance* (London, 1972), 410–413.

27. On Vitelleschi's entry as an evocation of a Roman triumph, see Charles Burroughs, *From Signs to Design: Environmental Process and Reform in Early Renaissance Rome* (Cambridge, MA, 1990), 141–142.

28. Infessura, *Diario della città di Roma*, 34–36.

29. Ludwig Pastor, *The History of the Popes from the Close of the Middle Ages*, trans. Frederick Antrobus (London, 1906), vol. 1, 299.

30. Carroll Westfall, *In this Most Perfect Paradise; Alberti, Nicholas V, and the Invention of Conscious Urban Planning in Rome, 1447–55* (University Park, PA, 1974), 63. D. S. Chambers, *Popes, Cardinals and War: The Military Church in Renaissance and Early Modern Europe* (London, 2006) 42–45.

31. Mario Caravale and Alberto Caracciolo, *Lo Stato pontificio da Martino V a Pio IX* (Torino, 1978), 56–65. Chambers, *Popes, Cardinals*, 45–46.

32. Infessura, *Diario della città di Roma*, 42.

33. Hofmann, ed. *Epistolae pontificae*, part 3, 96–99 and 105–108. It is not clear when the Council of Ferrara-Florence-the Lateran came to an end. Gill, *The Council of Florence*, 335–338.

34. On Frederick's shift of support from the Council to Eugenius, see Stieber, *Pope Eugenius IV,* 203–304. On the position of Charles VII and his court, see Heribert Müller, *Die Franzosen, Frankreich und das Basler Konzil (1431–1449)* (Paderborn, 1990), vol. 1, 345–471.

35. The concordat is recorded in the statutes of Paul II, Archivio Storico Capitolino, Rome, Cred. IV, tom. 88, f. 138r–143v. I consulted an incunabula of the statutes, INC Vatican City, Chig. II.362, f. 151v–165.

36. This is the longest section of the concordat. Ibid., 153v–163v. See Laurie Nussdorfer, *Brokers of Public Trust: Notaries in Early Modern Rome* (Baltimore, 2009), 45–47, 82–85, 93–96.

37. On Eugenius's changing attitude toward Rome's communal government, see Westfall, *In This Most Perfect Paradise*, 72–75; Caravale and Caracciolo, *Lo Stato pontificio*, 63–64.

38. Vespasiano da Bisticci, *Renaissance Princes, Popes, and Prelates: The Vespasiano Memoirs, Lives of Illustrious Men of the XVth Century*, trans. William George and Emily Waters (New York, 1963), 31; ———, *Le Vite*, ed. Aulo Greco (Firenze, 1970–76), vol. 1, 26–27.

39. On the disasters members of the Curia experienced as they fled from Rome in 1434, see Bracciolini, *De varietate fortune*, 135–136.

40. Elizabeth McCahill, "Rewriting Vergil, Rereading Rome: Maffeo Vegio, Poggio Bracciolini, Flavio Biondo, and early Quattrocento Antiquarianism," *Memoirs of the American Academy in Rome* 54 (2009): 184.

41. Marvin Becker, *Civility and Society in Western Europe, 1300–1600* (Bloomington, 1988), 57–58, 150–151; Franco Pignatti, "Studi recenti sulle *Facetiae* di Poggio Bracciolini," *Roma nel Rinascimento* (1996): 93–103.

42. On the ways in which stylistic imitation of Cicero and other ancient authors shaped humanist texts, see Michael Baxandall, *Giotto and the Orators: Humanist Observers of Painting in Italy and the Discovery of Pictorial Composition, 1350–1450.* (Oxford, 1971), 1–50; Ronald Witt, *In the Footsteps of the Ancients: The Origins of Humanism from Lovato to Bruni* (Leiden, 2000), 338–507.

43. Poggio Bracciolini, *Facezie*, trans. Marcello Ciccuto (Milano, 1983), 108–109.

44. Marcus Tullius Cicero, *De oratore*, trans. E. W. Sutton (Cambridge, MA, 1948), I.iii.12.

45. On the ways in which humanists transposed antiquity's claims for power of rhetoric from the spoken to the written word, see Hanna Gray, "Renaissance Humanism: the Pursuit of Eloquence," *JHI* 24 (1963): 503–505.

46. L. D. Reynolds, ed. *Texts and Transmission* (Oxford, 1983), 102–109.

47. Cicero, *De oratore*, II.lviii–lxxi; Aristotle, *The Poetics*, trans. W. Hamilton Fyfe (Cambridge, MA, 1953), v.1–7.

48. Cicero, *De oratore*, II.lviii.236–lix.239.

49. Ibid., II.liv.220; II.lxiv.260; II.lxix.280.

50. Bracciolini, *Facezie*, 250–251.

51. Cicero, *De oratore*, II.lviii.236.

52. Forty-five of the jokes of the *Facetiae* are attributed to a specific jokester.

53. Bracciolini, *Facezie*, 132–139.

54. Ibid., 226–229; 200–203.

55. Ibid., 238–239. Loschi's other three jokes are not directly related to a courtly context. Ibid., 208–211, 222–225, and 230–231.

56. Cicero, *De oratore*, II.lx.245–246; II.lxv.262.

57. Compare Norbert Elias, *The Established and the Outsiders: A Sociological Enquiry into Community Problems* (London, 1994), xviii–lii. See also Marcello Ciccuto, "Introduzione," in *Facezie*, 25–51; Peter Burke, *The Art of Conversation* (Ithaca, 1993), 67–68.

58. In saying that he wants to be read only by the witty and humane, Poggio issues a challenge of sorts. Bracciolini, *Facezie*, 110. Compare Leonardo Bruni, *Epistolarum libri VIII*, ed. James Hankins (Roma, 2007), 53–54.

59. Erving Goffman, *The Presentation of the Self in Everyday Life* (Garden City, NY, 1959), 22.

60. Compare Brian Krostenko, *Cicero, Catullus, and the Language of Social Performance* (Chicago, 2001), 202–232.

61. Goffman, *The Presentation of the Self*, 3–14.

62. Cicero, *De oratore*, III.i.1–ii.8; Bracciolini, *Facezie*, 408–409.

63. Francesco Tateo, "La raccolta delle 'Facezie' e lo stile 'comico' di Poggio," in *Poggio Bracciolini 1380–1980: Nel VI centenario della nascita* (Firenze, 1982), 229.

64. Armando Bisanti, *Tradizioni retoriche e letterarie nelle Facezie di Poggio Bracciolini* (Cosenza, 2011), 1–51. Bisanti does, however, identify rhetorical principles from Cicero's corpus in specific *facetiae*.

65. Cicero, *De oratore*, II.lxi.252.

66. Ibid, II.ii.5.

67. Ibid., II.lxvi.264.

68. Compare Nancy Struever, *The Language of History in the Renaissance: Rhetoric and Historical Consciousness in Florentine Humanism* (Princeton, NJ, 1970), 151–154.

69. Jennifer Richards, "Assumed Simplicity and the Critique of Nobility: Or,

How Castiglione Read Cicero," *RQ* 54 (2001): 460–486. Compare Daniel Javitch, *Poetry and Courtliness in Renaissance England* (Princeton, NJ, 1978), 20–49.

70. On the tension between Castiglione's memorialistic and didactic aims, see Wayne Rebhorn, "The Enduring Word: Language, Time, and History in 'Il Libro del Cortegiano,'" in *Castiglione: The Ideal and the Real in Renaissance Culture*, ed. Robert Hanning and David Rosand (New Haven, 1983), 69–90. On the way in which English humanists used Castiglione's text as a conversational guide, see Jennifer Richards, *Rhetoric and Courtliness in Early Modern Literature* (Cambridge, 2003), 43–64.

71. Baldesar Castiglione, *Il libro del Cortegiano*, ed. Walter Barberis (Torino, 1998), book 1, 58–60. For an excellent English translation, see ———, *The Book of the Courtier*, ed. Daniel Javitch, trans. Charles Singleton (New York, 2002). Hereafter "Barberis" and "Singleton." On the relation of *sprezzatura* to *grazia*, see Eduardo Saccone, "'Grazia, sprezzatura, affettazione' in 'The Courtier,'" in *Castiglione*, 45–67.

72. Javitch, *Poetry and Courtliness*, 36.

73. Barberis and Singleton, book 1 #40.

74. On the humanists' preoccupation with prudence, see Victoria Kahn, *Rhetoric, Prudence, and Skepticism in the Renaissance* (Ithaca, 1985), 29–46.

75. Joseph Falvo, *The Economy of Human Relations: Castiglione's* Il Libro del Cortegiano (New York, 1992), 51–69. On laughter as a form of social control, see Henri Bergson, "Le Rire," in *Comedy*, ed. Wylie Sypher (Garden City, NY, 1956), 73–74.

76. Lapo da Castiglionchio, "De curiae commodis," in *Renaissance Humanism and the Papal Curia: Lapo da Castiglionchio the Younger's* De curiae commodis, ed. Christopher Celenza (Ann Arbor, 1999), 160–161. Compare JoAnn Cavallo, "Joking Matters: Politics and Dissimulation in Castiglione's 'Book of the Courtier,'" *RQ* 53 (2000): 421.

77. Barberis and Singleton, book 1, #17; book 2, #132–136. On the anxiety produced by the ideal of *sprezzatura*, see Harry Berger, *The Absence of Grace: Sprezzatura and Suspicion in Two Renaissance Courtesy Books* (Stanford, 2000), 9–25. *De politia litteraria* offers another account of the competitive environment of early Renaissance courts. J. P Perry, "A Fifteenth-Century Dialogue on Literary Taste: Angelo Decembrio's Account of Playwright Ugolino Pisani at the Court of Leonello d' Este," *RQ* 39 (1986): 613–643; Anthony Grafton and Brian Curran, "A Fifteenth-Century Site Report on the Vatican Obelisk," *JWCI* 58 (1995): 234–248; Anthony Grafton, *Commerce with the Classics: Ancient Books and Renaissance Readers*, (Ann Arbor, 1997), 19–52; Christopher Celenza, "Creating Canons in Fifteenth Century Ferrara: Angelo Decembrio's 'De politia litteraria,' 1.10," *RQ* 57 (2004): 43–98.

78. Norbert Elias, *The Civilizing Process: Sociogenetic and Psychogenetic Investigations*, trans. Edmund Jephcott (Malden, MA, 2000), 397.

79. Aldo Scaglione, *Knights at Court: Courtliness, Chivalry, and Courtesy from Ottonian Germany to the Italian Renaissance* (Berkeley, CA, 1991), 13–14.

80. Barberis and Singleton, book 1, #4.

81. Barberis and Singleton, book 2, #42.

82. Several jokes have homosexual innuendos. Barberis and Singleton, book 2, #61 and #63. On the jokes' misogyny, see Valeria Finucci, *The Lady Vanishes: Subjectivity and Representation in Castiglione and Ariosto* (Stanford, 1992), 77–103.

83. See, for example, Bracciolini, *Facezie,* 120–121.

84. Ibid., 260–263.

85. Ibid., 188–189.

86. Compare Giuseppe Lombardi, "Locande e letteratura," in *Taverne, locande e stufe a Roma nel Rinascimento* (Roma, 1999), 98–99.

87. Sergio Bertelli and Giulia Calvi, "Rituale, cerimoniale, etichetta nelle corti Italiane," in *Rituale, cerimoniale, etichetta,* ed. Sergio Bertelli and Giuliano Crifò (Milano, 1985), 12.

88. On the relationship between the courtier's behavior and his role as political counselor, see Wayne Rebhorn, *Courtly Performances: Masking and Festivity in Castiglione's* Book of the Courtier (Detroit, 1978), 177–204; Daniel Javitch, "'Il Cortegiano' and the Constraints of Despotism," in *Castiglione,* 17–28; Virginia Cox, *The Renaissance Dialogue* (Cambridge, 1992), 47–60; Stephen Kolsky, "Learning Virtue, Teaching Politics: Some Notes on Book IV of the *Cortegiano,*" in *Courts and Courtiers in Renaissance Northern Italy* (Aldershot, 2003), 5–7.

89. Elias, *The Civilizing Process,* 63. On the reception of *The Civilizing Process,* see Ronald Asch, "Introduction: Court and Household from the Fifteenth to the Seventeenth Centuries," in *Princes, Patronage, and the Nobility: The Court at the Beginning of the Modern Age c. 1450–1650,* ed. Ronald Asch and Adolf Birke (Oxford, 1991), 1–38; Jeroen Duindam, *Myths of Power: Norbert Elias and the Early Modern Court* (Amsterdam, 1994); Dennis Smith, "'The Civilizing Process' and 'The History of Sexuality': Comparing Norbert Elias and Michel Foucault," *Theory and Society* 28 (1999): 79–100.

90. On Castiglione's dialogue as a representation of Eliasian civility, see Jorge Arditi, *A Genealogy of Manners: Transformations of Social Relations in France and England from the Fourteenth to the Eighteenth Century* (Chicago, 1998), 101–113.

91. C. Stephen Jaeger, *The Origins of Courtliness: Civilizing Trends and the Formation of Courtly Ideals 939–1210* (Philadelphia, 1985), 127–175; Arditi, *A Genealogy of Manners,* 54–85.

92. Becker, *Civility and Society;* ———. "An Essay on the Quest for Identity in the Early Italian Renaissance," in *Florentine Essays* (Ann Arbor, 2002).

93. Jaeger, *The Origins of Courtliness,* 7–9.

94. Bracciolini, *Facezie,* 306–307.

95. Riccardo Fubini, *Humanism and Secularization from Petrarch to Valla,* trans. Martha King (Durham, NC, 2003), 118.

96. Compare Kahn, *Rhetoric, Prudence, and Skepticism*, 36–46.

97. Annick Paternoster, "Decorum and Indecorum in the 'Seconda redazione' of Baldassare Castiglione's 'Libro del Cortegiano,'" *Modern Language Review* 99 (2004): 622–634.

98. Cicero, *De oratore*, II.lvi.219.

99. Ibid., II.lvi.232–233.

100. Antonius emphasizes the orator's unique ability to teach virtue at Cicero, *De oratore*, II.ix.35. Ludovico insists that the courtier must be "a man of honor and integrity." Barberis and Singleton, book 1, # 41.

101. Stephen Kolsky, "Making and Breaking the Rules: Castiglione's Cortegiano," in *Courts and Courtiers*, 358–380.

102. Fubini, *Humanism and Secularization*, 53, 72–74.

103. See Victoria Kahn, "Virtù and the Example of Agathocles in Machiavelli's *Prince*," *Representations* 13 (1986): 63–83; Timothy Hampton, "Montaigne and the Body of Socrates: Narrative and Exemplarity in 'Essais,'" *MLN* 104 (1989): 880–898; ———. *Writing from History: The Rhetoric of Exemplarity in Renaissance Literature* (Ithaca, 1990); Victoria Kahn, "Habermas, Machiavelli, and the Humanist Critique of Ideology," *PMLA* 105 (1990): 464–476; Francois Rigolot et al., "The Crisis of Exemplarity," *JHI* 59 (1998): 557–624. For signs of the "crisis of exemplarity" in the works of Petrarch and Boccaccio, see Karlheinz Stierle, "Three Moments in the Crisis of Exemplarity: Boccacio-Petrarch, Montaigne, and Cervantes," *JHI* 59 (1998): 581–595; Timothy Kircher, ed. *The Poet's Wisdom: The Humanists, the Church and the Formation of Philosophy in the Early Renaissance* (Leiden, 2006), 99–184.

104. Luca D'Ascia and Stefano Simoncini, "Momo a Roma: Girolamo Massaini fra L' Alberti ed Erasmo," *Albertiana* 3 (2000): 83–103; Cesare Vasoli, "Potere e folla nel *Momus*," in *Leon Battista Alberti: Actes du Congrès International de Paris*, ed. Francesco Furlan (Torin, 2000), vol. I, 443–463.

105. Leon Battista Alberti, *Momus*, trans. Sarah Knight, (Cambridge, MA, 2003), 2–11. Alberti emphasizes laughter again in the prefaces to books 3 and 4. See J. H. Whitfield, "Momus and the Language of Irony," in *The Languages of Literature in Renaissance Italy*, ed. Peter Hainsworth et al. (Oxford, 1988), 37–38.

106. On the ways in which the *Facetiae* and *Momus* differ in stylistic approach and tone, see Stefano Pittaluga, "Leon Battista Alberti e Poggio Bracciolini," in *Alberti e la cultura del Quattrocento: Atti del convegno internazionale del Comitato nazionale VI centenario della nascita di Leon Battista Alberti*, ed. Roberto Cardini and Mariangela Regoliosi (Firenze, 2007), 375–386. For discussion of the parallels between Alberti's arguments in *Momus* and those of Poggio in *De infelicitate principum*, see Stefano Borsi, *Leon Battista Alberti e Roma* (Firenze, 2003), 9–153; Davide Canfora, "Leon Battista Alberti modello di letteratura politica in età umanistica," in *Alberti e la cultura del Quattrocento*, 699–717.

107. The diversity of scholarly interpretations of *Momus* speaks to the complexity of the text. See, for example, Lorenza Begliomini, "Note sull'opera

dell'Alberti Il 'Momus' e il 'De re aedificatoria,'" *Rinascimento* 12 (1972): 267–283; Alessandro Perosa, "Considerazioni su testo e lingua del 'Momus' dell'Alberti," in *The Languages of Literature in Renaissance Italy,* 45–62; Luca Boschetto, "Ricerche sul 'Theogenius' e sul 'Momus' di Leon Battista Alberti," *Rinascimento* 33 (1993): 3–52; ———. "Democrito e la fisiologia della follia: La parodia della filosofia e della medicina nel 'Momus' di Leon Battista Alberti," *Rinascimento* 35 (1995): 3–29; David Marsh, *Lucian and the Latins: Humor and Humanism in the Early Renaissance* (Ann Arbor, 1998), 114–129; Mario Martelli, "Minima in 'Momo' libello adnotanda," *Albertiana* 1–2 (1998–99): vol. 1, 105–119, vol. 2, 121–136; David Marsh, "Alberti and Apuleius: Comic Violence and Vehemence in the 'Intercenales' and 'Momus,'" in *LBA: Actes du Congrès International de Paris,* 405–427; Rinaldo Rinaldi, "'Momus Christianus': Altre fonti albertiane," in *Leon Battista Alberti e il Quattrocento: Studi in onore di Cecil Grayson e Ernst Gombrich,* ed. Luca Chiavoni, Gianfranco Ferlisi, and Maria Vittoria Grassi (Firenze, 2001), 141–191; Rino Consolo, "Spunti Virgiliani e Oraziani nel *Momus,*" in *Alberti e la tradizione: per lo "smontaggio" dei "mosaici" albertiani,* ed. Roberto Cardini and Mariangela Regoliosi (Firenze, 2007), 287–304; Stefano Borsi, *Nicolò V e Roma: Alberti, Angelico, Manetti e un grande piano urbano* (Firenze, 2009), 521–623.

108. For readings of Jupiter as Nicholas V, see Borsi, *Leon Battista Alberti e Roma,* 55–75; Riccardo Fubini, "Papato e storiografia nel Quattrocento," in *Storiografia dell'umanesimo in Italia da Leonardo Bruni ad Annio da Viterbo* (Roma, 2003), 223; Manfredo Tafuri, *Interpreting the Renaissance: Princes, Cities, Architects,* trans. Daniel Sherer (New Haven, 2006), 23–58; Stefano Borsi, "Momenti di tangenza tra 'Momus' e "Porcaria coniuratio,'" *Albertiana* 10 (2006): 69–98. For a reading of Jupiter as Eugenius IV, see Giovanni Ponte, *Leon Battista Alberti: Umanista e scrittore* (Genova, 1981), 79–89.

109. Alberti, *Momus,* 44–45, 100–103.

110. See Olivia Catanorchi, "Tra politica e passione: Simulazione e dissimulazione in Leon Battista Alberti," *Rinascimento* 45 (2005): 137–177.

111. Alberti, *Momus,* 202–239.

112. Ibid., 336–337.

113. Ibid., 352–353.

114. For Cicero's praise of arguments *in utramque partem,* see Cicero, *De oratore,* III.xxvii.107.

115. For Quattrocento suggestions that Momus was supposed to represent Bartolomeo Facio or Filelfo, see Ponte, *Leon Battista Alberti,* 81; Perosa, "Considerazioni su testo e lingua," 49–50. Tafuri argues that Momus can be seen as a spokesman for Alberti himself. Tafuri, *Interpreting the Renaissance,* 42–52. Compare Anthony Grafton, *Leon Battista Alberti: Master Builder of the Italian Renaissance* (New York, 2000), 309–311.

116. For Garin's emphasis on the gloomy side of Alberti's oeuvre, see Eugenio Garin, "Il pensiero di Leon Battista Alberti: caratteri e contrasti," *Rinascimento* 12 (1972): 3–20; ———. *Rinascite e rivoluzioni: Movimenti culturali dal XIV al XVIII*

secolo (Roma, 1975); Sebastiano Gentile, "Eugenio Garin (1909–2004) e Leon Battista Alberti," *Albertiana* 9 (2006): 3–27.

117. Stephen Greenblatt, *Renaissance Self-Fashioning* (Chicago, 1980), 1–9; Jacob Burckhardt, *The Civilization of the Renaissance in Italy,* trans. S. G. C. Middlemore (New York, 1990), 98–119, 270–289.

118. John Martin, *Myths of Renaissance Individualism* (New York, 2004), 1–20.

119. For this analogy, see Saccone, *"Grazia, sprezzatura, affettazione,"* 64.

4. Curial Plans for the Reform of the Church

1. Lapo da Castiglionchio, "De curiae commodis," in *Renaissance Humanism and the Papal Curia: Lapo da Castiglionchio the Younger's* De curiae commodis, ed. Christopher Celenza (Ann Arbor, 1999), 126–127.

2. On the similarities between these texts, see Giorgio Pullini, *Burle e facezie del '400* (Pisa, 1958), 77–106.

3. Giovanni Boccaccio, *The Decameron,* trans. Mark Musa and Peter Bondanella (New York and London, 1982), Day 3, story 10. On the fortunes of this stereotype in the 20th century, see John Van Engen, "The Christian Middle Ages as a Historiographical Problem," *AHR* 91 (1986): 519–552.

4. John Van Engen, "Late Medieval Anticlericalism: The Case of the New Devout," in *Anticlericalism in Late Medieval and Early Modern Europe,* ed. Peter Dykema and Heiko Oberman (Leiden, 1993), 19–20.

5. On the importance of giving context to anticlerical texts, see Mahadev Apte, *Humor and Laughter: An Anthropological Approach* (Ithaca, 1985), 261; Donald Weinstein, "Writing the Book on Italian Anticlericalism," in *Anticlericalism,* 309–313.

6. For a fierce attack on all branches of the clergy, see Alfred Coville, ed. *Le traité de la ruine de l'église de Nicolas de Clamanges* (Paris, 1936), 111–156.

7. Mario Fois, "Vescovo e chiesa locale nel pensiero ecclesiologico," in *Vescovi e diocesi in Italia dal XIV all metà del XVI secolo,* ed. Giuseppina Gasparini, Antonio Rigon, Francesco Trolese, and Gian Maria Varanini (Roma, 1990), 61–65; Enzo Petrucci "Vescovi e cura d'anime nel Lazio," in *Vescovi,* 537–542.

8. For a contemporary attack on the Curia, see z Krakowa Mateusx, *De praxi romanae curiae,* ed. Wladyslaw Senko (Wrocław, 1969), 77–95. See also Peter Partner, *The Pope's Men: The Papal Civil Service in the Renaissance* (Oxford, 1990), 150–182.

9. On the ways in which Florence's priests failed to perform their duties, see Richard Trexler, *Synodal Law in Florence and Fiesole: 1306–1518* (Città del Vaticano, 1971), 35–78. On problems with male and female monasteries in the early Quattrocento, see Ambrogio Traversari, "Itinerarium," in *Ambrogio Traversari e i suoi tempi,* ed. Alessandro Dini-Traversari (Firenze, 1912), 11–139; Marianna Cipriani, "La visita pastorale di Ermolao Barbaro (1455–1456) ad

alcuni monasteri femminili veronesi," *Rivista di storia della Chiesa in Italia* 59 (2005): 475–495.

10. Carolus Cocquelines, ed. *Bullarum, privilegiorum ac diplomatum romanorum pontificum amplissima collectio : cui accessere pontificum omnium, vitæ, notæ & indices opportuni* (Roma,1739–1744), vol. 3, part 3, 4–7.

11. On clerical concubinage in the 15th century, see Andre Vauchez, "Clerical Celibacy and the Laity," in *Medieval Christianity,* ed. Daniel Bornstein (Minneapolis, 2009), 179–203.

12. Compare Thomas Izbicki, "Forbidden Colors in the Regulation of Clerical Dress from the Fourth Lateran Council (1215) to the Time of Nicholas of Cusa (d. 1464)," *Medieval Clothing and Textiles* 1 (2005): 105–114.

13. Studies published in the series *Italia Sacra* offer evidence of the vigor of late medieval and early modern Italian religious culture. See also Richard Trexler, *Public Life in Renaissance Florence* (Ithaca, 1980); David Peterson, "Out of the Margins: Religion and the Church in Renaissance Italy," *RQ* 53 (2000): 835–879.

14. Gerald Strauss, "Ideas of 'Reformatio' and 'Renovatio' from the Middle Ages to the Reformation," in *Handbook of European History 1400–1600,* ed. Thomas Brady, Heiko Oberman, and James Tracy (Leiden, 1995), 1–30.

15. Giles Constable, *The Reformation of the Twelfth Century* (Cambridge, 1996), 3.

16. Walter Ullmann, *A Short History of the Papacy in the Middle Ages* (London, 1972), 279–305; Giuseppe Alberigo, *Chiesa conciliare: identità e significato del conciliarismo* (Brescia, 1981), 68–71.

17. The phrase "in capite et membris" originated in the papal chancery during or before the reign of Innocent III (1198–1216). Philip Stump, "The Influence of Gerhart Ladner's 'The Idea of Reform,'" in *Reform and Renewal in the Middle Ages and the Renaissance: Studies in Honor of Louis Pascoe,* ed. Thomas Izbicki and Christopher Bellitto (Leiden, 2000), 15–16.

18. Heiko Oberman, *Forerunners of the Reformation: The Shape of Late Medieval Thought* (New York, 1966); ———. *The Dawn of the Reformation: Essays in Late Medieval and Early Reformation Thought* (Grand Rapids, MI, 1986). Compare Erika Rummel, "Voices of Reform from Hus to Erasmus," in *Handbook of European History 1400–1600,* 61–91.

19. Anthony Black, *Council and Commune: the Conciliar Movement and the Fifteenth-Century Heritage* (London, 1979), 45–48; Alberigo, *Chiesa conciliare,* 241–289.

20. Louis Pascoe, *Jean Gerson: Principles of Church Reform* (Leiden, 1973); Johannes Helmrath, *Das Basler Konzil, 1431–1449: Forschungsstand und Probleme* (Cologne, 1987), 327–352; Louis Pascoe, *Church and Reform: Bishops, Theologians, and Canon Lawyers in the Thought of Pierre d'Ailly, 1351–1420* (Leiden, 2005); Petra Weigel, "Reform als Paradigma: Konzilien und Bettelorden," in *Die Konzilien von Pisa (1409), Konstanz (1414–1418) und Basel (1431–1449): Institution und*

Personen, ed. Johannes Helmrath and Heribert Müller (Ostfildern, 2007), 289–335; Gerald Christianson, Thomas Izbicki, and Christopher Bellitto, eds., *The Church, the Councils, and Reform: The Legacy of the Fifteenth Century* (Washington, DC, 2008). Europe was not divided simply between papalists and conciliarists; even at Basel, there was a range of different perspectives. Michiel Decaluwe, *A Successful Defeat: Eugene IV's Struggle with the Council of Basel for Ultimate Authority in the Church, 1431–1449* (Bruxelles, 2009), 155–166.

21. Carol Richardson, *Reclaiming Rome: Cardinals in the Fifteenth Century* (Leiden, 2009), 144.

22. For Pastor's praise of Eugenius's reform program, see Ludwig Pastor, *The History of the Popes from the Close of the Middle Ages,* trans. Frederick Antrobus (London, 1923), vol. 1, 356. See also Denys Hay, "Eugenio IV," in *DBDI,* vol. 43, 500.

23. For Capranica's biography see A.A. Strnad, "Capranica, Domenico," in DBDI, vol. 19, 147–153. The cardinal's career is discussed at more length at the end of this chapter and in chapter 5.

24. Philip Stump, *The Reforms of the Council of Constance* (Leiden, 1994), 167–169; Francis Oakley, *The Conciliarist Tradition: Constitutionalism in the Catholic Church* (Oxford, 2003), 45–48.

25. Est enim perfacile loqui in publicum belle atque ornate, sub agni habitu hominum sermones et vulgi famam captantes; sed, nisi que ore profers comprobes operando, neque tibi quidquam profeceris neque illis. Maius quiddam est virtus, maius, inquam, quam aut verbis inanibus monstrari possit aut ostentatione dicendi. Actum requirit et exercitium sui, alioquin ridicule tractatur: primum quia plus oculis credunt homines quam verbis; deinde quia longum est iter per precepta, per exempla vero breve, efficax et apertum. Prospicere boni viri vitam, mores intueri, considerare vivendi normam, permagnum est imitande virtutis incitamentum. Poggio Bracciolini, "Oratio ad patres reverendissimos," in *Umanesimo e secolarizzazione da Petrarca a Valla* (Roma, 1990), 318–319. For a similar criticism of reformist conciliarists, see Thomas Izbicki, "Reform and Obedience in Four Conciliar Sermons by Leonardo Dati, O.P.," in *Reform and Renewal,* 174–192.

26. Compare Constable, *The Reformation of the Twelfth Century,* 1–43.

27. Alberto Melloni, "L'istituzione e la Christianità: Aspetti dell'ecclesiologia latina nel retroterra delle discussioni del Concilio di Ferrara-Firenze," in *Christian Unity: The Council of Ferrara-Florence 1438/39–1989,* ed. Giuseppe Alberigo (Leuven, 1991), 471–489.

28. Vespasiano da Bisticci, *Renaissance Princes, Popes, and Prelates: The Vespasiano Memoirs, Lives of Illustrious Men of the XVth Century,* trans. William George and Emily Waters (New York, 1963), 29; ———. *Le Vite,* ed. Aulo Greco (Firenze, 1970–76), vol. 1, 23.

29. Giacomo Filippo Tomasini, *Annales canonicorum secularium S. Georgii in Alga* (Utini, 1642), 30–36, 42–47.

30. Giorgio Cracco, "La fondazione dei canonici secolari di San Giorgio in Alga," *Rivista di storia della Chiesa in Italia* 13 (1959): 70–81; Silvio Tramontin, "Ludovico Barbo e la riforma di S. Giorgio in Alga," in *Riforma della Chiesa: Cultura e spiritualità nel Quattrocento Veneto,* ed. Francesco Trolese (Cesena, 1984) 91–107; Giorgio Picasso, *Tra umanesimo e "devotio:" Studi di storia monastica raccolti per il 50 di professione dell'autore* (Milano, 1999), 3–33.

31. For a bibliography on Barbo, see A. Pratesi, "Barbo, Ludovico," in *DBDI,* vol. 6, 244–249; Francesco Trolese, "Ludovico Barbo (1381–1443) e la congregazione monastica riformata di S. Giustina: Un settantennio di studi," *Fonte e ricerche di storia ecclesiastica padovana* 7 (1976): 35–80.

32. On the sorry state of Santa Giustina on Barbo's arrival, see Francesco Trolese, "Ricerche sui primordi della riforma di Ludovico Barbo," in *Riforma della Chiesa,* 109–133.

33. Gregorio Penco, "Vita monastica e società nel Quattrocento italiano," in *Riforma della Chiesa,* 16–18; Barry Collett, *Italian Benedictine Scholars and the Reformation: The Congregation of Santa Giustina of Padua* (Oxford, 1985), 1–4.

34. The other three monasteries in the original congregation were S. Maria di Firenze, S. Fiorfio Maggiore di Venezia, and SS Felice e Fortunato. Ildefonso Tassi, "La crisi della congregazione di S. Giustina tra il 1419 e il 1431," *Benedictina* 5 (1951): 95.

35. For studies of the Observant Movement in a range of regular orders, see Kaspar Elm, ed., *Reformbemühungen und Observanzbestrebungen im spätmittelalterichen Ordenswesen* (Berlin, 1989); Eric Saak, *Highway to Heaven: The Augustinian Platform between Reform and Reformation* (Leiden, 2002), 587–618; Bert Roest, "Observant reform in religious orders," in *The Cambridge History of Christianity, Volume IV: Christianity in Western Europe c. 1000–c. 1500,* ed. Miri Rubin and Walter Simons (Cambridge, 2009), 446–457.

36. Gregorio Penco, *Storia del monachesimo in Italia dalle origini alla fine del Medio Evo* (Roma, 1961), 320–321.

37. Alessandro Tomei, "Vicende della basilica sino al 1823," in *San Paolo fuori le mura a Roma,* ed. Carlo Pietrangeli (Firenze, 1988), 56; Enrico Bassan, "L'architettura del monastero e il chiostro dei Vassalletto," in *San Paolo,* 233.

38. Ildefonso Tassi, *Ludovico Barbo (1381–1443)* (Roma, 1952), 71.

39. On the interventions of Martin V, see Willibrord Witters, "La legislazione monastica della congregazione di S. Giustina nei suoi primordi (1419–1427)," in *Riforma della Chiesa,* 207–224.

40. Etsi ex solicitudinis debito pastoralis sub regulari observantia singulis Altissimo militantibus . . . nos favorabiles esse deceat pariter et benignos, praeclaram tamen dilectorum filiorum Monacorum de observantia Sanctae Justinae Congregationem Ordinis S. Benedicti, ad quos etiam antequam divina favente clementia ad apicem Summi Apostolatus assumeremur, specialem gessimus in Domino caritatis affectum. Spiritualis dono laetitiae vitam, et conversationem contemplantes, quibus eis aliisque proficiunt et salutaria piis fidelium

mentibus exempla transmittunt, tanto solertius ea prosequi, necnon instaurare studiis gerimus assiduis, per quae Congregationis huiusmodi status foeliciter adaugeri, solidarique poterit, quanto per assumptionem hujusmodi major nobis desuper attributa facultas est, et ampliorem Christicolis speramus jugiter provenire salutem. Attento itaque quod fel. rec. Martinus Papa Quintus praedecessor noster, nonnulla eisdem Monacis contulit privilegia, quae non usque adeo ad pleniorem ejusdem Congregationis soliditatem, augmentumve sunt sufficientia: idcirco nos propter dictorum Monacorum laudabilem vitam et exemplares mores nobis diu cognitos praefaturm praedecessorem nostrum sequentes, atque ubi opportunum fuerit nonnulla innovantes, et adiicientes, proprio motu, auctoritate Apostolica, et ex certa scientia, necnon irrefragabili, perpetuaque constitutione sancimus, et praesentium serie statuimus, volumus pariter, et ordinamus, quod omnes et singuli dictae Congregationis ordinem ipsum professi, praesentes et futuri, quamvis in diversis pro tempore Monasteriis sive locis morentur, unum tamen corpus, et una Congregatio existant. Quam quidem Congregationem auctoritate, et scientia similibus approbamus, et ut a Christifidelibus in reverentia et devotione habeatur hortamur, eamque sub Ordine et regula S. Benedicti esse declaramus, atque constituimus. Cocquelines, ed. *Bullarum, privilegiorum...collectio,* vol. 3, part 3, 7–8.

41. Tommaso Leccisotti, "La congregazione benedettina di Santa Giustina e la riforma della chiesa al secolo XV," *ASRSP* 67 (1944): 460.

42. Tassi, *Ludovico Barbo,* 65–71; Penco, *Storia del monachesimo,* 308–317; Collett, *Italian Benedictine Scholars,* 1–6.

43. On Barbo's career as bishop, see Luigi Pesce, *Ludovico Barbo vescovo di Treviso (1437–1443): Cura pastorale, riforma della Chiesa, spiritualità* (Padova 1969); ———. "Ludovico Barbo vescovo riformatore," in *Riforma della Chiesa* 135–159.

44. Mario Tubbini, "Il collegio Eugeniano e il Concilio del 1439," in *Firenze e il Concilio del 1439,* ed. Paolo Viti (Firenze, 1994), 175–189.

45. Ildefonso Tassi, "Un collaboratore dell'opera riformatrice di Eugenio IV: Giovanni de Primis" *Benedictina* 2 (1948): 3–26.

46. Picasso, *Tra umanesimo e "devotio,"* 38–56.

47. Gerhart Ladner, *The Idea of Reform: Its Impact on Christian Thought and Action in the Age of the Fathers* (Cambridge, MA, 1959), 2.

48. Dulcissime talis (exprime nomen eius) propter amorem quem habuisti in hoc misero seculo domino nostro Yesu Christo (si fuerit Martyr, dice) propter passionem quam ob eius amorem fortiter sustulisti (si fuerit confessori, dice) propter dilectionem et amorem quem habuisti ad Deum, pro quo multos sustinuisti labores, roga Deum pro me ut me faciat fidelem servum suum esse et perseverare usque ad mortem. Ad secundum sanctum eisdem dulcissimis deprecando verbis, ab eo pete ut intercedat pro te, ut sis constans et patiens in omnibus tribulationibus, adversitatibus, contrarietatibus et temptationibus; a tertio pete ut roget pro te ut dominus infundat tibi gratiam obediendi, non tantum patribus, sed et omnibus fratribus et minoribus seu inferioribus aut

iunioribus te; a quarto pete ut oret pro te ut sis humilis, pius, pacificus et omnibus benignus; a quinto pete ut Deus donet tibi gratiam abstinentie a superfluitatibus, diligere ieiunia, vigilias et silentia et alia sancta opera religionis que sunt porte ad dulcedinem contemplationis; a sexto pete ut oret pro te, ut Deus donet tibi gratiam amplius non peccandi saltem mortaliter, et donet tibi veram contritionem de preteritis, et satisfactionem ante mortem secundum quod ei placuerit. Ludovico Barbo, "Forma orationis et meditationis congregationi monachorum S. Iustine," in *Ludovico Barbo*, 144–145. On the importance of intercessory saints to late medieval Europeans, see Brad Gregory, "Late Medieval Religiosity and the Renaissance of Christian Martyrdom," in *Continuity and Change: the Harvest of Late Medieval and Reformation History*, ed. Robert Blast and Andrew Gow (Leiden, 2000), 391–394.

49. Bernard of Clairvaux, "The Steps of Humility and Pride" in *The Works of Bernard of Clairvaux* (Washington, DC, 1974).

50. Bonaventure, *The Journey of the Mind to God*, trans. Philotheus Boehner (Indianapolis, 1993), 7–8.

51. Frederick Artz, *The Mind of the Middle Ages* (Chicago, 1980), 421; Constable, *The Reformation of the Twelfth Century*, 36.

52. On the *Devotio Moderna*, see Hein Blommestijn, Charles Caspers, and Rijcklof Hofman, eds., *Spirituality Renewed: Studies on Significant Representatives of the Modern Devotion* (Leuven, 2003); Wybren Scheepsma, *Medieval Religious Women in the Low Countries: The "Modern Devotion," the Canonesses of Windesheim, and Their Writings*, trans. David Johnson (Woodbridge, 2004); John Van Engen, *Sisters and Brothers of the Common life: The* Devotio Moderna *and the World of the Later Middle Ages* (Philadelphia, 2008).

53. On the disputed authorship of the *Imitation* see John Van Engen, ed. *Devotio Modern: Basic Writings* (New York, 1988), 8–9.

54. Many manuscripts and incunabula of the *Imitation* were found in houses of the Congregation of Santa Giustina. See Giorgio Picasso, "L'Imitazione di Cristo' e l'ambiente di S. Giustina," in *Riforma della Chiesa*, 263–267.

55. Thomas à Kempis, *The Imitation of Christ*, trans. Aloysius Croft and Harold Bolton (Mineola, NY, 2003), chap. 3. Another critical difference between the two spiritual movements is that Barbo does not emphasize the evils of human existence, a repeated theme of the *Imitation of Christ*.

56. On saints and the language of patronage, see Guy Fitch Lytle, "Friendship and Patronage in Renaissance Europe," in *Patronage, Art, and Society in Renaissance Italy*, ed. F. W. Kent and Patricia Simons (Oxford, 1987), 48–55.

57. Compare Thomas à Kempis, *The Imitation of Christ*, book 1, chap 1.

58. Ibid., chaps 1, 11, 12, 56.

59. Charles Stinger, *Humanism and the Church Fathers: Ambrogio Traversari (1386–1439) and Christian Antiquity in the Italian Renaissance* (Albany, 1977), 167–202.

60. Thomas Izbicki, *Protector of the Faith: Cardinal Johannes de Turrecremata and the Defense of the Institutional Church* (Washington, DC, 1981), 1–17.

61. Mario Fois, "La chiesa di Venezia tra medioevo ed età moderna," *Contributi alla storia della chiesa di Venezia* 3 (1989): 147–150.

62. Mario Fois, "I Papi e l'Osservanza minoritica," in *Il rinnovamento del Francescanesimo l'Osservanza: Atti dei 'XI Convengno Internazionale* (Assisi, 1985), 31–45.

63. Duncan Nimmo, "The Franciscan Regular Observance: The Culmination of Medieval Franciscan Reform," in *Reformbemühungen und Observanzbestrebungen,* 189–205; Michael Robson, *The Franciscans in the Middle Ages* (Woodbridge, 2006), 205–208.

64. Vespasiano da Bisticci, *Renaissance Princes, Popes, and Prelates,* 22; ———. *Le Vite,* vol. 1, 13.

65. Eugenius promoted a similar innovation within the Dominican order. Joseph Gill, *Eugenius IV, Pope of Christian Union* (London, 1961), 187–188. On the extent of the differences between Observant and Conventual Dominicans, see Michael Tavuzzi, *Renaissance Inquisitors: Dominican Inquisitors and Inquisitorial Districts in Northern Italy, 1474–1527* (Leiden, 2007), 49–77.

66. Fois, "I Papi e l'Osservanza minoritica," 49–60.

67. Joachim Smet, "Pre-Tridentine Reform in the Carmelite Order," in *Reformbemühungen und Observanzbestrebungen,* 296–299; Franco dal Pino, "Tentativi di riforma e movimento di Osservanza presso i Servi di Maria nei secoli XIV–XV," in *Reformbemühungen* 363–368.

68. John O'Malley, "Was Ignatius Loyola a Church Reformer? How to Look at Early Modern Catholicism," *Catholic Historical Review* 77 (1991): 187.

69. Giovanni Lunardi, "L'ideale monastico di Ludovico Barbo," in *Riforma della Chiesa,* 59–71.

70. On the radical nature of Barbo's reforms, see Mario Fois, "I movimenti religiosi dell'Osservanza nel '400: I Benedettini," in *Riforma della Chiesa,* 231–246.

71. For helpful summaries of the reform goals of these popes, see F. Donald Logan, *A History of the Church in the Middle Ages* (London, 2002), 105–115, 184–201.

72. Jacob Burckhardt, *The Civilization of the Renaissance in Italy,* trans. S. G. C. Middlemore (New York, 1990), 313–323.

73. See also Marsuppini's comparison of hypocrites to dolphins fleeing a storm. Poggio Bracciolini, *Contra hypocritas,* ed. Davide Canfora (Roma, 2008), 20–21.

74. Numquid hoc Nicolai nostri pontificis tempore Romana curia septa, vel potius obsessa, est hypocritarum cohortibus velut apud Eugenium consuevit? Memini turbam illam redundantem intra palatii septa atque ita ex omnibus locis atque ordinibus tamquam formicas ex foraminibus scaturientem, ut multis

odio esset. Et certe, postea quam nunc verum fateri licet, bonus ille multis profecto in rebus pontifex fuit, sed in eo, sive ad extimationem vulgi sive quod
bonos illos viros putabat, paulum meo iudicio a via deflexit, quod nimium
hypocritis indulsit, adeo illis favens, ut multorum detexerit sua indulgentia
cicatrices. His primus ad pontificem aditus patebat, hi plurimum temporis cum
eo in rebus levissimis consumebant, hi aures illius depascebantur: quidam
somniis, alii revelationibus futurorum, nonnulli novis miraculis animum
illius demulcentes, adeo in mentem eius specie sanctitatis obrepserant, ut,
quicquid optarent aut peterent (plurima autem postulabant), sepius impe-
trarent. Ibid., 6–7.

75. Ibid., 18.

76. Dominici (1356–1420) was Archbishop of Ragusa and then cardinal.
He wrote a scathing critique of humanist studies, *Lucula noctis*. George Holmes,
The Florentine Enlightenment, 1400–50 (Oxford, 1992), 32–35.

77. Malatesta was bishop of Rimini from 1445 to 1448.

78. Bracciolini, *Contra hypocritas*, 27. Although he mentions Barbo by name,
Marsuppini goes on to say that the Bishop of Treviso should not be included
among hypocrites.

79. Poggio Bracciolini, "On Avarice," in *The Earthly Republic*, ed. Benjamin
Kohl and Ronald Witt (Philadelphia, 1978), 241–289; ———. *De avaritia*, trans.
Giuseppe Germano (Livorno, 1994). On the anticlericalism of *De avaritia*, see
John Oppel, "Poggio, San Bernardino of Siena and the Dialogue *On Avarice*,"
RQ 30 (1977): 564–587.

80. Helene Harth, "Niccolò Niccoli als literarischer Zensor: Untersuchungen
zur Textgeschichte von Poggios 'De Avaritia'," *Rinascimento* 7 (1967): 29–53.

81. Important studies of demonstrative rhetoric in the Renaissance include
Charles Trinkaus, "A Humanist's Image of Humanism: The Inaugural Orations
of Bartolomeo della Fonte," *Studies in the Renaissance* 7 (1960): 90–147; John
O'Malley, *Praise and Blame in Renaissance Rome: Rhetoric, Doctrine, and Reform in the
Sacred Orators of the Papal Court* (Durham, 1979); Anthony D'Elia, *The Renaissance
of Marriage in Fifteenth-Century Italy* (Cambridge, MA, 2004), 35–82. Three anal-
yses of Valla's *Encomium* on Aquinas demonstrate how demonstrative rhetoric
and a clear theological message could be combined. Hanna Gray, "Valla's
Encomium of St. Thomas Aquinas and the Humanist Conception of Christian
Antiquity," in *Essays in History and Literature Presented by the Fellows of the Newberry
Library to Stanley Pargellis*, ed. Heinz Bluhm (Chicago, 1965), 37–51; John
O'Malley, "The Feast of Thomas Aquinas in Renaissance Rome: A Neglected
Document and Its Import," *Rivista di storia della Chiesa in Italia* 35 (1981): 1–27;
Salvatore Camporeale, "Lorenzo Valla Tra Medioevo e Rinascimento," in *Lorenzo
Valla: Umanesimo, Riforma e orma* (Roma, 2002), 121–265.

82. For Zabarella's biography, see Gaspare Zonta, *Francesco Zabarella*
(Padova, 1915).

83. E. Pasztor, "Albergati, Niccolò," in *DBDI, vol. 1*, 619–621. On Albergati's

tenure as Bishop of Bologna, see Peter Partner, *The Papal State Under Martin V: The Administration and Government of the Temporal Power in the Early Fifteenth Century* (London, 1958), 50–52, 64–67, 89–93. For Cesarini's biography, see A. A. Strnad and K. Walsh, "Cesarini, Giuliano," in *DBDI*, vol. 24, 188–195. On his years at Basel, see Gerald Christianson, *Cesarini: The Conciliar Cardinal* (St. Ottilien, 1979); Decaluwe, *A Successful Defeat*, 64–276.

84. Poggio Bracciolini, "In Funere D. Francisci Cardinalis Florentini," in *Opera Omnia*, ed. Riccardo Fubini (Torino, 1964–1969), vol. 1, 253, 256, 259.

85. Almost one hundred members of the Council of Constance were students of Zabarella. Walter Brandmüller, *Das Konzil con Konstanz* (Paderborn, 1991–1997), vol. 1, 51, 171.

86. Bracciolini, "In Funere D. Francisci Cardinalis Florentini," 257.

87. Zabarella died in September 1417, and Poggio's *Oratio ad patres reverendissimos* was most likely delivered between July 16 and October 30 of the same year. Riccardo Fubini, *Umanesimo e secolarizzazione*, 304–305.

88. Ernst Walser, *Poggius Florentinus: Leben und Werke* (Leipzig, 1914), vol. 1, 45. On Zabarella's humanist credentials, see John McManamon, *Pier Paolo Vergerio the Elder: The Humanist as Orator* (Tempe, AZ, 1996), 48–59.

89. Poggio Bracciolini, "In funere reverendissimi cardinalis D. Iuliani de Caesarinis Romani," in *Opera Omnia*, vol. 2, 726–727, 730.

90. Itaque recte sapientes dixerunt, unum diem bene et cum virtute actum, peccanti immortalitati esse anteponendum. Hoc Iulianus cogitans, imbutusque per omnem vitam sapientum praeceptis, virtutem omnibus in rebus ducem habuit vitae: omnes suas actiones ad sapientiae normam direxit: nihil unquam sibi in vita praeter veram laudem et aeternam gloriam expetendam putavit: id egit semper ut sua dicta consilia facta consensu omnium probarentur. Ibid., 735.

91. Primum, summa religio, summa integritas, et sanctitas morum, cum nihil in eo reprehendi posset, cum per omnem vitam temperantia et continentia singularique doctrina praeditus erat, ac scientia rerum plurimarum, ut viris doctissimis aequari posset. Erat in eo denique agendorum usus ac experientia, quae in eo summam prudentiam efficiebant. Accedebat consilii gravitas, et animus in consultando omni passione vacuus, autoritas quantum in ullo homine esse potest, virtute et bene agendo contracta, mores probatissimi, aetas provectior, nullo unquam tempore ulla vel parva vitiorum labe notata.... His virtutibus addebatur humanitas quaedam et mansuetudo, quae eum summe gratum omnibus reddebant. Digne ergo sua opera in rebus arduis Pontifices utebantur, cum non ad questum aliquem, sed ad laborem officiosum, non ad propriam, sed ad communem utilitatem se inniti arbitraretur. Poggio Bracciolini, "Oratio secunda in funere Cardinalis S. Crucis," in *Opera Omnia*, vol. 1, 268.

92. Charles Trinkaus, *In Our Image and Likeness: Humanity and Divinity in Italian Humanist Thought* (Notre Dame, IN, 1995), xiii–xxvii.

93. Compare Karl Morrisson, *The Mimetic Tradition of Reform in the West* (Princeton, NJ, 1982), 200–202.

94. John McManamon, *Funeral Oratory and the Cultural Ideals of Italian Humanism* (Chapel Hill, NC, 1989), 11–16.

95. Poggio Bracciolini, *Lettere*, ed. Helene Harth (Firenze, 1984), 157–163.

96. In response, Bruni urged Poggio to write more cautiously. Leonardo Bruni, *Epistolarum libri VIII*, ed. James Hankins (Roma, 2007), 119–120.

97. Sed si recto iudicio ista examinarent, intelligerent eternum sibi exitium construere et interitum animorum. Non sunt hec Evangelii divina precepta, non sunt huiusmodi vestigia apostolorum et aliorum sanctorum patrum, quorum in hereditates intrastis. Illi enim sanguine sui hanc nobis Ecclesiam pepererunt, vos aliorum sanguinem exsorbetis; illi corporum tormenta sustinuerunt ob fidei corroborationem, vos ad ipsius desolationem tormenta pluribus hominibus infertis; illi sequebantur inopiam, vos opes queritis; gaudebant illi paupertate, vos divitiis; illi potentiam mundanam aspernabantur, humilitatem sequentes, vos dominia et elatio delectant; illi diligi et amari studebant, vos metui vultis, nescientes quod nunquam timor cum dilectione ac caritate miscetur; denique ad salutem illi nostram proficiebant, vos videmini ad perniciem constituti. Quid ergo mirandum est in tanta vite ac morum dissimilitudine, tanta nequitia, tanta perversitate personas ecclesiasticas iam esse odio hominibus cepisse, cum quisque bene loquatur male vivat? Bracciolini, "Oratio ad patres reverendissimos," 330–331.

98. Lorenzo Valla, *On the Donation of Constantine*, trans. G. W. Bowerscok, (Cambridge, MA, 2007), 30–43.

99. Valla also uses antithesis extensively in his oration on how Aquinas was inferior to the early Fathers. Lorenzo Valla, "Lorenzo Valla über Thomas von Aquino," in *Vierteljahrsschrift für Kultur und Literatur der Renaissance*, ed. J. Vahlen (Leipzig, 1886), 384–396; ———. "In Praise of Saint Thomas Aquinas," in *Renaissance Philosophy: New Translations*, ed. Leonard Kennedy (The Hague, 1973), 13–27.

100. Salvatore Camporeale, *Lorenzo Valla: Umanesimo e teologia* (Firenze, 1972), 311–403.

101. Fubini, *Humanism and Secularization from Petrarch to Valla*, trans. Martha King (Durham, NC, 2003), 90–91.

102. Bracciolini, *Lettere*, vol. 1, 5–7. See also Richard Newhauser, "Patristic Poggio?" *Rinascimento* 26 (1986): 231–239.

103. Burckhardt, *The Civilization of the Renaissance in Italy*, 102–104. For analysis of Burckhardt's picture of Alberti, see Anthony Grafton, *Leon Battista Alberti: Master Builder of the Italian Renaissance* (New York, 2000), 14–29.

104. On Alberti's use of ancient sources, see Massimo Danzi, "Governo della casa e 'scientia oeconomica' in Italia fra Medioevo e Rinascimento: Nota sulla 'Famiglia' di L.B. Alberti," in *Leon Battista Alberti: Actes du Congrès International de Paris*, ed. Francesco Furlan (Paris, Torino, 2000), 151–170; Piccardi, "Introduzione," in *Pontifex* (Firenze, 2007), 115–133.

105. Quis enim usque adeo temerarius ipsum hoc Dei tribunal vacuus terrore aggredietur? Iudicium, inquit, sibi assumit quisquis sacrificium id libarit indigne; impiisne his manibus altare Dei attrectabimus? Sed vix audeo de re ipsa proloqui, quod intelligerem per mortales homines, inter quos etiam qui iusti sunt omnino vitio non careant, non per incorruptissimos angelos Deum deorum hoc ut fieret sacrificium instituisse, quod in sanctorum sententia meminissem sacrificium esse medicinam animorum, quam egrotus, modo sibi in reliquis satis constet, non die singulo incommode suscipiat. Profecto de me ipso, qui non, ut ferunt, septies pecco, sed qui assidue admodum in via Domini pro humanitatis imbecillitate meme parum, ut pontificem par est, esse constantem sentio, fortassis longius consuluissem. Quo magis fit, mi pater, pontificiam hanc ipsam rem gravissimam esse existimem; nam sacrificandi quidem munus quovis cum alio vago atque nullis gregibus prefecto sacerdote mihi esse commune intelligo, purgande autem multitudinis a vitio, inseminandeque virtutis ac servandi in populo decoris cura mihi, quod sentiam commendata est. Quas quidem res, etsi litteris nonnihil sim tinctus, tamen, quia usum quemdam imperandi hic non minus quam peritiam bonarum artium requiri intelligam, novus ipse et inexpertus ac, prout convenit, recte inprimis agendi cupidus, quas dixi res, esse omnes supra vires meas deputo. Leon Battista Alberti, *Pontifex* ed. Andrea Piccardi (Firenze, 2007), 222–223.

106. Peter Brown, *The Rise of Western Christendom: Triumph and Diversity 200–1000* (Oxford, 1997), 141–144.

107. Elena Giannarelli, "Alberti e la letteratura Christiana antica: Linee di una Problema," and Andrea Piccardi, "Fonte cristiane nel *Pontifex*," in *Alberti e la tradizione: per lo "smontaggio" dei "mosaici" albertiani*, ed. Roberto Cardini and Mariangela Regoliosi (Firenze, 2007) 425–447 and 461–485.

108. Alberti, *Pontifex*, 278.

109. Grafton, *Leon Battista Alberti*, 194–196; Piccardi, "Introduzione," 55–63. On the importance of rewriting and cross-referencing in Alberti's works, see Roberto Cardini, *Mosaici: Il "nemico" dell'Alberti* (Roma, 1990), 4–5.

110. Eugenio Garin, "Leon Battista Alberti e l'autobiografia," in *Concordia discors: Studi su Niccolò Cusano e l'umanesimo europeo offerti a Giovanni Santinello*, ed. Gregorio Piaia (Padova, 1993), 361–376.

111. Hans Baron, *In Search of Florentine Civic Humanism: Essays on the Transition from Medieval to Modern Thought* (Princeton, NJ, 1988), vol. 1, 158–288. For context on humanist discussions of wealth, see A. D. Fraser-Jenkins, "Cosimo de' Medici's Patronage of Architecture and the Theory of Magnificence," *JWCI* 33 (1970), 162–170; Richard Goldthwaite, *Wealth and the Demand for Art in Italy, 1300–1600* (Baltimore, 1993), 149–255.

112. Alberti, *Pontifex*, 231.

113. Leon Battista Alberti, *I libri della Famiglia*, ed. Ruggiero Romano and Alberto Tenenti (Torino, 1969), 280, 290; ———. *The Family in Renaissance*

Florence Books I–IV, trans. Renee N Watkins (Long Grove, IL, 1969), 218, 225. Hereafter, "Romano and Tenenti" and "Watkins."

114. Romano and Tenenti, 21–22, 72; Watkins, 38, 73. See N. Bianchi Bensimon, "L'immagine paterna come modulo archetipico in alcuni dialoghi in volgare dell'Alberti," *Albertiana* 5 (2002): 77–88.

115. Romano and Tenenti, 267; Watkins, 209. Alberti, *Pontifex,* 230.

116. Alberti, *Pontifex,* 238.

117. Nempe haud nunc alia iam mihi in mentem redeunt, preter unum illud, ut Deum ipsum optimum maximum, priusquam negotiorum aliquid aggrediamur, ut a tam pestifero et mortifero inimicorum numero esse nos salvos velit, summis votis precemur. Eaque re hoc de me ipso profiteor: post annum etatis mee vigesimum, quo me a fervore iuvente pau   lisper ad mei cognitionem integriorem atque maturiorem recepi, nulla fuit unquam dies, qua non ceteris omissis rebus studuerim ad sacrificium interesse atque ut me ab adversis casibus ab omnique malo defenderet a summo Deo deprecarer. Quod ipsum laudo apud reliquos omnes pontifices pro more fieri, ut prima illorum sit opera, concelebrandi sacrificii, idque singulis atque inprimis ipsis pontificibus esse pernecessarium censeo. Ibid., 257.

118. Romano and Tenenti, 192–193, 296; Watkins 156, 229.

119. Aristotle, *The Nicomachean Ethics,* trans. David Ross (Oxford, 1980), II, 1–5. On Alberti's use of Aristotle, see James Lawson, "Giannozzo and Architecture in Alberti's Moral Writings," *Albertiana* 7 (2004): 83–85.

120. Romano and Tenenti, 77; Watkins, 76.

121. On Alberti's own religious beliefs, see Alberti Tenenti, "Riflessioni sul pensiero religioso di Leon Battista Alberti," in *LBA: Actes du Congrès International de Paris,* 305–315.

122. Romano and Tenenti, 211; Watkins, 169.

123. Alberti, *Pontifex,* 259.

124. Romano and Tenenti, 200; Watkins, 161.

125. Alberti, *Pontifex,* 262–263.

126. Compare Eugenius's 1432 bull to improve the moral character of episcopal households, discussed in Enrico Peverada, "La 'familia' del vescovo e la curia a Ferrara," in *Vescovi e diocesi,* 632, 653–654.

127. For two provocative readings of *Della famiglia* see Eugenio Garin, *Rinascite e rivoluzioni: Movimenti culturali dal XIV al XVIII secolo* (Roma, 1975), 165–167, 170–178; Grafton, *Leon Battista Alberti,* 152–182.

128. Rinaldo Rinaldi, "Melancholia albertiana: dalla 'Deifra' al 'Naufragus,'" *Lettere Italiane* 37 (1985): 41–82; Paolo Marolda, *Crisi e conflitto in Leon Battista Alberti* (Roma, 1988).

129. Leon Battista Alberti, *Intercenali inedite,* ed. Eugenio Garin (Firenze, 1965), 150–151; ———. *Dinner Pieces,* trans. David Marsh (Binghamton, NY, 1987), 75.

130. Stefano Pittaluga, "Leon Battista Alberti e Poggio Braccciolini," in *Alberti e la cultura del Quattrocento: Atti del Convegno internazionale del Comitato Nazionale*

VI centenario della nascita di Leon Battista Alberti, ed. Roberto Cardini and Mariangela Regoliosi (Firenze, 2007), 375–386.

131. A. A. Strnad, "Capranica, Domenico," in *DBDI,* vol 19, 147–153.

132. MS Vatican City, Vat. Lat. 4039, f. 16v–18. Only a part of the proposal survives.

133. The College welcomed its first thirty students in 1459, a year after Capranica's death. For more on the college, which is still functioning, see http://www.almocollegiocapranica.it/storia_eng.html

134. MS Vatican City, Vat. Lat. 7309, f. 1. A provisional edition of the Constitutions, with considerable critical apparatus is available at http://www.unifr.ch/cdc/constitutiones_de.php. Unless otherwise noted, all citations and quotations will follow this edition, which retains the original pagination of Vat. Lat. 7309.

135. Ibid., f. 8v.

136. Ibid., f. 1v.

137. Ibid., f. 2.

138. Ibid., f. 2v.

139. Ibid., f. 17v.

140. Pesce, "Ludovico Barbo vescovo riformatore," 145.

141. Niccolò Palmieri, Capranica's funeral eulogist, insists that his early education included the *studia humanitatis.* MS Vatican City, Vat. Lat. 5815 f. 15–16v. Vespasiano, however, does not attribute any love of humanistic learning to the cardinal. Vespasiano da Bisticci, *Renaissance Princes, Popes, and Prelates,* 133–137; ———. *Le Vite,* vol. 1, 159–167.

142. Bracciolini, *Lettere,* vol. 3, letters 5.9, 7.20, 7.32, 8.19, 8.27, 9.25.

143. MS Vatican City, Vat. Lat. 8184; A. V. Antonovics, "The Library of Cardinal Domenico Capranica," in *Cultural Aspects of the Italian Renaissance,* ed. Cecil H. Clough (Manchester, 1976), 141.

144. Vat. Lat. 8184, f. 36–43v. Other classicizing works are scattered throughout the collection.

145. Antonovics, "The Library of Cardinal Domenico Capranica," 145.

146. Vat. Lat. 8184, f. 3v–6v.

147. B. L. Ullman and P. A. Stadter, *The Public Library of Renaissance Florence* (Padua, 1982), 59–89. Antonio Manfredi, *I codici latini di Niccolò V: Edizione degli inventari e identificazione dei manoscritti* (Città del Vaticano, 1994), 63–127. ———. "S. Agostino, Niccoli e Parentucelli tra San Marco e la Vaticana: Rinnovamento delle biblioteche e diffusione di testi," *Italia Medioevale e Umanistica* 44 (2003): 27–64.

148. On Nicholas as the founder of the Vatican library, see Leonard Boyle, "Introduction," in *Rome Reborn,* ed. Anthony Grafton (Washington, DC, 1993), xi–xx; ———. "Per la fondazione della Biblioteca Vaticana," in *I codici latini di Niccolò V,* xiii–xxii. (Boyle begins by citing the works of Ruysschaert, who argued that Sixtus IV should be seen as the Library's true founder.) For other provoca-

tive studies of early Renaissance libraries, see Dora Thornton, *The Scholar in His Study: Ownership and Experience in Renaissance Italy* (New Haven, 1997); Anthony Grafton, *Commerce with the Classics: Ancient Books and Renaissance Readers*, (Ann Arbor, MI, 1997), 11–52; Luciano Gargan, "Biblioteche pubbliche in Italia nel secolo XV," in *Niccolò V nel sesto centenario della nascita*, ed. Franco Bonatti and Antonio Manfredi (Città del Vaticano, 2000), 9–20; Christopher Celenza, "Creating Canons in Fifteenth-Century Ferrara: Angelo Decembrio's 'De politia litteraria,' 1.10," *RQ* 57 (2004): 43–98.

149. The 1443 inventory of the papal library included 351 volumes. For more on the collection, see Jeannine Fohlen, *La Bibliothèque du Pape Eugène IV (1431–1447): Contribution à l'histoire du fonds Vatican latin* (Città del Vaticano, 2008). While Niccolò Niccoli's admirers claimed his collection included 800 manuscripts, only 403 were received by San Marco. Ullman and Stadter, *The Public Library of Renaissance Florence*, 59–60. Among Capranica's fellow cardinals, Bessarion alone is known to have had a larger library. Concetta Bianca, "La formazione della biblioteca latina del Bessarione," in *Scrittura, biblioteche e stampa a Rome nel Quattrocento*, ed. Concetta Bianca et al. (Città del Vaticano, 1980), 103–165; Lotte Labowsky, *Bessarion's Library and the Biblioteca Marciana: Six Early Inventories* (Roma, 1979).

150. Vat. Lat. 7309, f. 4–7.

151. Ibid, f. 4v.

152. Ibid., f. 7.

153. Ibid., f. 27v–28.

154. J. W. Clark, *The Care of Books: An Essay on the Development of Libraries and their Fittings from the Earliest Times to the End of the Eighteenth Century* (Cambridge, 1909), 69–71; Nathan Schachner, *The Mediaeval Universities* (New York, 1938), 329; Lynn Thorndike, *University Records and Life in the Middle Ages* (New York, 1944), 316.

155. Et quia tam theologis quam canonistis valde est utilis philosophia moralis, a qua iura trahunt originem, volumus, quod singulis diebus Dominicis et festivis, quibus non legitur in universitate, vel magister in theologia, qui assumendus est a collegio vel aliquis idoneus scolaris qui fuerit, legat unam lectionem libri ethicorum Aristotelis et illo libro completo legatur eius Economica et Politica, ad quam lectionem omnes scholares convenire habeant et si forenses vellent venire, salva semper honestate collegii, admittantur. Vat. Lat. 7309, f. 16v–17.

156. Robert Black, *Humanism and Education in Medieval and Renaissance Italy: Tradition and Innovation in Latin Schools from the Twelfth to Fifteenth Century* (Cambridge, 2001), 225–274; ———. *Education and Society in Florentine Tuscany, Volume I: Teachers, pupils and schools, 1250–1500* (Leiden, 2007), 48–52. For more on the limited teaching of moral philosophy in Italian Universities, see Paul Grendler, *Universities of the Italian Renaissance* (Baltimore, 2002), 393–402; Robert Black, "Review of Paul Grendler's 'Universities of the Italian Renaissance,'" *AHR* 108 (2003): 934–935.

157. Vat. Lat. 8184, f. 19.

158. John O'Malley, "Renaissance Humanism and the Religious Culture of the First Jesuits," *The Heythrop Journal* 31 (1990): 481.

159. John Van Engen, "The Church in the Fifteenth Century," in *Handbook of European History*, 307.

160. Pascoe, *Church and Reform*, 137–164.

161. Lorenzo Valla, "The Profession of the Religious," in *The Profession of the Religious and the principal arguments from The Falsely-Believed and Forged Donation of Constantine*, ed. Olga Pugliese (Toronto, 1985); ———. *De professione religiosorum*, ed. Mariarosa Cortesi (Patavii, 1986); Salvatore Camporeale, "Lorenzo Valla: Etica umanistica e prassi Christiana," *Memorie Domenicane* 22 (1991): 345–380.

162. Salvatore Camporeale, "Lorenzo Valla e il 'De falso credita Donatione': Rhetorica, libertà ed ecclesiologia nel '400," in *Lorenzo Valla: Umanesimo, riforma e controriforma*, 465–489; Christopher Celenza, "Lorenzo Valla, 'Paganism' and Orthodoxy," *Modern Language Notes* 119 (2004): 566–587.

163. Mariangela Regoliosi, "Salvatore Camporeale's Contribution to Theology and the History of the Church," *JHI* (2005): 537–539.

164. On the development of Roman confraternities in the 14th and 15th centuries, see Anna Esposito, "Apparati e suggestioni nelle feste e devotioni delle confraternite romane," *ASRSP* 106 (1983): 311–322; Giulia Barone, "Il movimento Francescano e la nascita delle confraternite romane," Paola Pavan, "La confraternita del Salvatore nella società romana del Tre-Quattrocento," and Anna Esposito, "Le confraternite del Gonfalone (secoli XIV–XV)," all in *Ricerche per la storia religiosa di Roma* 5 (1984): 71–136.

165. Alberto Monticone, "Le confraternite romane: una storia aperta," *Ricerche per la storia religiosa* 5 (1984): 19–23; Anna Esposito, "Uomini e donne nelle confraternite romane tra Quattro e Cinquecento: Ruoli, finalità, aspettative," *ASRSP* (2004): 111–131; Barbara Wisch, "Keys to Success: Propriety and Promotion of Miraculous Images by Roman Confraternities," in *The Miraculous Image in the Late Middle Ages and Renaissance*, ed. Erik Thuno and Gerhard Wolf (Rome, 2004), 161–184.

166. On the popularity of Francesca Romana, see Anna Esposito, "S. Francesca e la communità religiose femminili a Rome nel secolo XV," in *Culto dei santi: istituzioni e classi sociali in età preindustriale*, ed. Sofia B. Gajano and Lucia Sebastiani (L'Aquila, 1984), 537–562. On the social origins and impact of Francesca and her followers, see Arnold Esch, "Tre sante ed il loro ambiente sociale a Roma: S. Francesca Romana, S. Brigida di Svezia e S. Caterina da Siena," in *Atti del Simposio internazionale Cateriniano-Bernardiniano*, ed. Domenico Maffei and Paolo Nardi (Siena, 1982), 89–120.

167. P. D. Placido Tommaso Lugano, ed. *I processi inediti per Francesca Bussa dei Ponziani (Santa Francesca Romana)* (Città del Vaticano,1945), 18.

168. Tor de' Specchi was only one of sixty semireligious female houses in 15th-century Rome. On these communities generally, see Joyce Pennings,

"Semi-Religious Women in 15th-Century Rome," *Mededelingen van het Nederlands Instituut te Rome* 47 (1987): 115–145. Anna Esposito, "Il mondo della religiosità femminile Romana," ASRSP 132 (2009): 156–167.

169. For studies that emphasize the separation between lay and clerical religious culture, see Caroline Bynum, *Jesus as Mother: Studies in the Spirituality of the High Middle Ages* (Berkeley, CA, 1982), 1–21; R. W. Scribner, *Popular Culture and Popular Movements in Reformation Germany* (London, 1987), 17–47. Compare Daniel Bornstein, *The Bianchi of 1399: Popular Devotion in Late Medieval Italy* (Ithaca, 1993), 1–42.

170. Rather than distinguishing between the laity and the clergy, Van Engen writes of tension "between the Latinate elite and the vernacular peoples." Van Engen, "The Church in the Fifteenth Century," 319–322.

5. Acting as the One True Pope: Eugenius IV and Papal Ceremonial

1. Giannozzo Manetti, "Concerning the Secular and Papal Parades," in *Building the Kingdom: Giannozzo Manetti in the Material and Spiritual Edifice*, ed. Christine Smith and Joseph O'Connor (Tempe, AZ, 2006), 306–307.

2. Ibid., 317. For details on the walkway, see Leonardo Bruni, "Memoirs," in *History of the Florentine People*, ed. James Hankins (Cambridge, MA, 2007), vol. 3, 380–382.

3. Manetti, "Concerning the Secular and Papal Parades," 319.

4. Ibid., 318–321.

5. The literature on Renaissance and Baroque royal ceremony is immense. For a useful survey see J. Mulryne and Elizabeth Goldring, eds., *Court Festivals of the European Renaissance: Art, Politics and Performance* (Aldershot, 2002). Interesting studies, which approach the problem of ceremony from a variety of perspectives, include Ralph Giesey, *The Royal Funeral Ceremony in Renaissance France* (Geneva, 1960); Stephen Orgel, *The Illusion of Power: Political Theater in the English Renaissance* (Berkeley, CA, 1975); Gordon Kipling, *The Triumph of Honour: Burgundian Origins of the Elizabethan Renaissance* (The Hague, 1977); Roy Strong, *The Cult of Elizabeth: Elizabethan Portraiture and Pageantry* (London, 1977); Malcolm Smuts, *Court Culture and the Origins of a Royalist Tradition in Early Stuart England* (Philadelphia, 1987); John Elliot and Jonathan Brown, *A Palace for a King: The Buen Retiro and the Court of Philip IV* (New Haven, 2004). For additional bibliography, see Helen Watanabe-O'Kelly and Anne Simons, *Festivals and Ceremonies: A Bibliography of Works Relating to Court, Civic, and Religious Festivals in Europe 1500–1800* (New York, 2000).

6. On ekphrasis in the early Quattrocento, see Michael Baxandall, *Giotto and the Orators: Humanist Observers of Painting in Italy and the Discovery of Pictorial Composition, 1350–1450.* (Oxford, 1971), 78–96; Christine Smith, *Architecture in the Culture of Early Humanism: Ethics, Aesthetics and Eloquence, 1400–1470* (Oxford, 1992), 150–197.

7. Edward Muir, *Civic Ritual in Renaissance Venice* (Princeton, NJ, 1981), 59. For a helpful overview of ritual in the later part of this period, see ———. *Ritual in Early Modern Europe* (Cambridge, 1997).

8. Richard Trexler, *Public Life in Renaissance Florence* (Ithaca, 1980), 1–84.

9. Clifford Geertz, *The Interpretation of Cultures* (New York, 1973), 424.

10. Philippe Buc, *The Dangers of Ritual: Between Early Medieval Texts and Social Scientific Theory* (Princeton, NJ, 2001), 15–50.

11. David Cannadine, "The Context, Performance and Meaning of Ritual: The British Monarchy and the Invention of Tradition, c. 1820–1977," in *The Invention of Tradition*, ed. Eric Hobsbawm and Terence Ranger (Cambridge, 1983), 101–164.

12. Bonner Mitchell, *The Majesty of the State: Triumphal Progresses of Foreign Sovereigns in Renaissance Italy (1494–1600)* (Firenze, 1986); Irene Fosi, "Court and City in the Ceremony of the Possesso," in *Court and Politics in Papal Rome, 1492–1700*, ed. Gianvittorio Signorotto and Maria Visceglia (Cambridge, 2002), 31–52.

13. One exemplary exception is Maurice Bloch, *From Blessing to Violence: History and Ideology in the Circumcision Ritual of the Merina of Madagascar* (Cambridge, 1986).

14. Christine Smith and Joseph O'Connor, *Building the Kingdom*, 37–40, 43–45.

15. On Eugenius's support of the Medici regime, see Concetta Bianca, "I cardinali al Concilio di Firenze" in *Firenze e il Concilio del 1439*, ed. Paolo Viti (Firenze, 1994), 49–54. On Cosimo's support of Eugenius and his Curia, see George Holmes, "Cosimo and the Popes," in *Cosimo 'il Vecchio' de' Medici, 1389–1464*, ed. Francis Ames-Lewis (Oxford, 1992), 21–31.

16. Trexler, *Public Life in Renaissance Florence*, 331–547; Muir, *Civic Ritual in Renaissance Venice*, 1–61, 185–211; Amelie Kuhrt, "Usurpation, Conquest and Ceremonial: From Babylon to Persia," in *Rituals of Royalty: Power and Ceremonial in Traditional Societies*, ed. David Cannadine and Simon Price (Cambridge, 1987), 20–55.

17. For important studies of papal ceremony at Avignon, see Bernhard Schimmelpfennig, "Papal Coronations in Avignon," in *Coronations: Medieval and Early Modern Monarchic Ritual*, ed. J. M. Bak (Berkeley, CA, 1990), 179–196; Joëlle Rollo-Koster, "*Castrum Doloris*: Rites of Vacant See and the Living Dead Pope in Schismatic Avignon," in *Medieval and Early Modern Ritual: Formalized Behavior in Europe, China and Japan*, ed. Joëlle Rollo-Koster (Leiden, 2002), 245–277; ———. "The Politics of Body Parts: Contested Topographies in Late-Medieval Avignon," *Speculum* 78 (2003): 66–98; Bernhard Schimmelpfennig, "Der Einfluss des avignonesischen Zeremoniells auf den Vatikanpalast seit Nikolaus V," in *Functions and Decorations: Art and Ritual at the Vatican Palace in the Middle Ages and the Renaissance*, ed. Tristan Weddigen, Sible de Blaauw, and Bram Kempers (Città del Vaticano, 2003), 41–45; Joëlle Rollo-Koster, *Raiding*

Saint Peter: Empty Sees, Violence, and the Initiation of the Great Western Schism (Leiden, 2008).

18. Philip Stump, *The Reforms of the Council of Constance (1414–1418)* (Leiden, 1994), 20.

19. Peter Burke, *The Historical Anthropology of Early Modern Italy: Essays on Perception and Communication* (Cambridge, 1987), 182. See also Victor Turner, *The Anthropology of Performance* (New York, 1986), 21–32.

20. Compare Sergio Bertelli, *The King's Body: Sacred Rituals of Power in Medieval and Early Modern Europe,* trans. R. Burr Litchfield (University Park, PA, 2001).

21. Vespasiano da Bisticci, *Renaissance Princes, Popes, and Prelates: The Vespasiano Memoirs, Lives of Illustrious Men of the XVth Century,* trans. William George and Emily Waters (New York, 1963), 27; ———. *Le Vite,* ed. Aulo Greco (Firenze, 1970–76), vol. I, 21–22.

22. Pero Tafur, *Pero Tafur: Travels and Adventures (1435–1439),* trans. Malcolm Letts (New York, London, 1928), 225.

23. Bartolomeo del Corazza, *Diario Fiorentino (1405–1439),* ed. Roberta Gentile (Roma, 1991), 81–82.

24. Anna Benvenuti Papi, "Un Momento del Concilio di Firenze: La traslazione delle reliquie di San Zanobi," in *Firenze e il Concilio,* 191–220.

25. On St. John's Day, see Trexler, *Public Life in Renaissance Florence,* 240–270. On the celebration of union, see Vespasiano da Bisticci, *Renaissance Princes, Popes, and Prelates,* 25–26; ———. *Le Vite,* vol. I, 18–19.

26. On the ways in which the Council prompted innovations in Florentine ceremonial, see Paola Ventrone, "L'eccezione e la regola: Le rappresentazioni del 1439 nella tradizione Fiorentina delle Feste di Quartiere," in *Firenze e il Concilio,* 409–435.

27. John Baldovin, *The Urban Character of Christian Worship: The Origins, Development, and Meaning of Stational Liturgy* (Roma, 1987), 137–138. Candlemas occurs on February 2; it is the day of Christ's presentation at the temple and also of Mary's Purification.

28. Bernhard Schimmelpfennig, "Autorappresentazione e rappresentanza nel cerimoniale di Boniface VIII," in *Le culture de Bonifacio VIII* (Roma, 2006), 251–253. Compare Herbert Kessler and Johanna Zacharias, *Rome 1300: On the Path of the Pilgrim* (New Haven, 2000), 65–157.

29. On the naming of parts of the Avignon palace, see Carol Richardson, *Reclaiming Rome: Cardinals in the Fifteenth Century* (Leiden, 2009), 15.

30. Sible De Blaauw, *Cultus et Decor: Liturgia e architettura nella Roma tardoantica e medievale* (Città del Vaticano, 1994), vol. I, 40–41. Compare Joaquim Nabuco, "Introduction," in *Le Ceremonial Apostolique avant Innocent VIII,* ed. Filippo Tamburini (Roma, 1966), 12.

31. As a member of the vintner's guild, Corazza would have voted on some fiscal and military matters. Samuel Cohn, *Creating the Florentine State: Peasants and Rebellion 1348–1434* (Cambridge, 1999), 136.

32. The six cardinals are Branda da Castiglione, Tommasso Brancaccio (here, Corazza is mistaken as Brancaccio died in 1427), Angelotto Foschi, Lucido Conti, Prospero Colonna, and Francesco Condulmer.

33. Bartolomeo del Corazza, *Diario Fiorentino*, 77–78.

34. The performance perspective on ritual was first developed by Erving Goffman, Victor Turner, and Richard Schechner. See Erving Goffman, *The Presentation of the Self in Everyday Life* (Garden City, NY, 1959); ———. *Frame Analysis: An Essay on the Organization of Experience* (New York, 1974); Victor Turner, *From Ritual to Theatre* (New York, 1982); Richard Schechner, *Between Theatre and Anthropology* (Philadelpha, 1985); Turner, *The Anthropology of Performance;* Schechner, ed. *By Means of Performance: Intercultural Studies of Theatre and Ritual* (Cambridge, 1990). For a summary and analysis of their ideas and collaboration, see Ronald Grimes, "Performance Theory and the Study of Ritual," *New Approaches to the Study of Religion* 2 (2004): 112–121. More recent studies on ritual and performance include William Beeman, "The Anthropology of Theater and Spectacle," *Annual Review of Anthropology* 22 (1993): 369–393; Ronald Grimes, *Beginnings in Ritual Studies* (Columbia, SC, 1995), 161–266; Gavin Brown, "Theorizing Ritual as Performance: Explorations of Ritual Indeterminacy," *Journal of Ritual Studies* 17 (2003): 3–18; Jeffrey Alexander, "Cultural Pragmatics: Social Performance Between Ritual and Strategy," *Sociological Theory* 22 (2004): 527–573.

35. According to Turner, "Ritual is a mechanism that periodically converts the obligatory into the desirable." Victor Turner, *The Forest of Symbols* (Ithaca, 1967), 30.

36. Giorgio Vasari, *Le Opere di Giorgio Vasari con nuove annotazioni e commenti di Gaetano Milanesi* (Firenze, 1998), vol. 2, 236.

37. Anna Corbo, *Artisti e artigiani in Roma al tempo di Martino V e di Eugenio IV* (Roma, 1969), 141.

38. Archivio di Stato di Roma, Camerale I, Mandati 828, f. 121.

39. For the cost of these items, see Eugène Muntz, *Les arts à la cour des papes pendant* le xve et le xvie *siècle* (Paris, 1878), vol. 1, 20–25, 56–63; Corbo, *Artisti e artigiani,* 117–139. The first recorded papal gift of a rose was in 1096.

40. Rome, Biblioteca Corsiniana MS 41 E 22, f. 13–13v. Compare Pierre Ameil, "Le cérémonial de Pierre Ameil" in *Le cérémonial papal de la fin du Moyen Age à la Renaissance,* ed. Marc Dykmans (Bruxelles, 1985), vol. 4, 111–113. The golden rose symbolized Christ and identified the pope with Him. Agostino Paravicini-Bagliani, *The Pope's Body* trans. David Peterson (Chicago, 2000), 82–83.

41. Anna Corbo, *Cantori, artisti, e condottieri alla corte dei papi nel secolo XV* (Roma, 1999), 50–52.

42. Muntz, *Les arts à la cour des papes,* 57–58.

43. Each year, on the feast of the rose, Eugenius declared seven years and two hundred-eighty days of indulgences. MS Bibl. Cors. 41 E 22, f. 14.

44. Ulrich Richental, "Chronicle," in *The Council of Constance: The Unification of the Church*, trans. Louise Loomis (New York, 1961), 167–173.

45. On Eugenius's support of his musicians, see Adalbert Roth, "'Primus in Petri aede Sixtus perpetuae harmoniae cantores introduxit': Alcune ossservazioni sul patronato musicale di Sisto IV," in *Un pontificato ed una città: Sisto IV (1471–1484)*, ed. Massimo Miglio, et al. (Città del Vaticano, 1986), 223–224. For the musicians' wages, see Mandati 828, f. 108v, 110v, 114, 116, 119v, 121, 123v, 126, 128v, 135, 137, 139v.

46. On the music of Rome and the papal court in the Quattrocento, see Anthony Cummings, *The Politicized Muse: Music for Medici Festivals, 1512–1537* (Princeton, NJ, 1992), 59–66; Alejandro Planchart, "Music for the Papal Chapel in the Early Fifteenth Century," in *Papal Music and Musicians in Late Medieval and Renaissance Rome*, ed. Richard Sherr (Oxford, 1998), 93–124.

47. Margaret Bent, "Early Papal Motets" in *Papal Music and Musicians*, 5–43.

48. Manetti, "Concerning the Secular and Papal Parades," 320–321.

49. Ibid., 324–25.

50. Dufay was a singer in the papal chapel from January 1429 to June 1433 and from June 1435 to May 1437. Corbo, *Cantori, artisti, e condottieri*, 22–23.

51. Craig Wright, "Dufay's 'Nuper rosarum flores,' King Solomon's Temple, and the Veneration of the Virgin" *Journal of the American Musicological Society* 47 (1994): 399.

52. Ibid., 436.

53. Charles Warren, "Brunelleschi's Dome and Dufay's Motet," *The Musical Quarterly* 59 (1973): 92–105; Wright, "Dufay's 'Nuper rosarum flores'"; Marvin Trachtenberg, "Architecture and Music Reunited: A New Reading of Dufay's *Nuper rosarum flores* and the Cathedral of Florence," *RQ* 54 (2001): 740–775.

54. Geoffrey Chew, "The Early Cyclic Mass as an Expression of Royal and Papal Supremacy," *Music and Letters* 53 (1972): 267.

55. Giuseppe Coletti, "Dai diari di Stefano Caffari," *ASRSP* 8 (1885): 567.

56. Natalie Zemon Davis, *Society and Culture in Early Modern France* (Stanford, 1965), 91–123, 152–187; Emmanuel Le Roy Ladurie, *Carnival in Romans*, trans. Mary Feeney (New York, 1979); Peter Burke, *Popular Culture in Early Modern Europe* (Aldershot, 1994), 178–204; Robert Davis, *The War of the Fists: Popular Culture and Public Violence in Late Renaissance Venice* (Oxford, 1994); Edward Muir, *Mad Blood Stirring: Vendetta in Renaissance Italy* (Baltimore, 1998), 81–132.

57. In addition to the works already cited, see Bernhard Schimmelpfennig, "Die Krönung des Papstes im Mittalalter dargestellt am Beispiel der Krönung Pius II (3.9.1458)," *Quellen und Forschungen aus italienischen Archiven und Bibliotheken* 54 (1974): 192–270; Reinhard Elze, "'Sic transit gloria mundi': la morte del papa nel Medio Evo" *Annali dell' Istituto storico italo-germanico in Trento* 3 (1977), 23–41; Marcello Fagiolo, ed., *La festa a Roma: Dal Rinascimento al 1870* (Torino, (1977): Maria Visceglia, *La città rituale: Rome e le sue cerimonie in età moderna* (Roma, 2002); Richard Ingersoll, "The Ritual Use of Public Space in

Renaissance Rome" (Ph.D. diss., University of California, Berkeley, 1985). These and other works on papal ceremony say almost nothing about the pontificates of Eugenius IV and Martin V.

58. Burke, *Historical Anthropology,* 173.

59. Compare Averil Cameron, "The Construction of Court Ritual: The Byzantine *Book of Ceremonies,*" in *Rituals of Royalty,* 122–132.

60. On the development of the liturgy in the Middle Ages, see Theodor Klauser, *A Short History of the Western Liturgy: An Account and Some Reflections,* trans. John Halliburton (Oxford, 1979), 45–116; Josef Jungmann, *The Mass of the Roman Rite: Its Origins and Development,* trans. Francis Brunner (Westminster, MD, 1986), vol. 1, 7–141.

61. Bernhard Schimmelpfennig, *Die Zeremonienbücher der Römischen Kurie im Mittelalter* (Tübingen, 1973), 17–131; Marc Dykmans, *Le pontifical Romain révisé au XI siècle* (Città del Vaticano, 1985), 5–81; Eric Palazzo, *A History of Liturgical Books from the Beginning of the Thirteenth Century,* trans. Madeleine Beaumont (Collegeville, MN, 1998), 195–212.

62. Schimmelpfennig, *Die Zeremonienbücher,* 413.

63. R. Ricciardi, "Del Monte, Pietro," in *DBDI,* vol. 38, 141–146.

64. Jacopo Stefaneschi, *De Rome en Avignon ou le cérémonial de Jacques Stefaneschi,* in *Le cérémonial papal,* vol. 2; Pierre Amiel, "Le cérémonial de Pierre Amiel," in *Le cérémonial papal,* vol. 4, 68–251. Stefaneschi's pontifical is also known as Ordo XIV and Amiel's as Ordo XV. The earliest text incorporated into the Corsiniana manuscript dates from 1273 and the latest from the early Quattrocento. "Le cérémonial de Gregoire X," in *Le cérémonial papal,* vol. 1, 156–219; "Annexes du temps de Benoit XIII," in *Le cérémonial papal,* vol. 3, 336–355. For interesting studies of Stefaneschi's library and the sources for Ordo XIV, see Emma Condello, "I codici Stefaneschi: Uno scriptorum cardinalizio del Trecento tra Roma e Avignone," *ASRSP* 110 (1987): 22–61; ———. "I codici Stefaneschi: Libri e committenza di un cardinale Avignonese," *ASRSP* 112 (1989): 195–218.

65. For references to Martin, see MS Bibl. Cors. 41 E 22, f. 29, 185–185v. Del Monte signs one of his marginal notes. Ibid., f. 177v. The marginalia includes four other hands. Schimmelpfennig, *Die Zeremonienbücher,* 413.

66. Pietro comments that Eugenius IV received the blood of Christ differently on Corpus Domini than on other days and explains that he knows this because he stood and held the candle for the pope. MS Bibl. Cors. 41 E 22, 130v. He also describes Nicholas V's attire for the Sundays of Advent. Ibid., f. 45.

67. Franz Wasner, "Tor der Geschichte: Beiträge zum päpstlichen Zeremonienwesen im 15 Jahrhundert," *Archivium historiae pontificae* 6 (1968): 113–136.

68. The Corsiniana manuscipt opens with a section on the duties of the cardinal bishop or cardinal priest who assists the pope in celebrating the mass.

MS Bibl. Cors. 41 E 22, f. 1–2v. Compare "Le cérémonial cardinalice," in *Le cérémonial papal,* vol. 1, 264–266.

69. Compare Paravicini-Bagliani, *The Pope's Body,* 24–28.

70. Paratur una tobalea et extenditur super genua pape per duos capellanos eius lateribus assistentes et dictam tobaleam flexis genibus sic tenentes unus a dextris et alter a sinistris et duobus diaconibus cardinalibus antiquioribus domino pape more solite assistentibus. Et tunc prior episcoporum cardinalium deposita mitra sua stans pape sendenti in sede sua et cum mitra cereum non accensum "qui aliis maior est nichil" dicendo dat osculando manum pape. Et ibidem prior episcoporum vel subprior genuflexus recipit cereum de manu pape non accensum et osculatur genu dextrum domini pape. Et sic deinde omnes cardinales faciunt primo episcopi, secondo presbiteri, tertio diaconi et prelati omnes qui sunt parati mitris suis depositis et recipiunt cereum de manu pape et genu osculantur. Prelati vero non parati post receptionem cerei pedem osculantur non genu. Notandum vero quod si episcopus vel presbyter Cardinalis celebrat coram papa die praesenti et sit paratus antequam veniat ad receptione cerei non deponit planetam sed totus paratus recipit modo predicto cereum de manum pape. Camerarius vero, notarii, auditor contradictarum et corrector etiam si aliqui ipsorum essent archiepiscopi vel episcopi quia non consueverunt venire parati, sed cappis laneis induti et etiam capellani (tam commensales qui debent esse in cottis quam alii capellani) et similes necnon poenitentiarii et breviter omnes alii familiares pape etiam layci et quique alii non familiares etsi esset rex flexis genibus recipit cereum de manu pape et ipso recepto osculatur pedem et non genu. MS Bibl. Cors, 41 E 22, f. 3–3v. Compare Ameil, "Le cérémonial," 85–86.

71. Dykmans, *Le cérémonial papal,* vol. 4, 39.

72. This emphasis is not confined to performance theorists. See Pierre Bourdieu, "Rites as Acts of Institution," in *Honor and Grace in Anthropology,* ed. John Peristiany and Julian Pitt-Rivers (Cambridge, 1992), 79–89; Catherine Bell, *Ritual Theory, Ritual Practice* (Oxford, 1993), 94–101; Christopher Wulf, "Praxis," in *Theorizing Ritual,* ed. Jens Kreinath, Jan Snoek, and Michael Stausberg (Leiden, 2007), 395–411.

73. Roy Rappaport, *Ritual and the Religion in the Making of Humanity* (Cambridge, 1999), 117–124; Gerd Althoff, "The Variability of Rituals in the Middle Ages," in *Medieval Concepts of the Past,* ed. Gerd Althoff, Johannes Fried, and Patrick Geary (Cambridge, 2002), 82–87.

74. Michael Houseman, "Relationality," in *Theorizing Ritual,* 414–420.

75. Clifford Geertz, "Religion as a Cultural System," in *Anthropological Approaches to the Study of Religion,* ed. M. Banton (London, 1966), 1–46; Theodore Jennings, "On Ritual Knowledge," *Journal of Religion* 62 (1982): 111–127.

76. Bloch, *From Blessing to Violence,* 9–10; Grimes, "Performance Theory and the Study of Ritual," 113–116; Terence Turner, "Structure, Process, Form," in *Theorizing Ritual,* 229–234.

77. Bloch, *From Blessing to Violence*, 1–11, 181–183; Bell, *Ritual Theory*, 19–46.

78. Burke, *Historical Anthropology*, 168–220. Some representative studies on ritual as a form of communication include Maurice Bloch, "Symbols, Song, Dance, and Features of Articulation," *European Journal of Sociology* 15 (1974): 55–81; Babara Babcock, "Too Many, Too Few: Ritual Modes of Signification," *Semiotica* 23 (1978): 291–302; Frederick Bird, "Ritual As Communicative Action," in *Ritual and Ethnic Identity A Comparative Study of the Social Meaning of Liturgical Ritual in Synagogues*, ed. Jack Lightstone and Frederick Bird (Waterloo, 1995), 23–53; Solomon Harris, "Ritual: Communication and Meaning," *Journal of Ritual Studies* 11 (1997): 35–44; Thomas Gunter, "Communication," in *Theorizing Ritual*, 321–343. Compare Caroline Humphrey and James Laidlaw, *The Archetypal Actions of Ritual: A Theory of Ritual Illustrated by the Jain Rite of Worship* (Oxford, 1994).

79. Michel Andrieu, ed. *Pontifical romain au Moyen-Age* (Città del Vaticano, 1938), 206–207.

80. On the similarity of these services, see MS Bibl. Cors. 41 E 22, f. 42.

81. Compare Marc Bloch, "The Royal Bath in Madagascar," in *Rituals of Royalty*, 271–297.

82. For the most part, the Corsiniana MS is arranged by event (that is, Christmas, a papal election, etc); many events include non-liturgical as well as liturgical components. Compare Cameron, "The Construction of Court Ritual."

83. MS Bibl. Cors. 41 E 22 neglects to mention the seating arrangement for the cardinal priests and deacons, but a somewhat later copy of the manuscript (MS Vatican City, Borg. Lat. 409, f. 8) specifies that the cardinal priests sit at another table to the pope's right and the cardinal deacons at a table to his left, all according to the order of their elections. On the relation of these manuscripts, see Schimmelpfennig, *Die Zeremonienbücher*, 65.

84. Charles of Anjou was king of Naples from 1266 to 1282. He provided financial support to the exiled Byzantine emperor, Baldwin II.

85. Sedet autem papa in una mensa eminenti diversis et magnis vasis aureis et argenteis super mensa positis. In alia vero mensa, quae est a dextris pape . . . sedent episcopi cardinales (inter quos etiam sedent, si sint, patriarche quatuor principalium ecclesiarum patriarcalium) secundum ordinem prioritatis singulorum in statu in quo sunt cardinalatus. Nam priores primo sedent. Et post mensas cardinalium erunt mense aliorum prelatorum et nobilium. Coram papa servient laici maiores natu et nobiliores qui presentes erunt secundum officia illis distributa. Notandum tamen quod primum ferculum ponit coram pape aliquis de principalioribus nobilibus etiam si esset rex. Quo posito si rex foret, vadit ad sedendum in mensa a sinistris inter duos primos diaconos cardinales. Et sic faciebat dominus Karolus primus rex siciliae et descendentes ab eo reges. Maxime Imperator constantinopolitanus qui tunc temporis erat in curia

sedebat a dextris inter duos primos episcopos cardinales qui primum fortassis ferculum posuerat pape, secundum vero rex sicilie. Alii etiam nobiles maiores, etiam si essent filii imperatoris vel regum, pape serviunt in mensa. MS Bibl. Cors. 41 E22, f. 23–23v. Compare Ameil, "Le cérémonial," 142–143.

86. On the practical and ceremonial importance of this hierarchy, see Richardson, *Reclaiming Rome,* 235–261.

87. "Ritual is especially valuable to hierarchical organizations in communicating power relationships." David Kertzer, *Ritual, Politics & Power* (New Haven, 1988), 29.

88. For arguments that Valla's treatise was written at the instigation of Alfonso of Aragon as part of the king's campaign against Pope Eugenius see Mario Fois, *Il pensiero cristiano di Lorenzo Valla nel quadro strorico-culturale del suo ambiente* (Roma, 1969), 296–350; Jerry Bentley, *Politics and Culture in Renaissance Naples* (Princeton, 1987), 114.

89. Denys Hay, *The Church in Italy in the Fifteenth Century* (Cambridge, 1977), 83–84.

90. MS. Corsiniana 41 E 22, f. 6–6v.

91. Clement VI's ceremonial habits are also referenced vis-à-vis Ash Wednesday (Ibid., f. 8–11), Maundy Thursday (f. 25), Good Friday (f. 29), the feast of Agnus dei (f. 42), the Annunciation (f. 43–43v), Christmas (f. 48v–49), the creation of cardinals after the death of a pope (f. 50), the celebration of papal elections (f. 52–52v), the ceremony when a cardinal priest is made a cardinal bishop (f. 69), the giving of the rings of dead cardinals to those who are newly created (f. 70–70v), the creation of papal legates (f. 72), and the ceremony when a cardinal legate returns from his mission (73–73v). In the Corsiniana manuscript, there are three references to Clement V, four references to Innocent VI, four to Stefaneschi, six references to Benedict XII, eight references to John the XXII, and eight to Benedict XIII.

92. Hans-George Beck et al., *Handbook of Church History: From the High Middle Ages to the Eve of the Reformation,* trans. Anselm Biggs (New York, 1970), 324. On Cardinal Annibale di Ceccano's welcome of Clement VI, see Guillaume Mollat, *Les Papes d'Avignon (1305–1378)* (Paris, 1965), 313–314.

93. Benedict's ceremonial behavior is cited in reference to the feast of the Rose (MS Bibl. Cors. 41 E 22, f. 13v–14), Good Friday (f. 29, 30v), Easter (f. 41), Trinity Sunday (f. 44v), Corpus Christi (f. 44v), and what happens when the seat of a cardinal bishop falls vacant (f. 70).

94. On the ways in which Martin followed the precedents of Benedict XIII and John XXIII, see Marc Dykmans, "D'Avignon à Rome: Martin V et le cortege apostolique" *Bulletin de l'Institut Historique Belge de Rome* 39 (1968): 203–308.

95. Compare Bertelli, *The King's Body,* 10–61.

96. Carolus Cocquelines, ed. *Bullarum, privilegiorum, ac diplomatum Romanorum pontificum amplissima collectio: cui accessere pontificum omnium, vitæ, notæ & indices opportuni* (Rome, 1739–1744), vol. 3, parts 3, 5.

97. Germano Gualdo, "Le lettere concistoriali nel Quattrocento: Lettere concistoriali di Eugenio IV e Sisto IV," in *Cancelleria e cultura nel Medio Evo*, ed. German Gualdo (Città del Vaticano, 1990), 187–207; Ambrogio Piazzoni, *Storia delle elezioni pontificie* (Casale Monferrato, 2003), 179.

98. A. A. Strnad, "Capranica, Domenico," in *DBDI*, vol. 19, 149.

99. Joseph Gill, *Eugenius IV, Pope of Christian Union* (London, 1961), 45; Joachim Stieber, *Pope Eugenius IV, the Council of Basel and the Secular and Ecclesiastical Authorities in the Empire* (Leiden, 1978), 12.

100. Bianca, "I cardinali al Concilio di Firenze," 155.

101. M. Morpurgo-Castelnuovo, "Il Cardinale Domenico Capranica," *ASRSP* 52 (1928): 46–47. On Albergati's influence at Basel in 1433 and 1434, see Michiel Decaluwe, *A Successful Defeat: Eugene IV's Struggle with the Council of Basel for Ultimate Authority in the Church, 1431–1449* (Bruxelles, 2009), 198–204.

102. John A. F. Thomson, *Popes and Princes 1417–1517: Politics and Polity in the Late Medieval Church* (London, 1980), 64–66.

103. Hay, *The Church in Italy*, 33–35.

104. Francis Burkle-Young, *Passing the Keys: Modern Cardinals, Conclaves, and the Election of the Next Pope* (Lanham, 1999), xxii–xxiii.

105. Cocquelines, *Bullarum, privilegiorum...collectio*, vol 3, part 3, 21–24.

106. For the background to the confrontation, see Richardson, *Reclaiming Rome*, 101–104. On the chronology of events, see Margaret Harvey, "Eugenius IV, Cardinal Kemp and Archbishop Chichele," in *The Church and Sovereignty c. 590–1918: Essays in honour of Michael Wilks*, ed. Diana Wood (Oxford, 1991), 331–335.

107. Walter Ullmann, "Eugenius IV, Cardinal Kemp, and Archbishop Chichele," in *Medieval Studies Presented to Aubrey Gwynn*, ed. J. A. Watt (Dublin, 1961), 368–369.

108. For Innocent III's use of this passage, see Giuseppe Alberigo, *Cardinalato e collegialità: Studi sull'ecclesiologia tra l'XI e il XIV secolo* (Firenze, 1969), 72–84.

109. Cocquelines, *Bullarum, privilegiorum...collectio*, vol. 3, part 3, 22.

110. Alberigo, *Cardinalato e collegialità*, 14–49. On the earlier evolution of the cardinalate, see Stephan Kuttner, "Cardinalis: The History of a Canonical Concept," *Traditio* 3 (1945): 129–214.

111. Cocquelines, *Bullarum, privilegiorum...collectio*, vol. 3, part 3, 23.

112. Ibid., 24.

113. Ibid., 22.

114. MS Bibl. Cors. 41 E 22, f. 59v–67. Compare Stefaneschi, "De Rome en Avignon," 475–502.

115. Ms. Bibl. Cors. 41 E22, f. 60v.

116. Ibid., f. 61. If the candidate was not previously a prelate, the pope simply says that he is received as a cardinal priest or cardinal deacon.

117. Van Gennep's three phases of rites of initiation are separation, margin, and aggregation. Victor Turner, "Betwixt and Between: The Liminal Period in

Rites de Passage," in *The Forest of Symbols,* 94. On the ways in which Turner expanded Van Gennep's theory of liminality, see Rollo-Koster, *Raiding Saint Peter,* 80–81.

118. "Power is not a substance. Neither is it a mysterious property whose origin must be delved into. Power is a certain type of relation between individuals." Michel Foucault, *Power,* trans. Robert Hurley (New York, 1994), 324.

119. Bell, *Ritual Theory,* 199.

120. Michel Foucault, "The Subject and Power," in *Michel Foucault: Beyond Structuralism and Hermeneutics,* ed. Hubert L. Dreyfus and Paul Rabinow (Chicago, 1983), 220–221.

121. MS. Bibl. Cors. 41 E 22, f. 100–103. Compare "Le cérémonial de Gregoire X," 275–279.

122. MS. Bibl. Cors. 41 E 22, f. 64–64v. Compare Stefaneschi, "De Rome en Avignon," 482–483.

123. Poggio Bracciolini, *Two Renaissance Book Hunters: The Letters of Poggius Bracciolini to Nicolaus De Niccolis,* trans. Phyllis Gordan (New York, 1974), 180–181. ———. *Lettere,* ed. Helene Harth (Firenze, 1984), vol. 1, letter 44, 124–125.

124. MS. Bibl. Cors. 41 E 22, f. 142–148v. Compare Stefaneschi, "De Rome en Avignon," 437–447.

125. MS Bibl. Cors. 41 E 22, f. 147.

126. Schimmelpfennig, "Autorappresentazione e rappresentanza."

127. Stieber, *Pope Eugenius IV,* 19.

128. Bracciolini, *Two Renaissance Book Hunters,* 176.

129. Wasner, "Tor der Geschichte," 142–153.

130. Ibid., 158–159.

131. On the negotiations regarding the protocol for Charles VIII's visit to Rome, see Bonner Mitchell, *The Majesty of State: Triumphal Progress of Foreign Sovereigns in Renaissance Italy (1494–1600)* (Firenze, 1986), 71–76.

132. Giannozzo Manetti, "On the Achievements of Nicholas V, Supreme Pontiff," in *Building the Kingdom,* 369.

133. See, for example, Charles Stinger, *The Renaissance in Rome* (Bloomington, 1985), 46–52.

134. Marc Dykmans, *L'oeuvre de Patrizi Piccolomini* (Città del Vaticano, 1980), 30–31*. For more detail on what precedents Patrizi uses in different sections see Ibid., 98–162*, 164–241*.

135. Agostino Patrizi Piccolomini, "Texte," in *L'oeuvre de Patrizi Piccolomini,* 5–7.

136. Massimo Miglio, "Il ritorno a Roma," in *Roma centro ideale della cultura dell'Antico nei secoli XV e XVI: da Martino V al sacco di Roma, 1417–1527,* ed. Silvia Squarzina (Milano, 1989), 216–220.

137. Charles Stinger, "Roma Triumphans: Triumphs in the Thought and Ceremonies of Renaissance Rome," *Medievalia et Humanistica* 10 (1981): 189–210;

Ingrid Rowland, *The Culture of the High Renaissance: Ancients and Moderns in Sixteenth-century Rome* (Cambridge, 1998), 141–157.

138. Ingersoll, "The Ritual Use of Public Space in Renaissance Rome", 201–207; Stinger, *The Renaissance in Rome*, 235–254.

139. Frederick Hammond, *Music and Spectacle in Baroque Rome: Barberini Patronage under Urban VIII* (New Haven, 1994), 117–132; Visceglia, *La città rituale*, 53–117. For a ceremonial encounter that had to be restaged because of one party's dissatisfaction, see Peter Rietbergen, *Power and Religion in Baroque Rome: Barberini Cultural Practices* (Leiden, 2006), 181–217. For brief but vivid accounts of the "festivities and spectacles" of 17th-century Rome, see Torgil Magnuson, *Rome in the Age of Bernini* (Stockholm, 1982).

140. Dykmans, *L'Oeuvre de Patrizi Piccolomini*, v.

141. Althoff, "The Variability of Rituals in the Middle Ages," 73.

142. Smith and O'Connor, *Building the Kingdom*, 37–45.

143. In addition to the works of Foucault and Bell already cited, see David Cannadine, "Introduction: Divine Rites of Kings," in *Rituals of Royalty*, 1–19.

144. Clifford Geertz, *Negara: The Theatre State in Nineteenth-Century Bali* (Princeton, NJ, 1980).

145. While acknowledging his indebtedness to Geertz's model, Burke notes that the notion of a 'theater state' "assumes too easily that everyone in a given society believed in its myths." Peter Burke, *The Fabrication of Louis XIV* (New Haven, 1994), 12.

6. Eugenius IV, Biondo Flavio, Filarete, and the Rebuilding of Rome

1. The most important registers are Roma, Archivio di Stato di Roma, Camerale I, Mandati 824–830, Spese minute del palazzo 1468 and Fabbriche 1501. These records have been partially published. See Eugène Muntz, *Les arts à la cour des papes pendant* le xve et le xvie *siècle* (Paris, 1878), 32–52; Anna Corbo, *Artisti e artigiani in Roma al tempo di Martino V e di Eugenio IV* (Roma, 1969), 17–86.

2. On the dating of the doors' commission see Robert Glass, "Filarete at the Papal Court: Sculpture, Ceremony, and the Antique in early Renaissance Rome" (Ph.D. diss., Princeton University, 2011),183–187.

3. Horace, *Odes,* 3:30.

4. Iiro Kajanto, *Poggio Bracciolini and Classicism: A Study in Early Italian Humanism* (Helsinki, 1987), 37. For a compelling account of the antiquarianism of Poggio, Biondo, and their colleagues, see Brian Curran, *The Egyptian Renaissance: The Afterlife of Ancient Egypt in Early Modern Italy* (Chicago, 2007), 55–63.

5. For brief acknowledgments of the connection between *Roma instaurata* and the urban agenda of Eugenius IV, see Maria Blasio, "Memoria filologica e politica in Biondo: Il significatio della 'instauratio urbis,'" in *La memoria e la città: Scritture storiche tra Medioevo ed Età Moderna* ed. Claudia Bastia and Maria

Bolognani (Bologna, 1995), 307; Riccardo Fubini, *Storiografia dell'umanesimo in Italia da Leonardo Bruni ad Annio da Viterbo* (Roma, 2003), 56.

6. Compare Elizabeth McCahill, "Rewriting Vergil, Rereading Rome: Maffeo Vegio, Poggio Bracciolini, Flavio Biondo, and Early Quattrocento Antiquarianism," *Memoirs of the American Academy in Rome* 54 (2009): 165–199.

7. Arnaldo Momigliano, "Ancient History and the Antiquarian," *JWCI* 13 (1950): 290–291. For reappraisals of Momigliano's work, see M. H. Crawford and C. R. Ligota, eds., *Ancient History and the Antiquarian: Essays in Memory of Arnaldo Momigliano* (London, 1995); Peter Miller, ed., *Momigliano and Antiquarianism: Foundations of the Modern Cultural Sciences* (Toronto, 2007).

8. While Biondo claims that *Roma instaurata* is an archeological work and *Roma triumphans* is a study of institutions, both works include some archeology and some cultural history. Angelo Mazzocco, "Some Philological Aspects of Biondo Flavio's 'Roma triumphans,'" *Humanistica Lovaniensia* 28 (1979): 1–26; ———. "Rome and the Humanists: The case of Biondo Flavio," in *Rome in the Renaissance: The City and the Myth,* ed. P. A. Ramsey (Binghamton, NY, 1982), 183–195; ———. "Biondo Flavio and the Antiquarian Tradition," in *Acta Conventus Neo-Latini Bononiensis,* ed. R. J. Schoeck (Binghamton, NY, 1985), 128.

9. On humanist notebooks, see Anthony Grafton and Lisa Jardine, *From Humanism to the Humanities: Education and the Liberal Arts in Fifteenth and Sixteenth Century Europe* (Cambridge, MA, 1986), 1–28; Ann Moss, *Printed Common-Place Books and the Structuring of Renaissance Thought* (Oxford, 1996); Ann Blair et al., "Early Modern Information Overload," *JHI* 64 (2003): 1–72; Ann Blair, *Too Much to Know: Managing Scholarly Information Before the Modern Age* (New Haven, 2010), 62–116.

10. Compare Leonard Barkan, *Unearthing the Past: Archaeology and Aesthetics in the Making of Renaissance Culture* (New Haven 1999), 30.

11. On Biondo's literary sources and the ways in which he uses them see Anne-Raffarin-Dupuis, "Introduction" in *Rome restaurée* (Paris, 2005), vol. 1, L–LXXIX. Compare Dorothy Robathan, "Flavio Biondo's 'Roma instaurata'," *Medievalia et Humanistica* 1 (1970): 203–204; Anna Brizzolara, "La 'Roma instaurata' di Flavio Biondo: Alle origini del metodo archeologico," *Atti della Accademia della Scienze dell' Istituto di Bologna* 76 (1979–1980): 31–35.

12. For a detailed study of how Biondo read one particular ancient author, see Rita Cappelletto, *Recuperi Ammianei da Flavio Biondo* (Roma, 1983).

13. On Biondo's use of evidence, see Ottavio Clavuot, *Biondos* Italia Illustrata: *Summa oder Neuschopfung?: über die Arbeitsmethoden eines Humanisten* (Tubingen, 1990), 182–200. Compare Raffarin-Dupuis, "Introduction," L–LXIV, LXXIX–CX.

14. "Biondo was the forerunner of the systematic antiquarian handbooks, the founder of modern scientific research on the antiquities of all the countries

of Europe." Arnaldo Momigliano, *The Classical Foundations of Modern Historiography* (Berkeley, CA, 1990), 71. See also Roberto Weiss, *The Renaissance Discovery of Classical Antiquity* (Oxford, 1988), 66–72.

15. MS Vatican City, Vat. Lat. 3536, f. 15v.

16. Pudet uero pigetque quod a Capitolio incipientem eius deformitatem referre. Is et enim mons quem deorum domicilium M. Cicero cum saepe alias tum maxime in oratione ad Quirites habita pridie quam iret in exilium appellat, et Virgilius aureum dicit, qualis etiam anno post functos uita Ciceronem et Virgilium trecentesimo fuerit, Ammianus Marcellinus in Constantis filii Flauii Constantini Magni gestis rebus ostendit. Constans enim ex Constantinopoli, in qua natus et educatus erat, tunc primum Romam veniens ipsa urbe inspecta obstupuit. Suntque de illo haec Ammiani uerba libro XVI: Deinde intra septem montium culmina per accliuitates planitiemque posita urbis membra collustrans et suburbana, quicquid erat primum id eminere inter alia cuncta sperabat: Iouis Tarpei delubra quantum terrenis divina praecellunt . . . Eandem imitatus sententiam doctissimus optimusque uir Cassiodorus, in edicto Theodorici primi, Ostrogothorum regis, per quod formas aquarum urbis Romae iussit reparari, haec habet uerba: ". . . Capitolia celsa conscendere, hoc est humana ingenia superata uidere. Nunc uero praeter lateritiam domum a Bonifatio nono ruinis superaedificatam qualem mediocris olim fastidisset Romanus civis, usibus senatoris et causidicorum deputatam, praeter Arae Caeli fratrum beati Francisci ecclesiam in Feretrii Iouis templi fundamentis extructam, nihil habet is Capitolinus Tarpeiusue mons tantis olim aedificiis exornatus. Quae autem Capitolium olim habuerit loca superfluum scribere iudicamus. Nam cum fuerit rei diuinae in primis deputatus, aras, sacella, delubra, aedes et templa habuit supra sexaginta quorum nomina, si operi nostro expedire existimaremus, ex maiorum scriptis facile fuerit recensere. Flavio Biondo, *Roma instaurata*, ed. Anne Raffarin-Dupuis (Paris, 2012), vol. 1, 84–87.

17. In the chapter that follows, Biondo mentions the temples of Jove and Juno and discusses the Tarpeian rock, including two quotations from Livy and one from Vergil. Ibid., 86–89, 139.

18. For analysis of Biondo's account of the Forum, see Frances Muecke, "Humanists in the Roman Forum," *Proceedings of the British Academy* 71 (2003): 210–211.

19. Angelo Mazzocco, "Petrarca, Poggio, and Biondo: Humanism's Foremost Interpreters of Roman Ruins," in *Francis Petrarch, Six Centuries Later: A Symposium,* ed. Aldo Scaglione (Chapel Hill, NC, 1975), 361.

20. Fubini, *Storiografia dell' umanesimo,* 53–83.

21. Raffarin-Dupuis, "Introduction." See also G. M. Anselmi, "Città e civiltà in Flavio Biondo," *Atti della Accademia della Scienze dell' Istituto di Bologna* 76 (1979–1980): 5–28; Brizzolara, "La 'Roma instaurata' di Flavio Biondo;" Blasio, "Memoria filologica e politica in Biondo." On the humanists' tendency

to combine archeological and restorative impulses, see Thomas Greene, "Resurrecting Rome: The Double Task of the Humanist Imagination," in *Rome in the Renaissance*, 41–54.

22. Biondo was named a notary of the apostolic camera toward the end of 1432 and became a secretary in 1434. Riccardo Fubini, "Biondo, Flavio," in *DBDI*, vol. 10, 540–541.

23. Unde breui futurum apparet, ut Roma, ingeniorum parens, uirtutum alumna, celebritatis specimen, laudis et gloriae columen, ac omnium quae uniuersus orbis ubique habet bonarum rerum seminarium, in suis obscurata structuris, maiorem celebritatis et famae iacturam faciat, quam in rebus pridem factam ac potentia uideamus. Confirmauit etiam nostrum describendi propositum tuus in ipsam pontificatus tui sedem reditus, adeo illius conseruationi utilis atque necessarius, ut constet eam senio calamitatibusque confectam, si altero abfuisses decennio, paene funditus perituram. Neque enim sola comitantis curiae presentia quod semper ciuitatis opulentiae plurimum profuit, Romanos foues, sed collapsa deformataque aedificia multis in locis maximo instauras reficisque impendio . . . Quando ego itaque omnia, quae mihi adsunt, tuae Sanctitati debeo, cur non etiam ipse contendam, ut sic tu, Romam per ingenioli mei litterarum momumenta, sicuti caementariorum fabrorumque lignariorum opera, pergas instaurare? Accedet enim nostrae huic urbis instaurationi, quae dignitatis tuae sanctimoniam in primis deceat, et tuam gloriam maxime cumulet, pontificum romanorum qui te praecesserunt innouata operum commemoratio, dum urbis partes ad ueterem nouamque nominationem describens basilicas quoque templa et sacra, quas uocamus ecclesias, loca, per quos pontifices et alios christianos uel fundatae primo uel auctae uel fuerint instauratae, ostendam. Biondo, *Roma instaurata*, vol. 1, 10–13.

24. See, for example, Nicolò Signorili, "Descriptio urbis Romae eiusque excellentiae," in *Codice Topografico della città di Roma*, ed. Roberto Valentini and Giuseppe Zucchetti (Roma, 1953), vol. 4, 166–169; Anonymous, *I 'Mirabilia urbis Romae'*, ed. Maria Accame and Emy Dell'Oro (Roma, 2004), 110–111.

25. Biondo, *Roma instaurata*, vol. 1, 48–49.

26. Ibid., 48–51.

27. Ibid., 52–53.

28. Magnamque suscipiens ipsius et basilicae Beati Petri curam, multa fecit, quae in hoc annorum uixdum sexcentorum quot in haec tempora intercesserunt spatio, inueterata iam omnino corruerant, breui ad nihilum peruentura, nisi tua beatissime pater, Eugeni, opera factum esset, ut illa nunc laetemur cernere innouata. Ubi enim Leo donis ecclesiam ornauit, tu illam, suppellectile sacrorum ministerio pariter donatam, tecto insuper maiori ex parte innouato, nouisque sacristiae cameris exaedificatis reddidisti meliorem. Sola re una uideris a Leone superatus quod ualuas ille argenteas, tu aeneas basilicae dedisti, nisi par uideatur magnificentia, pro argenteis nullo exquisitiori artificio factis,

aeneas posuisse inauratas, tantisque insculptas historiis unionis Graecorum, Armeniorum, Aethiopum, Iacobinorum et aliorum populorum tua opera tuaque impensa ecclesiae conciliatorum, ut quadruplo aeris aurique impendium merces opificis superauerit. Quid quod ubi Leo campanarium turrim quae omnium prima in orbe terrarum fuit, tu aerarii officinam et proxime spetiosissimam palatii portam extruxisti. Strata uero palatii area et ipsa quae in urbem ducit uia in multas postea partes urbis diuisa, tanti sunt decoris, ut alia ab ea quae multis retro saeculis fuit urbs Roma uideatur reddita. Biondo, *Roma instaurata*, vol. 1, 66–69.

29. On Biondo's friendship with Alberti, see Anthony Grafton, *Leon Battista Alberti: Master Builder of the Italian Renaissance* (New York, 2000), 233–241.

30. On the revival of Rome under Leo IV, see Richard Krautheimer, *Rome: Profile of a City, 312–1308* (Princeton, NJ, 1980), 117–142.

31. Biondo identifies the restorers, as well as the founders, of Quattro Coronati, the Palace at San Lorenzo in Lucina, Santa Lucia, and San Lorenzo in Damaso. Biondo, *Roma instaurata*, vol. 1, 106–107, vol. 2, 24–27, 38–39, 118–121.

32. Compare Biondo's discussion of Theodoric in a letter to Sforza. Biondo Flavio, *Scritti inediti e rari di Biondo Flavio,* ed. Bartolomeo Nogara (Roma, 1927), 173–174.

33. Biondo, *Roma instaurata*, vol. 2, 102–103.

34. Biondo refers to Cassiodorus twenty times, and although he relies more extensively on ancient authors, his quotations of Cassiodorus tend to be especially long. Raffarin-Dupuis, "Introduction," LII–LVII

35. Biondo, *Roma instaurata*, vol. 2, 116–117. Translation from Cassiodorus, *The* Variae *of Magnus Aurelius Cassiodorus Senator,* trans. S. J. B. Barnish (Liverpool, 1992), 79–80.

36. Raffarin-Dupuis,"Introduction," XII–XVI.

37. Vetustatem uero tanti mali causam non fuisse hinc iudicamus, quod in annorum paulo plus mille quot a Gothorum excidio effluxerunt spatio, adeo corruisse ac penitus euanuisse non potuissent tam solidae extructiones quarum partes quae in agris a multitudinis commodo quando longe abfuerunt, integrae nunc uisuntur. Solae igitur incusandae ac detestandae sunt manus improbae illorum qui, ut priuata et quidem sordidissima erigerent aedificia, lapides aut in calcem decoquendos aut casarum muris abhibendos ab illa moenium maiestate non sunt ueriti asportare. Ut tamen nos etiam aliqua ex parte uetustati deferamus eam dicemus nulla ratione magis formas aquarum demolitam fuisse quam quod urbe Roma caeteris in gubernationis suae partibus senescente, seruandarum quoque formarum cura cessauit. Biondo, *Roma instaurata*, vol. 2, 106–109.

38. Ibid., vol. 1, 38–39; vol. 2, 148–151.

39. Blasio, "Memoria filologica e politica in Biondo," 313–316.

40. Compare Angelo Mazzocco, "Decline and Rebirth in Bruni and Biondo,"

in *Umanesimo a Roma nel Quattrocento,* ed. Paolo Brezzi and Maristella de Panizza Lorch (New York, 1984), 254–257.

41. Biondo, *Roma instaurata,* vol. 2, 12–15.

42. On Roman theater, see Ibid., vol. 2, 110–127; on the mimes, see Ibid., vol. 2, 126–129.

43. Ibid., vol. 2, 152–157. For an English translation of the complete letter, see Cassiodorus, *The Variae,* 90–93. On Biondo's mistake regarding Theodoric's supposed permission to despoil the Colosseum, see Raffarin-Dupuis, "Introduction," LXIII–LXIV.

44. Biondo, *Roma instaurata,* vol. 2, 88–91.

45. For Bruni's influence on Biondo, see Fubini, *Storiografia dell'umanesimo,* 21–22; Gary Ianziti, *Writing History in Renaissance Italy: Leonardo Bruni and the Uses of the Past* (Cambridge, MA, 2012), 20–23. Compare Mazzocco, "Decline and Rebirth in Bruni and Biondo."

46. Biondo, *Roma instaurata,* vol. 2, 210–211.

47. Charles Mitchell, "Archaeology and Romance in Renaissance Italy," in *Italian Renaissance Studies: A Tribute to the Late Cecilia M. Ady,* ed. E. F. Jacob (London, 1960), 462–463.

48. On the Ponte di Valentiniano, see Biondo, *Roma instaurata,* vol. 2, 82–83. Muntz records payments for the Ponte Salario, the Ponte Milvio, and the Ponte Mammolo between 1431 and 1433. Muntz, *Les arts à la cour des papes,* 51.

49. Biondo, *Roma instaurata,* vol. 2, 192–193. Compare Francesco Isoldi, ed. *La mesticanza di Paolo di Lello Petrone* (Città di Castello, 1910–1912), 62.

50. Biondo, *Roma instaurata,* vol. 2, 192–193; G. Cugnoni, "Diritti del capitolo di Santa Maria della Rotonda nell'eta di mezzo," *ASRSP* 8 (1885): 582–583. The Campo dei Fiori may also have been paved during Eugenius's pontificate. Charles Burroughs, *From Signs to Design: Environmental Process and Reform in Early Renaissance Rome* (Cambridge, MA, 1990), 88.

51. On the novelty of the efforts of Eugenius and Scarampo to protect the area around the Pantheon, see David Karmon, *The Ruin of the Eternal City: Antiquity and Preservation in Renaissance Rome* (New York, 2011), 152–154. It is extremely difficult to determine what repair work was done at the direct behest of the pope and what was organized and directed by various officials in the Curia. At times, "Eugenius" will be used as a short-hand for "the pope and his Curia" or "the Curia and those parts of the municipal government that cooperated with it."

52. Carroll Westfall, *In this Most Perfect Paradise; Alberti, Nicholas V, and the Invention of Conscious Urban Planning in Rome, 1447–55* (University Park, PA, 1974), 81; Anna Modigliani, *Disegni sulla città nel primo Rinascimento Romano: Paolo II* (Roma, 2009), 17–19.

53. On the continuity between Scarampo's promotion of order and cleanliness and the urban priorities of Nicholas V, see Burroughs, *From Signs to Design*, 87–91, 140–149.

54. Modigliani, *Disegni sulla città*, 20. Simonicini combines information from *Roma instaurata* and from other contemporary sources to give a compelling account of which parts of Rome were being improved and which were languishing during the last few years of Eugenius's reign. Giorgio Simoncini, *Roma: Le trasformazioni urbane nel Quattrocento*, vol. I *Topografia e urbanistica da Bonifacio IX ad Alessando VI* (Firenze, 2004), 86–92.

55. See note 1 of this chapter.

56. Given the dates of Fabbriche 1501, Cardinal Vitelleschi, rather than Eugenius himself, may have been the driving force behind these restorations. Corbo, *Artisti e artigiani*, 15–16.

57. Eugenius sponsored repair of the basilica's roof. Carlo Pietrangeli, ed., *La basilica romana di Santa Maria Maggiore* (Firenze, 1987), 30.

58. Muntz, *Les arts à la cour des papes*, 40–50.

59. Muntz calculates that the total sum expended was 3,384 ducats, 47 bolognesi, and 2 denari. Ibid., 37. For most of this period, there were 64 bolognesi to a ducat (at one point it changed to 66 bolognesi per ducat) and 17 denari to a bolognesi.

60. Peter Partner, "The 'Budget' of the Roman Church in the Renaissance Period," in *Italian Renaissance Studies*, ed. E. F. Jacob (London, 1960), 259–260. Simoncini argues that there were three distinct phases to Eugenius's pontificate. From 1431–1434 he worked to improve the condition of the city. After the pope's departure in 1434, Rome languished. Conditions began to improve again once Scarampo became Chamberlain in 1440, but the real revival of the city took place once Eugenius returned in 1442. Simoncini, *Topografia e urbanistica*, 82–92.

61. Simoncini argues that there were three distinct phases to Eugenius's pontificate. From 1431–1434 he worked to improve the condition of the city. After the pope's departure in 1434, Rome languished. Conditions began to improve again once Scarampo became Chamberlain in 1440, but the real revival of the city took place once Eugenius returned in 1442. Simoncini, *Topografia e urbanistica*, 82–92.

62. Over the course of 1434, there was a clear increase in military expenses. Archivio di Stato di Roma, Camerale I, Spese minute del palazzo, 1468. On the Curia's 1438 expenses relating to the Council of Florence, see Georg Hofmann, ed., *Acta Camerae Apostolicae et civitatum Venetiarum, Ferrariae, Florentiae, Ianuae de Concilio Florentino* (Roma, 1950), vol. 3, part 1, 25–55.

63. Ivana Ait, "Aspetti dell'attività edilizia a Roma: la fabbrica di S. Pietro nella seconda metà del 400," in *Maestranze e cantieri edili a Roma e nel Lazio*, ed. Ivana Ait and Angela Lanconelli (Roma, 2002), 39.

64. Maestro Giorgio, the head builder, received 16 bolognesi a day, as did the other skilled workers. Manual laborers received 10–12 bolognesi a day. Compare Richard Goldthwaite, *The Building of Renaissance Florence: An Economic and Social History* (Baltimore, 1980), 430, 436, 438.

65. Corbo, *Artisti e artigiani,* 26–62.

66. Eugenius also honored the Lateran by ordering that a tiara supposedly given by Sylvester to Constantine should be placed there and by a 1446 bull that emphasized the basilica's unique relics. Stefano Infessura, *Diario della città di Roma di Stefano Infessura scribasenato,* ed. Oreste Tommasini (Roma, 1890), 44; MS Vatican City, Vat. Lat. 8033, f. 113–113v.

67. Biondo, *Roma instaurata,* vol. 1, 108–109.

68. On the program of the Lateran frescoes, see Marina Tosti-Croce, "Pisanello a S. Giovanni in Laterano," in *Da Pisanello alla nascita dei musei capitolini* (Milano, 1988), 107–108.

69. D. Nicola Widloecher, *La congregazione dei canonici regolari lateranensi* (Gubbio, 1929), 74–92.

70. On the distinctive religiosity of Rome's canons see Andreas Rehberg, "Religiosità collettiva e private fra i canonici delle grande basiliche di Roma (secoli XIII–XVI)," ASRSP 132 (2009): 41–80.

71. Infessura, *Diario della città di Roma,* 41.

72. The saga of the Observants, henceforth known as the Lateran Canons, continued with increasing violence after Eugenius's death, and under Sixtus IV the secular canons were permanently reinstated. Denys Hay, *The Church in Italy in the Fifteenth Century* (Cambridge, 1977), 89–90; Burroughs, *From Signs to Design,* 145–148.

73. G. Ferri, "Le carte dell'Archivio Liberiano dal secolo X al XV," *ASRSP* 30 (1907): 159–160.

74. Burroughs, *From Signs to Design,* 142.

75. Michael Robson, *The Franciscans in the Middle Ages* (Woodbridge, 2006), 209–210.

76. A hospital was also built near the Castel Sant' Angelo during Eugenius's pontificate. Flavia Colonna, "Distribuzione urbana e tipologie degli edifice assistenziali" in *Roma: Le trasformazioni urbane nel Quattrocento,* vol. 2, *Fuzioni urbane e tipologie edilizie,* ed. Giorgio Simoncini (Firenze, 2004), 163.

77. Ottorino Montenovesi, "L'archiospedale di S. Spirito in Roma," *ASRSP* 62 (1939): 177–229; Anna Esposito, "Assistenza e organizzazione sanitaria nell' ospedale di S. Spirito," in *L'antico ospedale di Santo Spirito dall'istituzione papale alla sanità del terzo millennio,* ed. Renata Bizzotto (Roma, 2001), 201–214.

78. A. Canezza, *Gli arcispedali di Roma nella vita cittadina nel storia e nell'arte* (Rome, 1933), 30–31.

79. Andreas Rehberg, "L'ospedale di Santo Spirito nell'età Avignonese: Fra

la protezione della Curia e le vicende politiche a Roma," in *L'antico ospedale di Santo Spirito*, 95–104.

80. On the constitutions of the fraternity, see Mariano da Alatri, "Il Medio Evo," in *La carità cristiana in Roma*, ed. Vincenzo Monachino (Bologna, 1968), 149–150.

81. On Eugenius's expansion of the fraternity's land holdings, see Montenovesi, "L'archiospedale di S. Spirito in Roma," 204–215.

82. Anna Esposito, "Gli ospedali romani tra iniziative laicali e politica pontificia (sec. XIII–XV)," in *Ospedale e città: L'Italia del Centro-Nord, XIII–XVI secolo*, ed. Allen J. Grieco and Lucia Sandri (Firenze, 1997), 248–249. Cassiani offers a more benevolent reading of Sixtus's agenda. Maria Cassiani, "L'ospedale di Santo Spirito in Sassia," in *Sisto IV: Le arti a Roma nel primo Rinascimento*, ed. Fabio Benzi (Roma, 2000), 167–173.

83. On the uneven pace of work on the doors and the changes to their original program see Glass, "Filarete at the Papal Court," 183–224.

84. Charles Seymour, *Sculpture in Italy 1400–1500* (Harmondsworth, 1966), 115; Giorgio Vasari, *Le opere di Giorgio Vasari con nuove annotazioni e commenti di Gaetano Milanesi* (Firenze, 1998), vol. 2, 453–455. On Vasari's assessment of the doors and its enduring influence, see Robert Glass, "Filarete at the Papal Court," 12–47.

85. Westfall takes the former position and Nilgen the latter. Westfall, *In this Most Perfect Paradise*, 7–16; Ursula Nilgen, "Formeneklektizismus und Themenvielfalt als Programm in der römischen Frührenaissance: Filaretes Tür von St. Peter," in *Literarische Formen des Mittelalters: Florilegien, Kompilationen, Kollektionen*, ed. Kaspar Elm (Wiesbaden, 2000), 149–208. (Nilgen's essay has been translated into Italian, but the German version offers more visual support for her arguments. ———. "L'eclettismo come programma nel primo Rinascimento a Roma," in *Opere e giorni: Studi su mille anni di arte europea*, ed. Klaus Bergdolt and Giorgio Bonsanti (Venezia, 2001), 275–290.)

86. Westfall, *In this Most Perfect Paradise*, 9. Compare Nilgen, "Formeneklektizismus und Themenvielfalt," 154.

87. Seymour, *Sculpture in Italy 1400–1500*, 118.

88. Nilgen, "Formeneklektizismus und Themenvielfalt," 155–162.

89. On the relation between the traditional role of the *Porta Argentea* in imperial coronations and the new doors' program, see Glass, "Filarete at the Papal Court," 225–245.

90. Silvia Squarzina, "Pauperismo francescana e magnificenza antiquaria nel programma architettonico di Sisto IV," in *Sisto IV e Giulio II, mecenati e promotori di cultura: atti del convegno internazionale di studi, Savona*, ed. Silvia Bottaro, Anna Dagnino, and Giovanni Terminiello (Savona, 1989), 7–26; Fabio Benzi, *Sisto IV renovator urbis: Architettura a Roma 1471–1484* (Roma, 1990), 17–26. For a compelling study of how the fresco cycle he commissioned at Santo Spirito illustrated Sixtus's vision of papal *renovatio* see Diana Presciutti, "Dead Infants,

Cruel Mothers, and Heroice Popes: The Visual Rhetoric of Foundling Care at the Hospital of Santo Spirito, Rome" *RQ* 64 (2011): 752–799.

91. For positive assessments of the doors in the 15th through 17th centuries, see Glass, "Filarete at the Papal Court," 48–101.

92. For the traditional image of Nicholas V as a great patron and sponsor of culture, see Giannozzo Manetti, *Vita Nicolai V summi pontificis*, ed. and trans. Anna Modigliani (Roma, 2005). For a very different reading, in which Nicholas appears as a tyrannical despot, see Manfredo Tafuri, *Interpreting the Renaissance: Princes, Cities, Architects*, trans. Daniel Sherer (New Haven, 2006), 23–58. For more balanced explorations of Nicholas's pontificate, see Torgil Magnuson, *Studies in Roman Quattrocento Architecture* (Stockholm, 1958); Burroughs, *From Signs to Design;* Grafton, *Leon Battista Alberti*, 293–315.

93. Rome's population doubled between 1420 and 1526, from 30,000 to 60,000, largely because of an influx of immigrants. Anna Esposito, "La popolazione romana dalla fine del secolo XIV al Sacco: caratteri e forme di un'evoluzione demografica," in *Popolazione e società a Roma dal Medioevo all'età contemporanea*, ed. Eugenio Sonnino (Roma, 1998), 37–49.

94. Recent collections of essays that elucidate the range of work being done on the Renaissance papacy include Massimo Miglio et al., eds., *Un pontificato ed una città: Sisto IV (1471–1484)* (Roma, 1986); Silvia Bottaro et. al., *Sisto IV e Giulio II;* Giovanni Pesiri, ed. *Il Lazio e Alessandro VI: Civita Castellana, Cori, Nepi, Orte, Sermoneta* (Roma, 2003); Giovanna Terminiello and Giulio Nepi, eds., *Giulio II: papa, politico, mecenate: Savona, Fortezza del Priamar, Salla della Sibilla* (Genova, 2005); Luca D'Ascia, et. al., eds., *Conferenza su Pio II: nel sesto centenario della nascità di Enea Silvio Piccolomini (1405–2005)* (Siena, 2006); Flavia Cantatore et al., eds., *Guilio II e Savona* (Roma, 2009); ———. eds., *Metafore di un pontificato Giulio II (1503–1513)* (Roma, 2010); Paolo Procaccioli, ed., *Giulio II: La cultura non classicista* (Roma, 2010).

95. J. M. Huskinson, "The Crucifixion of St. Peter: A Fifteenth-Century Topographical Problem," *JWCI* 32 (1969): 135–161. See also Glass, "Filarete at the Papal Court," 116–126.

96. Biondo *Roma instaurata*, vol. 1, 60–63.

97. For Biondo's praise of Colonna as another Maecenas, see Ibid., vol. 1, 120–123.

98. Vocavit invitavitque ad cenam proximis diebus Sigismundum Pandulfum Malatestam, Armini principem, vir humanitatis virtutisque magis quam stemmate generis et cardinalatus fastigio summus, Prosper Columna noster. Vocatus et ego, non quidem, ut credidi, ad cenam, sed ad aliquod mei amantissimi principis Columnae obsequium, in Maecenatianos hortos concessi. Postquam discubitum est, referente Malatesta Sigismundo, primum intellexi cenam imprimis paratam constitutamque fuisse, ut perpetuo rerum Romanarum sermone, quantum paterentur temporis angustiae, potius a me

quam ciborum vel delicatissimorum affluentia a cardinalis architriclino repleretur. Cum itaque multa interrogatus respondissem, plurima a virorum, qui aderant, peritissimorum coetu audivissem, iucundissima quidem et tuis dignissima auribus, quae nedum epistulae, sed longiusculi libri volumine explicari non possent, fecit aerarii Romanorum suborta mentio, ut rem de te gratissimam cardinali et mihi Malatesta narraverit: nummos te ad decem millia aëneos vetustorum principum Romanorum more cudi curavisse, quibus altera in parte ad capitis tui imaginem tuum sit nomen inscriptum, altera autem pars quid habeat, cum diu oblivioni reluctatus voluerit dicere, nequivit. Laudavit Columna ingenium, laudavit vetusti moris imitationem, quae videatur te impulsura, ut, quorum, aemularis gloriae et famae amorem, vestigia quoque in ceteris, quae veram ac solidam afferunt gloriam, sequaris. Biondo, *Scritti inediti e rari*, 159–160.

99. Biondo Flavio, "De verbis romanae locutionis Biondi ad Leonardum Aretinum," in *Latino, grammatica, volgare*, ed. Mirko Tavoni (Padova, 1984), 198.

100. On Colonna's collection of ancient inscriptions and sculptures, see Kathleen Wren Christian, *Empire Without End: Antiquities Collections in Renaissance Rome c. 1350–1527* (New Haven, 2010), 48–61. On the abortive effort by Colonna and Alberti to raise two ancient ships submerged in Lake Nemi, see Philip Jacks, *The Antiquarian and the Myth of Antiquity: The Origins of Rome in Renaissance Thought* (Cambridge, 1993), 99–110; Grafton, *Leon Battista Alberti*, 240–253.

101. Poggio Bracciolini, *De varietate fortunae*, ed. Outi Merisalo (Helsinki, 1993), 91.

102. Virgil, *Aeneid VII–XII*, trans. H. R. Fairclough (Cambridge, MA, 2000), book 8.306–369.

103. On Rome as a part of heaven, see Giuseppe Lombardi, "La città, libro di pietra: Immagini umanistiche di Roma prima e dopo Costanza," in *Alle origini*, 23–26.

104. O quantum . . . Poggi haec Capitolia ab illis distant, quae noster Maro cecinit. "Aurea nunc, olim silvestribus horrida dumis." Ut quidem is versus merito possit converti: "Aurea quondam, nunc squalida spinetis vepribusque referta." Venit in mentem Marii illius per quem olim urbis imperium stetit, quem pulsum patria profugum atque egentem, cum in Africam appulisset, supra Carthaginis ruinas insedisse ferunt admirantem suam et Carthaginis vicem, simulque fortunam utriusque conferentem, addubitantemque utrius fortunae maius spectaculum extitisset. Ego vero immensam huius urbis stragem nulli alteri possum conferre; ita ceterarum omnium vel quas natura tulit rerum, vel quas manus hominum conflavit, haec una exuperat calamitatem. Evolvas licet hystorias omnes, omnia scripturarum monumenta pertractes, omnes gestarum rerum annales scruteris: nulla unquam exempla mutationis

suae maiora fortuna protulit, quam urbem Romam pulcherrimam olim ac magnificentissimam omnium, quae aut fuere aut futurae sunt, et ab Livanio doctissimo Graeco auctore, cum ad amicum suum scriberet Romam videre cupientem, non urbem sed quandam quasi caeli partem appellatam. Quo magis dictu mirabile est et acerbum aspectu, adeo speciem formamque ipsius immutasse fortunae crudelitatem, ut nunc omni decore nudata prostrata iaceat, instar gigantei cadaveris corrupti atque undique exesi. Bracciolini, *De varietate fortunae*, 91–92.

105. On the ways in which humanists highlighted Rome's decline in order to advertise their own knowledge, see Christian, *Empire without End*, 37–45.

106. Bracciolini, *De varietate fortunae*, 132.

107. On the environment of Rome and the Curia ca. 1527, see Andre Chastel, *The Sack of Rome, 1527*, trans. Beth Archer (Princeton, NJ, 1983); Kenneth Gouwens, *Remembering the Renaissance: Humanist Narratives of the Sack of Rome* (Leiden, 1998); Kenneth Gouwens and Sheryl Reiss, eds., *The Pontificate of Clement VII: History, Politics, Culture* (Burlington, VT, 2005).

108. Bracciolini, *De varietate fortunae*, 90.

109. John Monfasani, *George of Trebizond: A Biography and a Study of his Rhetoric and Logic* (Leiden, 1976), 109–113; Salvatore Camporeale, *Lorenzo Valla: Umanesimo e teologia* (Firenze, 1972), 311–403.

110. Denys Hay, "Flavio Biondo and the Middle Ages," *Proceedings of the British Academy* 45 (1959): 100–101; Fubini, "Biondo, Flavio," 548–550.

111. For a reading of Nicholas as tyrant, see Tafuri, *Interpreting the Renaissance*, 23–58.

112. On Nicholas's commitment both to collecting Greek texts and to having them translated, see Antonio Manfredi, "La sezione Greca nella Vaticana di Niccolò V," in *Niccolò V nel sesto centenario della nascita*, ed. Franco Bonatti and Antonio Manfredi (Città del Vaticano, 2000), 49–70.

113. On Nicholas's interest in promoting a new, humanist hagiography, see Alison Frazier, *Possible Lives: Authors and Saints in Renaissance Italy* (New York, 2005), 64–90.

114. On High Renaissance uses of curial scholarship, see John D'Amico, *Renaissance Humanism in Papal Rome: Humanists and Churchmen on the Eve of the Reformation* (Baltimore, 1983), 115–237; Charles Stinger, *The Renaissance in Rome* (Bloomington, 1985); Ingrid Rowland, *The Culture of the High Renaissance: Ancients and Moderns in Sixteenth-century Rome* (Cambridge, 1998). On persecution of wayward humanists, see Anthony D'Elia, "Stefano Porcari's Conspiracy Against Pope Nicholas V in 1453 and Republican Culture in Papal Rome," *JHI* 68 (2007): 207–231; ———. *A Sudden Terror: The Plot to Murder the Pope in Renaissance Rome* (Cambridge, MA, 2009).

115. Grafton, *Leon Battista Alberti*, 303–312.

116. On Poggio's increasing disenchantment with the Curia, see Riccardo Fubini, *Humanism and Secularization from Petrarch to Valla*, trans. Martha King (Durham, NC, 2003), 134–139.

117. Poggio Bracciolini, *Facezie*, trans. Marcello Ciccuto (Milano, 1983), 408–409.

Acknowledgments

This book has been the product of many years and many disparate experiences. A brief listing of acknowledgments cannot adequately recognize the contributions of the mentors, friends, colleagues, and family members who have helped me to bring it (finally) to completion. That said, there is no doubt as to its intellectual Genius; since I started graduate school in 1997, Anthony Grafton has served as a guide, critic, and inspiration in all matters related to classical scholarship. From correcting uninspired translations of Latin jokes to cheering the happy news of the manuscript's acceptance, Tony has participated in every stage of this project, demonstrating unexampled grace, patience, wit, understanding, and kindness as well as his extraordinary erudition. The Eternal City would never have been revived in this particular form without his help, for which the author is more grateful than she can say.

When I was fourteen, my parents first took me to Rome. I fell in love with the city, and unlike most teenage crushes, this one has endured and grown. Rome has inspired, challenged, and consoled me throughout the writing of this book, and while I have tried to keep my focus on the city in a specific historical moment, its other eras have all made their elusive magic felt. This book is an offering to the Eternal City, but it is a paltry one in comparison with the lessons in beauty, time, light, and life which Rome has given me.

More practically, this project would not have been possible without extensive time in Rome's libraries. Special thanks are due to the Biblioteca Apostolica Vaticana and its staff, most of all those in the Sala dei Manoscritti; again and again, they responded to the queries and confusion of a novice researcher with forbearance and humor. Thanks as well to the Vatican Bar, in its former incarnation, and to the scholars who enlivened many a panino with stimulating conversation. When I was not at the BAV, I enjoyed the hospitality and assistance of the Archivio di Stato di Roma, the Biblioteca Corsiniana, the École française de Rome, the Archivio Storico Capitolino, and the Archivio Segreto

Vaticano. For help in navigating these institutions, and the world of the Quattrocento city, I am indebted to a wonderful group of Italian scholars associated with Roma nel Rinascimento. They include Maurizio Campitelli, Paola Farenga, Massimo Miglio, and, most of all, Anna Modigliani.

I am grateful to Princeton University (especially the History Department, the Council on Regional Studies and the Committee on Italian Studies) and the Manuscript Society of America for funding my initial research trips to Rome. Many individuals at Princeton helped me to acquire the background knowledge and linguistic skills necessary for this project. Thanks to Paul Needham for his assistance with my Latin, to Eileen Reeves for broadening my understanding of the classical legacy and to Giles Constable for an exciting exploration of medieval intellectual life. I am especially grateful to Tia Kolbaba for introducing me to the Byzantine Empire and for her unfailing support. Members of my graduate cohort provided useful advice and criticism both inside and outside the classroom. My last years at Princeton were brightened by the arrival of Nicholas Popper and Amy Haley, whose conversations about scholarly and social networks helped me to think about intellectual elites in new ways and who have proved to be great friends as well as inspiring colleagues.

In addition to Tony, three remarkable advisers offered essential guidance as I began to consider the shape and focus of the present study. Peter Brown encouraged me to explore the ceremonial side of curial life and to envision Rome as a stage. Christopher Celenza urged me to question traditional definitions of humanism and to think more about the professional lives of my protagonists. And Leonard Barkan advised me to make Rome and its physical remains active players in my story. This book represents my best effort to follow their erudite and challenging advice.

Since graduate school, my colleagues at Keene State College, Sewanee, and the University of Massachusetts, Boston have offered encouragement and valuable feedback on drafts and ideas. UMass, Boston generously funded a research trip to Rome in 2010. My greatest institutional debt, however, is to the American Academy in Rome. In the summer of 2003, I participated in the Academy's Summer Program in Applied Palaeography, under the direction of Chris Celenza, and in 2008–2009, I was a Rome Prize Fellow. That year gave me the time to explore Roman collections besides the Vatican and to delve into new areas of scholarship; it also gave me the creative space and intellectual stimulation to move well beyond my graduate work. I am deeply grateful to the Academy, its then Director Carmela Franklin, the Arts Director, Martin Brody, and my fellow Fellows, most especially Carrie Beneš. Discussions with Carrie, her feedback on drafts, and her general support have been critical to this project's completion.

I have also benefitted from the intellectual camaraderie and fellowship of a wonderful group of Early Modern scholars, many of whom I know through the Renaissance Society of America. Special thanks to Tony D'Elia, Una D'Elia, Ken Gouwens, Pam Jones, Tim Kircher, Pamela Long, David Marsh, Angelo Mazzocco, Liz Mellyn, Margaret Meserve, Frances Muecke, Emily O'Brien, Sarah Ross, Malcolm Smuts, Walter Stephens, Ronald Witt, and the many other Renaissance enthusiasts who have been engaging interlocutors both during and after conference panels. Thanks also to Joelle Rollo-Koster for her helpful feedback on chapter five of this book.

Edward Muir was General Editor of the I Tatti Studies in Italian Renaissance History series when I submitted my manuscript, and he made the review process painless and even pleasant. Two readers for the series offered helpful comments and suggestions, especially in regards to the organization of my material. Since the manuscript's acceptance, I have relied heavily on the editorial acumen and friendly guidance of Ian Stevenson and Sam Spofford and the proofreading skills of Jason Amato and Charles Carroll. Thanks also to Philip Schwartzberg of Meridian Mapping for creating a map that captures the Rome of popes Martin V and Eugenius IV.

Other friends and family less interested in Quattrocento Italy have played a crucial role in this project, especially Claudia Esposito, Wilana Madden, Phoebe Milliken, Peter McCahill, and the late Elizabeth McCahill. Derek Jeter has been a bulwark of strength, cheer, humor, and patience throughout the composition and completion of this manuscript. If each of its endnotes included an acknowledgment of his love and encouragement, his contribution would still not be adequately recognized. Cecilia Jeter has filled the final stages of editing and proofreading with cuddles, giggles, and her ineffable sweetness.

With all these acknowledgments in mind, my greatest debt remains that to Michael and Barbara Ann McCahill. From the first, they taught me to enjoy history for itself, regardless of practical and professional considerations. Museum visits, elaborate costumes, endless stories, trips to England, assistance with papers, and unquestioning support (financial and otherwise) for my interest in the *studia humanitatis* motivated me before and during college and graduate school. In more recent years, Mum and Dad have tirelessly read and reread drafts, offered advice, encouragement, and the kind of commiseration that can only be expressed by fellow scholars. I dedicate this book to them with love and thanks.

Index